OCA Java® SE 8 Programmer I Study Guide

(Exam 1Z0-808)

OCA Java® SE 8 Programmer I Study Guide

(Exam 1Z0-808)

Edward Finegan
Robert Liguori

New York   Chicago   San Francisco
Athens   London   Madrid
Mexico City   Milan   New Delhi
Singapore   Sydney   Toronto

Cataloging-in-Publication Data is on file with the Library of Congress

McGraw-Hill Education books are available at special quantity discounts to use as premiums and sales promotions, or for use in corporate training programs. To contact a representative, please visit the Contact Us pages at www.mhprofessional.com.

OCA Java® SE 8 Programmer I Study Guide (Exam 1Z0-808)

1234567890 DOC DOC 1098765

ISBN: Book p/n 978-1-25-958750-4 and CD p/n 978-1-25-958752-8
of set 978-1-25-958751-1

MHID: Book p/n 1-25-958750-9 and CD p/n 1-25-958752-5
of set 1-25-958751-7

Sponsoring Editor Timothy Green	**Technical Editor** Ryan Cuprak	**Production Supervisor** James Kussow
Editorial Supervisor Jody McKenzie	**Copy Editor** Lisa Theobald	**Composition** Cenveo® Publisher Services
Project Editor LeeAnn Pickrell	**Proofreader** Lisa McCoy	**Illustration** Cenveo Publisher Services
Acquisitions Coordinator Amy Stonebraker	**Indexer** Rebecca Plunkett	**Art Director, Cover** Jeff Weeks

To AJ, Adalyn, and Shannon

—Edward G. Finegan

To Ashleigh, Patti, my family, and friends

—Robert J. Liguori

ABOUT THE AUTHORS

Edward Finegan is the founder of Dryrain Technologies. His company specializes in iOS software development supported by enterprise Java backends for the automatic identification and data capture (AIDC) industry. He has previously worked in the casino gaming industry, where he designed and implemented software for gaming machines. He also has previous experience in air traffic management systems and radar protocols.

Finegan has a bachelor's degree in computer science from Rowan University and a master's degree in computer science from Virginia Commonwealth University. His thesis, entitled *Intelligent Autonomous Data Categorization*, examined the possibility of using machine-learning algorithms to categorize data intelligently and autonomously.

Finegan is an avid Philadelphia sports fan. He enjoys spending time with his family, especially with his wife, Shannon, daughter, Adalyn, and son, AJ. He spends his free time partaking in outdoor activities and home-improvement projects, as well as tinkering with the latest technologies.

He can be contacted at edward@ocajexam.com.

Robert Liguori is the principal of Gliesian, LLC., a software development company. Liguori has a bachelor's degree in computer science and information technology from Richard Stockton College of New Jersey. He holds various Oracle certifications.

Liguori worked closely with Edward Finegan to produce the predecessors to this OCA book, with the earliest being the *SCJA Sun Certified Java Associate Study Guide (CX-310-019)* (McGraw-Hill Professional, 2009). Liguori and Ryan Cuprak produced the book *NetBeans IDE Programmer Certified Expert Exam Guide (Exam 310-045)* (McGraw-Hill Professional, 2010). Liguori and his wife, Patricia, co-authored a Java reference guide: *Java Pocket Guide* (O'Reilly Media, Inc., 2008). The book has matured through Java 7 and Java 8 versions and is now available in German and Polish.

Liguori enjoys spending time with his family, as well as bicycling and surf fishing. He is a rhythm guitarist for May and the Wandering Minstrels. He also regularly plays Google Ingress as part of the Enlightened team.

About the Technical Editor

Ryan Cuprak is an e-formulation analyst at Dassault Systèmes, and a co-author of two books: *EJB in Action, Second Edition* (Manning Publications, 2014) and *NetBeans IDE Programmer Certification Expert Exam Guide* (McGraw-Hill Professional, 2010). He has served as president of the Connecticut Java Users Group since 2003 and is a JavaOne Rock Star presenter. At Dassault Systèmes, he works on ENOVIA Enginuity chemical formulation software and is involved in desktop and backend server development as well as client data migrations. Prior to joining Dassault Systèmes, Cuprak worked for a distributed computing company, TurboWorx, and also Eastman Kodak's Molecular Imaging Systems group, now part of Burker. He earned a BS in computer science and biology from Loyola University Chicago.

He can be contacted at ryan@ocajexam.com.

CONTENTS AT A GLANCE

CONTENTS

The purpose of this study guide is to prepare you for the OCA Java SE 8 Programmer I (IZ0-808) exam to earn your Oracle Certified Associate, Java SE 8 Programmer (OCA Java SE 8 Programmer) certification. This preparation will be accomplished by familiarizing you with the necessary knowledge related to Java fundamentals, concepts, tools, and technologies that will be represented on the exam. In short, this book was written to help you pass the exam. As such, objective-specific areas are detailed throughout. Peripheral information, which is not needed to pass the exam, may not be included, or it may be presented in a limited fashion. Because this book covers a lot of information on the fundamentals of Java and related technologies, you may also want to use it as a general reference guide away from the certification process.

Achieving the OCA Java SE 8 Programmer certification will solidify your knowledge of the Java programming language, set the foundation for your evolvement through the related technologies, and identify you as a true Java professional. We strongly recommend the OCA Java SE 8 Programmer certification to matured programmers and software developers.

The Oracle certification series for Java includes various exams for both Java SE and Java EE. This study guide focuses on the first step of the Java SE–related exams.

Passing the Java SE 8 Programmer I (IZ0-808) exam enables you to achieve the Oracle Certified Associated, Java SE 8 Programmer certification. Once you've achieved this, you can take the Java SE 8 Programmer II (IZ0-809) exam to earn the Oracle Certified Professional, Java SE 8 certification. If you already have prior Java certification, you may opt for the upgrade to Java SE 8 Programmer (IZ0-810) exam to go directly for the Oracle Certified Professional, Java SE 8 certification.

In This Book

This book covers Java fundamentals, including development tools, basic constructs, operators, and strings. It also covers object-oriented principles and concepts, including classes and class relationships. A set of appendices covers Java keywords, bracket conventions, the Unicode standard, pseudo-code algorithms,

Java SE packages, and Unified Modeling Language (UML). A useful glossary is also provided. Enjoy.

On the CD-ROM

The CD-ROM includes the Oracle Press practice exam software, select source code represented in the book, and the Enterprise Architect project file containing the UML diagrams that were rendered and used as draft images for the book (shown in Figure 1). For more information on the CD-ROM, see Appendix I, "About the CD-ROM."

Exam Readiness Checklist

At the end of the "Introduction," you will find an "Exam Readiness Checklist." This table has been constructed to enable you to cross-reference the official exam objectives with the objectives as they are presented and covered in this book.

| FIGURE 1 | Enterprise Architect CASE tool |

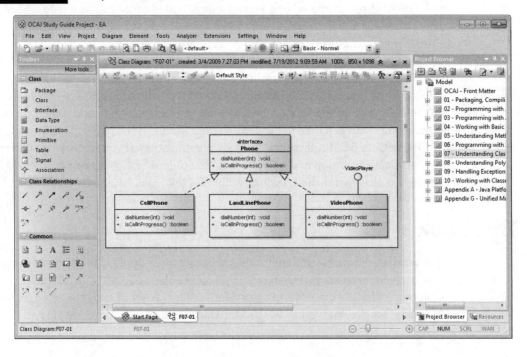

The checklist also helps you gauge your level of expertise on each objective at the outset of your studies so that you can check your progress and make sure you spend the time you need on more difficult or unfamiliar sections. References have been provided for the objective exactly as the vendor presents it, the section of the study guide that covers that objective, and a chapter and page reference.

In Every Chapter

We've created a set of chapter components that call your attention to important items, reinforce important points, and provide helpful exam-taking hints. Take a look at what you'll find in every chapter:

- Every chapter begins with **Certification Objectives**—what you need to know to pass the section on the exam dealing with the chapter topic. The objective headings identify the objectives within the chapter, so you'll always know an objective when you see it!

- **Exam Watch** notes call attention to information about, and potential pitfalls in, the exam. These helpful hints were written by authors who have taken the exams and received their certification. Who better to tell you what to worry about? They know what you're about to go through!

It is unlikely that you will see labeled statements on the exam. This coverage was simply intended for completeness of the transfer of control statement features.

- **Step-by-Step Exercises** are interspersed throughout the chapters. These are typically designed as hands-on exercises that enable you to get a feel for the real-world experience you'll need to pass the exams. They help you master skills that are likely to be an area of focus on the exam. Don't just read through the exercises—they are hands-on practice that you should be comfortable completing. Learning by doing is an effective way to increase your competency with a product.

- **On the Job** notes describe the issues that come up most often in real-world settings. They provide a valuable perspective on certification- and product-related topics. They point out common mistakes and address questions that have arisen from on-the-job discussions and experience.

■ **Inside the Exam** sidebars highlight some of the most common and confusing problems that students encounter when taking a live exam. Designed to anticipate what the exam will emphasize, getting inside the exam will help ensure that you know what you need to know to pass the exam. You can get a leg up on how to respond to those difficult-to-understand questions by focusing extra attention on these sidebars.

■ **Scenario & Solution** sections lay out potential problems and solutions in a quick-to-read format.

SCENARIO & SOLUTION

You want to use an AND operator that evaluates the second operand whether the first operand evaluates to true or false. Which would you use?	Boolean AND (&)
You want to use an OR operator that evaluates the second operand whether the first operand evaluates to true or false. Which would you use?	Boolean OR (|)
You want to use an AND operator that evaluates the second operand only when the first operand evaluates to true. Which would you use?	Logical AND (&&)
You want to use an OR operator that evaluates the second operand only when the first operand evaluates to false. Which would you use?	Logical OR (| |)

■ The **Certification Summary** presents a succinct review of the chapter and a restatement of salient points regarding the exam.

✓ ■ The **Two-Minute Drill** at the end of every chapter is a checklist of the main points of the chapter. Use it for last-minute review.

 ■ The **Self Test** offers questions similar to those found on the certification exams. The answers to these questions, as well as explanations of the answers, can be found at the end of each chapter. By taking the Self Test after completing each chapter, you'll reinforce what you've learned from that chapter while becoming familiar with the structure of the exam questions.

Some Pointers

Once you've finished reading this book, set aside some time to do a thorough review. You might want to return to the book several times and make use of all the methods it offers for reviewing the material:

- *Reread all the Two-Minute Drills,* or have someone quiz you. You also can use the drills as a quick cram before the exam. You may want to make some flash cards out of 3×5 index cards that contain Two-Minute Drill material.

- *Reread all the Exam Watch notes and Inside the Exam elements.* Remember that these notes are written by authors who have taken the exam and passed. They know what you should expect—and what you should be on the lookout for.

- *Review all the Scenario & Solution sections* for quick problem solving.

- *Retake the Self Tests.* Taking the tests right after you've read the chapter is a good idea because the questions help reinforce what you've just learned. However, it's an even better idea to go back later and consider all the questions in the book in one sitting. Pretend that you're taking the live exam. When you go through the questions the first time, you should mark your answers on a separate piece of paper. That way, you can run through the questions as many times as you need until you feel comfortable with the material.

- *Complete the exercises.* Did you do the exercises when you read through each chapter? If not, do them! These exercises are designed to cover exam topics, and there's no better way to get to know this material than by practicing. Be sure you understand why you are performing each step in each exercise. If you are not clear on a particular topic, reread that section in the chapter.

ACKNOWLEDGMENTS

The OCA exam covers a significant amount of information detailing areas from Java fundamentals to object-oriented concepts. To complete a voluminous project like this book, covering all of the related objectives, the authors decided to take the divide-and-conquer approach by splitting up the chapters based on their individual expertise. Finegan focused on the chapters covering object-oriented basic concepts. Liguori focused on the core Java fundamentals chapters.

OCA Java SE 8 Programmer Study Guide Project Team Acknowledgments

The McGraw-Hill Professional Support Team: Timothy Green, Amy Stonebraker, Jody McKenzie, Jim Kussow, LeeAnn Pickrell, Lisa Theobald, Lisa McCoy, and Rebecca Plunkett
Waterside Productions, Inc.: Carole Jelen McClendon
Technical Editor: Ryan Cuprak
Informal Reviewers: Shannon Reilly Finegan, Richard Tkatch (OCA 7 version), and Wayne Smith (SCJA version)

Personal Acknowledgements

Thank you to all of my family and friends. A project like this has a way of consuming more time than you ever expect. Their patience and encouragement has kept me motivated to accomplish this venture. I would like to give a special thanks to my wife, Shannon. She gave birth to our first child, Adalyn, during the second revision of this book. Right on schedule, during this third revision, our second child AJ joined our family. Shannon has always helped me balance the time between family and my professional endeavors. Without her support, this book would have never been completed.

I would also like to express my gratitude to my co-author, Robert Liguori. It has been an enriching experience collaborating with him on this project. Robert is a talented professional, and I sincerely thank him for keeping me on track. His enthusiasm and dedication to the Java community is truly remarkable and is evident in his work.

—Edward G. Finegan

I would like to thank my family, friends, and cousins for their friendship and support. Thanks again to my beautiful wife, Patti, and wonderful daughter, Ashleigh!

Also, thanks to my tech-savvy co-author Edward Finegan for working on this book with me; what a wonderful journey and endeavor this has been! Thanks also to our technical reviewer, Ryan Cuprak, and to all the folks at Waterside and McGraw-Hill Professional who made this book possible.

—Robert J. Liguori

INTRODUCTION

This *OCA Java SE 8 Programmer I Study Guide* has been designed to assist you in preparation of passing Oracle's Java SE 8 Programmer I exam to achieve the OCA Java SE 8 Programmer certification. The information in this book is presented through textual content, coding examples, exercises, and more. To the best extent possible, all code examples have been validated on Apple OS X, Microsoft Windows, and Linux operating systems. Information is covered in detail for all exam objectives.

The following topics are covered in this book:

- The Java SE platform
- Java development and support tools
- Java fundamentals, including statements, variables, method primitives, and operators
- String and StringBuilder class methods and functionality
- Basic Java elements, including primitives, arrays, enumerations, and objects
- Classes and interfaces, including class relationships
- Object-oriented principles
- Exception handling
- Date and Time API
- Lambda expressions

Various appendices are included as well to assist you with your studies.

Specifics About the OCA Java SE 8 Programmer Certification Exam

Specifics of the OCA Java SE 8 Programmer exam objectives are detailed on the Oracle Certification web site (http://education.oracle.com). Specifics about the exam registration process are supplied by Pearson VUE when you enroll for the exam. However, we do detail in the following sections the most important information you will need to know to enroll for and take the exam. Visit the Oracle Certification web site for the most current information on exam objectives.

Referring to the Exam

The formal name for this exam is the Java SE 8 Programmer I (IZ0-808) exam. If you pass the exam, you will receive the Oracle Certified Associate, Java SE 8 Programmer certification.

Googling online, you will see that people and resources are calling out this IZ0-808 exam as the *OCA exam*, the *OCAJ exam*, the *OCAJP exam*, and the *OCAJP8*. This would correlate to the OCA certification, OCAJ certification, OCAJP certification, and OCAJP8 certification.

For simplicity, we have made the best effort to refer to the exam as the *OCA exam* and the certification as the *OCA certification*.

Dynamics of the Java SE 8 Programmer I (IZ0-808) Exam

This exam is geared toward matured Java programmers and developers who want to achieve foundational Java certification. The prerequisite-free exam consists of 77 questions. A passing percentage of 65 percent is necessary—in other words, you must answer at least 50 of the 77 questions correctly to pass. The designated time limit is 120 minutes (2 hours).

The current cost to take the exam is U.S. $245. If you are employed by a technical organization, check to see if your company has an educational assistance policy.

Scheduling the OCA Exam

The exam must be given at a proctored Pearson VUE testing location. You may schedule your appointment for the exam via one of three methods:

- Online
- By phone
- Through the test center

You will find all of the information you need for these options at the Pearson VUE web site (www.pearsonvue.com/oracle/). For a quick look, Figure 2 shows the scheduling process on the site.

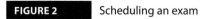

FIGURE 2   Scheduling an exam

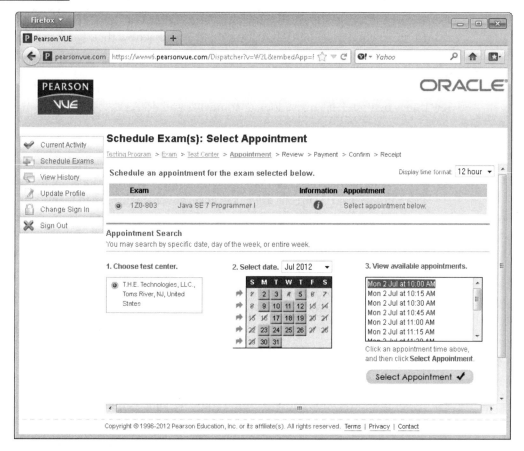

Pearson VUE Test Vouchers

Test Vouchers (prepaid exam certificates) may be available for purchase for the OCA exam. For more information about purchasing test vouchers, visit the voucher information page on the Pearson VUE web site at www1.pearsonvue .com/vouchers/, or visit the Pearson VUE voucher store at www1.pearsonvue.com/ contact/voucherstore/.

Pearson VUE Test Center Locator

If you are interested in finding a testing facility near you, without registering, you can use Pearson VUE's Test Center Locator at www.vue.com/vtclocator/.

Preparing for the OCA Exam

Getting a good night's rest before the exam and eating a healthy breakfast will contribute to good test marks, but you should already know that. Don't cram for the exam the night before. If you find you need to cram, you should reschedule the exam since you won't be ready for it.

You will need to bring a few things with you for the exam, *and* you'll be leaving a few things behind. Let's take a look at some do's and don'ts.

Do's

- *Do bring (at least) two forms of identification.* Valid identification includes a valid passport, current driver's license, government-issued identification, credit cards, or check-cashing cards. Two items must include your signature, and at least one item must include your photograph. Make sure you don't shorthand your signature when you sign in since it must match your identification.

- *Do show up early.* Plan to arrive 15 to 30 minutes before your exam's scheduled start time. You may find that the center needs to set up several people for exams. Getting in early may get you set up early—or at the least it will ensure that you don't start late.

- *Do use the restroom ahead of time.* The exam will take close to 2 hours to complete. Breaks are frowned upon and are most likely disallowed. In addition, you can't pause the time you have allocated if you take a break.

- *Do print out directions to the test facility.* Or get the address and punch it into your GPS navigator or directions app if you have one.

Don'ts

- *Don't bring your laptop, tablets, phone, or pager into the exam.* In addition, some facilities may ask that you do not enter the test area with your watch or wallet.

- *Don't bring books, notes, or writing supplies.* You may be given an erasable noteboard to use. Do not use the noteboard until the exam has started.
- *Don't bring large items.* Large storage may not be available for book bags and jackets. However, the testing facility may provide small securable lockers. Before storing your cell phone or other electronic device, turn it off.
- *Don't bring drinks or snacks to the exam.* But feel free to enjoy refreshments while you are studying for the exam.
- *Don't study in the test center.*

Taking the OCA Exam

Just prior to taking the exam, the proctor may take your photograph. Bring your best smile. You may be asked to sign in and wait while the proctor sets up your exam on a PC. In my case, the proctor adjusted the web cam in the room so it was facing me. There may be other people in the room taking other tests, so bring ear plugs if you are sensitive to the mouse clicks and general noises or people around you. The proctor should make sure that you get to the first question, and then he or she will leave room. Good luck!

After the exam, you may be presented with an optional computer-based survey, which will ask you about your technical background and other related information. A common misconception is that the questions are related to the exam questions you will be presented with; however, the survey is not related to the exam questions you will receive. The survey can take a few minutes to complete. The information gathered is important for those developing and refining future exams, so answer the questions honestly.

After you have completed the exam, your results will appear on the screen and will also be printed. Find the proctor (testing personnel) to retrieve your results from the printer and sign out. The point here is that *you should not leave* once you have completed the exam; stay and get your results.

Sharing Your Success

We would like to know how you did. You can send us an e-mail at results@ocajexam .com, or you can post your results on Java Ranch's Wall of Fame.

Rescheduling the OCA Exam

If you need to reschedule (or cancel) your exam, do so outside of 24 hours of the start of the exam. Use Pearson VUE's Test Taker Services page (www.vue.com/programs/) to assist with the rescheduling or contact Pearson VUE directly. Rescheduling within 24 hours before the scheduled exam is subject to a same-day forfeit exam fee. Refunds are not granted if you don't show up for the exam (that is, if you're a no-show).

Additional OCA Resources

You'll find numerous resources to supplement this book and assist with your goal of OCA certification. These resources include Java software utilities, Java community forums, language specifications and related documentation, OCA-related books, online and purchasable mock exams, and software tools (such as IDE's CASE tools, and so on). Although these peripheral tools and resources are highly beneficial and recommended, they are optional with regard to passing the OCA exam; this book attempts to cover all of the necessary material.

The following sections detail the previously mentioned resources.

Java Software

- Java Development Kits, www.oracle.com/technetwork/java/archive-139210 .html
- Java Enterprise Editions (out of scope of exam, provided here just FYI), www.oracle.com/technetwork/java/javaee/overview/index.html

Java Online Community Forums

- Java Ranch's Big Moose Saloon Java technology forums, www.coderanch .com/forums.
- Java Programming forums, http://javaprogrammingforums.com/
- </dream.in.code>, www.dreamincode.net/forums/forum/32-java/
- IBM - Java Technology Forums, www.ibm.com/developerworks/forums/ dw_jforums.jspa
- Tek Tips Java Forum, www.tek-tips.com/threadminder.cfm?pid=269

- Code Guru - Java Programming, http://forums.codeguru.com/forumdisplay .php?f=67
- Go4Expert, www.go4expert.com/forums/forumdisplay.php?f=21
- Java User Groups, http://home.java.net/jugs/java-user-groups

Java Tools and Technologies Specifications and Documentation

- The Java Tutorials, http://docs.oracle.com/javase/tutorial/
- Java Platform Standard Edition 8 Documentation, http://docs.oracle.com/ javase/8/docs/
- Java Platform, Standard Edition 8 API Specification, http://docs.oracle.com/ javase/8/docs/api/
- *The Java Language Specification: Java SE 8 Edition*, http://docs.oracle.com/ javase/specs/jls/se8/jls8.pdf

Books Covering Material Found on the OCA Exam

Although the book you are holding sufficiently covers everything you need to know to pass the exam, supplemental reading can only help. Consider reviewing the following books to refine your skills:

- *Java 8 Pocket Guide*, by Robert and Patricia Liguori (O'Reilly Media, Inc., 2014)
- *NetBeans IDE Programmer Certified Expert Exam Guide (Exam-310-045)*, by Robert Liguori and Ryan Cuprak (McGraw-Hill Professional, 2010)
- *Java: The Complete Reference*, by Herbert Schildt (McGraw-Hill Professional, 2014)

OCA Mock Exams

In addition to the CD and online mock exams associated with this book, various other free and commercial OCA mock exams exist. Various resources are listed here.

- Oracle certification practice exams, http://education.oracle.com/pls/web_ prod-plq-dad/db_pages.getpage?page_id=208
- Enthuware mock exams, http://enthuware.com/
- Whizlabs SCJA Preparation Kit, http://bit.ly/19h3fvg

- ExamsExpert, http://bit.ly/18Uw4hh
- Transcender, http://bit.ly/1NaCkyD

Integrated Development Environments

An *integrated development environment (IDE)* is a development suite that enables developers to edit, compile, debug, connect to version control systems, collaborate, and do much more depending on the specific tool. Most modern IDEs have add-in capabilities for various software modules to enhance the IDE's capabilities. There is no reason not to use an IDE. We (the authors) recommend that you use the NetBeans IDE for your test preparation because of its popularity, ease of use, and support from Oracle. However, any IDE from the following list would suffice:

- NetBeans IDE, www.netbeans.org
- Oracle JDeveloper IDE, http://bit.ly/19h29jc
- IntelliJ IDEA, www.jetbrains.com
- Eclipse IDE, www.eclipse.org
- JCreator IDE, www.jcreator.com
- BlueJ, www.bluej.org

Tools with UML Modeling Features

Several tools and IDEs have UML features. However, questions about UML are not included on the OCA. If you want to explore UML modeling, following are a few tools you may look into—but, again, this is not on the exam. We do believe, however, that software programmers and developers should learn UML early in their careers.

- NetBeans IDE, http://netbeans.org/features/uml/
- JDeveloper IDE, http://bit.ly/1N4bpq8
- Enterprise Architect CASE tool, www.sparxsystems.com/products/ea/
- Visual Paradigm for UML (provides plug-ins for the popular IDEs), www.visual-paradigm.com/product/vpuml/

Miscellaneous Resources

Various other resources, such as the following, include games and Java news outlets that can assist you with getting high marks on the exam.

■ Java Ranch Rules Round Up Game, www.javaranch.com/game/game2.jsp

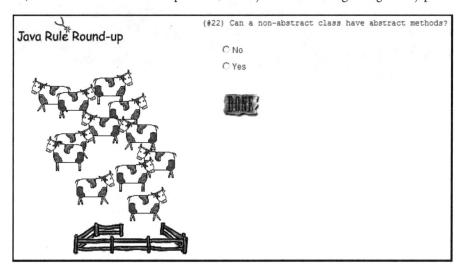

■ DZone, http://java.dzone.com
■ The Server Side, http://theserverside.com
■ OCA FAQs on Java Ranch, www.coderanch.com/how-to/java/OcajpFaq
■ Java Language Specifications, http://docs.oracle.com/javase/specs/

Oracle's Certification Program in Java Technology

This section maps the exam's objectives to specific coverage in the study guide.

Exam Readiness Checklist				Beginner	Intermediate	Expert
Official Objective	**Study Guide Coverage**	**Ch #**	**Pg #**			
Compare and contrast the features and components of Java such as platform independence, object orientation, encapsulation, etc.	The Java Platform	1	2			
Import other Java packages to make them accessible in your code	Understand Packages	1	4			
Define the structure of a Java class	Understand Class Structure	1	18			
Create executable Java applications with a main method; run a program from the command line; include console output	Compile and Interpret Java Code	1	22			
Create if and if/else constructs	Create and Use Conditional Statements	2	52			
Use a switch statement	Create and Use Conditional Statements	2	52			
Create and use for loops including the enhanced for loop	Create and Use Iteration Statements	2	62			
Create and use while loops	Create and Use Iteration Statements	2	62			
Create and use do/while loops	Create and Use Iteration Statements	2	62			
Compare loop constructs	Create and Use Iteration Statements	2	62			
Use break and continue	Create and Use Transfer of Control Statements	2	69			
Use Java operators, including parentheses to override operator precedence	Understand Fundamental Operators	3	88			
Create and manipulate strings	Use String Objects and Their Methods	3	102			

Exam Readiness Checklist

Official Objective	Study Guide Coverage	Ch #	Pg #	Beginner	Intermediate	Expert
Manipulate data using the StringBuilder class and its methods	Use StringBuilder Objects and Their Methods	3	116			
Test equality between strings and other objects using == and equals ()	Test Equality Between Strings and Other Objects	3	121			
Declare and initialize variables (including casting of primitive data types)	Understand Primitives, Enumerations, and Objects	4	150			
Develop code that uses wrapper classes such as Boolean, Double, and Integer	Understand Primitives, Enumerations, and Objects	4	150			
Differentiate between object reference variables and primitive variables	Use Primitives, Enumerations, and Objects	4	166			
Create methods with arguments and return values, including overloaded methods	Create and Use Methods	5	196			
Determine the effect upon object references and primitive values when they are passed into methods that change the values	Pass Objects by Reference and Value	5	203			
Define the scope of variables	Understand Variable Scope	5	206			
Explain an object's life cycle (creation, "dereference by reassignment," and garbage collection)	Understand Variable Scope	5	206			
Create and overload constructors, including impact on default constructors	Create and Use Constructors	5	212			
Use super and this to access objects and constructors	Use the this and super Keywords	5	215			
Apply the static keyword to methods and fields	Create Static Methods and Instance Variables	5	220			
Declare, instantiate, initialize, and use a one-dimensional array	Work with Java Arrays	6	250			
Declare, instantiate, initialize, and use a multi-dimensional array	Work with Java Arrays	6	250			
Declare and use an ArrayList of a given type	Work with ArrayList Objects and Their Methods	6	258			

Exam Readiness Checklist

Official Objective	Study Guide Coverage	Ch #	Pg #	Beginner	Intermediate	Expert
Describe inheritance and its benefits	Implement and Use Inheritance and Class Types	7	282			
Use abstract classes and interfaces	Implement and Use Inheritance and Class Types	7	282			
Apply access modifiers	Understand Encapsulation Principles	7	292			
Apply encapsulation principles to a class	Understand Encapsulation Principles	7	292			
Know how to read or write to object fields	Advanced Use of Classes with Inheritance and Encapsulation	7	298			
Develop code that demonstrates the use of polymorphism, including overriding and object type versus reference type	Understand Polymorphism	8	330			
Determine when casting is necessary	Understand Casting	8	346			
Describe the advantages of exception handling	Understand the Rationale and Types of Exceptions	9	368			
Differentiate among checked exceptions, unchecked exceptions, and errors	Understand the Rationale and Types of Exceptions	9	368			
Create and invoke a method that throws an exception	Understand the Nature of Exceptions	9	372			
Create a try-catch block and determine how exceptions alter normal program flow	Alter the Program Flow	9	375			
Recognize common exception classes (such as NullPointerException, ArithmeticException, ArrayIndexOutOfBoundsException, ClassCastException)	Recognize Common Exceptions	9	382			
Create and manipulate calendar data using classes from java.time.LocalDateTime, java.time.LocalDate, java.time.LocalTime, java.time.format.DateTimeFormatter, java.time.Period	Understand the Date and Time API	10	408			
Write a simple lambda expression that consumes a lambda predicate expression	Write Lambda Expressions	11	436			

1
Packaging, Compiling, and Interpreting Java Code

S ince you are holding this book, or reading an electronic version of it, you must have an affinity for Java. You must also have the desire to let everyone know through the Oracle Certified Associate, Java SE 8 Programmer (OCA), certification process that you are truly Java savvy. As such, you should either be—or have the desire to be—a Java programmer, and in the long term, a true Java developer. You may be or plan to be a project manager heading up a team of Java programmers and/or developers. In this case, you will need to acquire a basic understanding of the Java language and its technologies. In either case, this book is for you.

To start, you may be wondering about the core functional elements provided by the basic Java Standard Edition (SE) platform with regard to libraries and utilities, and how these elements are organized. This chapter answers these questions by discussing Java packages and classes, along with their packaging, structuring, compilation, and interpretation processes.

When you have finished this chapter, you will have a firm understanding of packaging Java classes, high-level details of common Java SE packages, and the fundamentals of Java's compilation and interpretation tools.

CERTIFICATION OBJECTIVE

The Java Platform

Exam Objective   Compare and contrast the features and components of Java, such as platform independence, object orientation, encapsulation, and so on

The Java language was first released in 1995 as a beta. At that time the Java team had a radical vision. They envisioned a language that was independent of the platform it was running on. They also wanted to create a language that was object oriented at its core and that used all the principles that this implied. Encapsulation, polymorphism, inheritance, and abstraction are all basic concepts upon which Java is built. This section will review the core philosophy that makes up the Java language.

Platform Independence

When the Java language is compiled, it is targeted for execution on the Java virtual machine, or JVM, instead of a specific hardware architecture. The compiled Java code is called *bytecode*. This is why it is possible to compile the Java language on a

Windows PC and execute the output on a Linux server. The only requirement for the code to work on any computer is the presence of a compatible JVM.

The Java language extends past the PC and server, however. Many mobile phones have embraced the power of Java as their recommended language for apps. This allows the hardware manufacturer to change the hardware between models without breaking the compatibility of the software. Java is even present in embedded systems and appliances. On devices such as Blu-ray players and car infotainment systems, Java software is often present.

It is important that you understand that platform independence does not mean your server code will run on your Blu-ray player. Java has a few different JVM specs for devices with different capabilities. For example, embedded systems use a JVM with only a subset of features, and mobile phones typically use a JVM with mobile optimized user interface libraries. All of these JVMs share a common Java core, but platform independence is limited to compatible versions.

Java's Object-Oriented Philosophy

Java was conceived as an object-oriented language, in contrast to the C language, which is procedural. An object-oriented language organizes related data and code together—a process called *encapsulation*. A properly encapsulated object uses data protection and exposes only some of its data and methods. The data and methods that are designed for internal use in the object are not exposed to other objects.

Object-oriented design also encourages *abstraction*, the ability to generalize algorithms. Abstraction facilitates code reuse and flexibility. These concepts are at the heart of the Java language. Inheritance and polymorphism are key concepts in creating reusable code. Both are covered in much more depth in Chapters 7 and 8 of this book.

Robust and Secure

Security and robustness were major design goals when Java was created. C and C++ suffered from the misuse of pointers, memory management, and buffer overruns. Java was architected to overcome these issues and many more.

Java was designed not to have explicit pointers. In the C language family, pointers store a memory address to an object. This memory address can be directly altered. Java variables store references to objects but do not allow access to, or modification of, the memory address stored in the reference. This simplified development and removed a level of complexity that was often the source of application instability.

Memory management was addressed in Java with the JVM's built-in garbage collector. When Java was introduced, many languages relied on explicit memory management. This meant that the developer was responsible for both allocating and deallocating the memory that was used for objects. This process could become tedious. If it was done incorrectly, the application could leak memory and/or crash. With Java, the JVM periodically runs the garbage collector, which looks for any objects that have gone out of scope or that are no longer referenced, and it automatically deallocates their memory. This frees the developer from this manual, error-prone task and increases robustness by ensuring that memory is properly managed.

Buffer overruns are a common exploit vector found in software that does not check for them. In a C program, when an array is created, the index used is never automatically checked to ensure it is in bounds. In fact, an out-of-bounds index may not even crash the program. The software will read or write to the memory address whether it is in bounds or out, and this can create unpredictable behavior. This can be used maliciously to alter the program in ways the developer never intended. Java automatically checks the bounds of arrays. If an index is out-of-bounds, an exception is thrown. This level of checking helps create both more robust and secure software.

CERTIFICATION OBJECTIVE

Understand Packages

Exam Objective   Import other Java packages to make them accessible in your code

Packaging is a common approach used to organize related classes and interfaces. Most reusable code is packaged. Unpackaged classes are commonly found in books and online tutorials, as well as in software applications with a narrow focus. This section will show you how and when to package your Java classes and how to import external classes from your Java packages. The following topics will be covered:

- Package design
- Package and import statements

Package Design

Packages are considered containers for classes, but they actually define where classes will be located in the hierarchical directory structure. Packaging is encouraged by Java coding standards to decrease the likelihood of classes colliding in the same

TABLE 1-1

Package
Attribute
Considerations

Package Attribute	Benefits of Applying the Package Attribute
Class coupling	Package dependencies are reduced with class coupling.
System coupling	Package dependencies are reduced with system coupling.
Package size	Typically, larger packages support reusability, whereas smaller packages support maintainability.
Maintainability	Often, software changes can be limited to a single package when the package houses focused functionality.
Naming	Consider conventions when naming your packages. Use a reverse domain name for the package structure. Use lowercase characters delimited with underscores to separate words in package names.

namespace. The package name plus the class names creates the *fully qualified class name*. Packaging your classes also promotes code reuse, maintainability, and the object-oriented principle of encapsulation and modularity.

When you design Java packages, such as the grouping of classes, consider the key areas shown in Table 1-1.

Let's take a look at a real-world example. As program manager, suppose you need two sets of classes with unique functionality that will be used by the same end product. You task Developer A to build the first set and Developer B to build the second. You do not define the names of the classes, but you do define the purpose of the package and what it must contain. Developer A is to create several geometry-based classes, including a point class, a polygon class, and a plane class. Developer B is to build classes that will be included for simulation purposes, including objects such as hot air balloons, helicopters, and airplanes. You send them off to build their classes (without having them package their classes).

Come delivery time, they both give you a class named `Plane.java`—that is, one for the geometry plane class and one for the airplane class. Now you have a problem, because both of these source files (class files, too) cannot coexist in the same directory because they have the same name. The solution is packaging. If you had designated package names to the developers, this conflict never would have happened (as shown in Figure 1-1). The lesson learned is this: Always package your code, unless your coding project is trivial in nature.

package and import Statements

You should now have a general idea of when and why to package your source files. Next, you need to know exactly how to do this. To place a source file into a package, you use the `package` statement at the beginning of that file. You may use zero or

FIGURE 1-1 Separate packaging of classes with the same names

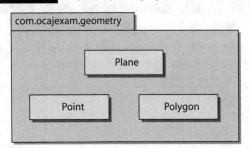
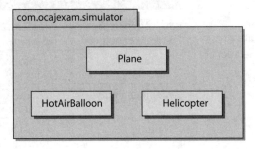

one `package` statements per source file. To import classes from other packages into your source file, you may use the `import` statement or you may precede each class name with its package name. The `java.lang` package that houses the core language classes is imported by default.

The following code listing shows usage of the `package` and `import` statements. You can return to this listing as we discuss the `package` and `import` statements in detail throughout the chapter.

```
package com.ocaj.exam.tutorial; // Package statement
/* Imports class ArrayList from the java.util package */
import java.util.ArrayList;
/* Imports all classes from the java.io package */
import java.io.*;
public class MainClass {
  public static void main(String[] args) {
    /* Creates console from java.io package - run outside your
IDE */
    Console console = System.console();
    String planet = console.readLine(" \nEnter your favorite
    planet: " );
    /* Creates list for planets */
    ArrayList planetList = new ArrayList();
    planetList.add(planet); // Adds users input to the list
    planetList.add("Gliese 581 c"); // Adds a string to the list
    System.out.println(" \nTwo cool planets: "  + planetList);
  }
}
$ Enter your favorite planet: Jupiter
$ Two cool planets: [Jupiter, Gliese 581 c]
```

The package Statement

The package statement includes the package keyword, followed by the package path delimited with periods. Table 1-2 shows valid examples of package statements. package statements have the following attributes:

- They are optional.
- They are limited to one per source file.
- Standard coding convention for package statements reverses the domain name of the organization or group creating the package. For example, the owners of the domain name ocajexam.com may use the following package name for a utilities package: com.ocajexam.utilities.
- Package names equate to directory structures. The package name com .ocajexam.utils would equate to the directory com/ocajexam/utils. If a class includes a package statement that does not map to the relative directory structure, the class will not be usable.
- The package names beginning with java.* and javax.* are reserved.
- Package names should be lowercase. Individual words within the package name should be separated by underscores.

The Java SE API contains several packages. These packages are detailed in Oracle's Online Javadoc documentation at http://docs.oracle.com/javase/8/docs/api/.

On the exam, you will see packages for the Java Abstract Window Toolkit API, the Java Swing API, the Java Basic Input/Output API, the Java Networking API, the Java Utilities API, and the core Java Language API. You will need to know the basic functionality that each package/API contains.

The import Statement

An import statement enables you to include source code from other classes into a source file at compile time. The import statement includes the import keyword followed by the package path delimited with periods and ending with a class

TABLE 1-2	Package Statement	Related Directory Structure
Valid package Statements	`package java.net;`	*[directory_path]\java\net*
	`package com.ocajexam .utilities;`	*[directory_path]\com\ocajexam\utilities*
	`package package_name;`	*[directory_path]\package_name*

| TABLE 1-3 | Valid import Statements |

Import Statement	Definition
`import java.net.*;`	Imports all the classes from the package `java.net`
`import java.net.URL;`	Imports only the URL class from the package `java.net`
`import static java.awt` `.Color.*;`	Imports all static members of the `Color` class of the package `java.awt` (J2SE 5.0 onward only)
`import static java.awt.` `color.ColorSpace.CS_GRAY;`	Imports the static member `CS_GRAY` of the `ColorSpace` class of the package `java.awt` (J2SE 5.0 onward only)

name or an asterisk, as shown in Table 1-3. These `import` statements occur after the optional `package` statement and before the class definition. Each `import` statement can relate to one package only.

on the **Job**

For maintenance purposes, it is better that you import your classes explicitly. This will allow the programmer to determine quickly which external classes are used throughout the class. For example, rather than using `import java`
`.util.*`, *use* `import java.util.Vector`. *In this real-world example, the coder would quickly see (with the latter approach) that the class imports only one class and it is a collection type. In this case, it is a legacy type and the determination to update the class with a newer collection type could be done quickly.*

SCENARIO & SOLUTION

To paint basic graphics and images, which package should you use?	Use the Java AWT API package. `import java.awt.*;`
To use data streams, which package should you use?	Use the Java Basic I/O package. `import java.io.*;`
To develop a networking application, which package should you use?	Use the Java Networking API package. `import java.net.*;`
To work with the collections framework, event model, and date/time facilities, which package should you use?	Use the Java Utilities API package. `import java.util.*;`
To utilize the core Java classes and interfaces, which package should you use?	Use the core Java Language package, which is imported by default. `import java.lang.*;`

C and C++ programmers will see some look-and-feel similarities between Java's import statement and C/C++'s #include statement, even though there is no direct mapping in functionality.

The static import Statement

Static import statements were introduced in Java SE 5.0. Simply put, static import statements allow you to import static members. The following example statements demonstrate this:

```
/* Import static member ITALY */
import static java.util.Locale.ITALY;
...
System.out.println("Locale: " + ITALY); // Prints "Local: it_IT"
...

/* Imports all static members in class Locale */
import static java.util.Locale.*;
...
System.out.println("Locale: " + ITALY); // Prints "Local: it_IT"
System.out.println("Locale: " + GERMANY); // Prints "Local: de_DE"
System.out.println("Locale: " + JAPANESE); // Print "Local: ja"
...
```

Without the static import statements shown in the example, the direct references to ITALY, GERMANY, and JAPANESE would be invalid and would cause compilation issues.

```
// import static java.util.Locale.ITALY;
...
System.out.println("Locale: " + ITALY); // Won't compile
```

EXERCISE 1-1

Replacing Implicit import Statements with Explicit import Statements

Consider the following sample application:

```
import java.io.*;
import java.text.*;
import java.time.*;
import java.time.format.*;
import java.util.*;
import java.util.logging.*;
```

```
public class TestClass {
  public static void main(String[] args) throws IOException {
    /* Ensure directory has been created */
    Files.createDirectories(Paths.get("logs"));
    /* Get the date to be used in the filename */
    DateTimeFormatter df
      = DateTimeFormatter.ofPattern("yyyyMMdd_hhmm");
    LocalDateTime now = LocalDateTime.now();
    String date = now.format(df);
    /* Set up the filename in the logs directory */
    String logFileName = "logs\\testlog-" + date + ".txt";
    /* Set up Logger */
    FileHandler myFileHandler = new FileHandler(logFileName);
    myFileHandler.setFormatter(new SimpleFormatter());
    Logger ocajLogger = Logger.getLogger("OCAJ Logger");
    ocajLogger.setLevel(Level.ALL);
    ocajLogger.addHandler(myFileHandler);
    /* Log Message */
    ocajLogger.info("\nThis is a logged information message. ");
    /* Close the file */
    myFileHandler.close();
  }
}
```

There can be implicit `import` statements that allow all necessary classes of a package to be imported:

```
import java.io.* ; // Implicit import example
```

There can be explicit `import` statements that allow only the designated class or interface of a package to be imported:

```
import java.io.File ; // Explicit import example
```

This exercise will have you using explicit `import` statements in lieu of the implicit `import` statements for all of the necessary classes of the sample application. If you are unfamiliar with compiling and interpreting Java programs, finish reading this chapter and then come back to this exercise. Otherwise, let's begin.

1. Type the sample application into a new file and name it *TestClass.java*. Save the file.

2. Compile and run the application to ensure that you have created the file contents without error: `javac TestClass.java` to compile, `java TestClass` to run. Verify that the log message prints to the screen. Also verify that a file has been created in the logs subdirectory with the same message in it.

3. Comment out all of the `import` statements:

```
//import java.io.*;
//import java.text.*;
// import java.time.*;
// import java.time.format.*;
//import java.util.*;
//import java.util.logging.*;
```

4. Compile the application: `javac TestClass.java`. You will be presented with several compiler errors related to the missing class imports. As an example, the following illustration demonstrates the errors that are displayed when only the `java.io` package has been commented out:

```
C:\Windows\system32\cmd.exe

c:\code>javac TestClass.java
TestClass.java:7: error: cannot find symbol
public static void main (String [] args) throws IOException {
                                                 ^
    symbol:   class IOException
    location: class TestClass
TestClass.java:9: error: cannot find symbol
new File ("TEST").mkdir();
    ^
    symbol:   class File
    location: class TestClass
2 errors

c:\code>
```

5. For each class that cannot be found, use the online Java Specification API to determine which package it belongs to and then update the source file with the necessary explicit `import` statement. Once completed, you will have replaced the four *implicit* `import` statements with nine *explicit* `import` statements.

6. Run the application again to ensure that the application works with the explicit `import` statements the same way it did with the implicit `import` statements.

Understand Package-Derived Classes

Oracle includes more than 200 packages in the Java SE 8 API. Each package has a specific focus. Fortunately, you need to be familiar with only a few of them for the OCA exam. These may include packages for Java utilities, basic input/output, networking, Abstract Window Toolkit (AWT), Swing, and data/time. The java data/time classes will be covered in more detail in Chapter 10.

The following sections address these APIs:

- Java Utilities API
- Java Basic Input/Output API
- Java Networking API
- Java Abstract Window Toolkit API
- Java Swing API
- JavaFX

Java Utilities API

The Java Utilities API is contained in the package `java.util`. This API provides functionality for a variety of utility classes. The API's key classes and interfaces can be divided into several categories. Categories of classes that may be seen on the exam include the Java Collections Framework, date and time facilities, internationalization, and some miscellaneous utility classes.

Of these categories, the Java Collections Framework pulls the most weight because it is frequently used and provides the fundamental data structures necessary to build valuable Java applications. Table 1-4 details the classes and interfaces of the Collections API that you may see referenced on the exam.

To assist collections in sorting where the ordering is not natural, the Collections API provides the `Comparator` interface. Similarly, the `Comparable` interface that resides in the `java.lang` package is used to sort objects by their natural ordering.

TABLE 1-4	Various Classes of the Java Collections Framework	

Interface	Implementations	Description
List	ArrayList, LinkedList, Vector	Data structures based on positional access.
Map	HashMap, Hashtable, LinkedHashMap, TreeMap	Data structures that map keys to values.
Set	HashSet, LinkedHashSet, TreeSet	Data structures based on element uniqueness.
Queue	PriorityQueue	Queues typically order elements in a first in, first out (FIFO) manner. Priority queues order elements according to a supplied comparator.

Various other classes and interfaces reside in the java.util package. Legacy date and time facilities are represented by the Date, Calendar, and TimeZone classes. Geographical regions are represented by the Locale class. The Currency class represents currencies per the ISO 4217 standard. A random-number generator is provided by the Random class. And StringTokenizer breaks strings into tokens. Several other classes exist within java.util, and these (and the collection interfaces and classes) are classes that you may find yourself commonly using on the job. These utilities classes are represented in Figure 1-2.

on the
ĵob

Many packages have related classes and interfaces with unique functionality, so they are included in their own subpackages. For example, regular expressions are stored in a subpackage of the Java utilities (java.util) package. The subpackage is named java.util.regex and houses the Matcher and Pattern classes. Where needed, consider creating subpackages for your own projects.

FIGURE 1-2   Various utility classes

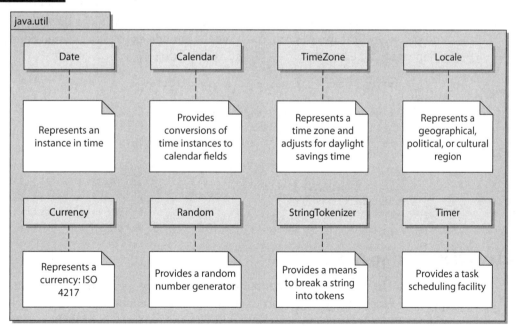

Java Basic Input/Output API

The Java Basic Input/Output API is contained in the package `java.io`. This API provides functionality for general system input and output in relation to data streams, serialization, and the file system. Data-stream classes include byte-stream subclasses of the `InputStream` and `OutputStream` classes. Data-stream classes also include character-stream subclasses of the `Reader` and `Writer` classes. Figure 1-3 depicts part of the class hierarchy for the `Reader` and `Writer` abstract classes.

Other important `java.io` classes and interfaces include `File`, `FileDescriptor`, `FilenameFilter`, and `RandomAccessFile`. The `File` class provides a representation of file and directory pathnames. The `FileDescriptor` class provides a means to function as a handle for opening files and sockets. The `FilenameFilter` interface, as its name implies, defines the functionality to filter filenames. The `RandomAccessFile` class allows for the reading and writing of files to specified locations.

In JDK 7, the NIO.2 API was introduced in the package `java.nio`. This included the useful `Paths` interface, the `Path` class, and the `Files` class. The `Files` class has `lines`, `list`, `walk`, and `find` methods that work hand-in-hand with the Stream API. All of this is beyond the scope of the exam but is useful to know. The following code snippet provides a quick look at what you can do with the API and other new features of Java. You'll see the lambda expression-related code in Chapter 11 (for example, `p -> { statements; }`).

```
// Print out .txt file names in a given folder
try {
  Files.walk(Paths.get("C:\\opt\\dnaProg\\users\\docs")).forEach(p -> {
    if (p.getFileName().toString().endsWith(".txt")) {
      System.out.println("Text doc:" + p.getFileName());
    }
  });
  } catch (IOException e) {
  e.printStackTrace();
}
```

The Java Networking API

The Java Networking API is contained in the package `java.net`. This API provides functionality in support of creating network applications. The API's key classes and interfaces are represented in Figure 1-4. You will probably see few, if any, of these classes on the exam, but the figure will help you conceptualize

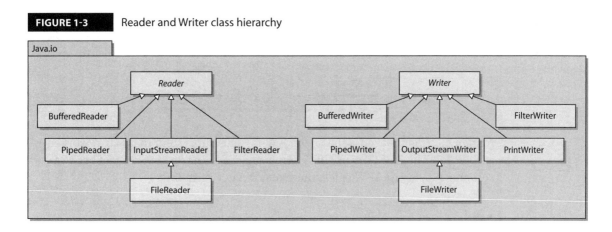

FIGURE 1-3   Reader and Writer class hierarchy

what's in the `java.net` package. The improved performance I/O API (`java.nio`) package, which provides for nonblocking networking and the socket factory support package (`javax.net`), is not included on the exam.

Java Abstract Window Toolkit API

The Java Abstract Window Toolkit API is contained in the package `java.awt`. This API provides functionality for creating heavyweight components with regard to creating user interfaces and painting associated graphics and images. The AWT API was Java's original GUI API and has been superseded by the Swing API. Where Swing has been recommended over AWT, certain pieces of the AWT API still

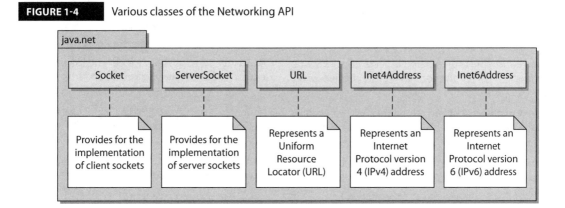

FIGURE 1-4   Various classes of the Networking API

FIGURE 1-5

AWT major
elements

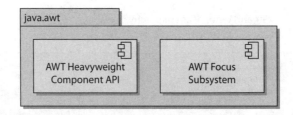

java.awt

AWT Heavyweight
Component API

AWT Focus
Subsystem

remain commonly used, such as the AWT Focus subsystem that was reworked in J2SE 1.4. The AWT Focus subsystem provides for navigation control between components. Figure 1-5 depicts these major AWT elements.

Java Swing API

The Java Swing API is contained in the package `javax.swing`. This API provides functionality for creating lightweight (pure-Java) containers and components. The Swing API, providing a more sophisticated set of GUI components, supersedes the AWT API. Many of the Swing classes are simply prefaced with the addition of "J" in contrast to the legacy AWT component equivalent. For example, Swing uses the class `JButton` to represent a button container, whereas AWT uses the class `Button`.

Swing also provides look-and-feel support, allowing for universal style changes of the GUI's components. Other features include tooltips, accessibility functionality, an event model, and enhanced components such as tables, trees, text components,

SCENARIO & SOLUTION

You need to create basic Java Swing components such as buttons, panes, and dialog boxes. Provide the code to import the necessary classes of a package.	`// Java Swing API package` `import javax.swing.*;`
You need to support text-related aspects of your Swing components. Provide the code to import the necessary classes of a package.	`// Java Swing API text subpackage` `import javax.swing.text.*;`
You need to implement and configure basic pluggable look-and-feel support. Provide the code to import the necessary classes of a package.	`// Java Swing API plaf subpackage` `import javax.swing.plaf.*;`
You need to use Swing event listeners and adapters. Provide the code to import the necessary classes of a package.	`// Java Swing API event subpackage` `import javax.swing.event.*;`

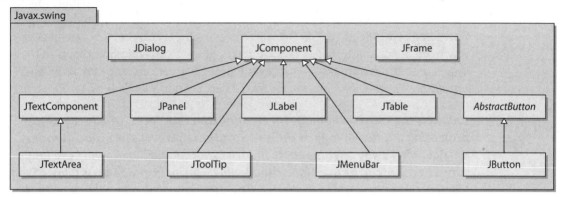

FIGURE 1-6   Various classes of the Swing API

sliders, and progress bars. Some of the Swing API's key classes are represented in Figure 1-6.

The Swing API makes excellent use of subpackages, with 18 of them in Java SE 8. As mentioned earlier, when common classes are separated into their own packages, code usability and maintainability are enhanced.

Swing takes advantage of the model-view-controller (MVC) architecture. The *model* represents the current state of each component. The *view* is the representation of the components on the screen. The *controller* is the functionality that ties the UI components to events. Although understanding the underlying architecture of Swing is important, it's not necessary for the exam. For comprehensive information on the Swing API, look to the book *Swing: A Beginner's Guide*, by Herbert Schildt (McGraw-Hill Professional).

on the
　　job

It's good to be familiar with the package prefixes `java` and `javax`. The prefix `java` is commonly used for the core packages. The prefix `javax` is commonly used for packages that comprise Java standard extensions. Take special notice of the prefix usage in the AWT and Swing APIs: `java.awt` and `javax.swing`. Also note that JavaFX will be replacing Swing as the GUI toolkit for Java SE. Its prefix is `javafx`.

JavaFX API

JavaFX is Java's latest technology for creating rich user interfaces. It is designed to provide lightweight, hardware-accelerated interfaces. JavaFX provides a similar set of features to the Swing library. JavaFX is intended to replace Swing in the same manner that Swing replaced AWT. The JavaFX libraries are part of the `javafx` package.

JavaFX best practices suggest that the MVC architecture be used when designing applications. FXML, an XML-based markup language, has been created for defining user interfaces. Many of the more than 60 UI controls can be styled by using Cascading Style Sheets (CSS). These features together represent a powerful new way to create user interfaces. JavaFX makes going from whiteboard design to implemented software faster than ever before. A great reference for JavaFX is *Introducing JavaFX 8 Programming,* by Herbert Schildt (Oracle Press).

on the job

JavaFX is the latest technology for creating user interfaces. Oracle is actively promoting this technology as the go-to tool kit. However, the Swing libraries are not going away anytime soon. In Java 8, both JavaFX and Swing are fully supported and can be used interchangeably. The `SwingNode` ***class allows Swing elements to be embedded in JavaFX. The*** `JFXPanel` ***will allow the reverse so that JavaFX elements can be used in a Swing applications.***

CERTIFICATION OBJECTIVE

Understand Class Structure

Exam Objective   Define the structure of a Java class

You must understand the structure of a Java class to do well on the exam and to have a promising career with Java. It would help to have a fundamental knowledge of Java naming conventions as well as knowledge of the typical separators that are seen in Java source code (such as comment separators and brackets for enclosing entities). These topics are covered in the following sections:

- Naming Conventions
- Separators and Other Java Source Symbols
- Java Class Structure

Naming Conventions

Naming conventions are rules for the usage and application of characters in creation of identifiers, methods, class names, and so forth, throughout your code base. If some of your team members are not applying naming conventions to their code, you should encourage them to do so, for the good of the effort and for maintainability aspects for after the code is deployed.

on the
Job

The popular article, "How to Write Unmaintainable Code," by Roedy Green, is worth reading (http://thc.org/root/phun/unmaintain.html). It brings to light, in a comical way, the challenges that can occur with maintaining code when there is a blatant or intentional disregard to software development best practices. On the flip-side, *The Passionate Programmer: Creating a Remarkable Career in Software Development,* ***by Chad Fowler (Pragmatic Bookshelf, 2009), encourages the software developer to be the best that he or she can be.***

You may encounter people who will come up with their own naming conventions. Although this is better than not applying any convention, an outsider trying to maintain that person's code would need to learn the original convention and apply it as well for consistency. Fortunately, the Java community does subscribe to a shared thought on how naming conventions should be applied to the many different elements in Java. Table 1-5 describes these conventions in a simple manner. When applying

TABLE 1-5	Java Naming Conventions		
Element	**Lettering**	**Characteristic**	**Example**
Class name	Begins uppercase, continues CamelCase	Noun	`SpaceShip`
Interface name	Begins uppercase, continues CamelCase	Adjective ending with "able" or "ible" when providing a capability; otherwise a noun	`Dockable`
Method name	Begins lowercase, continues CamelCase	Verb, may include adjective or noun	`orbit`
Instance and static variables names	Begins lowercase, continues CamelCase	Noun	`moon`
Parameters and local variables	Begins lowercase, continues CamelCase if multiple words are necessary	Single words, acronyms, or abbreviations	`lop` (line of position)
Generic type parameters	Single uppercase letter	The letter *T* is recommended	`T`
Constant	All uppercase letters	Multiple words separated by underscores	`LEAGUE`
Enumeration	Begins uppercase, continues CamelCase; the set of objects should be all uppercase	Noun	`enum Occupation {MANNED, SEMI_MANNED, UNMANNED}`
Package	All lowercase letters	Public packages should be the reversed domain name of the org	`com.ocajexam.sim`

naming conventions, you should strive to use meaningful and unambiguous names. And remember that naming conventions exist for the primary goal of making Java programs more readable, and therefore maintainable. The practice of using CamelCase—using uppercase letters for the first characters in compound words—is part of the Java naming conventions.

Separators and Other Java Source Symbols

The Java programming language makes use of several separators and symbols to aid in the structuring of the source code in a software program. Table 1-6 details these separators and symbols.

TABLE 1-6   Symbols and Separators

Symbol	Description	Purpose
( )	Parentheses	Encloses set of method arguments, encloses cast types, adjusts precedence in arithmetic expressions
{ }	Braces	Encloses blocks of codes, initializes arrays
[ ]	Box brackets	Declares array types, initializes arrays
< >	Angle brackets	Encloses generics
;	Semicolon	Terminates statement at the end of a line
,	Comma	Separates identifiers in variable declarations, separates values, separates expressions in a for loop
.	Period	Delineates package names, selects an object's field or method, supports method chaining
:	Colon	Follows loop labels
' '	Single quotes	Defines a single character
->	Arrow operator	Separates left-side parameters from the right-side expression
" "	Double quotes	Defines a string of characters
//	Forward slashes	Indicates a single-line comment
/* */	Forward slashes with asterisks	Indicates a blocked comment for multiple lines
/** */	Forward slashes with a double and single asterisk	Indicates Javadoc comments

Java Class Structure

Every Java program has at least one class. A Java class has a signature, optional constructors, optional data members (fields), and optional methods, as outlined here:

```
[modifiers] class classIdentifier [extends superClassIdentifier]
[implements interfaceIdentifier1, interfaceIdentifier2, etc.] {
    [data members]
    [constructors]
    [methods]
}
```

Each class may extend one and only one superclass. Each class may implement one or more interfaces. Interfaces are separated by commas.

The following SpaceShip class shows typical elements annotated with comments. The file containing this SpaceShip class must be called SpaceShip .java. Note that the class declaration extends the Ship class and implements the Dockable interface. The Dockable interface includes the dockShip method, which is overridden here. Ship class methods would be inherited by the SpaceShip class. Chapters 4–7 go into more comprehensive details about creating and working with classes.

The following code shows the structure of a typical class:

```
package com.ocajexam.craft_simulator;

public class SpaceShip extends Ship implements Dockable {

  // Data Members
  public enum ShipType {
    FRIGATE, BATTLESHIP, MINELAYER, ESCORT, DEFENSE
  }
  ShipType shipType = ShipType.BATTLESHIP;

  // Constructors
  public SpaceShip() {
    System.out.println("\nSpaceShip created with default ship type.");
  }
  public SpaceShip(ShipType shipType) {
    System.out.println("\nSpaceShip created with specified ship type.");
    this.shipType = shipType;
  }

  // Methods
  @Override
```

```
public void dockShip () {
  // TODO
}
@Override
public String toString() {
  String shipTypeRefined = this.shipType.name().toLowerCase();
  return "The pirate ship is a " + shipTypeRefined + " ship.";
}
}
```

This `SpaceShip` class can be instantiated as demonstrated in the following code:

```
package com.ocajexam.craft_simulator;
import com.ocajexam.craft_simulator.PirateShip.ShipType;
public class SpaceShipSimulator {

  public static void main(String[] args) {

    // Create SpaceShip object with default ship type
    SpaceShip ship1 = new SpaceShip ();
    // Prints "The pirate ship is a battleship."
    System.out.println(ship1);

    // Create SpaceShip object with specified ship type
    SpaceShip ship2 = new SpaceShip (ShipType.FRIGATE);
    // Prints "The pirate ship is a frigate ship."
    System.out.println(ship2);
  }
}
```

on the
job

The override annotation (@Override) indicates that a method declaration intends on overriding a method declaration in the class's supertype.

Compile and Interpret Java Code

Exam Objective   Create executable Java applications with a main method, run a program from the command line, including console output

The Java Development Kit (JDK) includes several utilities for compiling, debugging, and running Java applications. This section details two utilities from the kit: the Java compiler and the Java interpreter. For more information on the JDK and its other utilities, see Chapter 10.

Java Compiler

Because we'll need a sample application to use for our Java compiler and interpreter exercises, we'll employ the simple `GreetingsUniverse.java` source file, shown in the following listing, throughout the section. This sample includes the main method used as the entry point of the executed code. When the program is started, this is the first method to be called by the JVM. The main method shown here contains one line of code. This line,

```
System.out.println("Greetings, Universe!")
```

will print

```
Greetings, Universe!
```

to standard output. This output would typically be displayed on a Java application that was started from a console.

```java
public class GreetingsUniverse {
  public static void main(String[] args) {
    System.out.println("Greetings, Universe!");
  }
}
```

Let's take a look at compiling and interpreting simple Java programs along with their most basic command-line options.

Compiling Your Source Code

The Java compiler is only one of several tools in the JDK. When you have time, inspect the other tools resident in the JDK's bin folder, as shown in Figure 1-7. For the scope of the OCA exam, you will need to know the details surrounding only the compiler and interpreter.

The Java compiler simply converts Java source files into bytecode. The Java compiler's usage is as follows:

```
javac [options] [source files]
```

The most straightforward way to compile a Java class is to preface the Java source files with the compiler utility from the command line: `javac.exe FileName.java`. The `.exe` is the standard executable file extension on Windows machines

FIGURE 1-7   Java Development Kit utilities

and is optional. The `.exe` extension is not present on executables on UNIX-like systems.

```
javac GreetingsUniverse.java
```

This will result in a bytecode file being produced with the same preface, such as `GreetingsUniverse.class`. This bytecode file will be placed into the same folder as the source code, unless the code is packaged and/or it's been told via a command-line option to be placed somewhere else.

You will find that many projects use Apache Ant and/or Maven build environments. Understanding the fundamentals of the command-line tools is necessary for writing and maintaining the scripts associated with these build products.

Compiling Your Source Code with the -d Option

You may want to specify explicitly where you would like the compiled bytecode class files to go. You can accomplish this by using the `-d` option:

```
javac -d classes GreetingsUniverse.java
```

This command-line structure will place the class file into the classes directory, and since the source code was packaged (that is, the source file included a `package` statement), the bytecode will be placed into the relative subdirectories.

```
[present working directory]\classes\com\ocajexam\tutorial\
    GreetingsUniverse.class
```

INSIDE THE EXAM

Command-Line Tools

Most projects use integrated development environments (IDEs) to compile and execute code. The clear benefit in using IDEs is that building and running code can be as easy as stepping through a couple of menu options or clicking a hot key. The disadvantage is that even though you may establish your settings through a configuration dialog and see the commands and subsequent arguments in one of the workspace windows, you are not getting direct experience in repeatedly creating the complete structure of the

commands and associated arguments by hand. The exam is structured to validate that you have experience in scripting compiler and interpreter invocations. Do not take this prerequisite lightly. Take the exam only after you have mastered when and how to use the tools, switches, and associated arguments. At a later time, you can consider taking advantage of the "shortcut" features of popular IDEs such as those provided by NetBeans, Eclipse, IntelliJ IDEA, and JDeveloper.

Compiling Your Code with the -classpath Option

If you want to compile your application with user-defined classes and packages, you may need to tell the JVM where to look by specifying them in the classpath. This classpath inclusion is accomplished by telling the compiler where the desired classes and packages are with the -cp or -classpath command-line option. In the following compiler invocation, the compiler includes in its compilation any source files that are located under the 3rdPartyCode\classes directory, as well as any classes located in the present working directory (the period). The -d option (again) will place the compiled bytecode into the classes directory.

```
javac -d classes -cp 3rdPartyCode\classes\;. GreetingsUniverse
    .java
```

Note that you do not need to include the classpath option if the classpath is defined with the CLASSPATH environment variable, or if the desired files are in the present working directory.

On Windows systems, classpath directories are delimited with backward slashes and paths are delimited with semicolons:

```
-classpath .;\dir_a\classes_a\;\dir_b\classes_b\
```

On POSIX-based systems, classpath directories are delimited with forward slashes and paths are delimited with colons:

```
-classpath .:/dir_a/classes_a/:/dir_b/classes_b/
```

Again, the period represents the present (or current) working directory.

---

e x a m

ⓦatch

Know your switches. The designers of the exam will try to throw you by presenting answers with mix-matching compiler and interpreter switches. You may even see some make-believe switches that do not exist anywhere. For additional preparation, query the commands' complete set of switches by typing `java -help` *or* `javac -help`. *Switches are also known as command-line parameters, command-line switches, options, and flags.*

Java Interpreter

Interpreting the Java files is the basis for creating the Java application, as shown in Figure 1-8. Let's examine how to invoke the interpreter and its command-line options.

```
java [-options] class [args...]
```

Interpreting Your Bytecode

The Java interpreter is invoked with the `java[.exe]` command. Use it to interpret bytecode and execute your program.

You can easily invoke the interpreter on a class that's not packaged, as follows:

```
java MainClass
```

| FIGURE 1-8 | Bytecode conversion |

You can optionally start the program with the `javaw` command on Microsoft Windows to exclude the command window. This is a nice feature with GUI-based applications, because the console window is often not necessary.

```
javaw.exe MainClass
```

Similarly, on POSIX-based systems, you can use the ampersand to run the application as a background process:

```
java MainClass &
```

Interpreting Your Code with the -classpath Option

When interpreting your code, you may need to define where certain classes and packages are located. You can find your classes at runtime when you include the `-cp` or `-classpath` option with the interpreter. If the classes you want to include are packaged, then you can start your application by pointing the full path of the application to the base directory of classes, as in the following interpreter invocation:

```
java -cp classes com.ocajexam.tutorial.MainClass
```

The delimitation syntax is the same for the `-cp` and `-classpath` options, as defined earlier in the "Compiling Your Code with the -classpath Option" section.

Interpreting Your Bytecode with the -D Option

The `-D` command-line option allows for the setting of new property values. The usage is as follows:

```
java -D<name>=<value> class
```

The following single-file application comprising the `PropertiesManager` class prints out all of the system properties:

```java
import java.util.Properties;
public class PropertiesManager {
  public static void main(String[] args) {
    if (args.length == 0) {System.exit(0);}
    Properties props = System.getProperties();
      /* New property example */

      props.setProperty("new_property2", "new_value2");
      switch (args[0]) {
        case "-list_all":
          props.list(System.out); // Lists all properties
```

```
            break;
        case "-list_prop":
          /* Lists value */
          System.out.println(props.getProperty(args[1]));
          break;
        default:
          System.out.println("Usage: java
            PropertiesManager [-list_all]");
          System.out.println("          java
            PropertiesManager [-list_prop [property]]");
          break;
      }
    }
  }
```

Let's run this application while setting a new system property called new_property1 to the value of new_value1:

```
java -Dnew_property1=new_value1 PropertiesManager -list_all
```

You'll see in the standard output that the listing of the system properties includes the new property that we set and its value:

```
...
new_property1=new_value1
java.specification.name=Java Platform API Specification
...
```

Optionally, you can set a value by instantiating the Properties class and then setting a property and its value with the setProperty method.

To help you conceptualize system properties a little better, Table 1-7 details a subset of the standard system properties.

Retrieving the Version of the Interpreter with the -version Option

The -version command-line option is used with the Java interpreter to return the version of the JVM and exit. Don't take the simplicity of the command for granted, as the designers of the exam may try to trick you by including additional arguments after the command. Take the time to toy with the command by adding arguments and putting the -version option in various places. Do not make any assumptions about how you think the application will respond. Figure 1-9 demonstrates varying results based on where the -version option is used.

Check out the other JDK utilities at your disposal. Java Flight Recorder and Java Mission Control in particular are valuable GUI-based tools that are used to monitor, profile, and collect runtime information.

TABLE 1-7 Subset of System Properties

System Property	Property Description
file.separator	The platform-specific file separator (/ for POSIX, \ for Windows)
java.class.path	The classpath as defined for the system's environment variable
java.class.version	The Java class version number
java.home	The directory of the Java installation
java.vendor	The vendor supplying the Java platform
java.vendor.url	The vendor's Uniform Resource Locator
java.version	The version of the Java Interpreter/JVM
line.separator	The platform-specific line separator (\r on Mac OS 9, \n for POSIX, \r\n for Microsoft Windows)
os.arch	The architecture of the operating system
os.name	The name of the operating system
os.version	The version of the operating system
path.separator	The platform-specific path separator (: for POSIX, ; for Windows)
user.dir	The current working directory of the user
user.home	The home directory of the user
user.language	The language code of the default locale
user.name	The username for the current user
user.timezone	The system's default time zone

FIGURE 1-9

The -version command-line option

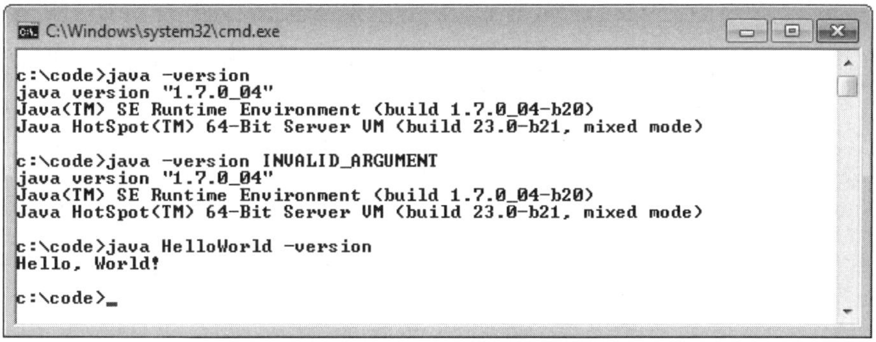

```
c:\code>java -version
java version "1.7.0_04"
Java(TM) SE Runtime Environment (build 1.7.0_04-b20)
Java HotSpot(TM) 64-Bit Server VM (build 23.0-b21, mixed mode)

c:\code>java -version INVALID_ARGUMENT
java version "1.7.0_04"
Java(TM) SE Runtime Environment (build 1.7.0_04-b20)
Java HotSpot(TM) 64-Bit Server VM (build 23.0-b21, mixed mode)

c:\code>java HelloWorld -version
Hello, World!

c:\code>_
```

EXERCISE 1-2

Compiling and Interpreting Packaged Software

When you compile and run packaged software from an IDE, the execution process can be as easy as clicking a run icon, as the IDE will maintain the classpath for you and will also let you know if anything is out of sorts. When you try to compile and interpret the code yourself from the command line, you will need to know exactly how to path your files. Consider our sample application that is placed in the com .ocajexam.tutorial package (that is, the com/ocajexam/tutorial directory).

```
package com.ocajexam.tutorial;
public class GreetingsUniverse {
  public static void main(String[] args) {
    System.out.println("Greetings, Universe!");
  }
}
```

This exercise will have you compiling and running the application with new classes created in a separate package.

1. Compile the program:

```
javac -d . GreetingsUniverse.java
```

2. Run the program to ensure it is error free:

```
java -cp . com.ocajexam.tutorial.GreetingsUniverse
```

3. Create three classes named Earth, Mars, and Venus and place them in the com.ocajexam.tutorial.planets package. Create constructors that will print the names of the planets to standard output. The details for the Earth class are given here as an example of what you will need to do:

```
package com.ocajexam.tutorial.planets;
public class Earth {
  public Earth {
    System.out.println("Hello from Earth!");
  }
}
```

4. Instantiate each class from the main program by adding the necessary code to the GreetingsUniverse class.

```
Earth e = new Earth();
```

5. Ensure that all of the source code is in the paths src/com/ocajexam/tutorial/ and src/com/ocajexam/tutorial/planets/.

6. Determine the command-line arguments needed to compile the complete program. Compile the program, and debug where necessary.

7. Determine the command-line arguments needed to interpret the program. Run the program.

The standard output will read as follows:

```
$ Greetings, Universe!
Hello from Earth!
Hello from Mars!
Hello from Venus!
```

CERTIFICATION SUMMARY

This chapter discussed packaging, structuring, compiling, and interpreting Java code. The chapter started with a discussion on the importance of organizing your classes into packages as well as using the `package` and `import` statements to define and include different pieces of source code. Through the middle of the chapter, we discussed the key features of commonly used Java packages: `java.awt`, `javax.swing`, `java.net`, `java.io`, and `java.util`. We discussed the basic structure of a Java class. We then concluded the chapter by providing detailed information on how to compile and interpret Java source and class files and how to work with their command-line options. At this point, you should be able to (outside of an IDE) package, build, and run basic Java programs independently.

✓ TWO-MINUTE DRILL

Understand Packages

- ☐ Packages are containers for classes.
- ☐ A package statement defines the directory path where files are stored.
- ☐ A package statement uses periods for delimitation.
- ☐ Package names should be lowercase and separated with underscores between words.
- ☐ Package names beginning with java.* and javax.* are reserved.
- ☐ There can be zero or one package statement per source file.
- ☐ An import statement is used to include source code from external classes.
- ☐ An import statement occurs after the optional package statement and before the class definition.
- ☐ An import statement can define a specific class name to import.
- ☐ An import statement can use an asterisk to include all classes within a given package.

Understand Package-Derived Classes

- ☐ The Java Abstract Window Toolkit API is included in the java.awt package and subpackages.
- ☐ The java.awt package includes GUI creation and painting graphics and images functionality.
- ☐ The Java Swing API is included in the javax.swing package and subpackages.
- ☐ The javax.swing package includes classes and interfaces that support lightweight GUI component functionality.
- ☐ The Java Basic Input/Output-related classes are contained in the java.io package.
- ☐ The java.io package includes classes and interfaces that support input/output functionality of the file system, data streams, and serialization.
- ☐ Java networking classes are included in the java.net package.

☐ The `java.net` package includes classes and interfaces that support basic networking functionality that is also extended by the `javax.net` package.

☐ Fundamental Java utilities are included in the `java.util` package.

☐ The `java.util` package and subpackages include classes and interfaces that support the Java Collections Framework, legacy collection classes, event model, date and time facilities, and internationalization functionality.

Understand Class Structure

☐ Naming conventions are used to make Java programs more readable and maintainable.

☐ Naming conventions are applied to several Java elements, including class names, interface names, method names, instance and static variable names, parameter and local variable names, generic type parameter names, constant names, enumeration names, and package names.

☐ The preferred order of presenting elements in a class is data members, followed by constructors, followed by methods. Note that the inclusion of each type of element is optional.

Compile and Interpret Java Code

☐ The Java compiler is invoked with the `javac[.exe]` command.

☐ The `.exe` extension is optional on Microsoft Windows machines and is not present on UNIX-like systems.

☐ The compiler's `-d` command-line option defines where compiled class files should be placed.

☐ The compiler's `-d` command-line option will include the package location if the class has been declared with a `package` statement.

☐ The compiler's `-classpath` command-line option defines directory paths in search of classes.

☐ The Java interpreter is invoked with the `java[.exe]` command.

☐ The interpreter's `-classpath` switch defines directory paths to use at runtime.

☐ The interpreter's `-D` command-line option allows for the setting of system property values.

☐ The interpreter's syntax for the `-D` command-line option is `-Dproperty=value`.

☐ The interpreter's `-version` command-line option is used to return the version of the JVM and exit.

☐ The `-h` command-line option can be applied either to the compiler or the interpreter to print out the tool's usage information.

SELF TEST

Understanding Packages

1. Which two `import` statements will allow for the import of the `HashMap` class?
   A. `import java.util.HashMap;`
   B. `import java.util.*;`
   C. `import java.util.HashMap.*;`
   D. `import java.util.hashMap;`

2. Which statement would designate that your file belongs in the package `com.ocajexam.utilities`?
   A. `pack com.ocajexam.utilities;`
   B. `package com.ocajexam.utilities.*`
   C. `package com.ocajexam.utilities.*;`
   D. `package com.ocajexam.utilities;`

3. Which of the following is the only Java package that is imported by default?
   A. `java.awt`
   B. `java.lang`
   C. `java.util`
   D. `java.io`

Understand Package-Derived Classes

4. The `JCheckBox` and `JComboBox` classes belong to which package?
   A. `java.awt`
   B. `javax.awt`
   C. `java.swing`
   D. `javax.swing`

5. Which package contains the Java Collections Framework?
   A. `java.io`
   B. `java.net`
   C. `java.util`
   D. `java.utils`

6. The Java Basic I/O API contains what types of classes and interfaces?

    A. Internationalization

    B. RMI, JDBC, and JNDI

    C. Data streams, serialization, and file system

    D. Collection API and data streams

7. Which API provides a lightweight solution for GUI components?

    A. AWT

    B. Abstract Window Toolkit

    C. Swing

    D. AWT and Swing

8. Consider the following illustration. What problem exists with the packaging? You may wish to reference Appendix G of the Unified Modeling Language (UML) for assistance.

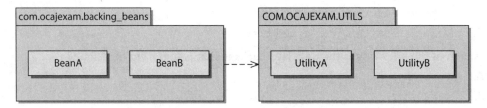

    A. You can have only one class per package.

    B. Packages cannot have associations between them.

    C. Package `com.ocajexam.backing_beans` fails to meet the appropriate package naming conventions.

    D. Package `COM.OCAJEXAM.UTILS` fails to meet the appropriate package naming conventions.

Understand Class Structure

9. When apply naming conventions, which Java elements should start with an uppercase letter and continue on using the CamelCase convention?

    A. Class names

    B. Interface names

    C. Constant names

    D. Package names

    E. All of the above

10. When instantiating an object with generics, should you use angle brackets, box brackets, curly brackets, or double-quotation marks to enclose the generic type? Select the appropriate answer.

    A. `List<Integer> a = new ArrayList<Integer>();`

    B. `List[Integer] a = new ArrayList[Integer]();`

    C. `List{Integer} a = new ArrayList{Integer}();`

    D. `List"Integer" a = new ArrayList"Integer"();`

11. When you're organizing the elements in a class, which order is preferred?

    A. Data members, methods, constructors

    B. Data members, constructors, methods

    C. Constructors, methods, data members

    D. Constructors, data members, methods

    E. Methods, constructors, data members

Compile and Interpret Java Code

12. Which usage represents a valid way of compiling a Java class?

    A. `java MainClass.class`

    B. `javac MainClass`

    C. `javac MainClass.source`

    D. `javac MainClass.java`

13. Which two command-line invocations of the Java interpreter return the version of the interpreter?

    A. `java -version`

    B. `java --version`

    C. `java -version ProgramName`

    D. `java ProgramName -version`

14. Which two command-line usages appropriately identify the classpath?

    A. `javac -cp /project/classes/ MainClass.java`

    B. `javac -sp /project/classes/ MainClass.java`

    C. `javac -classpath /project/classes/ MainClass.java`

    D. `javac -classpaths /project/classes/ MainClass.java`

15. Which command-line usages appropriately set a system property value?

A. `java -Dcom.ocajexam.propertyValue=003 MainClass`

B. `java -d com.ocajexam.propertyValue=003 MainClass`

C. `java -prop com.ocajexam.propertyValue=003 MainClass`

D. `java -D:com.ocajexam.propertyValue=003 MainClass`

SELF TEST ANSWERS

Understand Packages

1. Which two `import` statements will allow for the import of the `HashMap` class?

A. `import java.util.HashMap;`

B. `import java.util.*;`

C. `import java.util.HashMap.*;`

D. `import java.util.hashMap;`

> Answer:
>
> ☑   **A** and **B.** The `HashMap` class can be imported directly via `import java.util`
> `.HashMap` or with a wildcard via `import java.util.*;`.
>
> ☒   **C** and **D** are incorrect. **C** is incorrect because the answer is a static `import` statement that imports static members of the `HashMap` class, and not the class itself. **D** is incorrect because class names are case sensitive, so the class name `hashMap` does not equate to `HashMap`.

2. Which statement would designate that your file belongs in the package `com.ocajexam`
`.utilities`?

A. `pack com.ocajexam.utilities;`

B. `package com.ocajexam.utilities.*`

C. `package com.ocajexam.utilities.*;`

D. `package com.ocajexam.utilities;`

> Answer:
>
> ☑   **D.** The keyword `package` is appropriately used, followed by the package name delimited with periods and followed by a semicolon.
>
> ☒   **A, B,** and **C** are incorrect. **A** is incorrect because the word `pack` is not a valid keyword. **B** is incorrect because a `package` statement must end with a semicolon, and you cannot use asterisks in `package` statements. **C** is incorrect because you cannot use asterisks in `package` statements.

3. Which of the following is the only Java package that is imported by default?

A. `java.awt`

B. `java.lang`

C. `java.util`

D. `java.io`

Answer:

☑ **B.** The `java.lang` package is the only package that has all of its classes imported by default.

☒ **A, C,** and **D** are incorrect. The classes of packages `java.awt`, `java.util`, and `java.io` are not imported by default.

Understand Package-Derived Classes

4. The `JCheckBox` and `JComboBox` classes belong to which package?

A. `java.awt`

B. `javax.awt`

C. `java.swing`

D. `javax.swing`

Answer:

☑ **D.** Components belonging to the Swing API are generally prefaced with a uppercase *J*. Therefore, `JCheckBox` and `JComboBox` would be part of the Java Swing API and not the Java AWT API. The Java Swing API base package is `javax.swing`.

☒ **A, B,** and **C** are incorrect. **A** is incorrect because the package `java.awt` does not include the `JCheckBox` and `JComboBox` classes since they belong to the Java Swing API. Note that the package `java.awt` includes the `CheckBox` class, as opposed to the `JCheckBox` class. **B** and **C** are incorrect because the package names `javax.awt` and `java.swing` do not exist.

5. Which package contains the Java Collections Framework?

A. `java.io`

B. `java.net`

C. `java.util`

D. `java.utils`

Answer:

☑ **C.** The Java Collections Framework is part of the Java Utilities API in the `java.util` package.

☒ **A, B,** and **D** are incorrect. **A** is incorrect because the Java Basic I/O API's base package is named `java.io` and does not contain the Java Collections Framework. **B** is incorrect because the Java Networking API's base package is named `java.net` and also does not contain the Collections Framework. **D** is incorrect because there is no package named `java.utils`.

6. The Java Basic I/O API contains what types of classes and interfaces?

A. Internationalization

B. RMI, JDBC, and JNDI

C. Data streams, serialization, and file system

D. Collection API and data streams

Answer:

☑ **C.** The Java Basic I/O API contains classes and interfaces for data streams, serialization, and the file system.

☒ **A, B,** and **D** are incorrect. Internationalization (i18n), RMI, JDBC, JNDI, and the Collections framework are not included in the Basic I/O API.

7. Which API provides a lightweight solution for GUI components?

A. AWT

B. Abstract Window Toolkit

C. Swing

D. AWT and Swing

Answer:

☑ **C.** The Swing API provides a lightweight solution for GUI components, meaning that the Swing API's classes render using pure Java code and not native platform widgets.

☒ **A, B,** and **D** are incorrect. AWT and the Abstract Window Toolkit are one and the same and provide a heavyweight solution for GUI components.

8. Consider the following illustration. What problem exists with the packaging? You may wish to reference Appendix G of the Unified Modeling Language (UML) for assistance.

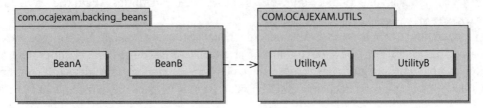

A. You can have only one class per package.

B. Packages cannot have associations between them.

C. Package com.ocajexam.backing_beans fails to meet the appropriate package naming conventions.

D. Package COM.OCAJEXAM.UTILS fails to meet the appropriate package naming conventions.

Answer:

☑   **D.** COM.OCAJEXAM.UTILS fails to meet the appropriate package naming conventions. Package names should be lowercase and should use an underscore between words. However, the words in ocajexam are joined in the URL; therefore, excluding the underscore here is acceptable. The package name should read com.ocajexam.utils.

☒   **A, B,** and **C** are incorrect. **A** is incorrect because being restricted to having one class in a package is ludicrous. There is no limit. **B** is incorrect because packages can and frequently do have associations with other packages. **C** is incorrect because com.ocajexam.backing_beans meets appropriate packaging naming conventions.

Understand Class Structure

9. When apply naming conventions, which Java elements should start with an uppercase letter and continue on using the CamelCase convention?

A. Class names

B. Interface names

C. Constant names

D. Package names

E. All of the above

Answer:

☑ **A and B.** Class names and interface names should start with an uppercase letter and continue on using the CamelCase convention.
☒ **C and D** are incorrect. **C** is incorrect because constant names should be all uppercase letters separated by underscores. **D** is incorrect because package names do not include uppercase letters, nor do they subscribe to the CamelCase convention.

10. When instantiating an object with generics, should you use angle brackets, box brackets, parentheses, or double-quotation marks to enclose the generic type? Select the appropriate answer.

A. `List<Integer> a = new ArrayList<Integer>();`
B. `List[Integer] a = new ArrayList[Integer]();`
C. `List{Integer} a = new ArrayList{Integer}();`
D. `List"Integer" a = new ArrayList"Integer"();`

Answer:

☑ **A.** Generics use angle brackets.
☒ **B, C,** and **D** are incorrect. Box brackets (**B**), curly brackets (**C**), and double quotation marks (**D**) are not used to enclose the generic type.

11. When you're organizing the elements in a class, which order is preferred?

A. Data members, methods, constructors
B. Data members, constructors, methods
C. Constructors, methods, data members
D. Constructors, data members, methods
E. Methods, constructors, data members

Answer:

☑ **B.** The preferred order in presenting elements in a class is to present the data members first, followed by constructors, followed by methods.
☒ **A, C, D,** and **E** are incorrect. Although ordering the elements in these manners will not cause any functional or compilation errors, none of these is the preferred order.

Compile and Interpret Java Code

12. Which usage represents a valid way of compiling a Java class?

    A. `java MainClass.class`

    B. `javac MainClass`

    C. `javac MainClass.source`

    D. `javac MainClass.java`

    > Answer:
    >
    > ☑ **D.** The compiler is invoked by the `javac` command. When compiling a Java class, you must include the filename, which houses the main classes, including the `.java` extension.
    >
    > ☒ **A, B,** and **C** are incorrect. **A** is incorrect because `MainClass.class` is bytecode that is already compiled. **B** is incorrect because `MainClass` is missing the `.java` extension. **C** is incorrect because `MainClass.source` is not a valid name for any type of Java file.

13. Which two command-line invocations of the Java interpreter return the version of the interpreter?

    A. `java -version`

    B. `java --version`

    C. `java -version ProgramName`

    D. `java ProgramName -version`

    > Answer:
    >
    > ☑ **A** and **C.** The `-version` flag should be used as the first argument. The application will return the appropriate strings to standard output with the version information and then immediately exit. The second argument is ignored.
    >
    > ☒ **B** and **D** are incorrect. **B** is incorrect because the version flag does not allow double dashes. You may see double dashes for flags in utilities, especially those following the GNU license. However, the double dashes do not apply to the version flag of the Java interpreter. **D** is incorrect because the version flag must be used as the first argument or its functionality will be ignored.

14. Which two command-line usages appropriately identify the classpath?

    A. `javac -cp /project/classes/ MainClass.java`

    B. `javac -sp /project/classes/ MainClass.java`

    C. `javac -classpath /project/classes/ MainClass.java`

    D. `javac -classpaths /project/classes/ MainClass.java`

Answer:

☑ **A** and **C.** The option flag that is used to specify the classpath is `-cp` or `-classpath`.

☒ **B** and **D** are incorrect. The option flags `-sp` (**B**) and `-classpaths` (**D**) are invalid.

15. Which command-line usages appropriately set a system property value?

    A. `java -Dcom.ocajexam.propertyValue=003 MainClass`

    B. `java -d com.ocajexam.propertyValue=003 MainClass`

    C. `java -prop com.ocajexam.propertyValue=003 MainClass`

    D. `java -D:com.ocajexam.propertyValue=003 MainClass`

Answer:

☑ **A.** The property setting is used with the interpreter, not the compiler. The property name must be sandwiched between the `-D` flag and the equal sign. The desired value should immediately follow the equal sign.

☒ **B, C,** and **D** are incorrect. The `-d` (**B**), `-prop` (**C**), and `-D:` (**D**) flags are invalid ways to designate a system property.

2

Programming with Java Statements

T he language statements within software applications allow the proper sequence of execution and associated functionality to occur. The more statement types a software language includes, the more effective the language can be. With Java, for example, the ability of programmatically allowing a system to stay up and running by supporting the code with exception handling statements is an effective benefit. Table 2-1 provides short definitions of the Java statement types defined in *The Java Language Specification: Java SE 8 Edition*, by James Gosling, Bill Joy, Guy Steele, Gilad Bracha, and Alex Buckley (Oracle, 2015). The statements covered on the exam and in this chapter are accompanied by a checkmark. You can refer to the language specification for more details on the statements that are not on the exam.

TABLE 2-1   Java Statements

Statement Name	Definition	On the Exam
The `assert` statement	Used to determine whether code is functioning as expected. When its expression is evaluated to false, an exception is thrown.	
The `break` statement	Used to exit the body of a `switch` statement or loop.	✓
The `case` statement	Used as part of the `switch` statement to execute statements when its value matches the `switch` statement's conditional value.	✓
The `continue` statement	Used to terminate the current iteration of a `do-while, while,` or `for` loop and continue with the next iteration.	✓
The `while` statement	Used for iteration based on a condition.	✓
The `do-while` statement	Used for iteration based on a condition. The body of the `do-while` statement is executed at least once.	✓
The `empty` statement	Used for trivial purposes where no functionality is needed. It is represented by a single semicolon.	
The expression statements	Used to evaluate expressions. See Table 2-2.	✓
The `for` loop statement	Used for iteration. Main components are an initialization part, an expression part, and an update part.	✓
The enhanced `for` loop statement	Used for iteration through an iterable object or array.	✓
The `if` statement	Used for the conditional execution of statements.	✓
The `if-then` statement	Used for the conditional execution of statements by providing multiple conditions.	✓
The `if-then-else` statement	Used for the conditional execution of statements by providing multiple conditions and fall-through when no conditions are met.	✓

TABLE 2-1	Java Statements *(continued)*	

Statement Name	Definition	On the Exam
The labeled statement	Used to give a statement a prefixed label.	
The `return` statement	Used to exit a method and return a specified value.	✓
The `switch` statement	Used for branching code based on conditions.	✓
The `synchronized` statement	Used for access control of threads.	
The `throw` statement	Used to throw an exception.	Chapter 9
The `try-catch-finally` statement	Used for exception handling.	Chapter 9

To be an effective Java programmer, you must master the basic statements. Oracle knows this and has included complete coverage of the basic statements on the exam. This chapter will teach you how to recognize and code Java statements.

We begin by understanding fundamental statements. The Java programming language contains a variety of statement types. Even though the various statement types serve different purposes, those covered in this chapter can be grouped into four main categories: expression statements, conditional statements, iteration statements, and transfer of control statements.

Expression statements are used for the evaluation of expressions. The assignment expression statements allow assignments to be performed on variables. *Conditional statements*, also known as decision statements, assist in directing the flow of control when a decision needs to be made. Conditional statements include the `if`, `if-then`, `if-then-else`, and `switch` statements. *Iteration statements* provide support in looping through blocks of code. Iteration statements include the `for` loop, the enhanced `for` loop, the `while` statement, and the `do-while` statement. *Transfer of control statements* provide a means of stopping or interrupting the normal flow of control. Transfer of control statements include the `continue`, `break`, and `return` statements. Transfer of control statements are always seen within other types of statements.

The goal of this chapter is for you to gain the knowledge of when and how to use all of the necessary types of Java statements that will be included in the OCA Java Associate SE 8 Programmer (OCA) exam.

CERTIFICATION OBJECTIVE

Understand Assignment Statements

An assignment statement sets a value within a variable. All assignment statements are considered to be expression statements. Although no explicit exam objective exists for this, you'll need to have a basic knowledge of expression statements and, in particular, assignment statements.

Let's start with the expression statement. Expression statements essentially work with expressions. Expressions in Java are anything that has a value or is reduced to a value. Typically, expressions evaluate to primitive types, such as in the case of adding two numbers—for example, (1+2). Concatenating strings together with the concatenation (+) operator results in a string and is also considered an expression. All expressions can be used as statements; the only requirement is that they end with a semicolon. Table 2-2 shows examples of some typical expression statements and where they are discussed in this book.

The Assignment Expression Statement

Assignment expression statements, commonly known simply as assignment statements, are designed to assign values to variables. All assignment statements must be terminated with a semicolon. The ability to use assignment statements is a core feature of Java development.

TABLE 2-2	Expression Statement	Expression Statement Example	Coverage
Expression Statements	Assignment	`variableName = 7;`	Chapter 2
	Prefix-increment	`++variableName;`	Chapter 3
	Prefix-decrement	`--variableName;`	Chapter 3
	Postfix-increment	`variableName++;`	Chapter 3
	Postfix-decrement	`variableName--;`	Chapter 3
	Method invocation	`performMethod();`	Chapter 5
	Object creation	`new ClassName();`	Chapter 4

Here is the general usage of the assignment statement:

```
variable = value;
```

Given the declaration of an integer primitive, let's look at an assignment in its most basic form. The assignment statement comprises three key elements. On the left is the variable that will be associated with the memory and type necessary to store the value. On the right is a literal value. If an expression is on the right, such as (1+2), it must be evaluated down to its literal value before it can be assigned. Lastly, an equal sign resides between the variable and value of an assignment statement. Here are some example statements:

```
int variableName; // Declaration of an integer
variableName = 100; // Assignment expression statement
```

As long as the application is running and the object in which the variable exists is still alive (that is, available in memory), the value for variableName will remain the assigned value, unless it is explicitly changed with another expression statement. The statement, illustrated in Figure 2-1, combines a declaration, an expression, and an assignment statement. In addition, it uses the values stored from previous assignment statements.

```
int fishInTank = 100;
int fishInCooler = 50;
int totalFish = fishInTank + fishInCooler;
```

Trying to save an invalid literal to a declared primitive type variable will result in a compiler error. For example, the compilation error Exception in thread "xxxx" java.lang.RuntimeException: Uncompilable source code - incompatible types... would appear for the following code:

```
int totalFish = "INVALID_USE_OF_A_STRING";
```

For more information about working with primitives, see Chapter 4.

FIGURE 2-1

Combined
statements

CERTIFICATION OBJECTIVE

Create and Use Conditional Statements

Exam Objective   *Create if and if/else and ternary constructs*
Exam Objective   *Use a switch statement*

Conditional statements are used when there is a need for determining the direction of flow based on conditions. Conditional statements include the if, if-then, if-then-else, and switch statements. The conditional statements represented in Table 2-3 will appear on the exam.

The if Conditional Statement

The if statement is designed to conditionally execute a statement or conditionally decide between a choice of statements. The if statement will execute only one statement upon the condition unless braces are supplied. Braces, also known as

TABLE 2-3   Conditional Statements

Formal Name	Keywords	Expression Types	Example
if	if, else (optional)	boolean	if (value == 0) {}
if-then	if, else if, else if (optional)	boolean	if (value == 0) {} else if (value == 1) {} else if (value >= 2) {}
if-then-else	if, else if (optional), else if (optional), else	boolean	if (value == 0) {} else if (value >=1) {} else {}
Ternary operator	?, : (not official Java keyword)	boolean	minVal = a < b ? a : b;

switch	switch,
	case,
	default (optional),
	break
	(optional)
		char, byte, short,
		int, Character,
		Byte, Short, String,
		Integer,
		enumeration
		types
			switch (100) {
			　case 100: break;
			　case 200: break;
			　case 300: break;
			　default: break;
			}

INSIDE THE EXAM

The if, if-then, and if-then-else Statements

The distinction between the if, if-then, and if-then-else statements may seem blurred. This is partially because the then keyword used in some other programming languages is not used in Java, even though the Java constructs are formally known as if-then and if-then-else. Let's clarify some confusing points about the if-related statements by providing some facts.

■ The if statement allows for the optional use of the else branch. This may be a little confusing since you may expect the if statement to stand alone without any branches.

■ The if-then statement must have at least one else if branch. Optionally, an unlimited number of else if branches may be included. You cannot use an else statement in an if-then statement or the statement would be considered an if-then-else statement.

■ The if-then-else statement must have at least one else if branch. The else if branch is not optional, because if it were not present, the statement would be considered to be an if statement that includes the optional else branch.

curly brackets, allow for multiple enclosed statements to be executed. This group of statements is also known as a *block*. The expression that is evaluated within if statements must evaluate to a boolean value or the application will not compile. The else clause is optional and may be omitted.

Here's the general usage of the if statement:

```
if (expression)
    statementA;
else
    statementB;
```

In the following example, we look at the most basic structure of an if statement. Here, we check to see if a person (isFisherman) is a fisherman, and, if so, the expression associated with the if statement would evaluate to true. Because it is true, the example's fishing trip value (isFishingTrip) is modified to true. No action would be taken if the isFisherman expression evaluated to false.

```
boolean isFisherman = true;
boolean isFishingTrip = false;
if (isFisherman)
    isFishingTrip = true;
```

Let's change the code a little bit. Next you will see that a fishing trip will occur only if there are one or more fishermen, as the expression reads (fishermen >= 1). See Chapter 3 for more details on relationship operators (for example, <, <=, >, >=, ==, !=). You also see that when "one or more fishermen" evaluates to true, a block of statements will be executed.

```
int fishermen = 2;
boolean isFishingTrip = false;
if (fishermen >= 1) {
    isFishingTrip = true;
    System.out.print("Going Fishing!");
}
$ Going Fishing!
```

Executing statements in relationship to false conditions is also common in programming. In the following example, when the expression evaluates to false, the statement associated with the else part of the if statement is executed:

```
boolean isFisherman = false;
if (isFisherman) System.out.println("Going fishing!");
else System.out.println("I'm doing anything but fishing!");
$ I'm doing anything but fishing!
```

The if-then Conditional Statement

The if-then conditional statement—also known as the if else if statement—is used when multiple conditions need to flow through a decision-based scenario.

Here's the general usage of the if-then statement:

```
if (expressionA)
    statementA;
else if (expressionB)
    statementB;
```

The expressions must evaluate to boolean values. Each statement may optionally be a group of statements enclosed in braces.

INSIDE THE EXAM

The if Statement

The most important thing you need to remember about the expression in the `if` statement is that it can accept any expression that returns a `boolean` value, and once the expression evaluates to `true`, all subsequent `else` statements are skipped. Note, too, that even though relational operators (such as >=) are commonly used, assignment statements are always allowed.

Review and understand the following code examples:

```
boolean b;
boolean bValue = (b = true);
// Evaluates to true
if (bValue) System.out
.println("TRUE");
else System.out.println("FALSE");
if (bValue = false) System.out
.println("TRUE");
else System.out.println("FALSE");
if (bValue == false) System.out
.println("TRUE");
else System.out.println("FALSE");
```

Output:

```
$ TRUE
$ FALSE
$ TRUE
```

You also need to know that the assignment statements of all primitives will return their primitive values. So, if it's not an assignment of a `boolean` type, the return value will not be `boolean`. As such, the following code will not compile:

```
int i; // Valid declaration
int iValue = (i=1);
// Valid evaluation to int
/* Fails here since a boolean value
is expected in the expression */
if (iValue) {};
```

Similarly, this code will not compile:

```
/* Fails here since a boolean value
is expected in the expression */
if (i=1) {};
```

The compiler error will look like the following:

```
Error: incompatible types; found:
int, required: boolean
```

Let's look at another example. (For those not familiar with surf fishing, when fishing off the beach, a lead pyramid-shaped sinker is used to keep the line on the bottom of the ocean.) In the following code segment, conditions are evaluated matching the appropriate pyramidSinker by weight against the necessary tide:

```
int pyramidSinker = 3;
System.out.print("A pyramid sinker that weighs " + pyramidSinker
  + "ounces is ");
if (pyramidSinker == 2)
  System.out.print("used for a slow moving tide. ");
else if (pyramidSinker == 3)
  System.out.print("used for a moderate moving tide. ");
else if (pyramidSinker == 4)
  System.out.print("used for a fast moving tide. ");
```

Output:

```
$ A pyramid sinker that weighs 3 ounces is used for a moderate
  moving tide.
```

We used the string concatenation (+) operator in this example. Although its functionality is straightforward, you'll find more information about its behavior in Chapter 3.

exam

ⓦatch
The if family of statements evaluates expressions that must result in a boolean type where the value is true or false. Be aware that an object from the Boolean wrapper class is also allowed, because it will go through unboxing in order to return the expected type. Unboxing is the automatic production of its primitive value in cases where it is needed. The following code demonstrates the use of a Boolean wrapper class object within the expression of an if statement:

```
Boolean wrapperBoolean = new Boolean ("true");
/* Valid */
boolean primitiveBoolean1 = wrapperBoolean.booleanValue();
/* Valid because of unboxing */
boolean primitiveBoolean2 = wrapperBoolean;
if (wrapperBoolean)
System.out.println("Works because of unboxing");
```

For more information on autoboxing and unboxing, see Chapter 4.

The if-then-else Conditional Statement

As with the `if` and `if-then` statements, all expressions must evaluate to `true` or `false` as the expected primitive type is `boolean`. The main difference in the `if-then-else` statement is that the code will fall through to the final stand-alone `else` when the expression fails to return `true` for any condition. Each statement may optionally be a group of statements enclosed in braces. There is no limit to the number of `else if` clauses.

Here's the general usage of the `if-then-else` statement:

```
if (expressionA)
    statementA;
else if (expressionB)
    statementB;
else if (expressionC)
    statementC;
...
else
    statementZZ;
```

In the following code listing, the method `getCastResult()` represents the efforts of a fisherman casting his line out into the ocean. The return value will be a `String` of value "fish," "shark," or "skate," and in this application the value is stored into the `resultOfCast` variable. This `String` value is evaluated against the stipulated string passed into the `equals` method. If the criteria are met for any `if` or `else if` condition, the associated block of code is executed; otherwise, the code related to the final `else` is executed. This code clearly demonstrates a complete `if-then-else` scenario.

```
...
private FishingSession fishingSession = new FishingSession();
...
public void castForFish() {
  fishingSession.setCatch();
  String resultOfCast = fishingSession.getCastResult();
  if (resultOfCast.equals("fish")) {
    Fish keeperFish = new Fish();
    keeperFish = fishingSession.getFishResult();
    String type = keeperFish.getTypeOfFish();
    System.out.println("Wahoo! Keeper fish: " + type);
  } else if (resultOfCast.equals("shark")) {
    System.out.println("Need to throw this one back!");
  } else if (resultOfCast.equals("skate")) {
```

```
      System.out.println("Yuck, Leo can take this one off the
         hook!");
   } else {
      System.out.println("Darn, no catch!");
   }
}
...
```

Output:

```
$ Wahoo! Keeper fish: Striped Bass
```

Note that the `Fish` class and associated methods are deliberately not shown since the scope of this example is the `if-then-else` scenario only.

on the job

If abrupt termination occurs (for example, due to an overflow error) during the evaluation of the conditional expression within an `if` statement, then all subsequent `if-then` (that is, `else if`) and `if-then-else` (that is, `else`) statements will end abruptly as well.

The Ternary Operator

The ternary operator is a variation of the `if-then-else` statement. It is also sometimes referred to as a conditional operator. The ternary operator derives its name from the fact that it is the only operator to use three operands. The `?` and `:` characters are used in this operation. The ternary operator behaves similarly to the `if-then-else` statement but never includes any optional `else if`.

The following is the general usage of the ternary operator:

```
result = testCondition ? value1 : value2
```

Let's take a look at the ternary operator in a real code example. In the following example, the variable `x` is set to `-5`. A ternary operator is then used to find the absolute value of the variable `x`. The first part must be an expression that results in a `boolean` value. In this case, `x` is tested to determine if it is greater than 0. If this expression is `true`, the ternary operation returns `value1`, the first value after the `?` character. A `false` will result in `value2`, the value after the `:` character, to be returned. In this example, −5 is not greater than 0. Therefore, the second value (the value following the `:`) will be used. In this case, that value flips the sign of the variable, changing −5 to 5.

```
int x = -5;
int absoluteValue = x > 0 ? x : -x;
System.out.println(absoluteValue);
```

Output:

```
$ 5
```

Here is the same example using a normal if-then-else statement:

```
int x = -5;
int absoluteValue;
if(x > 0){
    absoluteValue = x;
}
else{
    absoluteValue = -x;
}
System.out.println(absoluteValue);
```

on the

job

Ternary operators are great for checking and returning simple values. However, in a more complex situation, a normal if-then-else statement will often result in code that is easier to read.

The switch Conditional Statement

The switch conditional statement is used to match the value from a switch statement expression against a value associated with a case keyword. Once matched, the enclosed statement(s) associated with the matching case value are executed and subsequent case statements are executed, unless a break statement is encountered. The break statements are optional and will cause the immediate termination of the switch conditional statement.

When two case statements within the same switch statement have the same value, a compiler error will be thrown:

```
switch (intValue){
case 200: System.out.println("Case 1");
/* Compiler error, Error: duplicate case label */
 case 200: System.out.println("Case 2");
}
```

The expression of the switch statement must evaluate to byte, short, int, or char. Wrapper classes of type Byte, Short, Integer, and Character are also allowed because they are automatically unboxed to primitive types. Enumerated types (that is, enum) are permitted as well. Additionally, Java SE 7 added support for evaluation of the String object in the expression.

Here's the general usage of the `switch` statement:

```java
switch (expression) {
    case valueA:
        // Sequences of statements
        break;
    case valueB:
        // Sequences of statements
        break;
    default:
        // Sequences of statements
    ...
}
```

Let's take a look at a complete `switch` conditional statement example. In the following `generateRandomFish` method, we use a random number generator to produce a value that will be used in the `switch` expression. The number generated will be 0, 1, 2, or 3. The `switch` statement will use the value to match it to the value of a `case` statement. In the example, a `String` with the name `randomFish` will be set depending on the `case` matched. The only possible value that does not have a matching `case` statement is the number 3. Therefore, this condition will be handled by the `default` statement. Whenever a `break` statement is hit, it will cause immediate termination of the `switch` statement.

```java
public String generateRandomFish() {
    String randomFish;
    Random randomObject = new Random();
    int randomNumber = randomObject.nextInt(4);
    switch (randomNumber) {
        case 0:
            randomFish = "Blue Fish";
            break;
        case 1:
            randomFish = "Red Drum";
            break;
        case 2:
            randomFish = "Striped Bass";
            break;
        default:
            randomFish = "Unknown Fish Type";
            break;
    }
    return randomFish;
}
```

The case statements can be organized in any manner. The default case is often listed last for code readability. Remember that without break statements, the switch block will continue with its fall-through from the point that the condition has been met. The following code is a valid switch conditional statement that uses an enumeration type for its expression value:

```
private enum ClamBait {FRESH,SALTED,ARTIFICIAL}
...
ClamBait bait = ClamBait.SALTED;
switch (bait) {
default:
   System.out.println("No bait");
   break;
 case FRESH:
   System.out.println("Fresh clams");
   break;
 case SALTED:
   System.out.println("Salted clams");
   break;
 case ARTIFICIAL:
   System.out.println("Artificial clams");
   break;
 }
```

Knowing what you can and cannot do with switch statements will help expedite your development efforts.

SCENARIO & SOLUTION

To ensure that your statement is bug-free, which type of statements should you include within the switch?	Both break statements and the default statement are commonly used in the switch. Forgetting these statements can lead to improper fall-throughs or unhandled conditions. Note that many bug-finding tools will flag missing default statements.
You want to use a range in a case statement (for instance, case 7-35). Is this a valid feature in Java, as it is with other languages?	Ranges in case statements are *not* allowed. Consider setting up a condition in an if statement. For example: if (x >=7 && x <=35){}
You want to use the switch statement, using String values where the expression is expected, as is possible with other languages. Is this a valid feature in Java?	Strings are not valid at the decision point for switch statements prior to Java SE 7. For Java SE 6 and earlier, consider using an if statement instead. For example: if (strValue.equals("S1")){}

EXERCISE 2-1

Evaluating the String Class in the switch Statement

Build a small program that demonstrates the use of the `String` class being evaluated in a `switch` statement. Follow the model that is used for the `switch` statement with the other data types, and your application will run just fine.

CERTIFICATION OBJECTIVE

Create and Use Iteration Statements

Exam Objective   *Compare loop constructs*
Exam Objective   *Create and use for loops including the enhanced for loop*
Exam Objective   *Create and use while loops*
Exam Objective   *Create and use do/while loops*

Iteration statements are used when there is a need to iterate through pieces of code. Iteration statements include the `for` loop, enhanced `for` loop, and the `while` and `do-while` statements. The `break` statement is used to exit the body of any iteration statement. The `continue` statement is used to terminate the current iteration and continue with the next iteration. The iteration statements detailed and compared in Table 2-4 will appear on the exam.

The for Loop Iteration Statement

The `for` loop statement is designed to iterate through code. It has main parts that include an initialization part, an expression part, and an iteration part. The initialization does not need to declare a variable as long as the variable is declared before the `for` statement. So, for example, `int x = 0;` and `x=0;` are both acceptable in the initialization part. Be aware, though, that the scope of the variable declared within the initialization part of the `for` loop ends once the `for` loop terminates. The expression within the `for` loop statement must evaluate to a `boolean` value. The iteration, also known as the update part, provides the mechanism that will allow the iteration to occur. A basic update part is represented as `i++;`.

TABLE 2-4   Iteration Statements

Formal Name	Keywords	Main Expression Components	Example
`for loop`	`for,` `break` (optional), `continue` (optional)	Initializer, expression, update mechanism	`for (i=0; i<j; i++) {}`
Enhanced `for` loop	`for,` `break` (optional), `continue` (optional)	Element, array, or collection	`for (Fish f :` `listOfFish) {};`
`while`	`while,` `break` (optional), `continue` (optional)	Boolean expression	`while (value == 1) {` `}`
`do-while`	`do, while,` `break` (optional), `continue` (optional)	Boolean expression	`do {` `} while (value == 1);`

Here's the general usage of the `for` statement:

```
for ( initialization; expression; iteration) {
    // Sequence of statements
}
```

The following is an example of a basic `for` loop where the initialization variable is declared outside the `for` loop statement:

```
int m;
for (m = 1; m < 5; m++) {
  System.out.print("Marker " + m + ", ");
}
System.out.print("Last Marker " + m + "\n");
```

Output:

```
$ Marker 1, Marker 2, Marker 3, Marker 4, Last Marker 5
```

The following is a similar example, but with the variable declared in the `for` loop:

```
for (int m = 1; m < 5; m++) {
  System.out.print("Marker " + m + ", ");
}
```

Declaring the initialize variable in the `for` loop is allowed and is the common approach. However, you can't use the variable once you have exited the loop. The following will result in a compilation error:

```
for (int m = 1; m < 5; m++) {
  System.out.print("Marker " + m + ", ");
}
System.out.print("Last Marker " + m + "\n"); // m is out of scope
```

Compiler output:

```
# Error: variable m not found in class [ClassName].
```

The Enhanced for Loop Iteration Statement

The enhanced `for` loop is used to iterate through an array, a collection, or an object that implements the interface `iterable`. The enhanced `for` loop is also commonly known as the `for each` loop and the `for in` loop. Iteration occurs for each element in the array or iterable class. Remember that the loop can be terminated at any time by the inclusion of a `break` statement. And as with the other iteration statements, the `continue` statement will terminate the current iteration and start with the next iteration.

INSIDE THE EXAM

Exposing Corner Cases with Your Compiler

The exam designers were not satisfied with simply validating your knowledge of the fundamental Java material. They took the time to work in corner cases, as well as modify the structure of the code in such a slight manner that it appears to be correct but is not. When you work through the examples in this book, take the time to modify things a bit, intentionally introducing errors, to see how the compiler reacts. Your ability to think like the compiler will help you score higher on the exam.

Third-party developers of Java development kits can define their own text for compiler error messages. Where they will likely try to model the messages provided by Oracle's JDK, sometimes they will take care to make the messages more precise. Consider generating compiler errors with the latest Oracle JDK compiler, as well as a compiler provided by an integrated development environment (IDE) such as the Eclipse SDK. Compare the similarities and differences.

Here's the general usage of the `for` statement:

```
for (type variable : collection) statement-sequence
```

The following code segment demonstrates how a `for` loop can easily dump out the contents of an array. Here, the enhanced `for` loop iterates over each `hook` integer in the array `hookSizes`. For each iteration, the `hook` size is printed out.

```
int hookSizes[] = { 1, 1, 1, 2, 2, 4, 5, 5, 5, 6, 7, 8, 8, 9 };
for (int hook: hookSizes) System.out.print(hook + " ");
$ 1 1 1 2 2 4 5 5 5 6 7 8 8 9
```

The enhanced `for` loop is frequently used for searching through items in a collection. Here, the enhanced `for` loop iterates over each `hook` integer in the collection `hookSizesList`. For each iteration, the `hook` size is printed out. This example demonstrates the use of collections and generic interface.

```
List<Integer> hookSizesList = new ArrayList<>();
hookSizesList.add(1);
hookSizesList.add(4);
hookSizesList.add(5);
for (Integer hook : hookSizesList) System.out.print(hook + " ");
$ 1 4 5
```

See *Java Generics and Collections* by Maurice Naftalin and Philip Wadler (O'Reilly, 2006) for comprehensive coverage of the generics and collections frameworks.

EXERCISE 2-2

Iterating Through an ArrayList While Applying Conditions

In this exercise, you will iterate through an `ArrayList` of floats. Specifically, you will print out only the legal sizes of keeper fish.

1. Create an `ArrayList` of floats called `fishLengthList`. This list will represent the sizes of a few striped bass.

2. Add the following floats to the list: 10.0, 15.5, 18.0, 29.5, 45.5. These numbers represent the length in inches of the bass.

3. Iterate through the list, printing out only the numbers larger than the required length. Assume the required length is 28 inches.

To gain more knowledge on the `ArrayList` class, see Chapter 4.

Most IDEs support customizable formatting that can often be applied by selecting a format option from a menu. Using an IDE to ensure formatting is properly and consistently applied is a good idea.

The while Iteration Statement

The while statement is designed to iterate through code. The while loop statement evaluates an expression and executes the while loop body only if the expression evaluates to true. Typically, an expression within the body will affect the result of the expression.

Here's the general usage of the while statement:

```
while (expression) {
    // Sequences of statements
}
```

The following code example demonstrates the use of the while statement. Here, a fisherman will continue fishing until his fish limit has been reached. Specifically, when the fishLimit variable within the body of the while statement reaches 10, the fisherman's session will be set to inactive. Since the while statement demands that the session be active, its loop will terminate upon the change.

```
fishingSession.setSession("active");
/* WHILE STATEMENT */
while (fishingSession.getSession().equals("active")) {
 castForFish(); // Updates fishLimit instance variable
 if (fishLimit == 10) {
   fishingSession.setSession("inactive");
 }
}
```

When formatting your code, you can follow various formatting styles. Formatting considerations include indentation, whitespace usage, line wrapping, code separation, and braces handling. You should select a style and maintain it throughout your code. For demonstration purposes, here are two distinct ways that braces are handled.

Here is the K&R style braces handling:

```
while (x==y) {
  performSomeMethod();
}
```

Here is the Allman style braces handling:

```
while (x==y)
{
  performSomeMethod();
}
```

The do-while Iteration Statement

The do-while statement is designed to iterate through code. It is very similar to the while loop statement, except that it always executes the body at least once. The do-while loop evaluates an expression and continues to execute the body only if it evaluates to true. Typically, an expression within the body will affect the result of the expression.

Here's the general usage of the do-while statement:

```
do {
    // Sequence of statements
} while (expression)
```

EXERCISE 2-3

Performing Code Refactoring

In the following code example, we want to make sure the fisherman gets at least one cast in. Although this appears to make logical sense, you always need to think about corner cases. What if a fox steals the fisherman's bait before he gets a chance to cast? In this case, the piecesOfBait variable would equal zero, but the fisherman would still cast, as the body of the do-while loop is guaranteed at least one iteration. See if you can refactor this code with a while statement to avoid the possible condition of casting with no bait.

```
fishingSession.setSession("active");
int piecesOfBait = 5;
piecesOfBait = 0; // Fox steals the bait!
 do {
   castForFish();
   /* Check to see if bait is available */
   if (fishingSession.isBaitAvailable() == false) {
     /* Place a new piece of bait on the hook */
     fishingSession.setBaitAvailable(true);
     piecesOfBait--;
   }
 } while (piecesOfBait != 0);
```

SCENARIO & SOLUTION

You want to iterate though a collection. Which iteration statement would be the best choice?	Use the enhanced `for` loop statement.
You want to execute a statement based on the result of a `boolean` expression. Which conditional statement would be the best choice?	Use the `if` statement.
You want to provide conditional cases in relationship to enumeration values. What conditional statement would be your only choice?	Use the `switch` statement.
You want to execute a block of statements and then iterate through the block based on a condition. What iteration statement would be your only choice?	Use the `do-while` statement.
You want to exit a case statement permanently. What transfer of control statement would you choose?	Use the `break` statement.

Selecting the right statement types during development can make coding your algorithms easier. Proper statement selection will also promote the ease of software maintenance efforts if the code ever needs to be modified. It's important to realize that statements are used for different purposes, and one particular type of statement cannot solve all development needs. You will find it common to use a combination of statement types to implement the code for many algorithms. Having a strong foundation regarding the main purposes of the different types of statements will assist you when you need to use them together.

EXERCISE 2-4

Knowing Your Statement-Related Keywords

Table 2-5 represents all of the statement-related Java keywords. This exercise will enable you to use the table to assist in deducing the keywords you might see while using the various types of statements.

Let's start the exercise.

1. List the primary keywords you may see in conditional statements.

2. List the primary keywords you may see in iteration statements.

3. List the primary keywords you may see in transfer of control statements.

TABLE 2-5	Java Keywords				
Java Statement-Related Keywords	break	continue	else	if	throw
	case	default	finally	return	try
	catch	do	for	switch	while

4. Bonus: List the primary keywords you may see in exception handling statements.

CERTIFICATION OBJECTIVE

Create and Use Transfer of Control Statements

Exam Objective   Use break and continue

Transfer of control statements include the break, continue, and return statements. We've mentioned these statements in the previous sections, but we cover them directly here. In short, transfer of control statements provide a means to stop or interrupt the normal flow of control. They are always used within other types of statements. A transfer of control statement always works with the labeled statement. We'll examine working with the labeled statement after first looking at the most common way of using break, continue, and return statements.

The break Transfer of Control Statement

The break statement is used to exit or force an abrupt termination of the body of the switch conditional statement as well as the body of the do, for loop; enhanced for loop; and while and do-while iteration statements.

The general usage of the break statement is simple:

```
break;
```

In the following example, the for loop is completely exited when the break statement is called. The break statement is called when the total hours allowed fishing exceed the total hours fishing. In short, the method prints a statement for every hour allowed to be fished in a one-day period.

```java
public void fishingByHour() {
    int totalHoursFishing = 0;
    int hoursAllowedFishing = 4;
    for (int i = 1; i < 25; ++i) {
        totalHoursFishing = ++totalHoursFishing;
        if (totalHoursFishing > hoursAllowedFishing)
            break;
        System.out.println("Fishing for hour" + i + ".");
    }
}
```

Here's the result of executing this method:

```
Fishing for hour 1.
Fishing for hour 2.
Fishing for hour 3.
Fishing for hour 4.
```

The continue Transfer of Control Statement

The continue statement is used to terminate the current iteration of a do, for loop; enhanced for loop; or while or do-while loop and continue with the next iteration. The general usage of the continue statement is also simple:

```java
continue;
```

In the following example, the continue statement (when reached) immediately changes the flow to the next iteration of the for statement. The method prints a statement for each day allowed to go camping or camping and fishing. The fishing days start from day one and are defined by daysAllowedFishing. The continue statement is reached on days 1, 2, and 3, causing the rest of the iteration in the for loop to be skipped. On subsequent days, the continue statement is not reached, allowing the rest of the for loop to be exercised. The System.out .print statements are applied as reached.

```java
public void activitiesByDay() {
    int totalDaysCamping = 0;
    int daysAllowedFishing = 5;
    for (int i = 1; i < 8; ++i) {
        System.out.print("\nDay " + i + ": camping ");
        totalDaysCamping++;
```

```
            if (totalDaysCamping > daysAllowedFishing)
                continue;
            System.out.print("and fishing");
        }
    }
```

Here's the result of executing this method:

```
Day 1: camping and fishing
Day 2: camping and fishing
Day 3: camping and fishing
Day 4: camping and fishing
Day 5: camping and fishing
Day 6: camping
Day 7: camping
```

The return Transfer of Control Statement

The return statement is used to exit a method and optionally return a specified value as an expression. A return statement with no return value must have the keyword void in the method declaration.

Here's the general usage of the return statement:

```
return [expression];
```

In the following example, the getTotalFishTypes method returns the value of the fishTypesTotal int primitive that was computed in the method's assignment statement. The getTotalCaughtFish method returns an int as well; however, in this case, the expression is inline. In both cases, the int keyword is provided in the method declaration, as necessary.

```
public int getTotalFishTypes
    (int saltWaterFishTotal, int freshWaterFishTotal, int brackishFishTotal) {
    int fishTypesTotal = saltWaterFishTotal + freshWaterFishTotal
        + brackishFishTotal;
    return fishTypesTotal;
}
public int getTotalCaughtFish (int keeperFish, int throwBackFish) {
    return keeperFish + throwBackFish;
}
```

on the
job

If a return statement is the last statement in a method, and the method doesn't return anything, the return statement is optional. In this optional case, the return statement is typically not used.

The labeled Statement

The labeled statement is used to give a statement a prefixed label. It can be used in conjunction with the continue and break statements. Use labeled statements sparingly; you should use them over other approaches only on a few occasions.

The general usage of the labeled statement is the addition of a label followed by a colon with the appropriate statement immediately following it:

```
labelIdentifier:
              Statement (such as a for loop)
```

Here are the general usages of the break and continue statements in conjunction with the labeled statement:

```
break labelIdentifier;
```

and

```
continue labelIdentifier;
```

Let's look at a simple example of each. In the following example, the flow is transferred from the labeled break statement to the end of the labeled myBreakLabel outer loop:

```
public void labeledBreakTest() {
  myBreakLabel:
  while (true) {
    System.out.println("While loop 1");
    while (true) {
      System.out.println("While loop 2");
      while (true) {
        System.out.println("While loop 3");
        break myBreakLabel;
      }
    }
  }
}
```

Here's the result of executing this method:

```
While loop 1
While loop 2
While loop 3
```

In the following example, the flow is transferred from the labeled `continue` statement to the labeled `myContinueLabel` outer loop. Note that the fourth `while` loop is not reachable due to the `continue` statement.

```java
public void labeledContinueTest() {
  myContinueLabel:
  while (true) {
    System.out.println("While loop 1");
    while (true) {
      System.out.println("While loop 2");
      while (true) {
        System.out.println("While loop 3");
        continue myContinueLabel;
        while (true)
          System.out.println("While loop 4");
      }
    }
  }
}
```

The result of executing this method is the printing of the first three statements continuously repeated, as shown next:

```
While loop 1
While loop 2
While loop 3
While loop 1
While loop 2
While loop 3
While loop 1
While loop 2
While loop 3
...
```

It is unlikely that you will see labeled statements on the exam. This coverage was simply intended for ***completeness of the transfer of control statement features.***

CERTIFICATION SUMMARY

This chapter on fundamental statements discussed details related to the fundamental statement types. By studying this chapter, you should be able to recognize and develop the following types of statements:

- Expression statements, with a focus on the assignment statement
- Conditional statements (`if`, `if-then`, `if-then-else`, and `switch`)
- Iteration statements (`for`, enhanced `for`, `while`, and `do-while`)
- Transfer of control statements (`continue`, `break`, and `return`)

Throughout a Java developer's career, each of these statement types will be seen and used quite frequently. At this point, you should be well prepared for exam questions covering Java statements.

TWO-MINUTE DRILL

Understand Assignment Statements

- ☐ Assignment statements assign values to variables.
- ☐ Assignment statements that do not return `boolean` types will cause the compiler to report an error when used as the expression in an `if` statement.
- ☐ Trying to save an invalid literal to a declared primitive type variable will result in a compiler error.

Create and Use Conditional Statements

- ☐ Conditional statements are used for determining the direction of flow based on conditions.
- ☐ Types of conditional statements include the `if`, `if-then`, `if-then-else`, and `switch` statements.
- ☐ The ternary operator is another form of the `if-then-else` statement.
- ☐ The `default` case statement can be placed anywhere in the body of the `switch` statement.
- ☐ The expressions used in `if` statements must evaluate to `boolean` values, or the application will fail to compile.
- ☐ `Boolean` wrapper classes are allowed as expressions in `if` statements because they are unboxed. Remember that unboxing is the automatic production of primitive values from their related wrapper classes when the primitive value is required.

Create and Use Iteration Statements

- ☐ Iteration statements are designed for iterating over pieces of code.
- ☐ Iteration statements include the `for` loop, enhanced `for` loop, and the `while` and `do-while` statements.
- ☐ The `for` loop statement has main components that include an initialization part, an expression part, and an update part.
- ☐ The enhanced `for` loop statement is used for iteration through an iterable object or array.

☐ The while loop statement is used for iteration based on a condition.

☐ The do-while statement is used for iteration based on a condition. The body of this statement is always executed at least once.

Create and Use Transfer of Control Statements

☐ Transfer of control statements interrupt or stop the flow of execution.

☐ Transfer of control statements include continue, break, and return statements.

☐ The continue statement is used to terminate the current iteration of a do, for loop; enhanced for loop; and while or do-while loop and continue with the next iteration.

☐ The break statement is used to exit or force an abrupt termination of the body of the switch conditional statement as well as the body of the do, for loop, enhanced for loop, and while and do-while iteration statements.

☐ The return statement is used to exit a method and may return a specified value.

☐ The labeled statement is used to give a statement a prefixed label. It is used with the continue and break statements.

☐ A block is a sequence of statements within braces—for example, { int x=0; int y=1 }.

SELF TEST

The following questions will help you measure your understanding of the material presented in this chapter. Read all the choices carefully because there might be more than one correct answer. Choose all correct answers for each question.

Understand Assignment Statements

1. Which is not a type of statement?
   A. Conditional statement
   B. Assignment statement
   C. Iteration statement
   D. Propagation statement

2. What type of statement is the following equation: y = (m*x) + b?
   A. Conditional statement
   B. Assignment statement
   C. Assertion statement
   D. Transfer of control statement

3. Which statements correctly declare `boolean` variables?
   A. `Boolean isValid = true;`
   B. `boolean isValid = TRUE;`
   C. `boolean isValid = new Boolean (true);`
   D. `boolean isValid = 1;`

Create and Use Conditional Statements

4. Given x is declared with a valid integer, which conditional statement will not compile?
   A. `if (x == 0) {System.out.println("True Statement");}`
   B. `if (x == 0) {System.out.println("False Statement");}`
   C. `if (x == 0) {;} elseif (x == 1) {System.out.println("Valid Statement");}`
   D. `if (x == 0) ; else if (x == 1){} else {;}`

5. A `switch` statement works with which wrapper class/reference type(s)?

    A. `Character`

    B. `Byte`

    C. `Short`

    D. `Int`

6. Which of the following statements will not compile?

    A. `if (true) ;`

    B. `if (true) {}`

    C. `if (true) {;}`

    D. `if (true) {;;}`

    E. `if (true) ;{};`

    F. All statements will compile.

7. Given:

```java
public class Dinner {
  public static void main (String[] args)
  {
    boolean isKeeperFish = false;
    if (isKeeperFish = true) {
      System.out.println("Fish for dinner");
    } else {
      System.out.println("Take out for dinner");
    }
  }
}
```

What will be the result of the application's execution?

    A. `Fish for dinner` will be printed.

    B. `Take out for dinner` will be printed.

    C. A compilation error will occur.

8. Given:

```java
int x = 1;
String result = (x <= 1) ? "We are set for takeoff. " : "Launch Aborted!";
```

After this code is executed, what will be stored in the `result` variable?

    A. `We are set for takeoff.`

    B. `Launch Aborted!`

    C. A compilation error will occur.

9. Given:

```
int cartwheelsInAMinute = 30;
if (cartwheelsInAMinute > 48) {
  System.out.println("New world record!");
} else if (cartwheelsInAMinute > 30 && cartwheelsInAMinute <= 48) {
  System.out.println("Awesome Job!");
} else if (cartwheelsInAMinute > 0 && cartwheelsInAMinute <= 30) {
  System.out.println("Still impressive!");
} else {
  System.out.println("Keep trying!");
}
```

Select the correct answer.

A. `New world record!` will be printed.

B. `Awesome Job!` will be printed.

C. `Still impressive!` will be printed.

D. `Keep trying!` will be printed.

Create and Use Iteration Statements

10. You need to update a value of a hash table (that is, `HashMap`) where the primary key must equal a specified string. Which statements would you need to use in the implementation of this algorithm?

A. Iteration statement

B. Expression statement

C. Conditional statement

D. Transfer of control statement

Create and Use Transfer of Control Statements

11. Which keyword is part of a transfer of control statement?

A. `if`

B. `return`

C. `do`

D. `assert`

12. Given:

```
boolean isValid = true;
while (isValid){
  isValid = false;
  System.out.print("test1 ");
  if (isValid = true) {
    System.out.println("test2 ");
    break;
  }
  isValid = false;
  System.out.println("test3");
  }
}
```

What will be printed?

A.   Nothing will be printed.

B.   test1 will be printed.

C.   test1 test2 will be printed.

D.   test1 test2 test3 will be printed.

SELF TEST ANSWERS

Understand Assignment Statements

1. Which is not a type of statement?
   A. Conditional statement
   B. Assignment statement
   C. Iteration statement
   D. Propagation statement

> Answer:
>
> ☑ **D.** There is no such thing as a propagation statement.
> ☒ **A, B,** and **C** are incorrect. Conditional, assignment, and iteration are all types of statements.

2. What type of statement is the following equation: $y = (m*x) + b$?
   A. Conditional statement
   B. Assignment statement
   C. Assertion statement
   D. Transfer of control statement

> Answer:
>
> ☑ **B.** An assignment statement would be used to code the given example of $y = (m*x) + b$.
> ☒ **A, C,** and **D** are incorrect. The conditional, assertion, and transfer of control statements are not used to perform assignments.

3. Which statements correctly declare `boolean` variables?
   A. `Boolean isValid = true;`
   B. `boolean isValid = TRUE;`
   C. `boolean isValid = new Boolean (true);`
   D. `boolean isValid = 1;`

Answer:

☑ **A** and **C**. These statements properly declare `boolean` variables. Remember that the only valid literal values for the `boolean` primitives are `true` and `false`.

☒ **B** and **D** are incorrect. **B** is incorrect because `TRUE` is not a valid literal value. **D** is incorrect because you cannot assign the value 1 to a `boolean` variable.

Create and Use Conditional Statements

4. Given `x` is declared with a valid integer, which conditional statement will not compile?

   A. `if (x == 0) {System.out.println("True Statement");}`

   B. `if (x == 0) {System.out.println("False Statement");}`

   C. `if (x == 0) {;} elseif (x == 1) {System.out.println("Valid Statement");}`

   D. `if (x == 0) ; else if (x == 1){} else {;}`

   Answer:

   ☑ **C**. The statement will not compile. Without a space between the `else` and `if` keywords, the compiler will throw an error similar to `Error: method elseif (boolean) not found`....

   ☒ **A, B,** and **D** are incorrect. All of these conditional statements will compile successfully.

5. A `switch` statement works with which wrapper class/reference type(s)?

   A. `Character`

   B. `Byte`

   C. `Short`

   D. `Int`

   Answer:

   ☑ **A, B,** and **C**. The `switch` statements work with `Character`, `Byte`, and `Short` wrapper classes as well as the `Integer` wrapper class.

   ☒ **D** is incorrect. There is no such thing as an `Int` wrapper type. This was a trick question. The `switch` statement works with either the `int` primitive or the `Integer` wrapper type.

6. Which of the following statements will not compile?

A. `if (true) ;`

B. `if (true) {}`

C. `if (true) {;}`

D. `if (true) {;;}`

E. `if (true) ;{};`

F. All statements will compile.

Answer:

☑ **F.** All of the statements will compile.

7. Given:

```
public class Dinner {
  public static void main (String[] args)
  {
    boolean isKeeperFish = false;
    if (isKeeperFish = true) {
      System.out.println("Fish for dinner");
    } else {
      System.out.println("Take out for dinner");
    }
  }
}
```

What will be the result of the application's execution?

A. `Fish for dinner` will be printed.

B. `Take out for dinner` will be printed.

C. A compilation error will occur.

Answer:

☑ **A.** Because only one equal sign (that is, assignment statement) was used in the `if` statement, the `isKeeperFish` variable was assigned the value of `true`.

☒ **B** and **C** are incorrect.

8. Given:

    ```
    int x = 1;
    String result = (x <= 1) ? "We are set for takeoff. " : "Launch Aborted! ";
    ```

    After this code is executed, what will be stored in the `result` variable?

    A. `We are set for takeoff.`

    B. `Launch Aborted!`

    C. A compilation error will occur.

    Answer:

    ☑ **A.** The expression `(x <= 1)` evaluates to `true`. Therefore, the ternary operator returns the first value, which is the string "We are set for takeoff."

    ☒ **B** and **C** are incorrect.

9. Given:

    ```
    int cartwheelsInAMinute = 30;
    if (cartwheelsInAMinute > 48) {
      System.out.println("New world record!");
    } else if (cartwheelsInAMinute > 30 && cartwheelsInAMinute <= 48) {
      System.out.println("Awesome Job!");
    } else if (cartwheelsInAMinute > 0 && cartwheelsInAMinute <= 30) {
      System.out.println("Still impressive!");
    } else {
      System.out.println("Keep trying!");
    }
    ```

    Select the correct answer.

    A. `New world record!` will be printed.

    B. `Awesome Job!` will be printed.

    C. `Still impressive!` will be printed.

    D. `Keep trying!` will be printed.

    Answer:

    ☑ **C** is correct. The value stored in `cartwheelsInAMinute` meet the conditions to print this statement.

    ☒ **A, B,** and **D** are incorrect.

Create and Use Iteration Statements

10. You need to update a value of a hash table (that is, `HashMap`) where the primary key must equal a specified string. Which statements would you need to use in the implementation of this algorithm?

A. Iteration statement

B. Expression statement

C. Conditional statement

D. Transfer of control statement

Answer:

☑ **A, B,** and **C.** Iteration, expression, and conditional statements would be used to implement the algorithm. The following code segment demonstrates the use of these statements by programmatically replacing the ring on the little finger of a person's left hand. The statements are prefaced by comments that identify their types.

```
import java.util.HashMap;
public class HashMapExample {
  public static void main(String[] args) {
    HashMap<String,String> leftHand = new HashMap<String,String>();
    leftHand.put("Thumb", null);
    leftHand.put("Index finger", "Puzzle Ring");
    leftHand.put("Middle finger", null);
    leftHand.put("Ring finger", "Engagement Ring");
    leftHand.put("Little finger", "Pinky Ring");
    // Iteration statement
    for (String s : leftHand.keySet()) {
      // Conditional statement
      if (s.equals("Little finger")) {
        System.out.println(s + " had a " + leftHand.get(s));
        // Expression Statement
        leftHand.put("Little finger", "Engineer's Ring");
        System.out.println(s + " has an " + leftHand.get(s));
      }
    }
  }
}
$ Little finger had a Pinky Ring
$ Little finger has an Engineer's Ring
```

☒ **D** is incorrect. There is no transfer of control statement in the algorithm.

Create and Use Transfer of Control Statements

11. Which keyword is part of a transfer of control statement?

A. if

B. return

C. do

D. assert

Answer:

☑   **B.** The keyword `return` is used as part of a transfer of control statement.

☒   **A, C,** and **D** are incorrect. The keywords `if`, `do`, and `assert` are not part of any transfer of control statements.

12. Given:

```
boolean isValid = true;
while (isValid){
  isValid = false;
  System.out.print("test1 ");
  if (isValid = true) {
    System.out.println("test2 ");
    break;
  }
  isValid = false;
  System.out.println("test3");
  }
}
```

What will be printed?

A. Nothing will be printed.

B. `test1` will be printed.

C. `test1 test2` will be printed.

D. `test1 test2 test3` will be printed.

Answer:

☑   **C** is correct. `test1 test2` will print.

☒   **A, B,** and **D** are incorrect. **A** is incorrect because output is printed. **B** is incorrect because `test1` by itself is not printed. **D** is incorrect because `test1 test2 test3` is not printed.

3

Programming with
Java Operators and Strings

T wo of the most fundamental elements of the Java programming language are Java *operators* and *strings*. This chapter discusses Java operators and how they manipulate their operands. You will need a full understanding of the different types and groupings of operators and their precedence to score well on the exam. This chapter provides you with all of the operator-related information you need to know.

Strings are commonly used in Java, so they will also be present throughout the exam. This chapter details the `String` and `StringBuilder` classes and their related functionality. Topics include the string concatenation operator and the `toString` method, as well as a discussion of valuable methods from the `String` and `StringBuilder` classes. We wrap up the chapter discussing the testing of equality between strings.

After completing this chapter, you will have all the knowledge necessary to score well on the operator- and string-related questions on the exam.

CERTIFICATION OBJECTIVE

Understand Fundamental Operators

Exam Objective   Use Java operators, including parentheses, to override operator precedence

Java operators are used to return a result from an expression using one, two, or three operands. Operands are the values placed to the right or left side of the operators. Prefix- and postfix-increment and prefix- and postfix-decrement operators use one operand. The conditional ternary operator (`? :`) uses three operands. All other operators use two operands. Examples of operand use are shown in Figure 3-1. Note that the result of evaluating operands is typically a primitive value.

The following topics will be covered in these pages:

- Assignment operators
- Arithmetic operators
- Relational operators
- Logical operators
- Operator precedence

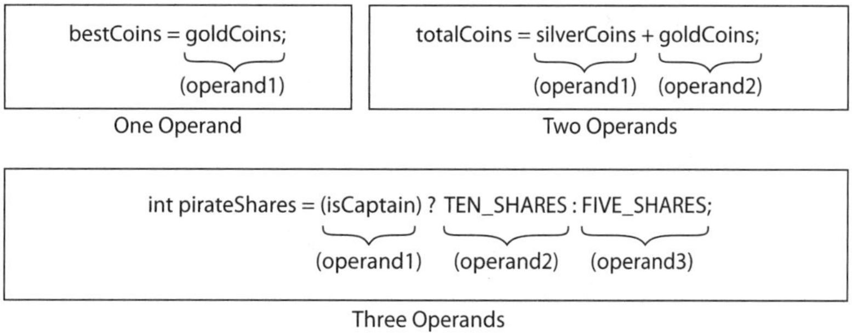

FIGURE 3-1

FIGURE 3-1

Operands

bestCoins = goldCoins;
(operand1)
One Operand

totalCoins = silverCoins + goldCoins;
(operand1)   (operand2)
Two Operands

int pirateShares = (isCaptain) ? TEN_SHARES : FIVE_SHARES;
(operand1)   (operand2)   (operand3)
Three Operands

Assignment Operators

Assignment operators are used to assign values to variables.

=	Assignment operator

The assignment operator is the equal sign (=). (Chapter 2 discusses assignment statements, and Chapter 4 discusses the assignment of literals into primitive data types and the creation of reference type variables.) At its simplest, the assignment operator moves valid literals into variables. Assignment operators cause compiler errors when the literals are not valid for the variable (that is, its associated type) to which they are assigned. The following are valid assignment statements using the assignment operator:

```
boolean hasTreasureChestKey = true;
byte shipmates = 20;
PirateShip ship = new PirateShip();
```

The following are invalid assignments and will cause compiler errors:

```
/* Invalid literal, TRUE must be lower case */
boolean hasTreasureChestKey = TRUE;
/* Invalid literal, byte value cannot exceed 127 */
byte shipmates = 500;
/*  Invalid constructor */
PirateShip ship = new PirateShip(UNEXPECTED_ARG);
```

Compound Assignment Operators

A variety of compound assignment operators exist. The exam covers only the addition and subtraction compound assignment operators.

+=	Assignment by addition operator
-=	Assignment by subtraction operator

Consider these two assignment statements:

```
goldCoins = goldCoins + 99;
pirateShips = pirateShips - 1;
```

The following two statements (with the same meaning and results as the preceding examples) are written with compound assignment operators:

```
goldCoins += 99;
pirateShips -= 1;
```

on the *Job*

Although the use of compound assignment operators cuts down on keystrokes, it is generally good practice to use the "longhand" approach since the code is clearly more readable.

EXERCISE 3-1

Using Compound Assignment Operators

This exercise will clear up any confusion you may have about compound assignment operators. The following application will be used for the exercise. (Don't run it until after step 3.)

```java
public class Main {
  public static void main(String[] args) {
    byte a;
    a = 10;
    System.out.println(a += 3);
    a = 15;
    System.out.println(a -= 3);
    a = 20;
    System.out.println(a *= 3);
    a = 25;
    System.out.println(a /= 3);
    a = 30;
    System.out.println(a %= 3);
    a = 35;
    // Optional as outside the scope of the exam
    System.out.println(a &= 3);
    a = 40;
    System.out.println(a ^= 3);
    a = 45;
    System.out.println(a |= 3);
```

```
a = 50;
System.out.println(a <<= 3);
a = 55;
System.out.println(a >>= 3);
a = 60;
System.out.println(a >>>= 3);
// End optional
    }
}
```

1. Grab a pencil and a piece of paper. Optionally, you can use Table 3-1 as your worksheet.

2. For each statement that has a compound assignment operator, rewrite the statement without the compound assignment operator and replace the variable with its associated value. For example, let's take the assignment statement with the addition compound assignment operator:

```
a = 5;
System.out.println(a += 3);
```

It would be rewritten as (a = a + 3)—specifically (a = 5 + 3);.

3. Evaluate the expressions without using a computer.

4. Compile and run the given application. Compare your results.

TABLE 3-1   Refactoring Compound Assignment Statements

Assigned Value of a	Compound Assignment	Refactored Statement	New Value of a
a = 10;	a += 3;	a = 10 + 3;	13
a = 15;	a -= 3;		
a = 20;	a *= 3;		
a = 25;	a /= 3;		
a = 30;	a %= 3;		
a = 35;	a &= 3;		
a = 40;	a ^= 3;		
a = 45;	a |= 3;		
a = 50;	a <<= 3;		
a = 55;	a >>= 3;		
a = 60;	a >>>= 3;		

(Note that many of these operators do not appear on the exam. The point of the exercise is to get you properly acquainted with compound assignment operators through repetition.)

on the **Job**

It is common to represent assignments in pseudo-code with the colon and equal sign characters (for example, A := 20). Notice that := looks similar to +=, -=, and other Java assignment operators such as *=, /=, and %=. Be aware, however, that the pseudo-code assignment representation (:=) is not a Java assignment operator, and if you see it in any Java code, it will not compile.

Arithmetic Operators

The exam will include nine arithmetic operators. Five of these operators are used for basic operations (addition, subtraction, multiplication, division, and modulus). The other four operators are used for incrementing and decrementing a value. We'll examine the five operators used for basic operations first.

Basic Arithmetic Operators

The five basic arithmetic operators are

+	Addition (sum) operator
-	Subtraction (difference) operator
*	Multiplication (product) operator
/	Division (quotient) operator
%	Modulus (remainder) operator

Adding, subtracting, multiplying, dividing, and producing remainders with operators is straightforward. The following examples demonstrate this:

```
/* Addition (+) operator example */
int greyCannonBalls = 50;
int blackCannonBalls = 50;
int totalCannonBalls = greyCannonBalls + blackCannonBalls; // 100
/* Subtraction (-) operator example */
int firedCannonBalls = 10;
totalCannonBalls = totalCannonBalls - firedCannonBalls; // 90
/* Multiplication (*) operator example */
int matches = 20;
```

```
int matchboxes = 20;
int totalMatches = matches * matchboxes; // 400
/* Division (/) operator example */
int pirates = 104;
int pirateShips = 3;
int assignedPiratesPerShip = pirates / pirateShips; // 34
/* Remainder (modulus) (%) operator example */
int pirateRemainder = pirates % pirateShips; // 2 (remainder)
```

Prefix-Increment, Postfix-Increment, Prefix-Decrement, and Postfix-Decrement Operators

Four operators allow incrementing or decrementing of variables:

++x	Prefix-increment operator
--x	Prefix-decrement operator
x++	Postfix-increment operator
x--	Postfix-decrement operator

Prefix-increment and prefix-decrement operators provide a shorthand way of incrementing and decrementing the variable by 1. Rather than creating an expression as y=x+1, you could write y=++x. Similarly, you could replace the expression y=x-1 with y=--x. This works because the execution of the prefix operators occurs on the operand prior to the evaluation of the whole expression. Postfix-increment and postfix-decrement characters execute the postfix operators after the expression has been evaluated. Therefore, y = x++ would equate to y=x followed by x=x+1. And y = x-- would equate to y=x followed by x=x-1.

Note that y=++x is not exactly equivalent to y=x+1, because the value of x changes in the former but not in the latter. This is the same for y=--x and y=x-1.

The prefix-increment operator increments a value by 1 before an expression has been evaluated.

```
int x = 10;
int y = ++x ;
System.out.println("x=" + x + ", y=" + y); // x= 11, y= 11
```

The postfix-increment operator increments a value by 1 after an expression has been evaluated.

```
int x = 10;
int y = x++ ;
System.out.println("x=" + x + ", y=" + y); // x= 11, y= 10
```

The prefix-decrement operator decrements a value by 1 before an expression has been evaluated.

```
int x = 10;
int y = --x ;
System.out.println("x=" + x + ", y=" + y); // x= 9, y= 9
```

The postfix-decrement operator decrements a value by 1 after an expression has been evaluated.

```
int x = 10;
int y = x-- ;
System.out.println("x=" + x + ", y=" + y); // x= 9, y= 10
```

Relational Operators

Relational operators return `boolean` values in relationship to the evaluation of their left and right operands. The six most common relational operators are on the exam. Four of them equate to the greater than and less than comparisons. Two are strictly related to equality, as we will discuss at the end of this section.

Basic Relational Operators

<	Less than operator
<=	Less than or equal to operator
>	Greater than operator
>=	Greater than or equal to operator

The less than, less than or equal to, greater than, and greater than or equal to operators are used to compare integers, floating points, and characters. When the expression used with the relational operators is true, the `boolean` value of `true` is returned; otherwise, `false` is returned. Here's an example:

```
/* returns true as 1 is less than 2 */
boolean b1 = 1 < 2;
/* returns false as 3 is not less than 2 */
boolean b2 = 3 < 2;
/* returns true as 3 is greater than 2 */
boolean b3 = 3 > 2;
/* returns false as 1 is not greater than 2 */
boolean b4 = 1 > 2;
/* returns true as 2 is less than or equal to 2 */
boolean b5 = 2 <= 2;
```

```
/* returns false as 3 is not less than or equal to 2 */
boolean b6 = 3 <= 2;
/* returns true as 3 is greater than or equal to 3 */
boolean b7 = 3 >= 3;
/* returns false as 2 is not greater than or equal to 3 */
boolean b8 = 2 >= 3;
```

So far, we've examined only the relationship of int primitives. Let's take a look at the various ways char primitives can be evaluated with relational operators, specifically the less than operator for these examples. Remember that characters (that is, char primitives) accept integers (within the valid 16-bit unsigned range), hexadecimal, octal, and character literals. Each literal in the following examples represents the letters "A" and "B." The left operands are character "A" and the right operands are character "B." Since each expression is essentially the same, they all evaluate to true.

```
boolean b1 = 'A' < 'B'; // Character literals
boolean b2 = '\u0041' < '\u0042'; // Unicode literals
boolean b3 = 0x0041 < 0x0042; // Hexadecimal literals
boolean b4 = 65 < 66; // Integer literals that fit in a char
boolean b5 = 0101 < 0102; //Octal literals
boolean b6 = '\101' < '\102'; // Octal literals
boolean b7 = 'A' < 0102; // Character and Octal literals
```

As mentioned, you can also test the relationship between floating points. The following are a few examples:

```
boolean b1 = 9.00D < 9.50D; // Floating points with D postfixes
boolean b2 = 9.00d < 9.50d; // Floating points with d postfixes
boolean b3 = 9.00F < 9.50F; // Floating points with F postfixes
boolean b4 = 9.0f < 9.50f; // Floating points with f postfixes
boolean b5 = (double)9 < (double)10; // Integers with explicit casts
boolean b6 = (float)9 < (float)10; // Integers with explicit casts
boolean b7 = 9 < 10; // Integers that fit into floating points
boolean b8 = (9d < 10f);
boolean b9 = (float)11 < 12;
```

Equality Operators

Relational operators that directly compare the equality of primitives (numbers, characters, booleans) and object reference variables are considered equality operators.

==	Equal to operator
!=	Not equal to operator

Comparing primitives of the same type is straightforward. If the right and left operands of the equal to operator are equal, the `boolean` value of `true` is returned; otherwise, `false` is returned. If the right and left operands of the not equal to operator are not equal, the `boolean` value of `true` is returned; otherwise, `false` is returned. The following code examples compare all eight primitives to values of the same type:

```
int value = 12;
/* boolean comparison, prints true */
System.out.println(true == true);
/* char comparison, prints false */
System.out.println('a' != 'a');
/* byte comparison, prints true */
System.out.println((byte)value == (byte)value);
/* short comparison, prints false */
System.out.println((short)value != (short)value);
/* integer comparison, prints true */
System.out.println(value == value);
/* float comparison, prints true */
System.out.println(12F == 12f);
/* double comparison, prints false */
System.out.println(12D != 12d);
```

on the job

You should actually use an epsilon when comparing floating-point numbers. See "Comparing Floating Point Numbers, 2012 Edition" for more information on comparing floating points for equality: http://randomascii.wordpress .com/2012/02/25/comparing-floating-point-numbers-2012-edition/.

Reference values of objects can also be compared. Consider the following code:

```
Object a = new Object();
Object b = new Object();
Object c = b;
```

The reference variables are a, b, and c. As shown, reference variables a and b are unique. Reference variable c refers to reference variable b, so for equality purposes, they are the same.

The following code shows the results of comparing these variables:

```
/* Prints false, different references */
System.out.println(a == b);
/* Prints false, different references */
System.out.println(a == c);
/* Prints true, same references */
System.out.println(b == c);
```

The following are similar statements, but they use the not equal to operator:

```
System.out.println(a != b); // Prints true, different references
System.out.println(a != c); // Prints true, different references
System.out.println(b != c); // Prints false, same references
```

Numeric Promotion of Binary Values   By this point, you may be wondering what the compiler does with the operands when they are of different primitive types. Numeric promotion rules are applied on binary values for the additive (+, -), multiplicative (*, /, %), comparison (<, <=, >, >=), equality (==, !=), bitwise (&, ^, |), and conditional (? :) operators. See Table 3-2.

Logical Operators

Logical operators return `boolean` values. There are three logical operators on the exam: logical AND, logical OR, and logical negation.

Logical (Conditional) Operators

Logical (conditional) operators evaluate a pair of `boolean` operands. Understanding their short-circuit principle is necessary for the exam.

&&	Logical AND (conditional AND) operator
||	Logical OR (conditional OR) operator

The logical AND operator evaluates the left and right operands. If both values of the operands have a value of true, then a value of `true` is returned. The logical AND is considered a short-circuit operator. If the left operand returns `false`, then there is no need to check the right operator since both would need to be true to return `true`; thus, it short-circuits. Therefore, whenever the left operand returns `false`, the expression terminates and returns a value of `false`.

TABLE 3-2	**Binary Numeric Promotion**	
Numeric Promotion of Binary Values	Check 1	Check if one and only one operand is a double primitive. If so, convert the non-double primitive to a double, and stop checks.
	Check 2	Check if one and only one operand is a float primitive. If so, convert the non-float primitive to a float, and stop checks.
	Check 3	Check if one and only one operand is a long primitive. If so, convert the non-long primitive to a long, and stop checks.
	Check 4	Convert both operands to `int`.

The following code demonstrates the usage of the logical AND operator:

```
/* Assigns true */
boolean and1 = true && true;
/* Assigns false */
boolean and2 = true && false;
/* Assigns false, right operand not evaluated */
boolean and3 = false && true;
/* Assigns false, right operand not evaluated */
boolean and4 = false && false;
```

The logical OR operator evaluates the left and right operands. If either value of the operands has a value of true, a value of `true` is returned. The logical OR is considered a short-circuit operator. If the left operand returns `true`, there is no need to check the right operator, since either needs to be true to return `true`; thus, it short-circuits. Again, whenever the left operand returns `true`, the expression terminates and returns a value of `true`.

The following code demonstrates the usage of the logical OR operator:

```
/* Assigns true, right operand not evaluated */
boolean or1 = true || true;
/* Assigns true, right operand not evaluated */
boolean or2 = true || false;
/* Assigns true */
boolean or3 = false || true;
/* Assigns false */
boolean or4 = false || false;
```

Logical Negation Operator

The logical negation operator is also known as the inversion operator or `boolean` invert operator. This is a simple operator, but don't take it lightly—you may see it quite often on the exam.

!	Logical negation (inversion) operator

The logical negation operator returns the opposite of a `boolean` value. The following code demonstrates the usage of the logical negation operator:

```
System.out.println(!false); // Prints true
System.out.println(!true); // Prints false
System.out.println(!!true); // Prints true
System.out.println(!!!true); // Prints false
System.out.println(!!!!true); // Prints true
```

Expect to see the logical negation operator used in conjunction with any method or expression that returns a `boolean` value. The following list details some of these expressions that return `boolean` values:

- Expressions with relational operators return `boolean` values.
- Expressions with logical (conditional) operators return `boolean` values.
- The `equals` method of the `Object` class returns `boolean` values.
- The `String` methods `startsWith` and `endsWith` return `boolean` values.

The following are some examples of statements that include the logical negation operator:

```
/* Example with relational expression */
int iVar1 = 0;
int iVar2 = 1;
if (!(iVar1 <= iVar2)) {};

/* Example with logical expressions */
boolean bVar1 = false; boolean bVar2 = true;
if ((bVar1 && bVar2) || (!(bVar1 && bVar2))){}

/* Example with equals method */
if (!"NAME".equals("NAME")) {}

/* Example with the String class's startsWith method */
String s = "Captain Jack";
System.out.println(!s.startsWith("Captain"));
```

The logical inversion operator cannot be used on a non-`boolean` value. The following code will not compile:

```
!10; // compiler error, integer use is illegal
!"STRING"; // compiler error, string use is illegal
```

Logical AND and logical OR are on the exam, but `boolean` AND and `boolean` OR, along with bitwise AND and bitwise OR, are not on the exam. You might, for example, want to use the nonlogical expressions associated with the right operand if a change occurs to a variable where the new result is used later in your code. The following Scenario & Solution details the specifics of this scenario.

SCENARIO & SOLUTION

You want to use an AND operator that evaluates the second operand whether the first operand evaluates to `true` or `false`. Which would you use?	Bitwise AND (&)
You want to use an OR operator that evaluates the second operand whether the first operand evaluates to `true` or `false`. Which would you use?	Bitwise OR (|)
You want to use an AND operator that evaluates the second operand only when the first operand evaluates to `true`. Which would you use?	Logical AND (&&)
You want to use an OR operator that evaluates the second operand only when the first operand evaluates to `false`. Which would you use?	Logical OR (||)

Understand Operator Precedence

Operator precedence is the order in which operators will be evaluated when several operators are included in an expression. Operator precedence can be overridden using parentheses. Know the basics surrounding operator precedence and you'll do well on the exam in this area.

Operator Precedence

Operators with a higher precedence are evaluated before operators with a lower precedence. Table 3-3 lists the Java operators from the highest precedence to the lowest precedence and their associations. The association (for example, left to right) defines which operand will be used (or evaluated) first.

Overriding Operator Precedence

Use parentheses to override operator precedence. When multiple sets of parentheses are present, the innermost set is evaluated first. Let's take a look at some basic code examples exercising operator precedence.

When operators have the same precedence, they are evaluated from left to right:

```
int p1 = 1; int p2 = 5; int p3 = 10;
/* Same precedence */
System.out.println(p1 + p2 - p3); // -4
```

When operators do not have the same precedence, the operator with the higher precedence is evaluated first:

```
int p1 = 1; int p2 = 5; int p3 = 10;
/* Lower, followed by higher precedence */
System.out.println(p1 + p2 * p3); // 51
```

| TABLE 3-3 | Java Operators |

Relative Precedence	Operator	Description	Association
1	`[ ]`	Array index	Left to right
	`( )`	Method call	
	`.`	Member access	
2	`++, --`	Postfix increment, postfix decrement	Right to left
	`+, -`	Unary plus, unary minus	Right to left
3	`++, --`	Prefix increment, prefix decrement	Right to left
	`!`	`boolean` (logical) NOT	
	`~`	Bitwise NOT	
4	`(type)`	Type cast	Right to left
	`new`	Object creation	Right to left
5	`*, /, %`	Multiplication, division, remainder (modulus)	Left to right
6	`+, -`	Addition, subtraction	Left to right
	`+`	String concatenation	
7	`<<, >>, >>>`	Left shift, right shift, unsigned right shift	Left to right
8	`<, <=, >, >=`	Less than, less than or equal to, greater than, greater than or equal to	Left to right
	`instanceof`	Reference test	
9	`==, !=`	Value equality and inequality / reference equality and inequality	Left to right
	`==, !=`		
10	`&`	Bitwise AND / `boolean` AND	Left to right
11	`^`	Bitwise XOR (exclusive OR) / `boolean` XOR	Left to right
12	`|`	Bitwise OR (inclusive OR) / `boolean` OR	Left to right
13	`&&`	Logical AND (aka conditional AND)	Left to right
14	`||`	Logical OR (aka conditional OR)	Left to right
15	`? :`	Conditional (ternary)	Right to left
16	`=, *=, /=, +=, -=, %=, <<=, >>=, >>>=, &=, ^=, |=`	Assignment and compound assignments	Right to left

When an expression includes parentheses, operator precedence is overridden:

```
int p1 = 1; int p2 = 5; int p3 = 10;
/* Parentheses overriding precedence */
System.out.println((p1 + p2) * p3); // 60
```

When an expression has multiple sets of parentheses, the operator associated with the innermost parentheses is evaluated first:

```
int p1 = 1; int p2 = 5; int p3 = 10; int p4 = 25;
/* Using innermost parentheses first */
System.out.println((p1 * (p2 + p3)) - p4); // -10
```

CERTIFICATION OBJECTIVE

Use String Objects and Their Methods

Exam Objective   Create and manipulate strings

Strings are commonly used in the Java programming language. This section discusses what strings are and how to concatenate separate strings, and then it details the methods of the `String` class. When you have completed this section, which covers the following topics, you should fully understand what strings are and how to use them:

- Strings
- String concatenation operator
- Methods of the `String` class

Strings

String objects are used to represent 16-bit Unicode character strings. Consider the 16 bits `000001011001` followed by `000001101111`. These bits in Unicode are represented as `\u0059` and `\u006F`. The value `\u0059` is mapped to the character "Y" and `\u006F` is mapped to the character "o". An easy way of concatenating 16-bit Unicode character strings together in a reusable element is by declaring the data within a string:

```
String exclamation = "Yo"; // 000001011001 and 000001101111
```

See Appendix C for more information on the Unicode standard.

Strings are *immutable* objects, meaning their values never change. For example, the following text, "Dead Men Tell No Tales", can be created as a string:

```
String quote = "Dead Men Tell No Tales";
```

In the following example, the value of the string does not change after a `String` method returns a modified value. Remember that strings are immutable. Here, we invoke the `replace` method on the string. Again, the new string is returned but will not change the value.

```
quote.replace("No Tales", "Tales"); // Returns new value
System.out.println(quote); // Prints the original value
$ Dead Men Tell No Tales
```

You can create strings in several ways. As with instantiating any object, you need to construct an object and assign it to a reference variable. As a reminder, a *reference variable* holds the value's address. Let's look at some of the things you can do with strings.

You can create a string without an assigned string object. Make sure you eventually give it a value, or you'll get a compiler error.

```
String quote1; // quote1 is a reference variable with no
assigned string object
quote1 = "Ahoy matey"; // Assigns string object to the reference
```

You can use a couple of basic approaches to create a string object with an empty string representation:

```
String quote2a = new String(); // quote2a is a reference variable
String quote2b = new String(""); // Equivalent statement
```

You can create a string object without using a constructor:

```
String quote3 = "The existence of the sea means the existence"
  + " of Pirates! -- Malayan proverb";
```

You can create a string object while using a constructor:

```
/* quote4 is a reference variable to the new string object */
String quote4 = new String("Yo ho ho!");
```

You can create a reference variable that refers to a separate reference variable of a string object:

```
String quote5 = "You're welcome to my gold. -- William Kidd";
String quote6 = quote5; // quote6 refers to the quote5 reference
```

SCENARIO & SOLUTION

You want to use an object that represents an immutable character string. Which class will you use to create the object?	The `String` class
You want to use an object that represents a mutable character string. Which class will you use to create the object?	The `StringBuilder` class
You want to use an object that represents a thread-safe mutable character string. Which class will you use to create the object?	The `StringBuffer` class

You can assign a new string object to an existing string reference variable:

```
/*Assigns string object to the reference variable */
String quote7 = "The treasure is in the sand.";
/* Assigns new string to the same reference variable */
quote7 = "The treasure is between the rails.";
```

If you want to use a mutable character string, consider `StringBuffer` or `StringBuilder` as represented in the preceding Scenario & Solution.

The String Concatenation Operator

The string concatenation operator concatenates (joins) strings together. The operator is denoted with the + sign.

+	String concatenation operator

If you have been programming for at least six months, odds are you have glued two strings together at some time. Java's string concatenation operator makes the act of joining two strings very easy. For example, `"doub"` + `"loon"` equates to `"doubloon"`. Let's look at some more complete code:

```
String item = "doubloon";
String question = "What is a " + item + "? ";
System.out.println ("Question: " + question);
```

Line 2 replaces the `item` variable with its contents, `"doubloon"`, and so the question string becomes

```
What is a doubloon?
```

Notice that the question mark was appended as well.

Line 3 replaces the `question` variable with its contents and so the following string is returned:

```
$ Question: What is a doubloon?
```

It is that simple. But wait! What happens when primitives are added to the concatenation? The Java language specification reads, "The + operator is syntactically left-associative, no matter whether it is determined by type analysis to represent string concatenation or numeric addition." We can examine this behavior in the following examples:

```
float reale = .007812f; // percent of one gold doubloon
float escudo = .125f; // percent of one gold doubloon

/* Prints "0.132812% of one gold doubloon" */
System.out.println
  (reale + escudo + "% of one gold doubloon"); // values added

/* Prints "0.132812% of one gold doubloon" */
System.out.println
  ((reale + escudo) + "% of one gold doubloon"); // includes parentheses

/* Prints "% of one gold doubloon: 0.132812" */
System.out.println
  ("% of one gold doubloon: " + (reale + escudo)); // includes parentheses

/* Prints "Coin values concatenated: 0.0078120.125" */
System.out.println
  ("Coin values concatenated:" + reale + escudo); // values not added
```

The toString Method

The `Object` class has a method that returns a string representation of objects. This method is appropriately named the `toString` method. All classes in Java extend the `Object` class by default; therefore, every class inherits this method. When you're creating classes, it is common practice to override the `toString` method to return the data that best represents the state of the object. The `toString` method makes common use of the string concatenation operator.

Let's take a look at the `TreasureMap` class with the `toString` method overridden.

```
public class TreasureMap {
  private String owner = "Blackbeard";
  private String location = "Outer Banks";
```

```
public String toString () {
  return "Map Owner: " + this.owner + ", treasure location: "
  + this.location;
 }
}
```

Here, the `toString` method returns the contents of the class's instance variables. Now let's print out the representation of a `TreasureMap` object:

```
TreasureMap t = new TreasureMap();
System.out.println(t);
$ Map Owner: Blackbeard, treasure location: Outer Banks
```

Concatenation results may be unexpected if you are including variables that are not initially strings. You should become very comfortable with working with the string concatenation operator, so let's take another look at it.

Consider a string and two integers:

```
String title1 = " shovels.";
String title2 = "Shovels: ";
int flatShovels = 5;
int roundPointShovels = 6;
```

The compiler performs left-to-right association for the additive and string concatenation operators.

For the following two statements, the first two integers are added together. Next, the concatenation operator takes the `toString` representation of the result and concatenates it with the other string:

```
/* Prints '11 shovels' */
System.out.println(flatShovels + roundPointShovels + title1);

/* Prints '11 shovels' */
System.out.println((flatShovels + roundPointShovels) + title1);
```

Next, moving from left to right, the compiler takes the `title2` string and joins it with the string representation of the `flatShovels` integer variable. The result is a string. Now this result string is joined to the string representation of the `roundPointShovels` variable. Note that the `toString` method is used to return the string.

```
/* Prints 'Shovels: 56' */
System.out.println(title2 + flatShovels + roundPointShovels);
```

Parentheses take precedence, so you can join the sum of the integer values with the string if you code it as follows:

```
/* Prints 'Shovels: 11' */
System.out.println(title2 + (flatShovels + roundPointShovels));
```

Uncovering Bugs that Your Compiler May Not Find

Consider the strings in the following application:

```
public class StringTest {
  public static void main(String[] args) {
    String s1 = new String ("String one");
    String s2 = "String two";
    String s3 = "String " + "three";
  }
}
```

One of the strings is constructed in an inefficient manner. Do you know which one? Let's find out using the FindBugs application from the University of Maryland.

1. Create a directory named "code" somewhere on your computer.
2. Create the StringTest.java source file.
3. Compile the StringTest.java source file: `javac StringTest.java`.
4. Download the FindBugs software from http://findbugs.sourceforge.net/.
5. Extract, install, and run the FindBugs application. Note that the Eclipse and NetBeans IDEs have plug-ins for the FindBugs tool as well as other software quality tools such as PMD and Checkstyle.
6. Create a new project in FindBugs by choosing File | New Project.
7. Add the project name (for instance, OCA String Test).
8. Click the Add button for the text area associated with the Class Archives And Directories To Analyze. Find and select the StringTest.class file in the code directory and click Choose.
9. Click the Add button for the text area associated with the Source Directories. Find and select the code directory (not the source file) and then click Choose.

10. The New Project dialog box will look similar to the following illustration, with the exception of your personal directory locations. Click Finish.

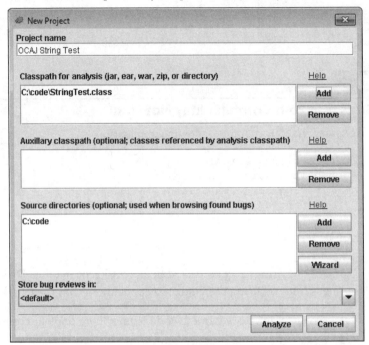

11. You will see that two bugs are returned. We are concerned with the first one. Drill down in the window that shows the bugs (Bugs | Performance | [...]). The application will detail the warning and show you the source code with the line in error highlighted.

12. Fix the bug by not calling the constructor.

13. Rerun the test.

Methods of the String Class

Several methods of the String class are commonly used, such as the following: charAt, indexOf, length, concat, replace, startsWith, endsWith, substring, trim, toLowerCase, toUpperCase, and ensureIgnoreCase(). These methods are detailed in Figure 3-2 and in the following sections.

In the following sections, you'll find a description of each method, followed by the method declarations and associated examples.

Commonly used
methods of the
String class

String
+ charAt(int) : char
+ concat(String) : String
+ endsWith(String) : boolean
+ equalsIgnoreCase(String) : boolean
+ IndexOf(int) : int
+ IndexOf(int, int) : int
+ IndexOf(String) : int
+ IndexOf(String, int) : int
+ length() : int
+ replace(char, char) : String
+ replace(CharSequence, CharSequence) : String
+ startsWith(String, int) : boolean
+ startsWith(String) : boolean
+ toLowerCase(Locale) : String
+ toLowerCase() : String
+ toString() : String
+ toUpperCase(Locale) : String
+ toUpperCase() : String
+ trim() : String

First, consider the following string:

```
String pirateMessage = "  Buried Treasure Chest! ";
```

The string has two leading blank spaces and one trailing blank space. This is
important in relationship to the upcoming examples. The string is shown again in
Figure 3-3 with the index values shown in relationship to the individual characters.
Let's use each method to perform some action with the string `pirateMessage`.

The charAt Method

The `String` class's `charAt` method returns a primitive `char` value from a
specified `int` index value in relationship to the referenced string object.
There is one `charAt` method declaration:

```
public char charAt(int index) {…}
```

FIGURE 3-3   String object

	B	u	r	i	e	d		T	r	e	a	s	u	r	e		C	h	e	s	t	!	
0	1	2	3	4	5	6	7	8	9	10	11	12	13	14	15	16	17	18	19	20	21	22	23	24

Here are some examples:

```
/* Returns the 'blank space' character from location 0 */
char c1 = pirateMessage.charAt(0);
/* Returns the character 'B' from location 2 */
char c2 = pirateMessage.charAt(2);
/* Returns the character '!' from location 23 */
char c3 = pirateMessage.charAt(23);
/* Returns the 'blank space' character from location 24 */
char c4 = pirateMessage.charAt(24);
/* Throws a StringIndexOutOfBoundsException exception*/
char c5 = pirateMessage.charAt(25);
```

The indexOf Method

The String class's indexOf method returns primitive int values representing the index of a character or string in relationship to the referenced string object.

Four public indexOf method declarations exist:

```
public int indexOf(int ch) {…}
public int indexOf(int ch, int fromIndex) {…}
public int indexOf(String str) {…}
public int indexOf(String str, int fromIndex) {…}
```

Here are some examples:

```
/* Returns the integer 3 as it is the first 'u' in the string. */
int i1 = pirateMessage.indexOf('u'); // 3
/* Returns the integer 14 as it is the first 'u' in the string past
 * location 9.
 */
int i2 = pirateMessage.indexOf('u', 9); // 14
/* Returns the integer 13 as it starts at location 13 in the
 * string.
 *
int i3 = pirateMessage.indexOf("sure"); // 13
/* Returns the integer -1 as there is no Treasure string on or
 *past location 10
 */
int i4 = pirateMessage.indexOf("Treasure", 10); // -1!
/* Returns the integer -1 as there is no character u on or past
 * location 10
 */
int i5 = pirateMessage.indexOf("u", 100); // -1!
```

The length Method

The String class's length method returns a primitive int value representing the length of the referenced string object.

There is one `length` method declaration:

```
public int length() {…}
```

Here are some examples:

```
/* Returns the string's length of 25 */
int i = pirateMessage.length(); // 25
// Use of String's length method
String string = "box";
int value1 = string.length(); // 3
// Use of array's length attribute
String[] stringArray = new String[3];
int value2 = stringArray.length; // 3
```

e x a m
ⓦ a t c h
The String class uses the `length` method (for example, `string .length()`). Arrays reference an instance variable in their state (for example, `array .length`). Therefore, the string methods use the set of parentheses to return their length and arrays do not. This is a gotcha that you will want to look for on the exam.

The concat Method

The `String` class's `concat` method concatenates the specified string to the end of the original string.

The sole `concat` method declaration is

```
public String concat(String str) {…}
```

Here's an example:

```
/* Returns the concatenated string
 *" Buried Treasure Chest! Weigh anchor!"
 */
String c = pirateMessage.concat ("Weigh anchor!");
```

The replace Method

The `String` class's `replace` method returns strings, replacing all characters or strings in relationship to the referenced string object. The `CharSequence` interface allows for the use of either a `String`, `StringBuffer`, or `StringBuilder` object.

Two `replace` method declarations can be used:

```
public String replace(char oldChar, char newChar) {…}
public String replace(CharSequence target, CharSequence
replacement) {…}
```

Here are some examples:

```
/* Returns the string with all characters 'B' replaced with 'J'. */
String s1 = pirateMessage.replace
   ('B', 'J'); // Juried Treasure Chest!
/* Returns the string with all blank characters ' ' replaced
 * with 'X'.
 */
String s2 = pirateMessage.replace
   (' ', 'X'); // XXBuriedXTreasureXChest!X
/* Returns the string with all strings 'Chest' replaced
 *  with 'Coins'.
 */
String s3 = pirateMessage.replace
   ("Chest", "Coins"); // Buried Treasure Coins!
```

The startsWith Method

The `String` class's `startsWith` method returns a primitive `boolean` value representing the results of a test to see if the supplied prefix starts the referenced string object.

Two `startsWith` method declarations can be used:

```
public boolean startsWith(String prefix, int toffset) {…}
public boolean startsWith(String prefix) {…}
```

Here are some examples:

```
/* Returns true as the referenced string starts with the
compared string. */
boolean b1 = pirateMessage.startsWith
   (" Buried Treasure"); // true
/* Returns false as the referenced string does not start with
 * the compared string.
 */
boolean b2 = pirateMessage.startsWith(" Discovered"); // false
/* Returns false as the referenced string does not start with
 * the compared string at location 8.
 */
boolean b3 = pirateMessage.startsWith("Treasure", 8); // false
/* Returns true as the referenced string does start with
 * the compared string at location 9.
 */
boolean b4 = pirateMessage.startsWith("Treasure", 9); // true
```

The endsWith Method

The String class's endsWith method returns a primitive boolean value representing the results of a test to see if the supplied suffix ends the referenced string object.

There is one endsWith method declaration:

```
public boolean endsWith(String suffix) {…}
```

Here are some examples:

```
/* Returns true as the referenced string ends with the compared
 * string.
 */
boolean e1 = pirateMessage.endsWith("Treasure Chest! "); // true
/* Returns false as the referenced string does not end with the
 * compared string.
 */
boolean e2 = pirateMessage.endsWith("Treasure Chest "); // false
```

The substring Method

The String class's substring method returns new strings that are substrings of the referenced string object. The substring begins with the value in the begin argument and, if supplied, ends with the endIndex -1 argument. The String class's substring method returns new strings that are substrings of the referenced string object.

Two substring method declarations exist:

```
public String substring(int beginIndex) {…}
public String substring(int beginIndex, int endIndex) {
```

Here are some examples:

```
/* Returns the entire string starting at index 9. */
String ss1 = pirateMessage.substring(9); // Treasure Chest!
/* Returns the string at index 9. */
String ss2 = pirateMessage.substring(9, 10); // T
/* Returns the string at index 9 and ending at index 23. */
String ss3 = pirateMessage.substring(9, 23); // Treasure Chest
/* Produces runtime error. */
String ss4 = pirateMessage.substring(9, 8); // out of range
/* Returns a blank */
String ss5 = pirateMessage.substring(9, 9); // Blank
```

The trim Method

The String class's trim method returns the entire string minus leading and trailing whitespace characters in relationship to the referenced string object. The whitespace character corresponds to the Unicode character \u0020.

```
System.out.println(" ".equals("\u0020")); // true
```

The sole trim method declaration is

```
public String trim() {…}
```

Here is an example:

```
/* "Buried Treasure Chest!" with no leading or trailing
 * whitespaces
 */
String t = pirateMessage.trim();
```

The toLowerCase Method

The String class's toLowerCase method returns the entire string as lowercase characters.

Two toLowerCase method declarations can be used:

```
public String toLowerCase () {…}
public String toLowerCase (Locale locale) {…}
```

Here is an example:

```
/* Returns all lowercase characters "  buried treasure chest!  " */
String l1 = pirateMessage.toLowerCase();
```

The toUpperCase Method

The String class's toUpperCase method returns the entire string as uppercase characters.

Two toUpperCase method declarations can be used:

```
public String toUpperCase () {…}
public String toUpperCase (Locale locale) {…}
```

Here is an example:

```
/* Returns all uppercase characters "  BURIED TREASURE CHEST!  " */
String u1 = pirateMessage.toUpperCase();
```

INSIDE THE EXAM

Chaining

Java allows for methods to be chained together. Consider the following message from the captain of a pirate ship:

```
String msg = "  Maroon the First
Mate with a flagon of water and a
pistol!  ";
```

We want to change the message to read, "Maroon the Quartermaster with a flagon of water."

Three changes need to be made to adjust the string as desired:

1. Trim the leading and trailing whitespace.

2. Replace the substring `First Mate` with `Quartermaster`.

3. Remove `and a pistol!`.

4. Add a period at the end of the sentence.

A variety of methods and utilities can be used to make these changes. We will use the trim, replace, and substring methods, in this order:

```
msg = msg.trim(); // Trims whitespace
msg = msg.replace("First Mate",
"Quartermaster");// Replaces text
msg = msg.substring(0,47);
// Returns first 48 characters.
```

Rather than writing these assignments individually, we can have one assignment statement with all of the methods chained. For simplicity, we also add the period with the string concatenation operator:

```
msg = msg.trim().replace("First Mate",
"Quartermaster").substring(0,47) +
".";
```

Whether methods are invoked separately or chained together, the end result is the same:

```
System.out.println (msg);
$  Maroon the Quartermaster with a
flagon of water.
```

Look for chaining on the exam.

The equalsIgnoreCase Method

The `String` class's `equalsIgnoreCase` method returns a `boolean` value after comparing two strings while ignoring case consideration.

The `equalsIgnoreCase` method declaration is

```
public boolean equalsIgnoreCase (String str) {…}
```

Here are some examples:

```
/* Compares " Buried Treasure Chest! " with
 * " Buried TREASURE Chest! "
 */
Boolean b1 = pirateMessage.equalsIgnoreCase
  (" Buried TREASURE Chest! "); // true
/* Compares " Buried Treasure Chest! " with
 * " Buried XXXXXXX Chest! "
 */
Boolean b2 = pirateMessage.equalsIgnoreCase
  (" Buried XXXXXXX Chest! "); // false
```

CERTIFICATION OBJECTIVE

Use StringBuilder Objects and Their Methods

Exam Objective   Manipulate data using the StringBuilder class and its methods

An object of the StringBuilder class represents a mutable character string, whereas an object of the StringBuffer class represents a thread-safe mutable character string. Remember that an object of the String class represents an immutable character string. In regard to the StringBuilder class and the exam, you need to familiarize yourself with the class's most common methods and constructors.

Methods of the StringBuilder Class

Several methods of the StringBuilder class are commonly used: append, insert, delete, deleteCharAt, and reverse. These methods are included in Figure 3-4 and discussed in the following sections.

Coming up, you'll see a description of each method, followed by the method declarations and associated examples.

First, consider the following string:

```
StringBuilder mateyMessage = new StringBuilder ("Shiver Me Timbers!");
```

The string is shown again in Figure 3-5 with the index values shown in relationship to the individual characters. This message is used for many of the examples throughout this section.

Let's now look at some of the StringBuilder methods.

Commonly used
methods of the
StringBuilder
class

StringBuilder
+ append(Object) : StringBuilder
+ append(String) : StringBuilder
– append(StringBuilder) : StringBuilder
+ append(StringBuffer) : StringBuilder
+ append(CharSequence) : StringBuilder
+ append(CharSequence, int, int) : StringBuilder
+ append(char[]) : StringBuilder
+ append(char[], int, int) : StringBuilder
+ append(boolean) : StringBuilder
+ append(char) : StringBuilder
+ append(int) : StringBuilder
+ append(long) : StringBuilder
+ append(float) : StringBuilder
+ append(double) : StringBuilder
+ appendCodePoint(int) : StringBuilder
+ delete(int, int) : StringBuilder
+ deleteCharAt(int) : StringBuilder
+ indexOf(String) : int
+ indexOf(String, int) : int
+ insert(int, char[], int, int) : StringBuilder
+ insert(int, Object) : StringBuilder
+ insert(int, String) : StringBuilder
+ insert(int, char[]) : StringBuilder
+ insert(int, CharSequence) : StringBuilder
+ insert(int, CharSequence, int, int) : StringBuilder
+ insert(int, boolean) : StringBuilder
+ insert(int, char) : StringBuilder
+ insert(int, int) : StringBuilder
+ insert(int, long) : StringBuilder
+ insert(int, float) : StringBuilder
+ insert(int, double) : StringBuilder
+ lastIndexOf(String) : int
+ lastIndexOf(String, int) : int
– readObject(java.io.ObjectInputStream) : void
+ replace(int, int, String) : StringBuilder
+ reverse() : StringBuilder
+ StringBuilder()
+ StringBuilder(int)
+ StringBuilder(String)
+ StringBuilder(CharSequence)
+ toString() : String
– writeObject(java.io.ObjectOutputStream) : void

StringBuilder
object

S	h	i	v	e	r		M	e		T	i	m	b	e	r	s	!
0	1	2	3	4	5	6	7	8	9	10	11	12	13	14	15	16	17

The append Method

The StringBuilder class's append method appends the supplied data as a character string.

There are 13 append method declarations. These overloaded methods are shown here to provide coverage of the different Java types:

```
public StringBuilder append(Object o) {…}
public StringBuilder append(String str) {…}
public StringBuilder append(StringBuffer sb) {…}
public StringBuilder append(CharSequence s) {…}
public StringBuilder append(CharSequence s, int start, int end)
{…}
public StringBuilder append(char[] str) {…}
public StringBuilder append(char[] str, int offset, int len) {…}
public StringBuilder append(boolean b) {…}
public StringBuilder append(char c) {…}
public StringBuilder append(int i) {…}
public StringBuilder append(long l) {…}
public StringBuilder append(float f) {…}
public StringBuilder append(double d) {…}
```

Here are some examples:

```
StringBuilder mateyMessage;
mateyMessage = new StringBuilder ("Shivers!");
/* Prints out "Shivers! Bad Storm!" */
System.out.println(mateyMessage.append(" Bad Storm!"));

StringBuilder e = new StringBuilder ("Examples:");
e.append(" ").append("1"); // String
e.append(" ").append(new StringBuffer("2"));
e.append(" ").append('\u0031'); // char
e.append(" ").append((int)2); // int
e.append(" ").append(1L); // long
e.append(" ").append(2F); // float
e.append(" ").append(1D); // double
e.append(" ").append(true); // true

/* Prints out "Examples: 1 2 1 2 1 2.0 1.0 true" */
System.out.println(e);
```

The insert Method

The StringBuilder class's insert method inserts the string representation of the supplied data starting at the specified location.

There are 12 `insert` method declarations, though you need to be familiar with only the most basic declarations:

```
public StringBuilder insert
    (int index, char[]str, int offset, int len) {…}
public StringBuilder insert(int offset, Object obj) {…}
public StringBuilder insert(int offset, String str) {…}
public StringBuilder insert(int offset, char []str) {…}
public StringBuilder insert(int dstOffset, CharSequence) {…}
public StringBuilder insert
    (int dstOffset, CharSequence s, int start, int end) {…}
public StringBuilder insert(int offset, boolean b) {…}
public StringBuilder insert(int offset, char c) {…}
public StringBuilder insert(int offset, int i) {…}
public StringBuilder insert(int offset long l) {…}
public StringBuilder insert(int offset float f) {…}
public StringBuilder insert(int offset, double d) {…}
```

Here is an example:

```
StringBuilder mateyMessage;
mateyMessage = new StringBuilder ("Shiver Me Tim");
/* Prints out "Shiver Me Timbers and Bricks! */
System.out.println(mateyMessage.insert(17, " and Bricks"));
```

The delete Method

The `StringBuilder` class's `delete` method removes characters in a substring of the `StringBuilder` object. The substring begins with the value in the `start` argument and ends with the `end` - `1` argument.

There is one `delete` method declaration:

```
public StringBuilder delete(int start, int end) {…}
```

Here is an example:

```
StringBuilder mateyMessage;
mateyMessage = new StringBuilder ("Shiver Me Timbers!");
/* Prints out "Shivers!" */
System.out.println(mateyMessage.delete(6,16));
```

The deleteCharAt Method

The `StringBuilder` class's `deleteCharAt` method removes the character from the specified index.

There is one deleteCharAt method declaration:

```
public StringBuilder deleteCharAt (int index) {…}
```

Here is an example:

```
StringBuilder mateyMessage;
mateyMessage = new StringBuilder ("Shiver Me Timbers!");
/* Removes the '!' and prints out "Shiver Me Timbers" */
System.out.println(mateyMessage.deleteCharAt(17));
```

The reverse Method

The StringBuilder class's reverse method reverses the order of the character sequence.

There is one reverse method declaration:

```
public StringBuilder reverse () {…}
```

Here is an example:

```
StringBuilder r = new StringBuilder ("part");
r.reverse();
/* Prints out "It's a trap!" */
System.out.println("It's a " + r + "!");
```

EXERCISE 3-3

Using Constructors of the StringBuilder Class

It's a good idea to get familiar with the different constructors of the StringBuilder class. Review the Javadoc documentation to determine when you would use the different constructors and perform the following steps:

1. Create StringBuilder instances with the StringBuilder () constructor.

2. Create StringBuilder instances with the StringBuilder (CharSequence seq) constructor.

3. Create StringBuilder instances with the StringBuilder (int capacity) constructor.

4. Create StringBuilder instances with the StringBuilder (String str) constructor.

Test Equality Between Strings and Other Objects

Exam Objective   Test equality between strings and other objects using == and equals ()

One way to compare objects in Java is by performing a comparison by using the equals method. Note that the equals method in a class that will be used in a comparison must override the equals method of the Object class. The hashCode method also needs to be overridden, but this method is outside the scope of the test. For this objective, we'll explore the equals method and the == operator a little further. The String class overrides the equals method, as is shown in the following code sample:

```
/** The value is used for character storage. */
private final char value[];
/** The offset is the first index of the
storage that is used. */
private final int offset;
…
public boolean equals(Object anObject) {
if (this == anObject) {
  return true;
}
if (anObject instanceof String) {
  String anotherString = (String)anObject;
  int n = count;
if (n == anotherString.count) {
  char v1[] = value;
  char v2[] = anotherString.value;
  int i = offset;
  int j = anotherString.offset;
    while (n-- != 0) {
      if (v1[i++] != v2[j++])
        return false;
      }
      return true;
    }
  }
  return false;
}
```

equals Method of the String Class

When comparing character strings among two separate strings, the `equals` method should be used:

```
String msg1 = "WALK THE PLANK!";
String msg2 = "WALK THE PLANK!";
String msg3 = ("WALK THE PLANK!");
String msg4 = new String ("WALK THE PLANK!");

System.out.println(msg1.equals(msg2)); // true
System.out.println(msg1.equals(msg3)); // true
System.out.println(msg1.equals(msg4)); // true
System.out.println(msg2.equals(msg3)); // true
System.out.println(msg3.equals(msg4)); // true
```

When comparing object references, the == operator should be used:

```
String cmd = "Set Sail!";
String command = cmd;
System.out.println(cmd == command ); // true
```

Do not attempt to compare character sequence values of strings with the == operator. Even though the result may appear to be correct, this is an inappropriate use of the operator, because the == operator is designed to check whether two object references refer to the same instance of an object, and not the character sequences of strings. Literal strings are pooled in the JVM and reused when possible. Here's an example that does return `true` due to string reuse. This equality-testing approach should not be practiced:

```
String interjection1 = "Arrgh!";
String interjection2 = "Arrgh!";
System.out.println(interjection1 == interjection2); // Bad
```

If you do make this mistake, modern IDEs will typically flag the issue as a warning and give you the option to refactor the code to use the `equals` method, as shown here:

```
System.out.println(interjection1.equals(interjection2));
```

In addition, the IDE, such as NetBeans, may give you the option of refactoring in the `equals` method with null checks while using the ternary operator.

```
System.out.println((interjection1 == null ? interjection2 ==
null : interjection1.equals(interjection2)));
```

Working with the compareTo Method of the String Class

Given the following code that prints "0":

```
String eggs1 = "Cackle fruit";
String eggs2 = "Cackle fruit";
System.out.println(eggs1.compareTo(eggs2));
```

1. Modify the string(s) so that a value greater than 0 is printed, and explain why this happens.

2. Modify the string(s) so that a value less than 0 is printed, and explain why this happens.

CERTIFICATION SUMMARY

This chapter discussed everything you need to know about operators and strings for the exam.

Operators of type assignment, arithmetic, relational, and logical were all presented in detail. Assignment operators included the general assignment, assignment by addition, and assignment by subtraction operators. Arithmetic operators included the addition, subtraction, multiplication, division, and remainder (modulus) operators, as well as the prefix increment, prefix decrement, postfix increment, and postfix decrement operators. Relational operators included the less than, less than or equal to, greater than, greater than or equal to, equal to, and not equal to operators. Logical operators included the logical negation, logical AND, and logical OR operators.

We explored operator precedence and overriding operators. The concepts here were rather simple, and knowing the precedence of the common operators and the purposing of the parentheses in overriding precedence is all you'll need to retain.

Strings were discussed in three main areas: creating strings, the string concatenation operator, and methods of the String class. The following methods of the String class were covered: charAt, indexOf, length, concat, replace, startsWith, endsWith, substring, trim, toLowerCase, toUpperCase, and equalsIgnoreCase. The StringBuilder class was discussed in comparison to the String class. The following methods of the `StringBuilder` class were covered: `append`, `insert`, `delete`, `deleteCharAt`, and `reverse`.

Testing object and `String` equality using the `equals` method was also discussed. The `==` operator was also discussed and we explained when to and when not to use it.

Knowing the fine details of these core areas related to operators and strings is necessary for the exam.

TWO-MINUTE DRILL

Understand Fundamental Operators

- ☐ The exam covers the following assignment and compound assignment operators: =, +=, and -=.
- ☐ The assignment operator (=) assigns values to variables.
- ☐ The additional compound assignment operator is used for shorthand. As such, a=a+b is written a+=b.
- ☐ The subtraction compound assignment operator is used for shorthand. As such, a=a-b is written a-=b.
- ☐ The exam covers the following arithmetic operators: +, -, *, /, %, ++, and --.
- ☐ The addition operator (+) is used to add two operands together.
- ☐ The subtraction operator (-) is used to subtract the right operand from the left operand.
- ☐ The multiplication operator (*) is used to multiply two operands together.
- ☐ The division operator (/) is used to divide the right operand into the left operand.
- ☐ The modulus operator (%) returns the remainder of a division.
- ☐ The prefix-increment (++) and prefix-decrement (--) operators are used to increment or decrement a value before it is used in an expression.
- ☐ The postfix-increment (++) and postfix-decrement (--) operators are used to increment or decrement a value after it is used in an expression.
- ☐ The exam covers the following relational operators: <, <=, >, >=, ==, and !=.
- ☐ The less than operator (<) returns true if the left operand is less than the right operand.
- ☐ The less than or equal to operator (<=) returns true if the left operand is less than or equal to the right operand.
- ☐ The greater than operator (>) returns true if the right operand is less than the left operand.
- ☐ The greater than or equal to operator (>=) returns true if the right operand is less than or equal to the left operand.
- ☐ The equal to equality operator (==) returns true if the left operand is equal to the right operand.

- ☐ The not equal to equality operator (!=) returns true if the left operand is not equal to the right operand.
- ☐ Equality operators can test numbers, characters, `boolean`s, and reference variables.
- ☐ The exam covers the following logical operators: !, &&, and ||.
- ☐ The logical negation (inversion) operator (!) negates the value of the `boolean` operand.
- ☐ The logical AND (conditional AND) operator (&&) returns true if both operands are true.
- ☐ The logical AND operator is known as a short-circuit operator because it does not evaluate the right operand if the left operand is false.
- ☐ The logical OR (conditional OR) operator (||) returns true if either operand is true.
- ☐ The conditional OR operator is known as a short-circuit operator because it does not evaluate the right operand if the left operand is true.

Understand Operator Precedence

- ☐ Operators with a higher precedence are evaluated before operators with a lower precedence.
- ☐ Operator precedence is overridden by the use of parentheses.
- ☐ When multiple sets of parentheses are present relative to operator precedence, the innermost set is evaluated first.
- ☐ Operators in an expression that have the same precedence will be evaluated from left to right.

Use String Objects and Their Methods

- ☐ An object of the `String` class represents an immutable character string.
- ☐ *Mutable* means changeable. Java variables such as primitives are mutable by default and can be made immutable by using the `final` keyword.
- ☐ The `CharSequence` interface is implemented by the `String` class as well as the `StringBuilder` and `StringBuffer` classes. This interface can be used as an argument in the `String` class's `replace` method.
- ☐ The string concatenation operator (+) joins two strings together and creates a new string.

☐ The string concatenation operator will join two operands together, as long as one or both of them are strings.

☐ The `String` class's `charAt` method returns a primitive `char` value from a specified `int` index value in relationship to the referenced string.

☐ The `String` class's `indexOf` method returns a primitive `int` value representing the index of a character or string in relationship to the referenced string.

☐ The `String` class's `length` method returns a primitive `int` value representing the length of the referenced string.

☐ The `String` class's `concat` method concatenates the specified string to the end of the original string.

☐ The `String` class's `replace` method returns strings replacing all characters or strings in relationship to the referenced string.

☐ The `String` class's `startsWith` method returns a primitive `boolean` value representing the results of a test to see if the supplied prefix starts the referenced string.

☐ The `String` class's `endsWith` method returns a primitive `boolean` value representing the results of a test to see if the supplied suffix ends the referenced string.

☐ The `String` class's `substring` method returns new strings that are substrings of the referenced string.

☐ The `String` class's `trim` method returns the entire string minus leading and trailing whitespace characters in relationship to the referenced string.

☐ The `String` class's `toLowerCase` method returns the entire string as lowercase characters.

☐ The `String` class's `toUpperCase` method returns the entire string as uppercase characters.

☐ The `String` class's `equalsIgnoreCase` method returns a `boolean` value after comparing two strings while ignoring case consideration.

Use StringBuilder Objects and Their Methods

☐ An object of the `StringBuilder` class represents a mutable character string.

☐ An object of the `StringBuffer` class represents a thread-safe mutable character string.

☐ The StringBuilder class makes use of the following methods that the String class has also declared: charAt, indexOf, length, replace, startsWith, endsWith, and substring.

☐ The StringBuilder class's append method appends the supplied data as a character string.

☐ The StringBuilder class's insert method inserts the string representation of the supplied data starting at the specified location.

☐ The StringBuilder class's delete method removes characters in a substring of the StringBuilder object.

☐ The StringBuilder class's deleteCharAt method removes the character from the specified index.

☐ The StringBuilder class's reverse method reverses the order of the character sequence.

Test Equality Between Strings and Other Objects

☐ Use the equals method of the String class (overridden from the Object class) to test the equality of the character sequence values of string objects.

☐ Use the == operator to test to see if the object references (for example, the memory addresses) of strings are equal.

☐ Use the == operator to test the equality of primitives.

SELF TEST

Understand Fundamental Operators

1. Given:

```
public class ArithmeticResultsOutput {
    public static void main (String[] args) {
        int i = 0;
        int j = 0;
        if (i++ == ++j) {
            System.out.println("True: i=" + i + ", j=" + j);
        } else {
            System.out.println("False: i=" + i + ", j=" + j);
        }
    }
}
```

What will be printed to standard output?

A. `True: i=0, j=1`
B. `True: i=1, j=1`
C. `False: i=0, j=1`
D. `False: i=1, j=1`

2. Which set of operators represents the complete set of valid Java assignment operators? (Note that shift operators include <<, >>, and >>>.)

A. `%=, &=, *=, $=, :=, /=, ^=, |=, +=, <<=, =, -=, >>=, >>>=`
B. `%=, &=, *=, /=, ^=, |=, +=, <<=, <<<=, =, -=, >>=, >>>=`
C. `%=, &=, *=, /=, ^=, |=, +=, <<=, =, -=, >>=, >>>=`
D. `%=, &=, *=, $=, /=, ^=, |=, +=, <<=, <<<=, =, -=, >>=, >>>=`

3. Given the following Java code segment, what will be printed, considering the usage of the modulus operators?

```
System.out.print(49 % 26 % 5 % 1);
```

A. 23
B. 3
C. 1
D. 0

4. Given:

```java
public class BooleanResultsOutput {
  public static void main (String[] args) {
    boolean booleanValue1 = true;
    boolean booleanValue2 = false;
    System.out.print(!(booleanValue1 & !booleanValue2) + ", ");
    System.out.print(!(booleanValue1 | !booleanValue2) + ", ");
    System.out.print(!(booleanValue1 ^ !booleanValue2));
  }
}
```

What will be printed, considering the usage of the logical `boolean` operators?

A. `false, false, true`

B. `false, true, true`

C. `true, false, true`

D. `true, true, true`

5. Given:

```java
public class ArithmeticResultsOutput {
  public static void main (String[] args) {
    int i1 = 100; int j1 = 200;
    if ((i1 == 99) & (--j1 == 199)) {
      System.out.print("Value1: " + (i1 + j1) + " ");
    } else {
      System.out.print("Value2: " + (i1 + j1) + " ");
    }
    int i2 = 100; int j2 = 200;
    if ((i2 == 99) && (--j2 == 199)) {
      System.out.print("Value1: " + (i2 + j2) + " ");
    } else {
      System.out.print("Value2: " + (i2 + j2) + " ");
    }
    int i3 = 100; int j3 = 200;
    if ((i3 == 100) | (--j3 == 200)) {
      System.out.print("Value1: " + (i3 + j3) + " ");
    } else {
      System.out.print("Value2: " + (i3 + j3) + " ");
    }
    int i4 = 100; int j4 = 200;
    if ((i4 == 100) || (--j4 == 200)) {
      System.out.print("Value1: " + (i4 + j4) + " ");
    } else {
      System.out.print("Value2: " + (i4 + j4) + " ");
    }
  }
}
```

What will be printed to standard output?

A. `Value2: 300 Value2: 300 Value1: 300 Value1: 300`

B. `Value2: 299 Value2: 300 Value1: 299 Value1: 300`

C. `Value1: 299 Value1: 300 Value2: 299 Value2: 300`

D. `Value1: 300 Value1: 299 Value2: 300 Value2: 299`

6. Given the following code segment:

```
public void validatePrime() {
    long p = 17496; // 'prime number' candidate
    Double primeSquareRoot = Math.sqrt(p);
    boolean isPrime = true;
    for (long j = 2; j <= primeSquareRoot.longValue(); j++) {
        if (p % j == 0) {
            // Print divisors
            System.out.println(j + "x" + p / j);
            isPrime = false;
        }
    }
    System.out.println("Prime number: " + isPrime);
}
```

Which of the following is true? Hint: 17496 is not a prime number.

A. The code will not compile due to a syntactical error somewhere in the code.

B. The code will not compile since the expression `(p % j == 0)` should be written as `((p % j) == 0)`.

C. Divisors will be printed to standard output (for example, 2x8478, and so on), along with `Prime number: false` as the final output.

D. Divisors will be printed to standard output (for example, 2x8478, and so on), along with `Prime number: 0` as the final output.

7. Given:

```
public class EqualityTests {
    public static void main (String[] args) {
        Integer value1 = new Integer("312");
        Integer value2 = new Integer("312");
        Object object1 = new Object();
        Object object2 = new Object();
        Object object3 = value1;
    }
}
```

Which expressions evaluate to `true`?

A. `value1.equals(value2)`

B. `value1.equals(object1)`

C. `value1.equals(object3)`

D. `object1.equals(object2)`

8. Given:

```
System.out.print( true | false & true + "," );
System.out.println( false & true | true );
```

What will be printed to standard output?

A. `true, true`

B. `true, false`

C. `false, true`

D. `false, false`

E. `Compilation error`

9. In the following code segment, what is printed to standard output?

```
int score = 10;
System.out.println("score: " + score++);
```

A. 9

B. 10

C. 11

D. A compiler error will occur.

E. A runtime error will occur.

10. From highest precedence to lowest, which list of operators is ordered properly?

A. `*, +, &&, =`

B. `*, &&, +, =`

C. `*, =, &&, +`

D. `+, *, &&, =`

Use String Objects and Their Methods

11. Given:

```
System.out.print(3 + 3 + "3");
System.out.print(" and ");
System.out.println("3" + 3 + 3);
```

What will be printed to standard output?

A. 333 and 333
B. 63 and 63
C. 333 and 63
D. 63 and 333

12. Consider the interface `CharSequence` that is a required argument in one of the `replace` method declarations:

```
public String replace(CharSequence target, CharSequence
replacement) {
    ...
}
```

This `CharSequence` interface is a super interface to which concrete classes?

A. `String`
B. `StringBoxer`
C. `StringBuffer`
D. `StringBuilder`

13. Which statement is false about the `toString` method?

A. The `toString` method is a method of the `Object` class.
B. The `toString` method returns a string representation of the object.
C. The `toString` method must return the object's state information in the form of a string.
D. The `toString` method is commonly overridden.

14. Which `indexOf` method declaration is invalid?

A. `indexOf(int ch)`
B. `indexOf(int ch, int fromIndex)`
C. `indexOf(String str, int fromIndex)`
D. `indexOf(CharSequence str, int fromIndex)`

15. Given:

```
String tenCharString = "AAAAAAAAAA";
System.out.println(tenCharString.replace("AAA", "LLL"));
```

What is printed to the standard output?

A. AAAAAAAAAA
B. LLLAAAAAAA
C. LLLLLLLLLA
D. LLLLLLLLLL

16. Consider the following illustration. Which statements, also represented in the illustration, are true?

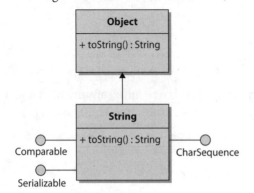

A. The String class implements the Object interface.
B. The String class implements the Comparable, Serializable, and CharSequence interfaces.
C. The toString method overrides the toString method of the Object class, allowing the string object to return its own string.
D. The toString method is publicly accessible.

Use StringBuilder Objects and Their Methods

17. Which declaration of the StringBuilder class exists?
    A. public StringBuilder reverse (String str) {…}
    B. public StringBuilder reverse (int index, String str) {…}
    C. public StringBuilder reverse () {…}
    D. All of the above

Test Equality Between Strings and Other Objects

18. Given:

```
String name1 = new String ("Benjamin");
StringBuilder name2 = new StringBuilder ("Benjamin");
System.out.println (name2.equals (name1));
```

Are the String and StringBuilder classes of comparable types? Select the correct statement.
A. The String and StringBuilder classes are comparable types.
B. The String and StringBuilder classes are incomparable types.

19. Which append declaration does not exist in Java 8?

    A. `public StringBuilder append (short s) {...}`

    B. `public StringBuilder append (int i) {...}`

    C. `public StringBuilder append (long l) {...}`

    D. `public StringBuilder append (float f) {...}`

    E. `public StringBuilder append (double d) {...}`

SELF TEST ANSWERS

Understand Fundamental Operators

1. Given:

```
public class ArithmeticResultsOutput {
    public static void main (String[] args) {
        int i = 0;
        int j = 0;
        if (i++ == ++j) {
            System.out.println("True: i=" + i + ", j=" + j);
        } else {
            System.out.println("False: i=" + i + ", j=" + j);
        }
    }
}
```

What will be printed to standard output?

A. `True: i=0, j=1`

B. `True: i=1, j=1`

C. `False: i=0, j=1`

D. `False: i=1, j=1`

Answer:

☑ **D.** The value of j is prefix-incremented before the evaluation; however, the value of i is not. Therefore, the expression is evaluated with a `boolean` value of `false` as a result, since 0 does not equal 1 (that is, `i=0` and `j=1`). After the expression has been evaluated, but before the associated print statement is executed, the value of i is postfix-incremented (that is, (`i=1`)). Therefore, the correct answer is `False: i=1, j=1`.

☒ **A, B,** and **C** are incorrect answers as justified by the correct answer's explanation.

2. Which set of operators represents the complete set of valid Java assignment operators? (Note that shift operators include <<, >>, and >>>.)

A. `%=, &=, *=, $=, :=, /=, ^=, |=, +=, <<=, =, -=, >>=, >>>=`

B. `%=, &=, *=, /=, ^=, |=, +=, <<=, <<<=, =, -=, >>=, >>>=`

C. `%=, &=, *=, /=, ^=, |=, +=, <<=, =, -=, >>=, >>>=`

D. `%=, &=, *=, $=, /=, ^=, |=, +=, <<=, <<<=, =, -=, >>=, >>>=`

Answer:

☑   **C.** The complete set of valid Java assignment operators is represented.

☒   **A, B,** and **D** are incorrect answers. **A** is incorrect because $= and : = are not valid Java assignment operators. **B** is incorrect because <<<= is not a valid Java assignment operator. **D** is incorrect because $= and <<<= are not valid Java assignment operators.

3. Given the following Java code segment, what will be printed, considering the usage of the modulus operators?

```
System.out.print(49 % 26 % 5 % 1);
```

A.   23

B.   3

C.   1

D.   0

Answer:

☑   **D.** The remainder of 49/26 is 23. The remainder of 23/5 is 3. The remainder of 3/1 is 0. The answer is 0.

☒   **A, B,** and **C** are incorrect answers as justified by the correct answer's explanation.

4. Given:

```
public class BooleanResultsOutput {
  public static void main (String[] args) {
    boolean booleanValue1 = true;
    boolean booleanValue2 = false;
    System.out.print(!(booleanValue1 & !booleanValue2) + ", ");
    System.out.print(!(booleanValue1 | !booleanValue2)+ ", ");
    System.out.print(!(booleanValue1 ^ !booleanValue2));
  }
}
```

What will be printed, considering the usage of the logical `boolean` operators?

A.   `false, false, true`

B.   `false, true, true`

C.   `true, false, true`

D.   `true, true, true`

Answer:

☑   **A.** The first expression statement (`!(true & !(false))`) evaluates to `false`. Here, the right operand is negated to `true` by the (`boolean invert`) operator, the `boolean` AND operator equates the expression of the two operands to `true`, and the (`boolean invert`) operator equates the resultant value to `false`. The second expression statement (`!(true | !(false))`) evaluates to `false`. Here, the right operand is negated to `true` by the (`boolean invert`) operator, the `boolean` OR operator equates the expression of the two operands to `true`, and the (`boolean invert`) operator equates the resultant value to `false`. The third expression statement (`!(true ^ !(false))`) evaluates to `true`. Here, the right operand is negated to `true` by the (`boolean invert`) operator, the `boolean` XOR operator equates the expression of the two operands to `false`, and the (`boolean invert`) operator equates the resultant value to `true`.

☒   **B, C,** and **D** are incorrect answers as justified by the correct answer's explanation.

5.   Given:

```java
public class ArithmeticResultsOutput {
  public static void main (String[] args) {
    int i1 = 100; int j1 = 200;
    if ((i1 == 99) & (--j1 == 199)) {
      System.out.print("Value1: " + (i1 + j1) + " ");
    } else {
      System.out.print("Value2: " + (i1 + j1) + " ");
    }
    int i2 = 100; int j2 = 200;
    if ((i2 == 99) && (--j2 == 199)) {
      System.out.print("Value1: " + (i2 + j2) + " ");
    } else {
      System.out.print("Value2: " + (i2 + j2) + " ");
    }
    int i3 = 100; int j3 = 200;
    if ((i3 == 100) | (--j3 == 200)) {
      System.out.print("Value1: " + (i3 + j3) + " ");
    } else {
      System.out.print("Value2: " + (i3 + j3) + " ");
    }
    int i4 = 100; int j4 = 200;
    if ((i4 == 100) || (--j4 == 200)) {
      System.out.print("Value1: " + (i4 + j4) + " ");
    } else {
      System.out.print("Value2: " + (i4 + j4) + " ");
    }

    }
  }
```

What will be printed to standard output?

A. `Value2: 300 Value2: 300 Value1: 300 Value1: 300`

B. `Value2: 299 Value2: 300 Value1: 299 Value1: 300`

C. `Value1: 299 Value1: 300 Value2: 299 Value2: 300`

D. `Value1: 300 Value1: 299 Value2: 300 Value2: 299`

Answer:

☑ **B.** `Value2: 299 Value2: 300 Value1: 299 Value1: 300` will be printed to the standard output. Note that `&&` and `||` are short-circuit operators. When the first operand of a conditional AND (`&&`) expression evaluates to `false`, the second operand is not evaluated. When the first operand of a conditional OR (`||`) expression evaluates to `true`, the second operand is not evaluated. Thus, for the second and fourth `if` statements, the second operand isn't evaluated. Therefore, the prefix increment operators are never executed and do not affect the values of the `j[x]` variables.

☒ **A, C,** and **D** are incorrect answers as justified by the correct answer's explanation.

6. Given the following code segment:

```
public void validatePrime() {
   long p = 17496; // 'prime number' candidate
   Double primeSquareRoot = Math.sqrt(p);
   boolean isPrime = true;
   for (long j = 2; j <= primeSquareRoot.longValue(); j++) {
     if (p % j == 0) {
        // Print divisors
        System.out.println(j + "x" + p / j);
        isPrime = false;
     }
   }
   System.out.println("Prime number: " + isPrime);
}
```

Which of the following is true? Hint: 17496 is not a prime number.

A. The code will not compile due to a syntactical error somewhere in the code.

B. The code will not compile since the expression `(p % j == 0)` should be written as `((p % j) == 0)`.

C. Divisors will be printed to standard output (for example, `2x8478`, and so on), along with `Prime number: false` as the final output.

D. Divisors will be printed to standard output (for example, `2x8478`, and so on), along with `Prime number: 0` as the final output.

Answer:

☑   **C.** Divisors will be printed to standard output followed by `Prime number: false`. For those who are curious, the complete list of divisors printed are 2x8748, 3x5832, 4x4374, 6x2916, 8x2187, 9x1944, 12x1458, 18x972, 24x729, 27x648, 36x486, 54x324, 72x243, 81x216, and 108x162.

☒   **A, B,** and **D** are incorrect. **A** is incorrect because there are no syntactical errors in the code. **B** is incorrect because a set of parentheses around `p % j` is not required. Answer **D** is incorrect because the code does not print out the character 0; it prints out the `boolean` literal value `false`.

7. Given:

```
public class EqualityTests {
  public static void main (String[] args) {
    Integer value1 = new Integer("312");
    Integer value2 = new Integer("312");
    Object object1 = new Object();
    Object object2 = new Object();
    Object object3 = value1;
  }
}
```

Which expressions evaluate to `true`?

A. `value1.equals(value2)`

B. `value1.equals(object1)`

C. `value1.equals(object3)`

D. `object1.equals(object2)`

Answer:

☑   **A** and **C.** **A** is correct because the class `Integer` implements the `Comparable` interface, allowing use of the `equals` method. **C** is correct because the `Integer` object was used to create the `Object` reference.

☒   **B** and **D** are incorrect because the code cannot equate two objects with different references.

8. Given:

```
System.out.print( true | false & true + "," );
System.out.println( false & true | true );
```

What will be printed to standard output?

A. `true, true`

B. `true, false`

C. `false, true`

D. `false, false`

E. `Compilation error`

Answer:

☑ **E.** Concatenation of a `boolean` and a string is not allowed in the first print statement. Therefore, the first line will not compile. Changing the statement by adding parentheses around the `boolean` evaluations would allow the line to compile:

```
System.out.print( (true | false & true) + ", " );
```

Once the line was compilable, the correct answer would have been A, considering operating precedence with the `boolean` AND (`&`) operator having a higher precedence over the `boolean` OR (`|`) operator.

☒ **A, B, C,** and **D** are incorrect. **A** is incorrect because the code will not compile. **B, C,** and **D** are incorrect because if the code were refined to be compilable, the answer would have been A.

9. In the following code segment, what is printed to standard output?

```
int score = 10;
System.out.println("score: " + score++);
```

A. `9`

B. `10`

C. `11`

D. A compiler error will occur.

E. A runtime error will occur.

Answer:

☑ **B.** This variable score is not incremented until the operation is completed since it is a postfix-increment operator, so 10 is printed.

☒ **A, C, D,** and **E** are incorrect. **A** would be correct if this were a prefix-decrement operator. **C** would be correct if this were a prefix-increment operator. **D** and **E** are incorrect because the code contains no errors.

10. From highest precedence to lowest, which list of operators is ordered properly?

A. *, +, &&, =

B. *, &&, +, =

C. *, =, &&, +

D. +, *, &&, =

Answer:

☑ **A.** In order of precedence, the following is correct: multiplication (*), addition (+), conditional AND (&&), assignment (=).

☒ **B, C,** and **D** are incorrect because they are improperly ordered.

Use String Objects and Their Methods

11. Given:

```
System.out.print(3 + 3 + "3");
System.out.print(" and ");
System.out.println("3" + 3 + 3);
```

What will be printed to standard output?

A. 333 and 333

B. 63 and 63

C. 333 and 63

D. 63 and 333

Answer:

☑ **D.** The + operators have left-to-right association. The first two operands of the first statement are numeric, so the addition (+) operator is used. Therefore, 3 + 3 = 6. Since 6 + "3" uses a string as an operand, the string concatenation (+) operator is used. Therefore, concatenating the strings 6 and 3 renders the string 63. The last statement is handled a little differently. The first operand is a String; therefore, the string concatenation operator is used with the other operands. Thus, concatenating strings "3" + "3" + "3" renders the string 333. The correct answer is 63 and 333.

☒ **A, B,** and **C** are incorrect. Note that changing ("3" + 3 + 3) to ("3" + (3 + 3)) would have rendered 36.

12. Consider the interface CharSequence that is a required argument in one of the replace method declarations:

```
public  String  replace(CharSequence  target,  CharSequence
replacement) {
    ...
}
```

This CharSequence interface is a super interface to which concrete classes?

A. String
B. StringBoxer
C. StringBuffer
D. StringBuilder

Answer:

☑ **A, C,** and **D.** The concrete classes String, StringBuffer, and StringBuilder all implement the interface CharSequence. These classes can all be used in a polymorphic manner in regard to CharSequence being an expected argument in one of the String class's replace methods.

☒ **B** is incorrect. There is no such thing as a StringBoxer class.

13. Which statement is false about the toString method?
    A. The toString method is a method of the Object class.
    B. The toString method returns a string representation of the object.
    C. The toString method must return the object's state information in the form of a string.
    D. The toString method is commonly overridden.

Answer:

☑ **C.** While the `toString` method is commonly used to return the object's state information, any information that can be gathered may be returned in the string.

☒ **A, B,** and **D** are incorrect answers because they all represent true statements. **A** is incorrect because the `toString` method is a method of the `Object` class. **B** is incorrect because the `toString` method returns a string representation of the object. **D** is incorrect because the `toString` method is also commonly overridden.

14. Which `indexOf` method declaration is invalid?

A. `indexOf(int ch)`

B. `indexOf(int ch, int fromIndex)`

C. `indexOf(String str, int fromIndex)`

D. `indexOf(CharSequence str, int fromIndex)`

Answer:

☑ **D.** The method declaration including `indexOf(CharSequence str, int fromIndex)` is invalid. `CharSequence` is not used as an argument in any `indexOf` method. Note that `String`, `StringBuffer`, and `StringBuilder` all declare their own `indexOf` methods.

☒ **A, B,** and **C** are incorrect because they are all valid method declarations.

15. Given:

```
String tenCharString = "AAAAAAAAAA";
System.out.println(tenCharString.replace("AAA", "LLL"));
```

What is printed to the standard output?

A. AAAAAAAAAA

B. LLLAAAAAAA

C. LLLLLLLLLA

D. LLLLLLLLLL

Answer:

☑ **C.** The `replace` method of the `String` class replaces all instances of the specified string. The first three instances of AAA are replaced by LLL, making LLLLLLLLLA correct.

☒ **A, B,** and **D** are incorrect answers as justified by the correct answer's explanation.

16. Consider the following illustration. Which statements, also represented in the illustration, are true?

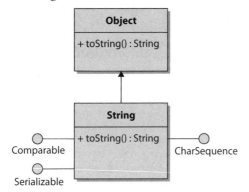

A. The `String` class implements the `Object` interface.
B. The `String` class implements the `Comparable`, `Serializable`, and `CharSequence` interfaces.
C. The `toString` method overrides the `toString` method of the `Object` class, allowing the string object to return its own string.
D. The `toString` method is publicly accessible.

Answer:

☑ **B, C,** and **D.** These answers all represent true statements. **B** is correct because the `String` class implements the `Comparable`, `Serializable`, and `CharSequence` interfaces. **C** is correct because the `toString` method overrides the `toString` method of the `Object` class, allowing the string object to return its own string. **D** is correct because the `toString` method is also publicly accessible.

☒ **A** is incorrect. The `Object` class is a concrete class. Therefore, the `String` class does not implement an `Object` interface since there is no such thing as an `Object` interface. The `String` class actually extends an `Object` concrete class.

Use StringBuilder Objects and Their Methods

17. Which declaration of the `StringBuilder` class exists?
    A. `public StringBuilder reverse (String str) {…}`
    B. `public StringBuilder reverse (int index, String str) {…}`
    C. `public StringBuilder reverse () {…}`
    D. All of the above

> **Answer:**
>
> ☑ **C.** The `reverse` method of the `StringBuilder` class does not have any arguments.
> ☒ **A, B,** and **D** are incorrect answers as justified by the correct answer's explanation.

Test Equality Between Strings and Other Objects

18. Given:

    ```
    String name1 = new String ("Benjamin");
    StringBuilder name2 = new StringBuilder ("Benjamin");
    System.out.println(name2.equals(name1));
    ```

    Are the `String` and `StringBuilder` classes of comparable types? Select the correct statement.
    A. The `String` and `StringBuilder` classes are comparable types.
    B. The `String` and `StringBuilder` classes are incomparable types.

> **Answer:**
>
> ☑ **B.** The `String` and `StringBuilder` classes are incomparable types.
> ☒ **A** is incorrect because the `String` and `StringBuilder` classes are incomparable types.

19. Which append declaration does not exist in Java 8?
    A. `public StringBuilder append (short s) {…}`
    B. `public StringBuilder append (int i) {…}`
    C. `public StringBuilder append (long l) {…}`
    D. `public StringBuilder append (float f) {…}`
    E. `public StringBuilder append (double d) {…}`

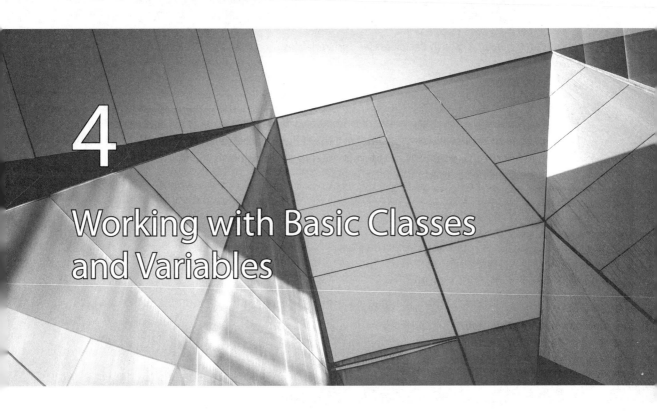

4
Working with Basic Classes and Variables

T his chapter will cover the basics of primitive variables and objects. OCA questions will require that the test taker understand the difference between primitives and objects and how each is used. The next few chapters will build on this foundation. The following topics will be covered in this chapter:

- Primitives
- Objects
- Arrays
- Enumerations
- Java's strongly typed nature
- Naming conventions

CERTIFICATION OBJECTIVE

Understand Primitives, Enumerations, and Objects

Exam Objective   *Declare and initialize variables (including casting of primitive data types)*
Exam Objective   *Develop code that uses wrapper classes such as Boolean, Double, and Integer*
Exam Objective   *Differentiate between object reference variables and primitive variables.*

An application is made up of *variables* that store data and code that manipulates the data. Java uses *primitive* variables to store its most basic data. These primitives are then used in more advanced data types called *objects*. This is what makes Java an object-oriented language: it allows the developer to organize related code and data together in discrete objects.

This is a very important and fundamental concept that you must understand to know how the Java language truly works.

Primitive Variables

Java primitives are a special subset of Java data types. They are the foundation of storing data in a program. It is important that you understand what a primitive is and what it is not for the OCA exam. The Java language has eight primitives. The important thing to remember about each primitive is what kind of value you would store in it. The size in memory and minimum/maximum value sizes are good to know, but you will not be required to memorize them for the exam.

What Is a Primitive?

A primitive is the most basic form of data in a Java program, hence its name. When a primitive is declared, it reserves a certain number of bits in memory. The size of the memory allocation is dependent on the type of primitive. Each primitive data type has a set size that it will always occupy in memory.

The eight primitive data types are

- `boolean` (boolean)
- `char` (character)
- `byte` (byte)
- `short` (short integer)
- `int` (integer)
- `long` (long integer)
- `float` (floating point)
- `double` (double precision floating point)

Remember that something represented in code as an `Integer` (which refers to an object) is different from an `int` (which refers to a primitive containing an integer value).

While working with a primitive variable, you may only set it or read it. Calculations performed with primitives are much faster than calculations performed with similar objects.

Declaring and Initializing Primitives

Like all variables in Java, primitives need to be declared before they can be used. When a variable is declared, its type and name are set. The following code shows a primitive `int` being declared:

```
int gallons;
```

The `gallons` variable is now declared as an `int`. This variable can store only an integer and cannot be broken down into any smaller elements. Now that the variable is declared, it can only be set or read—that is all. No methods can be called using this variable because it is a primitive.

This will be discussed in more depth later in the chapter when objects are explored. Primitives that are declared as instance variables get assigned a default value of 0 or false if they are a boolean. When primitives are used in the body of a method, they must be assigned a value before being used. If they are not assigned a value, a compile time error will be generated.

This code uses the new integer:

```
int gallons = 13;
System.out.println("Gallons: " + gallons);
```

boolean Primitive

A boolean primitive is used to store a value of true or false. They store a 1-bit value and will default to false as an instance variable. Although they represent only 1 bit of information, their exact size is not defined in the Java standard and may occupy more space on different platforms. Valid literals include true and false.

```
boolean hasTurboCharger = true;
hasTurboCharger = false;
```

char Primitive

The char primitive is used to store a single 16-bit Unicode character and requires 16 bits of memory. The range of a char corresponds to the minimum and maximum as defined by the Unicode specification '\u0000' (or 0) and '\uffff' (or 65,535 inclusive), respectively. When a char is set with a character in code, single quotes should be used—'Y', for example. A char has a default value of '\u0000', or 0, when used as an instance variable. This primitive is always unsigned.

The following code segments demonstrate the uses of char. Valid literals include individual characters, special characters, Unicode characters, and hexadecimal and octal representations:

```
char c1 = 'S'; // S as a character
char c2 = '\u0068'; // h in Unicode
char c3 = 0x0065; // e in hexadecimal
char c4 = 0154; // l in octal
char c5 = (char) 131170; // b; from cast to 98
char c6 = (char) 131193; // y; from cast to 121
char c7 = '\''; // ' apostrophe special character
```

```
char c8 = 's'; // s as a character
char[] autoDesignerArray = {c1, c2, c3, c4, c5, c6, c7, c8};
System.out.println(new String(autoDesignerArray) + "Mustang"); // Shelby's Mustang
```

See Table E-1 in Appendix E of the Unicode standard for representation of printable and nonprintable ASCII characters as Unicode values.

byte Primitive

A byte is a Java primitive that is normally used to store small, signed numbers up to 1 byte in size. As an instance variable, it has a default value of 0. A byte occupies 8 bits of memory and can store an 8-bit signed two's complement non–floating-point number. It has a maximum value of 127 and a minimum value of –128, inclusive. When a literal integer is stored in a byte primitive, it is implicitly cast to 1 byte. The following code segments demonstrate the uses of byte:

```
byte passengers = 4; // implicit cast from integer to byte
byte doors = (byte) 2; // explicit cast from integer to byte
```

short Primitive

A short is a Java primitive used for small numbers. It is most commonly used when the developer wants to save memory space over an int. As an instance variable, it has a default value of 0. A short occupies 16 bits of memory and can store a 16-bit signed two's complement non–floating-point number. It has a maximum value of 32,767 and a minimum value of –32,768, inclusive. The following code segments demonstrate the uses of short:

```
short unladenWeightInLbs = 2350; // implicit cast to two bytes
short capacityInCu = (short) 427; // explicit cast to two bytes
```

int Primitive

An int is the most commonly used Java primitive. An int is used to store most whole numbers. As an instance variable, it has a default value of 0. An int occupies 32 bits of memory and can store a 32-bit signed two's complement non–floating-point number. It has a maximum value of 2,147,483,647 and a minimum value of –2,147,483,648, inclusive. Java 8 has added helper methods to the Integer class that enable the developer to treat the int as if it were unsigned. However, when dealing with the int primitive directly, the Java virtual machine (JVM) will always assume it to be a signed value. The following code segments demonstrate the uses of `int`:

```
int auctionPrice = 7800000;

char cylinders = '\u0008';
int cyl = cylinders; // implicit cast from char to integer

byte wheelbase = 90;
int wBase = wheelbase; // implicit cast from byte to integer

short horsepower = 250;
int hPower = horsepower; // implicit cast from short to integer

int length = (int) 151.5F; // floats must be explicitly casted
int powerToWeightRatio = (int) 405.1D; // doubles must be
                                       // explicitly casted
```

long Primitive

A `long` is a Java primitive used for whole numbers that are larger than an `int` can store. As an instance variable, it has a default value of 0L. The `l` or `L` appended to this number indicates that it is a `long` and not an `int`. A `long` occupies 64 bits of memory and can store a 64-bit signed two's complement non–floating-point number. It has a maximum value of 9,223,372,036,854,775,807 and a minimum value of –9,223,372,036,854,775,808, inclusive. Java 8 has added helper methods to the `Long` class that enable the developer to treat the `long` as if it were unsigned. However, when dealing with the `long` primitive directly, the JVM will always assume it to be a signed value. The following code segments demonstrate the uses of `long`:

```
long mustangBingResults = 146000000L;
long mustangGoogleResults = 405000001;
/* explicit cast to long */
long mustangAmazonBookResults = (long) 5774;
/* implicit cast to long */
long mustangAmazonManualResults = 2380;
```

float Primitive

A `float` primitive is used to store decimal values. It has a default value of 0.0f when used as an instance variable. This value is equal to 0, but the `f` or `F` appended to the end indicates that this value is a `float`, not a `double`. A `float` requires 32 bits of memory and may contain a 32-bit value with a maximum of $3.4e^{+38}$ and a minimum positive nonzero value of $1.4e^{-45}$, inclusive. (These values are rounded for simplicity. The exact size of a `float` is a formula that can be found in section 4.2.3 of *The Java Language Specification: Java SE 8 Edition,* by James Gosling, Bill Joy, Guy Steele, Gilad Bracha, and Alex Buckley [Oracle, 2014], but this is beyond the scope of this book and the OCA exam.) The following code segments demonstrate the uses of `float` (notice the use of f or F to denote that the number is a `float`):

```
float currentBid = 80100.99F;
float openingBid = 20000.00f;
float reservePrice = (float) 92000;
float myBid = 36000;  // implicit cast from integer to float
```

double Primitive

A `double` primitive is used to store large decimal values. The `double` primitive is the default primitive that most developers use to store floating-point numbers. It has a default value of 0.0 as an instance variable. A `double` occupies 64 bits of memory and may contain a 64-bit value with a maximum of $1.8e^{+308}$ and a minimum positive nonzero value of $5e^{-324}$, inclusive. (These values are rounded for simplicity. The exact size of a `double` is a formula that can be found in section 4.2.3 of *The Java Language Specification*, but this is beyond the scope of this book and the OCA exam.) The following code segments demonstrate the uses of `double`:

```
double leafSpringCobraEngine = 4.7D;
double chyrsler331Engine = 5.4d;
double ford427Engine = (double)7;
double ford428Engine = 7.01;
double fordV8Engine = 5; // implicit cast from integer to double
```

Why So Many Primitives?

There are eight Java primitives. The astute reader will likely be wondering why Java has so many, and why most seem to store the same data. This is a very good observation. The primitives `byte`, `short`, `int`, and `long` all store whole numbers. These primitives are listed in size order from smallest to largest. If a number such as 32 were to be stored, all four primitives would work without issue, since 32 is small enough to fit into a `byte`, which is the smallest type. The only negative to using a larger type such as a `short`, `int`, or `long` would be the space that it occupies in memory.

The primitives for storing floating-point numbers are `float` and `double`. A small number such as 5.3 can be stored in either, with the only difference being the memory that the primitive consumes. However, as a floating-point number grows, it can lose precision. A `double` has double the precision of a `float`.

The `char` and `boolean` primitives are each unique. A `boolean` is the only primitive that can store a `true` or `false` value. And a `char` is the only primitive that stores an unsigned whole number.

Floating-Point Math

As a developer, you must be careful when using floating-point numbers. A floating-point number will lose precision as the number becomes larger. The following code is a simple example of two `floats` being added and printed to standard output:

```
float a = 19801216.0f;
float b = 20120307.12f;
float c = a + b;
//Format the float into US Currency format.
String  d = NumberFormat.getCurrencyInstance().format(c);
System.out.println(d);
//Print the number directly as it is stored.
System.out.println(c);
```

It is easy to expect the output of this code segment to be $39,921,523.12 after the `NumberFormat` class formats the number as U.S. currency. However, this is not the correct output. The code will instead output the following:

```
$39,921,524.00
3.9921524E7
```

The output is off by 0.88. This is an example of the `float` primitive losing the precision of a number. Although the output is not correct, it is expected based on how `floats` work. If the code segment is changed to use the `double` primitive, the correct output will be displayed. The following code segments use `double`, which increases the precision of the numbers:

```
double x = 19801216.0;
double y = 20120307.12;
double z = x + y;
//Format the double into US Currency format.
String  s = NumberFormat.getCurrencyInstance().format(z);
System.out.println(s);
//Print the number directly as it is stored.
System.out.println(z);
```

This code segment will output the following:

```
$39,921,523.12
3.9921523120000005E7
```

This is the correct output. Notice that the raw `double`, 3.9921523120000005E7, is much more precise then the raw `float`, 3.9921524E7. However, it is important for you to understand that the `double` does not solve all problems like this. In this case, the precision needed was more than the `float` was able to provide, but it was within the bounds of a `double`. If the required precision grew or the number got larger, a `double` would have the same problem. This example illustrates why currency should never be stored as a `double` or `float`. The proper way to store currency, or any other floating-point number that needs guaranteed precision, is to use the Java class `BigDecimal`. `BigDecimal` can store any number, with the only limit being the memory your application is able to use. `BigDecimal` is not as fast to work with as primitives are, but it provides accuracy that primitives cannot provide. For more information on how `BigDecimal` works, see the Java Platform, Standard Edition 8 API Specification.

The following Scenario & Solution details each of the primitives that will appear on the OCA exam. It is important that you understand this content.

Primitives vs. Their Wrapper Class

You know that primitives are the basic building blocks in Java and are one of the few things that are not objects. Java has a built-in wrapper class for each primitive that can convert a primitive to an object. The wrapper classes are `Integer`, `Double`, `Boolean`, `Character`, `Short`, `Byte`, `Long`, and `Float`. Notice that each of these classes starts with a *capital* letter, whereas a primitive begins with a *lowercase* letter.

SCENARIO & SOLUTION	
What primitive would you use to store a value that will be `true` or `false`?	`boolean`
What primitive would you use to store a value that will be a whole number?	`int`
What primitive would you use to store a Unicode value?	`char`
What primitive would you use to store a value that may not be a whole number if you are concerned with memory size?	`float`
What primitive would you use to store large or high precision floating-point numbers? This also tends to be the default primitive for floating-point numbers.	`double`
What primitive would you use to store a very large whole number?	`long`
What primitive would you use to store a byte of data?	`byte`
What primitive would you use to store a value of 3000, without using any more memory than needed?	`short`

If you see a data type `Float`, it is referring to the object, while the data type `float` refers to the primitive. As of J2SE 5.0, a primitive will automatically be converted in either direction between its wrapper class and associated primitive. This feature is called *autoboxing* and *unboxing*.

The following is an example of an `Integer` object being initialized:

```
// An Integer is created and initialized to 5
Integer valueA = new Integer(5);
/*A primitive int is set to the int
value stored in the Integer object*/
int num = number.intValue();
// Autoboxing is used to convert an int to an Integer
Integer valueB = num;
```

Primitives and their equivalent objects can, in most cases, be used interchangeably. However, this is a bad coding practice. When performing math operations, using primitives will result in much faster calculations. Primitives also consume a smaller memory footprint.

Reviewing All Primitives

Table 4-1 details all eight Java primitives. For the OCA exam, it is most important that you remember what data type you would use for the data you are storing. The size and range are nice to know but are not required for the exam.

	Data Type	Used for	Size	Range
TABLE 4-1	`boolean`	`true` or `false`	1 bit	N/A
	`char`	Unicode character	16 bits	\u0000 to \uFFFF (0 to 65,535)
Java Primitive Data Types	`byte`	integer	8 bits	−128 to 127
	`short`	integer	16 bits	−32768 to 32767
	`int`	integer	32 bits	−2,147,483,648 to 2,147,483,647
	`long`	integer	64 bits	-2^{63} to $2^{63}-1$
	`float`	floating point	32 bits	positive $1.4e^{-45}$ to $3.4e^{+38}$
	`double`	floating point	64 bits	positive $5e^{-324}$ to $1.8e^{+308}$

When you're reading Java code that other developers have created, you will mostly see the primitives `int`, `double`, and `boolean`. These three primitives cover most standard cases and are the default choice of most developers. Developers tend to worry only about optimizing the size of primitives when they are used repeatedly in arrays or in data structures that remain persistent for a long period of time.

Objects

Java is an object-oriented language, and your understanding of what objects are and how they work is fundamental and very important. Almost everything you work with in Java is an object. Primitives are one of the few exceptions to this rule. You will learn what is stored in objects and how objects help keep code organized.

Understanding Objects

Objects are a more advanced data type than primitives. They internally use primitives and other objects to store their data and contain related code. The data is used to maintain the state of the object, while the code is organized into methods that perform actions on this data. A well-designed class should be clearly defined and easily reused in different applications. This is the fundamental philosophy of an object-oriented language.

Objects vs. Classes and the New Operator

The distinction between objects and classes is important for you to understand. When a developer writes code, he or she is creating or modifying a class. A class is the file containing the code that the developer writes. It is a tangible item. A class is like a blueprint to tell the JVM how to create an object at runtime. The new operator tells the JVM to use the blueprint to create a new instance of this class, the result of which is an object. Many objects can be built from one class. The following is an example of a class that is employed to create an object used to represent a car:

```java
public class Car {
    int topSpeed;
    boolean running;
    Car(int topSpeed, boolean running){
        this.running = running;
        this.topSpeed = topSpeed;
    }
    public boolean isRunning(){
        return running;
    }
}
```

The preceding class can be used to represent a `Car` object. The class can store a `boolean` value that represents whether the car is running and an `int` value that represents the top speed. From this class, the JVM can create one or many instances of the `Car` class. Each instance will become its own `Car` object.

In the following code segment, two `Car` objects are created:

```
Car fastCar = new Car(200,true);
Car slowCar = new Car(100,true);
```

Both `fastCar` and `slowCar` are instances of the `Car` class. To initialize an object, the `new` operator must be used. The `new` operator tells the JVM that it needs to create a `Car` object with the arguments given to the constructor. The `new` operator will always return a new and independent instance of the class.

Initializing Objects

Earlier in the chapter, you learned how each primitive has a finite predetermined size. Unlike a primitive, an object's size is not clearly defined. An object's size depends on the size of all the primitives and objects that it stores. Because objects store other objects, their size must also be considered. When an object is initialized, the JVM makes a reference in memory to the location of the object. Objects also have the ability to change in size as the objects they store grow or shrink. An object is declared in the same manner as a primitive, but it cannot be used until it has been initialized, with the `new` operator or set equal to an existing object.

In the following example, we use the `Car` class again:

```
/* This is legal. You can use the method isRunning because
the object has been initialized. */
Car bigCar;
bigCar = new Car(125,true);
boolean running = bigCar.isRunning();

/* This is legal. You can use the method isRunning because
the object smallCar has been set to the same initialized
object as bigCar. This will make smallCar and bigCar the same object. */
Car smallCar;
smallCar = bigCar;
boolean running = smallCar.isRunning();

/* This is an illegal example. You cannot use a method on an
uninitialized object. */
Car oldCar;
boolean running = oldCar.isRunning();
```

Notice that, unlike a primitive, an object must be initialized with the new operator. Before initialization, an object is set to null by default. If a null object is used, it will throw a null pointer exception.

When to Use Objects

Primitives are used to store simple values. Integers or floating-point numbers within the bounds of a primitive data type are easy to store. Unfortunately, not all applications deal with values that fit neatly in the bounds of a primitive. For example, if an integer value is very large and has the potential to become even larger, the primitive int or long may not be appropriate. Instead, the developer may have to use one of the classes from the built-in Java packages for handling large numbers. These classes are BigInteger and BigDecimal. BigInteger is able to store a whole number and is limited in size only by the memory that the application can use. BigDecimal is similar to BigInteger except that it can store a floating-point number.

Objects can and should be created to store data that is similar. Remember that it is good object-oriented design to group together like code and data in a distinct class. Objects should be used to store complex related data.

Null Objects

Before an object is assigned or initialized, it is given the null value. A NullPointerException is a runtime exception that is thrown when an object is used that is null. This is a very common runtime error and can cause an application to terminate. It can be very frustrating and time consuming to track down. The best way to prevent this is to be careful, initialize your objects, and use a condition statement to check objects that may have been set to null elsewhere in code.

Here is an example of how to check whether an object is null:

```
Truck truck = null; // Initializes to null
  if(truck != null){
    truck.startEngine();
  }
```

Here, a Truck object is declared and called truck. The variable truck is then checked to determine whether it is null. If it is not null, it proceeds inside of the if statement and executes the startEngine method. In this case, truck is never initialized, so it would not pass the condition of the if statement. The flow of execution would skip the body of the if statement, and the startEngine method would never be called. This prevents a NullPointerException from being thrown.

It is a good habit to check to see if unknown variables are `null` before they are used. Even if your application is in an error state, checking the variable will allow a better log message to be recorded before the application exits.

Compile and Run an Object

This exercise will get you more familiar with objects. You will use the `Car` class and then add more functionality to it.

1. Copy the `Car` class into a text file and save it as Car.java.

2. Create a new text file and name it Main.java. This will be your main class. Copy the following code into this file:

```
public class Main {
  public static void main(String[] args) {
    // Your code goes here
  }
}
```

3. Use the following code to create a `Car` object:

```
Car yourCar = new Car(230,true);
```

4. Use the following code to display to the user whether or not the car is running:

```
System.out.println(yourCar.isRunning());
```

5. Go back to the `Car` class and add a method to get the car's top speed.

6. Add a line to your Main.java file that will display the car's top speed.

Arrays

An array is a series of variables of the same type that can be accessed by an index. Arrays are useful when all the variables in a set of data will be used in a similar way. Arrays can be made from primitive data types or objects. Even if an array is made of primitive data types, the `new` operator must be used.

The following is an example of an array made up of the `int` data type:

```
int[] testScore = new int[3];
```

In this example, we declare a variable named `testScore` to be an integer array. This is done by adding box brackets to the end of the data type: `int []` is the result. The `[]` after the data type means it will be an array. The box brackets should follow the data type, but it is valid for them to follow the variable name instead. Standard Java coding conventions suggest they should be used only with the data type. Regardless of whether the new array is of primitives or objects, it must be initialized with `new` and then with the data type. The number in brackets indicates the size of the array. In this example, the array has three items. Each item is of type `int`. Individual elements in the array can be accessed or modified; they can also be placed in another `int`. The index for an array is zero based. This means that the first element has an index of zero.

The example that follows demonstrates how an array can be used:

```
int[] testScore = new int[3];
testScore[0] = 98;
testScore[1] = 100;
testScore[2] = 72;
int shannonsTestScore = testScore[1];
```

Arrays are useful in loops. It is very common to access an array in a loop with a variable as the index. This variable would be incremented each time through the loop until the end of the array. The developer must take caution not to use an index that is out of bounds. An out-of-bounds index will cause the JVM to throw an exception at runtime. Once the size of an array is set, it cannot be changed. This makes arrays less useful for situations in which the data set may grow. Figure 4-1 shows a basic array declaration.

Arrays can also be multidimensional. A multidimensional array has more than one index. Arrays and their uses will be discussed in more detail in Chapter 6.

Enumerations

Enumerations are a special data type in Java that allows for a variable to be set to predefined constants. The variable must equal one of the values that have been predefined for it. An enumeration is useful when there is a limited set of options that a variable can equal and it is restricted to these known values. For example,

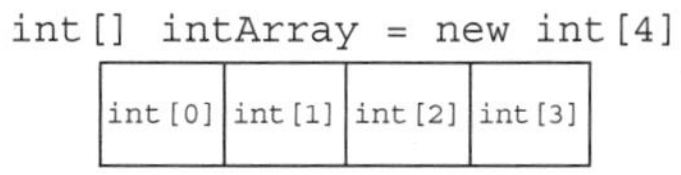

FIGURE 4-1

Array declaration

```
int[] intArray = new int[4]
```

| int[0] | int[1] | int[2] | int[3] |

a deck of playing cards will always have four suits: clubs, diamonds, hearts, and spades. If a developer wanted to represent a card, an enumeration could be used to represent the suit:

```
enum Suit { CLUBS, DIAMONDS, HEARTS, SPADES }
```

This is an example of an enumeration that would be used to store the suit of a playing card. It is defined with the keyword `enum`. The `enum` keyword is used in the same manner as the `class` keyword. It can be defined in its own Java file or embedded in a class.

The next example demonstrates the use of an enumeration. The variable `card` is declared as a `Suit`. `Suit` was defined earlier as an enumeration. The `cardSuit` variable can now be used to store one of the four predefined suit values.

```
Suit cardSuit;
cardSuit = Suit.CLUBS;
if(cardSuit == Suit.CLUBS){
   System.out.println("The suit of this card is clubs.");
}
```

Benefits of Using Enumerations

An object can be created to work in the same manner as an enumeration. In fact, enumerations were not even included in the Java language until version 5.0. However, enumerations make code more readable and provide less room for programmer error.

Java Is Strongly Typed

Java is a *strongly typed* programming language. Java requires that a developer declare the data type of each variable used. Once a variable is declared as one type, all data stored in it must be compatible with that type. Think back to the primitive data types we reviewed earlier in the chapter. For example, once a variable is declared as an `int`, only `int` data can be stored within it. Data can be converted, by casting, from one type to another, as discussed in the following sections.

Understanding Strongly Typed Variables

Strongly typed variables help to create more reliable code. In most cases, the Java compiler will not allow the developer to store mismatched data types. Only variables with the same data type are compatible with each other. For example, a `float` cannot be stored in any other data type other than a `float`. The same is true for all primitives and objects. The JVM will perform some automatic conversions for the developer. It is important that you understand that the types are not compatible and that the code will work only because of the conversion that is happening.

An example of a conversion would be going from an `int` to a `float`. The JVM will allow for an `int` to be placed into a `float` because it can convert an `int` to a `float` without losing precision. However, the converse is not true. A `float` cannot be converted to an `int` without the loss of precision.

Casting Variables to Different Types

Java does allow a variable to be cast to a different type. Casting tells the compiler that a variable of one type is intended to be used as a different type. To cast a variable, place the new data type in parentheses in front of the data or variable. Data can be cast only to types with which it is compatible. If data is illegally cast, the program will throw an exception at runtime.

An object can be cast to any parent or child object if the object was initialized as that child object. (This is an advanced concept of object-oriented languages and will be discussed in more detail in later chapters.) Primitives can also be cast to other primitives or compatible objects. For example, a `float` can be cast to an `int`. In this scenario, the cast would truncate the `float` to a whole number. Following are some examples of casting variables and data:

```
float floatNum = 1.5f;
int wasFloat = (int) floatNum;
```

The variable `wasFloat` would be equal to `1` since the `.5` would be truncated to make the data compatible.

on the job

Developers should use casting variables lightly. There are times when variables must be cast, and some advanced programming techniques even rely on it. However, casting variables adds unneeded complexity to the code. Cast data only when you have a good reason to do so.

Naming Conventions

Using the correct naming conventions while creating a Java application is a critical step in creating easily readable and maintainable code. Java does not have many restrictions on how classes and objects can be named. However, nearly every experienced Java developer uses a single naming convention suggested by Oracle. For all the conventions, see Oracle's *Code Conventions for the Java Programming Language* specification. This section will cover the common conventions that will be seen on the OCA exam.

When you are creating a class, the class name should be a noun. The first letter should be capitalized along with each internal word after the first. Names should be short, yet descriptive. Shown next are some examples of good class names that follow the naming convention:

```
class SportsCar {...}
class BaseballPlayer {...}
class Channel {...}
```

Variables should also have short but meaningful names. However, it is okay to use one-letter names for temporary variables. A variable's name should give an outside observer some insight as to what the variable is used for. The name should start with a lowercase letter, but each sequential internal word should be capitalized. Shown next is a sample of some variable names that follow the convention:

```
int milesPerGallon;
float price;
int i;
Car raceCar;
```

e x a m

ⓦatch
The OCA exam will ask questions about which variable is a primitive data type and which is an object. If you don't have a firm understanding of each, you may find the answers confusing. Remember that the OCA exam will always follow proper Java naming conventions and start object data types with a capital letter and begin primitive data types with a lowercase letter. For example, a `float` *is a primitive data type and a* `Float` *is an object.*

CERTIFICATION OBJECTIVE

Use Primitives, Enumerations, and Objects

Exam Objective   Differentiate between object reference variables and primitive variables

This section will build on the fundamental concepts that were discussed in the previous sections. The OCA exam will not require that you write code from scratch. However, the exam creators have decided to present scenarios in which the candidate will need to determine the best-suited code from a list of segments. The exam will also present segments of code and ask varying questions about its elements. This section specifically covers literals and practical examples of primitives, enumerations, and objects.

Literals

A *literal* is a term used for a hard-coded value used within code. A literal is any value that is not a variable. The following example demonstrates the use of literals:

```
int daysInMay = 31;
int daysInJune;
daysInJune = 30;
char y   = 'Y';
```

As used here, 31, 30, and 'Y' are examples of literals. Valid literal value formats for all primitives except the boolean type include character, decimal, hexadecimal, octal, and Unicode. Literals values for booleans must be true or false.

on the
Job

Starting in Java 7, it is possible to insert underscores in numeric literals. This allows the developer to create more readable code. The underscores are ignored at runtime and are used solely to make the code easier to read. The underscores can be placed in both whole and floating-point numbers. They cannot be placed before the first number, or after the last number, or adjacent to a decimal point. They also cannot be placed prior to the f and l suffixes for a float or long. The following are some examples of underscores in use:

```
long creditCardNumber = 5555_5555_5555_5555L;
int largeNumber = 1_000_000;
float pi = 3.14_159_265f;
```

Examples of Primitives, Enumerations, and Objects

This section will provide a few examples of all the topics covered in this chapter so far. Each example will be accompanied by an explanation. These examples will mimic the types of scenarios likely found on the OCA exam.

Primitives in Action

Primitives are the most basic data types in Java. As stated, they can only be set or read. The following sample program uses each primitive that will be on the OCA exam. This program calculates a baseball pitcher's earned run average (ERA).

```
public class EraCalculator{
  public static void main(String[] args) {
    int earnedRuns = 3;
    int inningsPitched = 6;
    int inningsInAGame = 9;
    float leagueAverageEra = 4.25f;
    float era = ((float)earnedRuns / (float)inningsPitched) *
      inningsInAGame;
    boolean betterThanAverage;
    if (era < leagueAverageEra) {
      betterThanAverage = true;
    } else {
      betterThanAverage = false;
    }
    char yesNo = betterThanAverage ? 'Y' : 'N';
    System.out.println("Earned Runs\t\t" + earnedRuns);
    System.out.println("Innings Pitched\t\t" + inningsPitched);
    System.out.println("ERA\t\t\t" + era);
    System.out.println("League Average ERA\t"+leagueAverageEra);
    System.out.println("Is player better than league average "+
      yesNo);
  }
}
```

Notice that on the line where the variable ERA is calculated, the two int variables, earnedRuns and inningsPitched, are cast to a float. The cast to a float is needed so the division will be performed on variables of type float instead of their original type of int. The variables earnedRuns, inningsPitched, inningsInAGame, and leagueAverageEra are all set by literals. The preceding program shows how primitives are used. When the code is executed, it will produce the following output:

```
Earned Runs                            3
Innings Pitched                        6
ERA                                    4.5
League Average ERA                     4.25
Is player better than league average   N
```

Primitives and Their Wrapper Class

The code segment that follows shows four variables being declared. Of the four, two are primitives and two are objects. The objects are instances of primitive wrapper classes. On the exam, pay close attention to how the variables are declared. There will likely be a segment where the question will ask how many of the variables are primitives.

```
Integer numberOfCats;
Float averageWeightOfCats;
int numberOfDogs;
float averageWeightOfDogs;
```

In the preceding example, int and float are primitives and Integer and Float are objects. Note that the capital F in Float signifies an object.

Enumerations

Enumerations are used for variables that can have the value of only a few predefined constants. The following example demonstrates a small class. This class has an enumeration defined that contains three different shoe types. The createRunningShoes() method is used to set the shoe variable to the enumerated type of a running shoe:

```
public class EnumExample {
  enum TypeOfShoe { RUNNING, BASKETBALL, CROSS_TRAINING }
  TypeOfShoe shoe;
  void createRunningShoes(){
    shoe = TypeOfShoe.RUNNING;
  }
}
```

Objects

The OCA exam does not require that you develop your own objects, but it is important that you understand the content of an object and be able to recognize it in code. It is also important that you understand how to use methods that an object contains. In the following example, a class is defined. This class is the Thermostat class. As its name suggests, it would be used to represent a thermostat for a heater or furnace. This is a very basic class, because it has only two methods and one instance variable. A more useful class would have many more of both.

```
class Thermostat {
  int temperatureTrigger;
  int getTemperatureTrigger() {
    return temperatureTrigger;
```

```
    }
    public void setTemperatureTrigger(int temperatureTrigger) {
        this.temperatureTrigger = temperatureTrigger;
    }
}
```

The preceding `Thermostat` class stores the temperature that will trigger the system to turn on in the variable named `temperatureTrigger`. The two methods are used to get the value and set the value. These are called *getters* and *setters* and will be discussed in Chapter 7.

The following code segments will use the `Thermostat` class to create an object:

```
Thermostat houseThermostat = new Thermostat ();
houseThermostat.setTemperatureTrigger(68);
System.out.println(houseThermostat.getTemperatureTrigger());
```

This code segment declares a new variable as a `Thermostat` object. The object is then initialized with the new keyword. The next line uses the `setTemperatureTrigger` method to modify the state of the object. The final line uses the `getTemperatureTrigger` method to read this value and display it to the user. For the OCA exam, it is important that you be familiar with this syntax and understand how the methods are used.

EXERCISE 4-2

Creating Getters and Setters

Creating a dozen getter and setter methods by hand could take you a while to complete. Fortunately, most modern IDEs have an automated way of creating getter and setter methods. Using this automated feature produces the methods with just a few mouse clicks. Follow along with this exercise to get a feel for how this works in the Eclipse IDE.

1. Create a few instance variables.

2. If you are using Eclipse, do the following:

   a. Highlight the desired instance variable you want to produce getters and setters for, and then right-click the mouse.

   b. A pop-up menu will be displayed. Select Source followed by Generate Getters and Setters....

   c. Another dialog box will be displayed with additional options that are not needed for this example. Finally, click the OK button to generate the methods.

3. If you are using NetBeans, do the following:

    a. In the NetBeans text editor, highlight the instance variable and right-click.

    b. From the drop-down box, select Refactor | Encapsulate Fields....

    c. A pop-up box will display the highlighted instance variable already selected. You can then click the Refactor button to add the getter and setter with the default settings.

See Chapter 7 for more information on getter and setter methods.

CERTIFICATION SUMMARY

In this chapter, some of the most fundamental concepts of Java were discussed in relationship to basic classes and variables. Even though the OCA exam includes only two objectives covering these concepts, many advanced concepts and objectives are built upon the content of this chapter. Your understanding of this chapter will result in a better understanding of the next few chapters.

Java primitives were examined first. Primitives are the basic building blocks of a Java program. The eight primitive variable data types that will appear on the OCA are `int`, `double`, `boolean`, `char`, `byte`, `short`, `long`, and `float`. It is important that you remember these primitives and what type of data they are designed to store.

Objects were then discussed. Objects are a very important concept for you to understand for the OCA exam. Objects are an advanced Java data type that can be custom created or found in the many Java packages that are included with the Java Virtual Machine. Objects are the pieces that interact to make up an application. Java is an object-oriented language, which means that nearly every aspect of the program is represented as objects, and the interaction between the objects is what gives an application its functionality.

Arrays were then discussed. Arrays are good for keeping like data together. They use a zero-based index to access the individual elements of the array. Arrays can be of objects or primitives and must be initialized.

Enumerations were the last group of data types discussed. Enumerations are special objects that are used to denote a value among a defined set of values. Although regular objects can be used to achieve the same results, enumerations provide a way to limit the data set without implementing a lot of custom code.

Next, the details of what makes Java a strongly typed language were examined. In general, the Java language allows for variables to change data type only by explicitly casting them to a new data type. If a variable is cast to a data type that it is not compatible with, an exception will be generated.

The final Java concept covered was Java naming conventions. Even though there are very few limitations on how variables and classes can be named, it is good coding practice to follow the conventions used by nearly every Java developer. Not following these conventions is a quick way to test the patience of your fellow developers.

The chapter concluded with a group of examples and explanations. These examples are important for you to understand. The OCA will not ask you to write large sections of code, but you must be able to understand code segments and determine what the output will be or if errors are present in the code.

TWO-MINUTE DRILL

Understand Primitives, Enumerations, and Objects

- ☐ Primitives are the fundamental data type in Java.
- ☐ `int` is a primitive data type that is used to store integer values. It is the default value for whole numbers.
- ☐ `double` is a primitive data type for large floating-point values. It is the default value for floating-point numbers.
- ☐ `boolean` is a primitive data type that is used to store `true` or `false` values.
- ☐ `char` is a primitive data type that is used to store a single Unicode character.
- ☐ `byte` is a primitive used to store small numbers that are 1 byte (8 bits) or smaller.
- ☐ `short` is a primitive used to store whole numbers up to 16 bits.
- ☐ `long` is a primitive used to store large whole numbers up to 64 bits.
- ☐ `float` is a primitive data type used to store floating-point values.
- ☐ Primitive data types all start with a lowercase letter, while classes start with a capital letter.
- ☐ Each primitive data type has a corresponding wrapper class: `Integer`, `Double`, `Boolean`, `Character`, `Byte`, `Short`, `Long`, and `Float`. Notice the capital letters.
- ☐ Objects are more advanced data types. They may be defined by a developer or found in a built-in Java package.

Use Primitives, Enumerations, and Objects

- ☐ Objects must be initialized by using the `new` keyword.
- ☐ Arrays allow you to store multiple variables together that can be accessed by an index.
- ☐ Enumerations allow a developer to create a predefined set of constants. A variable can then be set only to one of the predefined values.
- ☐ Java is a strongly typed language. Variables must be declared as a type, and any value that is stored must be compatible with this type.

☐ It is possible to cast a variable to a different data type. If incompatible types are cast, an exception will be thrown.

☐ A literal is a value that is hard-coded in code as the value itself.

☐ Java naming conventions dictate that a class should be named with the first letter capitalized, along with each sequential word in the name.

☐ Java naming conventions dictate that a variable should be named with the first letter lowercased and with each sequential word in the name beginning with a capital letter.

SELF TEST

Understand Primitives, Enumerations, and Objects

1. You need to create an application that is used to calculate the attendance at a baseball game. What data type would be most appropriate for storing the attendance?

   A. `boolean`

   B. `char`

   C. `float`

   D. `int`

2. What is the best data type to use if you are required to perform many addition, subtraction, and multiplication calculations on a whole number?

   A. `double`

   B. `Double`

   C. `int`

   D. `Integer`

3. You are writing a class that will store the status of an on/off switch. Which data type is most appropriate for storing this value?

   A. `boolean`

   B. `char`

   C. `short`

   D. `int`

4. You have decided on the data type for a variable that will store the information about the on/off switch. Now you must determine a name for it. Which of the following names follows the Java naming conventions?

   A. `LIGHTSWITCHENABLED`

   B. `LightSwitchEnabled`

   C. `lightSwitchEnabled`

   D. `x`

5. What is the best data type to use when storing a status code that may have one of the following values: success, failed, success with errors, or undetermined?

   A. `Object`

   B. `Class`

   C. `boolean`

   D. `enum`

   E. `int`

6. A system has three sensors attached to it. You need a way to represent this system in your program. What would be the best data type to use to model this system and sensors?

    A. `Object`

    B. `boolean`

    C. `enum`

    D. `int`

7. The new keyword is used to initialize which of the following data types? (Choose all that apply.)

    A. `Object`

    B. `boolean`

    C. `Boolean`

    D. `Float`

    E. `float`

    F. `float[]`

8. In the following line of code, what does the `(int)` represent?

```
number = (int)sensorReading;
```

    A. Rounding the `sensorReading` variable to the nearest `int`.

    B. Casting the `sensorReading` variable to the `int` data type.

    C. Nothing; it is there as a comment.

9. Given the following line of code, which of the next lines of code listed are incorrect? (Choose all that apply.)

```
char c;
```

    A. `c = new char();`

    B. `c = 'Y';`

    C. `c = '\u0056';`

    D. `c = "Yes";`

10. When dealing with currency, what data type should be used?

    A. `float`

    B. `double`

    C. `BigDecimal`

    D. `BigNumber`

11. Complete the sentence. The `Integer` class _____.
    A. is the same as an `int` primitive
    B. is the primitive wrapper class for all whole numbers
    C. is the primitive wrapper class for just `int` primitives
    D. None of these statements is valid.

12. Which of the statements are correct? (Choose all that apply.)
    A. `3.0` is a valid literal for an `int`.
    B. `3.0` is a valid literal for a `float`.
    C. `3` is a valid literal for an `int`.
    D. `3` is a valid literal for a `float`.
    E. `3f` is a valid literal for an `int`.
    F. `3f` is a valid literal for a `float`.

13. What literal values are acceptable to use with the `boolean` primitive?
    A. `true` and `false`
    B. `true`, `false`, and `null`
    C. `true`, `false`, `TRUE`, and `FALSE`
    D. `TRUE` and `FALSE`

Use Primitives, Enumerations, and Objects

14. Which of the following variables are being set with the use of a literal? (Choose all that apply.)
    A. `int tvChannel = 4;`
    B. `char c = '5';`
    C. `char d = '\u0123';`
    D. `char e = c;`
    E. `int oldChannel = tvChannel;`

15. Given the following line of code, what next lines are valid? (Choose all that apply.)

```
enum Sports { FOOTBALL, BASKETBALL, BASEBALL, TRACK }
```

    A. `Sports sport = FOOTBALL;`
    B. `Sports sport = Sports.FOOTBALL;`
    C. `Sports sport = Sports.HOCKEY;`
    D. `Sports sport = 'TRACK'`

16. What is wrong with the following method?

```
public double interestDue(double currentBalance, float interestRate){
double interestDue = currentBalance * interestRate;
return interestDue;
}
```

A. It should use all `float` primitives.
B. It should use all `Float` objects.
C. It should use all `double` primitives.
D. It should use all `Double` objects.
E. It should use `BigDecimal` objects.
F. Nothing is wrong with this method.
G. It does not compile because you cannot do math operations with primitives that are not the same type.

17. What is the correct way to create an array with five `int` data types? (Choose all that apply.)

A. `int intArray = new int[5];`
B. `int intArray = new int(5);`
C. `int[] intArray = new int[5];`
D. `int intArray[] = new int[5];`

18. What is the correct way to initialize a variable declared with the data type of `Book` as a new `Book` object?

A. `Book b;`
B. `Book b = new Book();`
C. `Book b = new Book[];`
D. `Book b = Book();`

19. What is the difference between an `int` and an `Integer`?

A. Nothing. They are both fully interchangeable.
B. An `int` is an object and `Integer` is a primitive. An `int` is fastest when performing calculations.
C. An `int` is a primitive and `Integer` is an object. An `int` is fastest when performing calculations.
D. This is a trick question. There is no such thing as an `Integer`.
E. This is a trick question. An `Integer` can be defined to be anything a developer wants it to be.

20. What is the result of using a method of an uninitialized object?

A. Null is returned.

B. The object is automatically initialized and an appropriate value is returned.

C. A `NullPointerException` is thrown from the Java virtual machine.

21. What is wrong with the following code segment? (Choose all that apply.)

```
1:      float a = 1.2f;
2:      int b = 5;
3:      short c = 9;
4:      long d = 6;
5:      double e = b;
6:      Double f = e;
7:      Short g;
8:      Float h = g.floatValue();
```

A. Nothing is wrong.

B. There is an error on line 1.

C. There is an error on line 2.

D. There is an error on line 3.

E. There is an error on line 4.

F. There is an error on line 5.

G. There is an error on line 6.

H. There is an error on line 7.

I. There is an error on line 8.

22. What is the value of variable x in the following code segment?

```
float x =0.0f;
int y = 5;
long z;
x = y + 3.3f;
x = x + z;
```

A. 0

B. 0.0f

C. 5.0f

D. 8.3f

E. 8.3

F. This code will not compile.

23. Which integer declaration uses a valid octal literal?

A. `int value1 = 0000;`

B. `int value2 = '\u0777 ';`

C. `int value3 = '\01111 ';`

D. `int value4 = '\x0123 ';`

24. Given:

```
int b1 = 0b_0101_0101_0101_0101;
int b2 = 0b_1010_1010_1010_1010;
int b3 = b1 & b2;
System.out.println("Value:" + b3);
```

What will be the result?

A. `Value:  0` will be printed.

B. `Value:  65535` will be printed.

C. `0b_1111_1111_1111_1111` will be printed.

D. A compiler error will occur.

25. Which code example makes use of arrays without producing a compiler or runtime error?

A.
```
public class Actor {
    String[] characterName = new String[3];
    {
      characterName[0] = "Captain Video";
      characterName[1] = "Quizmaster";
      characterName[2] = "J.C. Money";
      characterName[3] = "Jersey Joe";
    }
}
```

B.
```
public class Actor {
    String[] characterName = new String[1..4]
    {
      characterName[0] = "Captain Video";
      characterName[1] = "Quizmaster";
      characterName[2] = "J.C. Money";
      characterName[3] = "Jersey Joe";
    }
}
```

C. ```
    public class Actor {
        String characterName = new String[4];
      {
          characterName[0] = "Captain Video";
          characterName[1] = "Quizmaster";
          characterName[2] = "J.C. Money";
          characterName[3] = "Jersey Joe";
      }
    }
    ```

D.  ```
    public class Actor {
        String [] characterName = new String[4];
        {
        characterName[0] = "Captain Video";
        characterName[1] = "Quizmaster";
        characterName[2] = "J.C. Money";
        characterName[3] = "Jersey Joe";
        }
    }
    ```

SELF TEST ANSWERS

Understand Primitives, Enumerations, and Objects

1. You need to create an application that is used to calculate the attendance at a baseball game. What data type would be most appropriate for storing the attendance?
   A. `boolean`
   B. `char`
   C. `float`
   D. `int`

   Answer:

   ☑ **D.** The attendance of a baseball game is going to be a whole number within the range of an `int`.

   ☒ **A, B,** and **C** are incorrect. **A** is incorrect because `boolean` variables are used to store literals with values of `true` or `false`. **B** is incorrect because the `char` data type is used to store a single Unicode character. **C** is incorrect because `float` is used to store floating-point numbers.

2. What is the best data type to use if you are required to perform many addition, subtraction, and multiplication calculations on a whole number?
   A. `double`
   B. `Double`
   C. `int`
   D. `Integer`

   Answer:

   ☑ **C.** An `int` is used to store whole numbers and is a primitive. Primitive variables perform calculations faster than their associated wrapper class.

   ☒ **A, B,** and **D** are incorrect. **A** is incorrect because a `double` is used for floating-point numbers. **B** is incorrect because `Double` is a primitive wrapper class used for floating-point numbers. **D** is incorrect because the `Integer` data type is the wrapper class for an `int`. You can tell that it is not a primitive because the first letter is capitalized like all class names. Performing calculations with an `Integer` would be much slower than doing so with the primitive `int`.

3. You are writing a class that will store the status of an on/off switch. Which data type is most appropriate for storing this value?

A. `boolean`

B. `char`

C. `short`

D. `int`

> Answer:
>
> ☑ **A**. A `boolean` primitive is used to store `true` or `false`, which can be applied to a switch.
>
> ☒ **B, C**, and **D** are incorrect. They are all primitives used for different types of data.

4. You have decided on the data type for a variable that will store the information about the on/off switch. Now you must determine a name for it. Which of the following names follows the Java naming conventions?

A. `LIGHTSWITCHENABLED`

B. `LightSwitchEnabled`

C. `lightSwitchEnabled`

D. `x`

> Answer:
>
> ☑ **C**. A variable should begin with a lowercase letter, with each sequential word capitalized. The name should also be descriptive of what the variable is used for.
>
> ☒ **A, B**, and **D** are incorrect. **A** is incorrect because all capitals is not a correct naming convention for a variable. **B** is incorrect because it starts with a capital letter. **D** is incorrect because it is not descriptive.

5. What is the best data type to use when storing a status code that may have one of the following values: success, failed, success with errors, or undetermined?

A. `Object`

B. `Class`

C. `boolean`

D. `enum`

E. `int`

Answer:

☑ **D**. An enum, or enumeration, is used to store data that has the possibility to be one of a few predefined data types.

☒ **A, B, C**, and **E** are incorrect. **A** is incorrect because objects are used to store complex data structures. **B** is incorrect because classes are used to create objects. **C** and **E** are incorrect because both are primitives and not suitable for this specific application.

6. A system has three sensors attached to it. You need a way to represent this system in your program. What would be the best data type to use to model this system and sensors?
   A. `Object`
   B. `boolean`
   C. `enum`
   D. `int`

Answer:

☑ **A**. An `Object` data type is one that the developer can define to represent the system and its state in the application's code.

☒ **B, C**, and **D** are incorrect. None of them is a primitive type, and none can be defined to hold complex data structures.

7. The new keyword is used to initialize which of the following data types? (Choose all that apply.)
   A. `Object`
   B. `boolean`
   C. `Boolean`
   D. `Float`
   E. `float`
   F. `float[]`

Answer:

☑ **A, C, D**, and **F** are correct. New is used to initialize any variable that is not a primitive.

☒ **B** and **E** are incorrect. Both `boolean` and `float` are primitive data types.

8. In the following line of code, what does the `(int)` represent?

```
number = (int)sensorReading;
```

A. Rounding the `sensorReading` variable to the nearest `int`.
B. Casting the `sensorReading` variable to the `int` data type.
C. Nothing; it is there as a comment.

Answer:

☑ **B**. It is casting the variable `sensorReading` to an `int`.
☒ **A** and **C** are incorrect. **A** is incorrect because casting to an `int` will not round the value but instead result in loss of precision. **C** is incorrect because this is not used as a comment.

9. Given the following line of code, which of the next lines of code listed are incorrect? (Choose all that apply.)

```
char c;
```

A. `c = new char();`
B. `c = 'Y';`
C. `c = '\u0056';`
D. `c = "Yes";`

Answer:

☑ **A** and **D**. **A** is a correct answer because the new keyword cannot be used with the primitive `char`. **D** is a correct answer because `char` cannot store a string.
☒ **B** and **C** are incorrect. Both are valid lines of code.

10. When dealing with currency, what data type should be used?
A. `float`
B. `double`
C. `BigDecimal`
D. `BigNumber`

Answer:

☑   **C.** The `BigDecimal` class can handle large floating-point numbers without loss of precision.

☒   **A, B,** and **D** are incorrect. **A** and **B** are incorrect because their precision is limited by their size and would require the use of floating-point math. **D** is incorrect because the `BigNumber` class is limited to whole numbers.

11. Complete the sentence. The `Integer` class _____.
   A.   is the same as an `int` primitive
   B.   is the primitive wrapper class for all whole numbers
   C.   is the primitive wrapper class for just `int` primitives
   D.   None of these statements is valid.

Answer:

☑   **C.** The `Integer` class is used as a wrapper class only for `int` primitives.

☒   **A, B,** and **D** are incorrect. **A** is incorrect because an `int` and `Integer` classes are not the same. `Integer` is an object, and `int` is a primitive. However, they may appear to be the same since autoboxing and auto unboxing allow them to be used interchangeably. **B** is incorrect because the `Integer` class is the primitive wrapper class for the `int` primitive.

12. Which of the statements are correct? (Choose all that apply.)
   A.   `3.0` is a valid literal for an `int`.
   B.   `3.0` is a valid literal for a `float`.
   C.   `3` is a valid literal for an `int`.
   D.   `3` is a valid literal for a `float`.
   E.   `3f` is a valid literal for an `int`.
   F.   `3f` is a valid literal for a `float`.

Answer:

☑ **C, D**, and **F. C** is correct because an `int` is used to store an integer number. **D** is correct because the compiler will automatically convert 3 to a floating-point number. **F** is also correct because when an `f` is appended to a number, it implies that that number is a floating-point number, even if it does not have a decimal.

☒ **A, B**, and **E** are incorrect. **A** is incorrect because an `int` cannot store a decimal number. **B** is incorrect because `3.0f` would be a valid literal for a float, but `3.0` would not (the compiler treats `3.0` as a double). **E** is incorrect because an `int` cannot have `f` appended to it.

13. What literal values are acceptable to use with the `boolean` primitive?
    A. `true` and `false`
    B. `true`, `false`, and `null`
    C. `true`, `false`, `TRUE`, and `FALSE`
    D. `TRUE` and `FALSE`

Answer:

☑ **A**. Valid literal values for the `boolean` primitive are `true` and `false`.

☒ **B, C**, and **D** are incorrect. `TRUE`, `FALSE`, and `null` are all invalid literals for the `boolean` primitive. The `null` value is a valid literal for the `Boolean` wrapper class.

Use Primitives, Enumerations, and Objects

14. Which of the following variables are being set with the use of a literal? (Choose all that apply.)
    A. `int tvChannel = 4;`
    B. `char c = '5';`
    C. `char d = '\u0123';`
    D. `char e = c;`
    E. `int oldChannel = tvChannel;`

Answer:

☑ **A, B,** and **C.** A literal is a value that is not a variable. **A** has the literal 4. **B** has the literal '5'. **C** has the literal '\u0123'.

☒ **D** and **E** are incorrect. **D** is incorrect because the variable c is used to set this char. **E** is incorrect because tvChannel is a variable.

15. Given the following line of code, what next lines are valid? (Choose all that apply.)

```
enum Sports { FOOTBALL, BASKETBALL, BASEBALL, TRACK }
```

A. `Sports sport = FOOTBALL;`

B. `Sports sport = Sports.FOOTBALL;`

C. `Sports sport = Sports.HOCKEY;`

D. `Sports sport = 'TRACK'`

Answer:

☑ **B.** This is the only line that uses a sport that is in the enumeration and that uses the correct syntax.

☒ **A, C,** and **D** are incorrect. **A** is incorrect because it uses incorrect syntax. **C** is incorrect because HOCKEY is not defined as a sport type. **D** is incorrect because the syntax is incorrect.

16. What is wrong with the following method?

```
public double interestDue(double currentBalance, float interestRate){
double interestDue = currentBalance * interestRate;
return interestDue;
}
```

A. It should use all float primitives.

B. It should use all Float objects.

C. It should use all double primitives.

D. It should use all Double objects.

E. It should use BigDecimal objects.

F. Nothing is wrong with this method.

G. It does not compile because you cannot do math operations with primitives that are not the same type.

Answer:

☑   **E.** Primitives should not be used when working with currency on any value that cannot lose precision. Instead, objects such as `BigDecimal` should be used.

☒   **A, B, C, D, F,** and **G** are incorrect. **A, B, C,** and **D** are incorrect because they can all lose precision and cause unexpected rounding errors. **F** is incorrect because the method will produce rounding errors in some cases. **G** is incorrect because this code will compile.

17. What is the correct way to create an array with five `int` data types? (Choose all that apply.)
A. `int intArray = new int[5];`
B. `int intArray = new int(5);`
C. `int[] intArray = new int[5];`
D. `int intArray[] = new int[5];`

Answer:

☑   **C** and **D. C** is the preferred way to declare an array. **D** is correct, but it does not follow standard conventions.

☒   **A** and **B** are incorrect ways to declare an array.

18. What is the correct way to initialize a variable declared with the data type of `Book` as a new `Book` object?
A. `Book b;`
B. `Book b = new Book();`
C. `Book b = new Book[];`
D. `Book b = Book();`

Answer:

☑   **B.** The correct way to declare an object is to use `new` and then the object name followed by parentheses. The parentheses are used to pass arguments to the constructor if needed.

☒   **A, C,** and **D** are incorrect. **A** is incorrect because it does not initialize a new `Book` object. **C** is incorrect because the incorrect square brackets are used instead of parentheses. **D** is incorrect because the `new` keyword is missing.

19. What is the difference between an int and an Integer?

    A. Nothing. They are both fully interchangeable.

    B. An int is an object and Integer is a primitive. An int is fastest when performing calculations.

    C. An int is a primitive and Integer is an object. An int is fastest when performing calculations.

    D. This is a trick question. There is no such thing as an Integer.

    E. This is a trick question. An Integer can be defined to be anything a developer wants it to be.

Answer:

☑ **C.** An int is a primitive, and primitives are faster when performing calculations. An Integer is an object. The capital letter *I* should help you distinguish objects from primitives.

☒ **A, B, D,** and **E** are incorrect. **A** is incorrect because an int and Integer are distinctly different. Auto boxing and unboxing will automatically preform conversions between the two, but this does not make them them same. **B** is incorrect because an int is the primitive and Integer is an object. **D** and **E** are incorrect because this is not a trick question.

20. What is the result of using a method of an uninitialized object?

    A. Null is returned.

    B. The object is automatically initialized and an appropriate value is returned.

    C. A NullPointerException is thrown from the Java virtual machine.

Answer:

☑ **C.** A NullPointerException is thrown from the Java virtual machine.

☒ **A** and **B** are incorrect. **A** is incorrect because a method cannot be called on an uninitialized object. However, an uninitialized object has a value of null and can be checked before a method is called. **B** is incorrect because an object cannot be automatically initialized, because it may need special parameters for its constructor or other custom initialization.

21. What is wrong with the following code segment? (Choose all that apply.)

```
1:      float a = 1.2f;
2:      int b = 5;
3:      short c = 9;
4:      long d = 6;
5:      double e = b;
```

```
6:        Double f = e;
7:        Short g;
8:        Float h = g.floatValue();
```

A. Nothing is wrong.
B. There is an error on line 1.
C. There is an error on line 2.
D. There is an error on line 3.
E. There is an error on line 4.
F. There is an error on line 5.
G. There is an error on line 6.
H. There is an error on line 7.
I. There is an error on line 8.

Answer:

☑ **I**. In line 8, the object g is never initialized. Therefore, when a method is called, it causes a compile time error.
☒ **A, B, C, D, E, F, G**, and **H** are incorrect. These are all valid lines of code.

22. What is the value of variable x in the following code segment?

```
float x =0.0f;
int y = 5;
long z;
x = y + 3.3f;
x = x + z;
```

A. 0
B. 0.0f
C. 5.0f
D. 8.3f
E. 8.3
F. This code will not compile.

Answer:

☑ **F**. The primitive z is never assigned a value. Therefore, this code will not compile.
☒ **A, B, C, D**, and **E** are incorrect. **D** would be correct if z were initialized to 0.

23. Which integer declaration uses a valid octal literal?

A. `int value1 = 0000;`

B. `int value2 = '\u0777 ';`

C. `int value3 = '\01111 ';`

D. `int value4 = '\x0123 ';`

Answer:

☑ **A.** Octal literals must start with a `0`.

☒ **B, C,** and **D** are incorrect. **B** is incorrect because octal literals do not start with `\u`. **C** is incorrect because octal literals do not start with `\0`. **D** is incorrect because octal literals do not start with `\x`.

24. Given:

```
int b1 = 0b_0101_0101_0101_0101;
int b2 = 0b_1010_1010_1010_1010;
int b3 = b1 & b2;
System.out.println("Value:" + b3);
```

What will be the result?

A. `Value: 0` will be printed.

B. `Value: 65535` will be printed.

C. `0b_1111_1111_1111_1111` will be printed.

D. A compiler error will occur.

Answer:

☑ **D.** A compilation error will occur because an underscore cannot be used after the `b` in the literal. The other underscores are allowed.

☒ **A, B,** and **C** are incorrect. **A** is incorrect because a compiler error occurs. If the underscores after the b's were removed in the literal, this would have been the correct answer. **B** is incorrect because a compiler error occurs. If the underscores after the b's were removed in the literal, this still would have been an incorrect answer. Note that with the underscores removed, `65535` would have resulted if the exclusive OR (|) was used in place of the `&`. **C** is incorrect because an integer value representation would be expected as output if the binary literals were used appropriately.

25. Which code example makes use of arrays without producing a compiler or runtime error?

A.
```
public class Actor {
      String[] characterName = new String[3];
      {
        characterName[0] = "Captain Video";
        characterName[1] = "Quizmaster";
        characterName[2] = "J.C. Money";
        characterName[3] = "Jersey Joe";
      }
}
```

B.
```
public class Actor {
      String[] characterName = new String[1..4]
      {
        characterName[0] = "Captain Video";
        characterName[1] = "Quizmaster";
        characterName[2] = "J.C. Money";
        characterName[3] = "Jersey Joe";
      }
}
```

C.
```
public class Actor {
      String characterName = new String[4];
      {
        characterName[0] = "Captain Video";
        characterName[1] = "Quizmaster";
        characterName[2] = "J.C. Money";
        characterName[3] = "Jersey Joe";
      }
}
```

D.
```
public class Actor {
      String [] characterName = new String[4];
      {
        characterName[0] = "Captain Video";
        characterName[1] = "Quizmaster";
        characterName[2] = "J.C. Money";
        characterName[3] = "Jersey Joe";
      }
}
```

Answer:

☑ **D.** The array declaration and element assignments are used appropriately and compile without error.

☒ **A**, **B**, and **C** are incorrect. **A** compiles with an `ArrayIndexOutOfBoundsException` exception thrown at runtime. This is because the array index `characterName[3]` is out of bounds. **B** fails to compile because only an integer is expected in the box brackets. **C** fails to compile because the box brackets that are needed to create the array are missing.

5
Understanding Methods and Variable Scope

CERTIFICATION OBJECTIVES

- Create and Use Methods
- Pass Objects by Reference and Value
- Understand Variable Scope
- Create and Use Constructors
- Use the this and super Keywords

- Create Static Methods and Instance Variables
- ✓ Two-Minute Drill
- Q&A Self Test

T his chapter will look at some of the details of methods and variable scoping. You are likely familiar with methods; this chapter will review the nuances of method and constructor creation. The effect of a static variable and method will be reviewed and demonstrated with code samples. The `this` and `super` keywords and their effects on the flow of execution will also be covered.

CERTIFICATION OBJECTIVE

Create and Use Methods

Exam Objective   Create methods with arguments and return values, including overloaded methods

This section will explore the construction and use of methods. Methods operate on data encapsulated within an object. They make up the backbone of your application. The way objects interact with methods defines the functionality of the software. Some of the OCA exam questions require that you understand how methods work. They present code segments that use many different methods. You must understand the flow of the code as well as determine whether it is valid. This section will demonstrate how to create and use methods:

- Using method syntax
- Making and calling a method
- Overloading a method

Using Method Syntax

All methods must be defined inside of a class. Methods are made up of five parts: the access modifier, the return type, the method identifier, the parameter list, and the body. Some of these parts can be empty. The following example shows the parts of a method and then a few valid examples:

```
//Parts of a method
<Access Modifier> <Return Type> <Method Identifier > (<Parameter List>) {<Body>}
//Valid examples
```

```
public int getAttendance(){/*Method Body*/}
private double average(double firstNum, double secondNum){/*Method Body*/}
void saveToDisk(){/*Method Body*/}
```

Notice that although the first example does not include any parameters, it is valid. A method that has no parameter list means that it does not need any outside input to perform its action. The last example has no access modifier. In this case, the method is using the default access modifier; this method is also valid.

Access Modifier

The Java language allows for methods to be given access modifiers that indicate to the compiler and Java virtual machine (JVM) what other objects can access this code. Java has four access modifiers. They are, in order of most restrictiveness, `private`, default (*package-private*), `protected`, and `public`.

The `private`, `protected`, and `public` access modifiers are all indicated by placing them at the start of the method declaration. If no access modifier is declared, the method will use the default modifier. Here is an example of all four being used:

```
private int getScore(){/*Method Body*/}
/*No access modifier is declared so
this will use default (package-private)*/
int getScore(){/*Method Body*/}
protected int getScore(){/*Method Body*/}
public int getScore(){/*Method Body*/}
```

Access modifiers, and what they do, will be discussed in more detail in Chapter 7. For now, it is important that you understand that every method has an access modifier, even if it is the default modifier. For the rest of this chapter, all of the methods will use the least restrictive `public` access modifier for simplicity.

Return Type

Methods can return data to the code that has called them. A method can return either one variable or none at all. The returned variable may be an object or a primitive. Every method must declare a return type or use the `void` keyword to indicate that nothing will be returned to the caller from this method. Once a method declares that it will return a value, a `return` statement must be included in the method body to pass the data back to the calling code. A `return` statement must include the keyword `return` followed by a variable or a literal of the declared return type. Once the `return` statement is executed, the method is finished. No code will execute after the `return` statement.

The following example shows a few methods; notice the return type in the method declaration:

```
public boolean isActive(){return true;}
public int getCurrentTotal(){return 5;}
public void processPendingData(){/*Method Body*/}
public ArrayList getAllAccounts(){return new ArrayList();}
```

In this example, we see a `boolean`, an `int`, and an `ArrayList` all being returned by the different methods. The `void` indicates that the method does not return any data. In this simple example, the literal `true`, an `int` `5`, and a new `ArrayList` are returned.

Method Identifier

The method identifier, sometimes called method name, is the text that is used to reference the method later in code. The identifier should be descriptive as to what the method does. Chapter 7 provides details about standard Java naming conventions.

The next example demonstrates a method with the identifier `sampleMethod`:

```
public void sampleMethod(){/*Method Body*/}
```

Parameter List

A method's parameter list follows the method identifier. It is enclosed in parentheses and is a comma-delimited list. A method may have no parameters, in which case the parentheses are empty. Methods can contain up to 255 parameters, though it is best not to use this upward limit, since passing more than a handful of parameters is often a sign of bad design.

Parameters can be objects, enumeration types, or primitives. When creating the parameter list, the type is placed in front of the variable name. This is continued for each parameter, separated by commas. Following are a few examples of method declarations with various sized parameter lists:

```
public double areaOf3dRectangle(double height,
    double width, double length) {/*Method Body*/}
public double areaOfCube(double sideLength){/*Method Body*/}
public void drawCube(){/*Method Body*/}
```

The first example has three parameters: `(double height, double width, double length)`. The next example has only one parameter, `(double sideLength)`, and the final example has no parameters.

Method Body

The method body is the main part of the method and contains all the code that makes up the functionality of the method. It may contain as few as one line of code or several hundred lines. If the method declares a return type, it must have a `return` statement that returns a literal or variable to match that type. If the return type is void, no `return` statement is required; however, the method can be used without a variable or literal to exit the method.

Following are two examples of a simple method with a complete body:

```
public int sum(int num1, int num2){
    int sum = num1 + num2;
    return sum;
}

public void printString(String stringToPrint){
    System.out.println(stringToPrint);
}
```

The first example demonstrates using the `return` statement to return a value. The second example does not return any data, which is indicated by the void keyword.

on the **job**

When you are creating methods, keep them focused and concise. If your method includes more than a few hundred lines of code, you may want to consider refactoring it into more than one method.

Making and Calling a Method

A class comprises variables and methods. The instance variables make up the state of the object, and the methods are responsible for all actions. When a class is created, the author must decide what its purpose is and implement that functionality as methods. Keep in mind the syntax rules discussed earlier in this chapter while we look at some scenarios.

The class for this example will be used to perform some simple math calculations. The first method that we'll create will determine the lower value of two `int` primitives. The `public` access modifier will be included since we do not want any restrictions on where this method can be used. This method should return to the caller the `int` that is smaller. Therefore, this method must have a return type of `int`. The method will be called `findLowerValue`. This method will accept two parameters; both are `int` primitives and will be called `number1` and `number2`.

The method body will use conditional statements to determine what variable has a lower value. Here is this method:

```
public class MathTools {
    public int findLowerValue(int number1, int number2){
        int result;
        if(number1 < number2)
            result = number1;
        else
            result = number2;
        return result;
    }
}
```

The parameters in this example are compared, and then the int with the lower value is stored in the result variable. This variable is then returned.

Methods are contained in objects. A method must be called from an instance of the object it is part of. The findLowerValue method in the preceding code is part of the MathTools class. To use this method, you must create an instance of MathTools. The syntax for calling a method is object name followed by a dot (.), and then the method identifier with its parameter list. The following code segment calls the findLowerValue method:

```
MathTools mTools = new MathTools();
int x = 8;
int y = 13;
int lowestInt = mTools.findLowerValue(x,y);
System.out.println("Result1 : " + lowestInt);
System.out.println("Result2 : " + mTools.findLowerValue(x,y));
```

First, this example must create a MathTools object and call it mTools. Two int primitives are then created. Next, the findLowerValue method is called. The x and y variables are passed to this method. Notice that the variable names in the parameter list do not have to match names in the method definition; however, they must be a compatible type. The findLowerValue method returns the parameter that has the least value. This is stored in the lowestInt variable. Then the results are printed to standard output. The results are printed twice to highlight the fact that a method call with a return value can also be used in place of a variable of the same type. The output is as follows:

```
Result1: 8
Result2: 8
```

If a method has no parameters, the parameter list is left empty. Methods that do not return any data, return type void, cannot be used to set a variable as we did in the preceding example. However, the data from methods that do return a variable does not have to be used. In that case, the caller would be interested only in the action that the method performs.

on the
Job

The NetBeans IDE provides refactoring support allowing for automated actions such as safely renaming methods, moving methods to superclasses or subclasses, introducing a new method from an existing block of code (where the existing block of code is replaced with a call to the method), and generating accessor (getters) and mutator (setters) methods. For more information on using the refactoring features of the NetBeans IDE, see NetBeans IDE Programmer Certified Expert Exam Guide (Exam 310-045), *by Robert Liguori and Ryan Cuprak (McGraw-Hill Professional, 2010).*

Overloading a Method

When several methods share the same identifier, but have different parameter lists, the methods are said to be overloaded. The parameter list may comprise more or fewer parameters than the other methods, or different types. This is a useful feature when a method may, for example, have five parameters; three of them are nearly always defaulted to a certain value, however. In this case, a method can be provided with all five parameters, plus another for convenience that has just two, which sets the other three to their defaults. Additionally, overloaded methods are not required to have the same return type.

Overloading methods can also be useful when a method can produce a similar result using different data types as its parameters. In the previous example of the findLowerValue method, two int primitives were compared to find the one with the lower values. This method can be overloaded to work the same with double primitives. Here is an example of this method overloaded:

```
public double findLowerValue(double number1, double number2){
   double result;
   if(number1 < number2)
      result = number1;
   else
      result = number2;
   return result;
}
```

This method can be added to the `MathTools` class. The `findLowerValue` is now overloaded to work with both `int` and `double` primitives. The compiler determines what method is called by matching the parameter lists. If two `double` primitives are used, it executes the code in the second method; two `int` primitives would still use the original method.

The next example is a class called `LogManager` that can be used to perform some basic log management. It has two methods for printing log information to standard output. Here is this class:

exam

watch   *Pay close attention to overloaded methods on the exam. It is easy to mistake which method is being used.*

```
public class LogManager {
    public void logInfo(String message, int errorNumber){
        System.out.println("Error: " + errorNumber + " | " + message);
    }
    public void logInfo(String message){
        logInfo(message, -1);
    }
}
```

The first method in this class has two parameters: the first is a `String` and is the message to be printed, and the second is a corresponding error number. This method will then print a line to standard output. The second method has only a `String` as a parameter. The `logInfo` method is overloaded since there is more than one method with the same identifier. The second `logInfo` method will be used when a specific error number for the message is not included. In these cases, the error number will default to `-1`. Instead of implementing most of the same code as the first method, the second method will simply call the first method and pass in its default value.

The following code segment uses this case:

```
LogManager logManager = new LogManager();
logManager.logInfo("First log message", -299);
logManager.logInfo("Second log message");
```

Here's the output:

```
Error: -299 | First log message
Error: -1 | Second log message
```

A good design habit is to ensure that any overloaded methods behave in a similar manner. Your code will be confusing if two methods with the same identifier but different parameters have vastly different results.

Pass Objects by Reference and Value

Exam Objective   Determine the effect upon object references and primitive values when they are passed into methods that change the values

This section will explore the way that Java passes data between methods. A variable will be passed by value if it's a primitive and by reference if it's an object. The differences between these two concepts are subtle but can have a big effect on application design. The following is covered:

- Passing primitives by value to methods
- Passing objects by reference to methods

Passing Primitives by Value to Methods

When a primitive is used as an argument, a copy of the value is made and provided to the method. If the method sets the value of the parameter to a different value, it has no effect on the variable that was passed to the method. The following is an example of a method that adds 2 to the `int` primitive that is passed to it:

```
void addTwo(int value) {
  System.out.println("Parameter: value = " + value);
  value = value + 2;
  System.out.println("Leaving method: value = " + value);
}
```

Because primitives are passed by value, a copy of the variable value is passed to the method. Even though the method modifies the parameter (since it is just a copy of the original argument used to invoke the method), the original argument remains unchanged from the perspective of the calling code. The following is a code segment that could be used to call this method:

```
int value = 1;
System.out.println("Argument: value = " + value);
addTwo(value);
System.out.println("After method call: value = " + value);
```

If this code segment were executed, it would produce the following results. Read the output that follows and walk through the code.

```
Argument: value = 1
Parameter: value = 1
Leaving method: value = 3
After method call: value = 1
```

Passing Objects by Reference to Methods

A *reference* is basically an internal index that represents the object. Objects are passed by reference to a method. This means that instead of making a copy of the object and passing it, a reference to the original object is passed to the method.

This section can start a very technical conversation, which is beyond the scope of this book. The OCA is not going to drill into the details of how an object is passed internally. In short, for the OCA exam, it is important that you understand that any object is passed by reference.

The following example is similar to the example that demonstrated how primitives were passed by value. Instead of passing an `int` this time, it will pass a custom `Number` object. The following is the `Number` class:

```
public class Number {
  int number;
  public Number(int number) {
    this.number = number;
  }
  int getNumber() {
    return this.number;
```

```
  }
  void setNumber(int number) {
    this.number = number;
  }
}
```

Here is the method that will be called; this time, it will add 3 to the value passed to it:

```
void addThree(Number value) {
  System.out.println("Parameter: value = " + value.getNumber());
  value.setNumber(value.getNumber() + 3);
  System.out.println("Leaving method: value = " + value.getNumber());
}
```

Finally, here's the code segment used to call this method:

```
Number value = new Number(1);
System.out.println("Argument: value = " + value.getNumber());
addThree(value);
System.out.println("After method call: value = " + value.getNumber());
```

This example is almost identical to the earlier one. The only difference is that now an object is passed by reference and the method adds 3 instead of 2. If this code segment were executed, the following would be the output. Notice that, this time, when the method returns to the calling code, the object has been modified.

```
Argument: value = 1
Parameter: value = 1
Leaving method: value = 4
After method call: value = 4
```

CERTIFICATION OBJECTIVE

Understand Variable Scope

Exam Objective   Define the scope of variables
Exam Objective   Explain an object's lifecycle (creation, "dereference by reassignment," and garbage collection)

This section will explore the way variables are organized in your code. As you can imagine, any nontrivial application will have countless variables. If variables could be accessed anywhere in the code, it would be difficult to find unique names that still conveyed a meaning. This scenario would also promote bad coding practices, and a programmer may try to access a variable that is in a completely different part of the program. To solve these problems, Java has variable scope. *Scope* refers to the section of code that has access to a declared variable. The scope may be as small as a few lines, or it may include the entire class.

In this section, we will cover the following topics:

■ Local variables
■ Method parameters
■ Instance variables

Local Variables

Local variables are declared inside of methods. As the name implies, these variables are used locally in code. They are commonly declared at the start of a method and in loops, but they can be declared anywhere in code. A local variable may be a temporary variable that is used just once, or it can be used throughout a method.

The block of code in which a variable is declared determines the scope of the local variable. A block of code is determined by braces: {   }. For example, if the variable is declared at the start of a method after the left brace ({), it would remain in scope until the method is closed with the right brace (}). Once a variable goes out of scope, it can no longer be used and its value is lost. The JVM may reallocate the memory that it occupies at any time.

A block of code can be created anywhere. A block can also be nested inside another block. A variable is in scope for the code block in which it is declared and for all code blocks that exist inside it. The most common blocks are if statements and for or while loops.

The following example demonstrates the use of local variables in code blocks:

```
void sampleMethod() { // Start of code block A
  int totalCount = 0;
    for (int i = 0; i < 3; i++) { // Start of code block B
      int forCount = 0;
      totalCount++;
      forCount++;
      { // Start of code block C
        int block1Count = 0;
        totalCount++;
        forCount++;
        block1Count++;
      } // End of code block C
      { // Start of code block D
        int block2Count = 0;
        totalCount++;
        forCount++;
        block2Count++;
      } // End of code block D
    /* These two variables have no relation to the above ones of
       the same name */
    int block1Count;
    int block2Count;
  }  // End of code block B
}  // End of code block A
```

Code block A is the method. Any variable that is declared in this block is in scope for the entire method. The variable totalCount is declared in block A; therefore, it can be accessed from anywhere else in the example method.

Code block B starts with the for loop. The variable i is declared in this block; even though it is not between the brackets, because it was declared in the for statement, it is considered to be in code block B. The variable forCount is also declared in block B. Because both of these variables are declared in block B, they are in scope only for block B and any blocks contained within B. They are out of scope for block A, and a compiler error would be generated if they were accessed from this block.

Contained inside block B is code block C. This block is started arbitrarily. In Java, it is valid to start a block of code at any time, although this is not often done in practice. The variable block1Count is declared in this block. It is in scope only for block C. However, any code inside block C also has access to the variables that have been declared in blocks A and B.

Block C is closed, and block D is created in block B. Block D contains the variable `block2Count`. This variable is in scope only for block D. Like block C, block D can also access variables that have been declared in blocks A and B. Understand that the variables in block C are not in scope for block D, and variables in D are not in scope for C.

In block B, the line after the closure of block D, two new variables are declared: `block1Count` and `block2Count`. These variables happen to have the same names as the variables that were declared in blocks C and D. Because the variables in blocks C and D are now out of scope, these two new variables have no relationship with the scope variables. Giving variables the same names as others that are out of scope is valid in Java; however, it is not good coding practice because it can make the code difficult to maintain.

Figure 5-1 represents another way to visualize this code example. Each code block represents scope. This figure shows each variable as it is declared in the code example. A variable is in scope from where it is declared until the end of its block; nested code blocks are included. These blocks correspond to the braces in the code example.

FIGURE 5-1

Code blocks
visualized

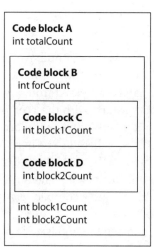

A local variable is used when data needs to be accessed in only a certain part, or locally, in your code. For example, a variable used as a counter should be a local variable. Often times, a variable that you want to return will start as a local variable.

on the
ⓙob *When developing Java source code, variables should be declared with the most limited scope possible. This coding practice helps reduce programming mistakes and improves code readability.*

Method Parameters

Method parameters are the variables that are passed to the method from the calling segment of code. They are passed as arguments to the method. Method parameters may be primitives or objects. A method can have as many parameters as the developer defines, up to 255. These variables are in scope for the entire method block. Method parameters are defined in the declaration for the method.

The following example contains two method parameters:

```
float findMilesPerHour(float milesTraveled, float hoursTraveled) {
   return milesTraveled / hoursTraveled;
}
```

In this example, `milesTraveled` and `hoursTraveled` are both method parameters. They are declared in the method's declaration. In this example, they are declared as `floats`. When this method is called, two `floats` must pass to the method as arguments. These two variables may be accessed anywhere in this method.

Instance Variables

Instance variables are declared in the class. They are called *instance variables* because they are created and remain in memory for as long as the instance of the class exists. Instance variables store the state of the object. They are not within the scope of any one particular method; instead, they are in scope for the entire class. They exist and retain their value from the time a class is initialized until that class is either reinitialized or no longer referenced.

The following example demonstrates two instance variables:

```
public class Television {
  int channel = 0;
  boolean on = false;
  void setChannel(int channelValue) {
    this.channel = channelValue;
  }
  int getChannel() {
    return this.channel;
  }
  void setOn(boolean on) {
    this.on = on;
  }
  boolean isOn() {
    return this.on;
  }
}
```

In this example, channel is declared as an int, and on is declared as a boolean. These are both instance variables. Remember that instance variables must be declared in the class, not in a method. The four methods in this class each access one of the instance variables. The setChannel method is used to set the instance variable channel to the value of the int that was passed to it as an argument. The getChannel and isOn methods return the values that are stored in the two instance variables, respectively. Notice that the setOn method has a parameter that has the same name as an instance variable. This is valid code. In a method that has these conditions, if the variable is referenced, it will be the method argument. To reference the instance variable, use the this keyword, which will be discussed in detail later in this chapter.

The following code segment demonstrates the Television class in use:

```
Television tv1 = new Television();
Television tv2 = new Television();
tv1.setChannel(2);
tv2.setChannel(7);
System.out.println("Television channel for tv1: " + tv1.getChannel());
System.out.println("Television channel for tv2: " + tv2.getChannel());
```

The first two lines of this example create two unique instances of the Television class. When the instance of the class is created, each object gets an instance variable

FIGURE 5-2

Two instances of
the tv class

: tv 1

channel = 2
on = false

: tv 2

channel = 7
on = false

that will store a channel. The next two lines use the `setChannel` method to set the channel to 2 and 7, respectively.

Figure 5-2 represents the two objects that have been created and the value of both of their instance variables. The last two lines of code use the `getChannel` method to retrieve the value stored in the channel instance variable.

If the code was executed, the following would be the output. Remember that each `tv` object has a unique set of instance variables.

```
Television channel for tv1: 2
Television channel for tv2: 7
```

The following Scenario & Solution covers types of variable scope and a likely use for each.

SCENARIO & SOLUTION

What variable scope would be best suited for a counter in a loop?	Local variable
What variable scope must be used to store information about the state of an object?	Instance variable
What variable scope must be used to pass information to a method?	Method parameter

An Object's Lifecycle

Objects are created and destroyed many times during the course of an application. This cycle is known as an object's *lifecycle*. Objects start out by being declared, when the data type and variable name are assigned. At this point, the code is telling the compiler that a variable of a certain name and type can be referenced in other places.

An object must then be *instantiated* and *initialized*. Instantiation of an object occurs when the `new` operator is used. At this point, the JVM allocates space for the object. Then the object is initialized with the object's *constructor*. The constructor sets all of the object's initial values and prepares the object to be used.

The object next enters the main part of its life. It is ready to have its methods called, which will perform actions and will store the data it was intended to store. As long as other active objects retain a reference to the object, it remains in this state. This is where the object will spend most of its time.

An object continues to exist until no other object holds a reference to it. An object can be deallocated when all its variables go out of scope, are set to reference a different object, are set to null, or any combination of these conditions. Once there are no other active references to the object, it is eligible to be removed from memory by the Java garbage collector. At this point, the object can no longer be called. The garbage collector will eventually reclaim the memory used for the discarded object, making it available for other uses.

CERTIFICATION OBJECTIVE

Create and Use Constructors

Exam Objective   Create and overload constructors, including impact on default constructors

A *constructor* is a special type of method in Java that, as its name implies, is used to construct an object. Every class in Java has a constructor. A class may have one or more user-defined constructors, or it may use the compiler-added default constructor. This section will look at how to create and use constructors:

- Making a constructor
- Overloading a constructor
- Using the default constructor

Making a Constructor

The constructor is a special method that is used to initialize an object. The constructor is called after the new operator. The next example shows the constructor for the Integer object being called, with one parameter:

```
Integer intObj = new Integer(7);
```

Every class is required to have at least one constructor, which may be user defined or the implicated default constructor that is added by the Java compiler. By defining a constructor, the developer is able to initialize the object any way he or she sees fit. This may mean initializing the instance variables to predetermined defaults and/or setting up resources such as a database connection.

A constructor always shares the name of the class, including the capitalized first letter. It is possible for a constructor to use any of the four access modifiers. However, only more common public access modifiers will be included on the OCA exam. Other modifiers tend to be used only in more advanced design patterns, and these patterns are not a part of the exam. Unlike a method, a constructor does not declare any return value, including `void`.

Here is an example of a constructor being defined in a class:

```java
public class LoanDetails {
    private int term;
    private double rate;
    private double principal;

    public LoanDetails() {
        term = 180;
        rate = .0265; //Interest rate as a decimal
        principal = 0;
    }

    public void setPrincipal(double p) {
        principal = p;
    }

    public double monthlyPayment(){
        return (rate * principal / 12)
            / (1.0 - Math.pow(((rate / 12) + 1.0), (-term)));
    }
}
```

This class is used to calculate details about a basic loan. The constructor is called `LoanDetails`. It does not accept any parameters. Notice that it has no return type declared. When a `LoanDetails` object is created, the constructor sets the term, rate, and principal instance values to their default settings. This class assumes that the user will later set the principal amount based on the loan in question— that is why the setter, `setPrincipal`, for the principal instance variable is included with this

watch   *Remember that constructors have no return type declared, not even the* `void` *keyword.*

class. This class includes another method for calculating the monthly payment of a loan. (You do not need to understand the details of this calculation, but it is accurate and based on industry-standard formulas.)

The following code segment demonstrates the use of this class:

```
LoanDetails ld = new LoanDetails();
ld.setPrincipal(150000);
System.out.println("Payment: " + ld.monthlyPayment());
```

This segment will produce the following output:

```
Payment: 1010.809999701624
```

Overloading a Constructor

Just as methods can be overloaded, so can constructors. To overload a constructor, the programmer must declare another constructor with the same name but a different parameter list. This is useful when a class wants to provide a simple constructor for most cases and a more advanced one for when it is needed. Continuing with the preceding example, the LoanDetails constructor can be overloaded to provide parameters for setting the term, rate, and principal. The next example shows the constructor that can be added to the LoanDetails class:

```
public LoanDetails(int t, double r, double p){
    term = t;
    rate = r;
    principal = p;
}
```

This new constructor has three parameters, (int t, double r, double p), and allows the entire object to be set up and initialized directly from the constructor.

The next code segment demonstrates both constructors in use:

```
LoanDetails firstLD = new LoanDetails();
firstLD.setPrincipal(150000);
System.out.println("Payment 1 : " + firstLD.monthlyPayment());
LoanDetails secondLD = new LoanDetails(10, .025, 125000);
System.out.println("Payment 2 : " + secondLD.monthlyPayment());
```

This code is valid since the constructor is overloaded. The new constructor allows for the object to be initialized with the parameters passed to it. It is possible to overload the constructor as many times as needed, as long as each constructor has a unique set of parameters. The parameters are considered unique if the data types do not match any of the other constructors' data types.

The output is as follows:

```
Payment 1 : 1010.809999701624
Payment 2 : 12643.676288957713
```

Using the Default Constructor

Every class must have a constructor. If no constructor is defined by the developer, the Java compiler adds one at compile time. This is called the *default constructor.*

This constructor has no parameters. When called, it simply calls the superclass's constructor. This constructor is always named the same as the class. The default constructor is accessed in code the same way a user-defined constructor is called if it has no parameters. In fact, the calling code does not know whether the constructor is user defined or the default.

If one user-defined constructor is defined, the compiler will not add a default one. This means methods are not guaranteed to have a constructor that takes no parameters.

CERTIFICATION OBJECTIVE

Use the this and super Keywords

Exam Objective   Use super and this to access objects and constructors

The this and super keywords are used to access Java elements explicitly in relation to the current class. This section will look at how each works and when they should be used.

The this Keyword

The this keyword is used to refer explicitly to the current object. It is most commonly used when accessing instance variables. If a method or local variable has the same name as an instance variable, this can be used to refer explicitly to the instance variable. Following is an example of a class with one method that uses `this` to set the instance variable from the method parameter:

```java
public class ScoreKeeper {
    private int currentScore;
    public void setCurrentScore(int currentScore) {
        this.currentScore = currentScore;
    }
}
```

In this example the class contains an instance variable, `currentScore`. The setter for this variable has a parameter by the same name. To access the instance variable, `this` is used. If `this` were not used, any reference to `currentScore` in the setter would refer to the parameter.

The `this` keyword can also be used to call constructors from inside of the method. The next example rewrites the `LoanDetails` class using the `this` keyword:

```java
public class LoanDetails {
    private int term;
    private double rate;
    private double principal;

    public LoanDetails() {
        term = 180;
        rate = 0.0265;
        principal = 0;
    }

    public LoanDetails(int term, double rate, double principal){
        this.term = term;
        this.rate = rate;
        this.principal = principal;
    }

    public void setPrincipal(double principal) {
        this.principal = principal;
    }

    public double monthlyPayment(){
        return (rate * principal / 12)
            / (1.0 - Math.pow(((rate / 12) + 1.0), (-term)));
    }
}
```

In this example, the parameter names of the constructor and setter have been changed to make the code more readable. However, they are now named the same as the instance variable. In both, `this` is used to access the instance variable. If `this` were not used, the parameter would be accessed instead.

o n t h e J o b

It is always good practice to use the `this` keyword to access instance variables. It provides clarity when reading the code and lets the reader know immediately that an instance variable is being accessed.

The `this` keyword can also be used to refer to methods and constructors in the same object. Oftentimes, when a class has an overloaded constructor, the constructor that accepts the most parameters will do all of the initialized work and the other constructors will call it with sensible defaults. We can further rewrite the `LoanDetails` class to demonstrate this. The next code segment shows the constructor that does not accept any parameters rewritten:

```
public LoanDetails() {
    this(180,0.025,0);
}
```

This new constructor uses `this` to call the other constructor and passes it three parameters. It is valid to use `this` only in the first line of the constructor. A compiler error will be generated if `this` is used after that. This new constructor has the same effect as the original version of this method. However, this version is a better design. In some cases, the constructors may include many lines of code. It is easier to maintain one constructor and have the others call it than to maintain many different constructors.

The `this` keyword can also be used in front of methods in the same manner it is used with instance variables. However, this is not often used. An example is the following line of code, which would have to be in the `LoanDetails` class to be valid:

```
System.out.println("Payment " + this.monthlyPayment);
```

The super Keyword

The `super` keyword is used to refer to an object's superclass. It can be used to access methods that have been overridden in the current class or the constructor of a superclass. When the default constructor is used, it automatically calls its parent class's constructor by using `super`. A user-defined constructor can call its parent's constructor by using super on the first line. A compiler error will be generated if it is used past the first line. If a user-defined method does not use super, the compiler will automatically make a call with super to the parent class's constructor with no parameters. If this constructor does not exist in the parent class, a compile time error will be generated.

The following two classes show the super keyword in use:

```java
public class ParentClass {
    public ParentClass() {
        System.out.println("ParentClass Constructor");
    }
    public ParentClass(String s) {
        System.out.println("ParentClass Constructor " + s);
    }
}

public class ChildClass extends ParentClass{
    public ChildClass() {
        System.out.println("ChildClass Constructor");
    }
    public ChildClass(String s) {
        super(s);
        System.out.println("ChildClass Constructor " + s);
    }
}
```

Both classes have two constructors. One accepts no parameters and the other accepts a string.

The ChildClass extends the ParentClass. The following code segment shows these classes in use:

```java
ChildClass childClass1 = new ChildClass();
ChildClass childClass2 = new ChildClass("test");
```

The first line in this code segment calls the first constructor in the ChildClass class. Since there is no reference to super, the compiler automatically calls the constructor with no parameters of the parent class. The second line of code calls the ChildClass class's constructor that accepts a string as a parameter. This constructor then uses super to call its parent class's constructor that also accepts a string. Here is the output of this code segment:

```
ParentClass Constructor
ChildClass Constructor
```

```
ParentClass Constructor test
ChildClass Constructor test
```

Trace through the code and ensure that you understand the flow of execution. The concepts presented here may be confusing at first, but are important to grasp, because they will be seen in some form on the OCA exam.

The super keyword works with methods in a way similar to how it works with constructors. When a method has been overridden, super can be used to gain access to the method from the parent class. Following is an example of this. This method would be added to the ParentClass:

```
public String className(){
    return " ParentClass ";
}
```

This method would be added to the ChildClass:

```
public String className(){
    return "ChildClass -> " + super.className();
}
```

Notice how this method is called super.*methodIdentifer*. That will call the method that is overridden from the parent class. Here is a code segment to demonstrate this:

```
ChildClass childClass = new ChildClass();
System.out.println(childClass.className());
```

This segment creates a new object and then prints the results of the className method to standard output. The result of this code is as follows:

```
ParentClass Constructor
ChildClass Constructor
ChildClass -> ParentClass
```

The same text from the constructor is displayed as before. The className method appends its current name to that of its parent class by using super. Finally, it is printed to standard output.

exam

ⓦatch *The this and super keywords can be used only on the first line of* *the constructor. Otherwise, a compile-time error will be generated.*

CERTIFICATION OBJECTIVE

Create Static Methods and Instance Variables

Exam Objective   Apply the static keyword to methods and fields

A static method and field are also known as *class methods* and *class variables*. Both use the static keyword to indicate that they belong to the class and not an instance of the class. This section will look at how the static keyword is used to create class methods, class variables, and a common form for creating constants in Java.

Static Methods

The static keyword can be used to indicate that a method is a static, or class, method instead of a standard method. A static method belongs to the class and not to an object or the instances of the class. Because these methods do not belong to the instance of an object, they cannot access any instance variables or standard methods. Static methods are also unable to use the this and super keywords. However, they can access other static methods or static variables. A static method is accessed by using the class name in place of the object's instance name. Here is an example of a class with a static method:

```
public class Tools {
    public static String formatDate(){
        Date date = new Date();
        Format formatter = new SimpleDateFormat("MMM-dd-yy");
        return formatter.format(date);
    }
}
```

The Tools class has one method called formatDate. The static keyword is used to indicate that this is a static method. As shown in this example, the static keyword must be placed after the access modifier.

The next code segment is an example of this static method being used.

```
System.out.println(Tools.formatDate());
```

This single line of code prints the output of the method to standard output. Notice how the class name is used to call the method instead of an object. This is able to happen because the method is static and therefore belongs to the class, not to an object. Here is the output for this line of code:

```
Feb-27-15
```

Static methods are most commonly used as utility methods. For example, if you look though the Java API you will find that many of the methods in the Math class are static. This is because these methods are intended to perform a single task and have no reason to maintain the state of their own object. For example, the sin method in the Math class is used to find the trigonometric sine of an angle. It has no need for instance variables and is used more as a utility, or helper, method.

on the job

Next time you start a project, take a look at the main method. Notice that it is a static method.

Static Variables

The static keyword can also be used to create class variables. A class variable is similar to an instance variable, but instead of belonging to the instance of the object, it belongs to the class. The key difference between the two is that every instance of an object has access to the same class variable, but each instance has access to its own set of unique instance variables.

This example will demonstrate a class that is used to assign tracking numbers to packages. Each package must have a unique number. This class is called ShippingPackage and is shown next:

```java
public class ShippingPackage {
    public static int nextTrackingNumber = 100000;
    private int packageTrackingNumber;

    public ShippingPackage() {
        this.packageTrackingNumber = nextTrackingNumber;
        nextTrackingNumber++;
    }
    public int getPackageTrackingNumber() {
        return packageTrackingNumber;
    }
}
```

This class has a static class variable that is called nextTrackingNumber. It is used to store the next available number for a package. This variable is set to 100000 initially, representing the first valid tracking number. The class also has an instance variable that is used to store the assigned tracking number. When the constructor is called, it sets the instance variable, packageTrackingNumber, to the next available number stored in nextTrackingNumber. It then increments this variable. Since the nextTrackingNumber is static, every instance of the ShippingPackage class will access the same variable and data that it contains.

The next code segment will use the ShippingPackage class:

```
ShippingPackage packageOne = new ShippingPackage();
ShippingPackage packageTwo = new ShippingPackage();
ShippingPackage packageThree = new ShippingPackage();

System.out.println("Package One Tracking Number: " +
    packageOne.getPackageTrackingNumber());
System.out.println("Package Two Tracking Number: " +
    packageTwo.getPackageTrackingNumber());
System.out.println("Package Three Tracking Number: " +
    packageThree.getPackageTrackingNumber());
```

This code segment creates three instances of the ShippingPackage class. It then prints to standard output the tracking number that was assigned to each from the ShippingPackage constructor.

The output of the code is as follows:

```
Package One Tracking Number: 100000
Package Two Tracking Number: 100001
Package Three Tracking Number: 100002
```

In this output, notice how each tracking number is incremented by 1. This happens because the static variable, nextTrackingNumber, is a class variable and therefore common between all instances of the object.

Class variables with less restrictive access modifiers can be accessed in code similar to how class methods are accessed. The method identifier can be used. In the preceding example, the nextTrackingNumber variable is public. The following line of code can be used to get the variable and print it to standard output:

```
System.out.println("Next Tracking Number: " +
    ShippingPackage.nextTrackingNumber);
```

Notice how the class name is used to access this public variable. The following will be output from this example:

```
Next Tracking Number: 100003
```

Constants

Static variables can also be used to create constants in code. A *constant* is simply a variable that has a set value at compile time that can never be changed. A Java constant is made by adding the `final` keyword to a class variable. The `final` keyword simply indicates that this variable can never have its value changed. Here is an example of a Java constant:

```
public static final double PI = 3.14;
```

This constant is for the value of `PI`. This can be accessed anywhere in your code by using its class name. This constant is already defined in the Java API, but to a much higher precision.

CERTIFICATION SUMMARY

Most of the objectives in this chapter cover a smaller section of the Java language. However, they are equally important to understand if you want to become a great developer.

This chapter began by discussing methods. Method syntax was reviewed, and each part of a method declaration was examined. You must understand methods or you will find it difficult to understand deeper topics. Overloading methods is another critical topic covered in the first section. It is important that you remember that methods that are overloaded, which means they have the same identifier, must each have a unique parameter list.

The difference between passing objects to methods and passing primitives was also examined in this chapter. When a primitive is passed as an argument, a copy is made and the original will remain unchanged. However, when an object is passed as an argument, a reference of the object is passed to the method, and any changes made to the object in the method will be present in the original calling object.

Mastering the scope of variables is important as you design and read large Java applications. The next section covered these topics. First, local variables were discussed. These are the variables that should be used when the data needs to be stored for only a short amount of time and accessed from only one place in a class. The scope of these variables is the block of code in which they are declared.

Method parameters are the variables passed to the method. These variables will be used only when the method needs outside input from the calling code. They are declared in the method's signature and have a scope of the entire method.

Finally, instance variables were discussed. These variables are declared inside of a class, but outside of a method. These variables are accessible throughout the entire class. They provide the state of an object and retain their value through the lifecycle of the object. Different methods may access them to read or modify the instance variables' data.

Class constructors are a lot like normal methods, except that they are used only with the new operator to initialize an object. Unlike methods, constructors do not have any return type, including void. Every class must have a constructor. It may be user defined, or a default constructor will be added if none has been defined. Like methods, constructors can also be overloaded.

The this and super keywords are used to reference objects that are in relation to the current object. The this keyword will reference the current object, and the super keyword will reference the parent, or superclass, of the current object. The this keyword can be used on the first line of a constructor to call other constructors from the same class. The super keyword can similarly be used on the first line of a constructor, but it will call the parent class constructor.

Finally, this chapter reviewed the use of the static keyword. Java allows for variables and methods to be declared static, and the method or object belongs to the class, and not an object instance. Static methods, or class methods, can access only other static methods and variables. Static variables, or class variables, are shared between all instances of an object. Java constants are defined by creating a static variable and marking it final by using the final keyword.

This chapter covered different material that may not always seem to be tightly related. However, your understanding all of these concepts will help you create rich applications that use sophisticated design patters. An OCA test taker is expected to understand these concepts. They will not all make up a huge part of this test, but a good understanding will help push your score higher.

TWO-MINUTE DRILL

Create and Use Methods

- ☐ Methods may return one variable or none at all.
- ☐ A method return type can be a primitive or an object.
- ☐ A method must declare the data type of any variable it returns.
- ☐ If a method does not return any data, it must use `void` as its return type.
- ☐ The syntax for a method is `<Access Modifier> <Return Type> <Method Identifier> (<Parameter List>) {<Body>}`.
- ☐ Methods can be overloaded by creating another method with the same identifier but a different parameter list.
- ☐ Methods can be overloaded as much as needed.

Pass Objects by Reference and Value

- ☐ Primitives are passed by value.
- ☐ When passing a primitive by value, the value is copied into the method.
- ☐ Objects are passed by reference.
- ☐ When passing an object by reference, a reference to the object is copied into the method. Changes to the object will be present in all references to that object.

Understand Variable Scope

- ☐ A variable's scope defines what parts of the code have access to that variable.
- ☐ An instance variable is declared in the class, not inside a method. It is in scope for the entire method and remains in memory for as long as the instance of the class it was declared in remains in memory.
- ☐ Method parameters are declared in the method declaration; they are in scope for the entire method.
- ☐ Local variables may be declared anywhere in code. They remain in scope as long as the execution of code does not leave the block in which they were declared.

Create and Use Constructors

- ☐ Constructors are used to initialize an object.
- ☐ If you do not define a constructor, the complier will add a default one for you.
- ☐ A constructor can be overloaded with a unique parameter list as many times as needed.

Use the this and super Keywords

- ☐ The this keyword is a reference to the current object.
- ☐ It is good practice to append this in front of instance variables.
- ☐ this() can be used to access other constructors in the current class.
- ☐ this() can be used only on the first line of a constructor.
- ☐ The super keyword is a reference to the parent object of the current object.
- ☐ super can be used to access the overridden methods of a parent.
- ☐ super() can be used to call the constructor of the parent class.
- ☐ super() can be used only on the first line of a constructor.

Create Static Methods and Instance Variables

- ☐ The static keyword can be used to create static methods and variables.
- ☐ A static method is also known as a class method.
- ☐ A static variable is also known as a class variable.
- ☐ Static methods belong to the class, not an object instance.
- ☐ Static variables belong to the class, not an object instance.
- ☐ Static methods can access only other static methods and variables.
- ☐ Every object of a class has access to the same variable if it is static.
- ☐ The static keyword with the final keyword can be use to create Java constants.

SELF TEST

Create and Use Methods

1. A method needs to be created that accepts an array of `floats` as an argument and does not return any variables. The method should be called `setPoints`. Which of the following method declarations is correct?

   A. `setPoints(float[] points) {...}`
   B. `void setPoints(float points) {...}`
   C. `void setPoints(float[] points) {...}`
   D. `float setPoints(float[] points) {...}`

2. When the `void` keyword is used, which of the following statements are true? (Choose all that apply.)

   A. A `return` statement with a value following it must be used.
   B. A `return` statement with a value following it can optionally be used.
   C. A `return` statement with a value following it should never be used.
   D. A `return` statement by itself must be used.
   E. A `return` statement by itself can optionally be used.
   F. A `return` statement by itself should never be used.
   G. A `return` statement must be omitted.
   H. A `return` statement can optionally be omitted.
   I. A `return` statement should never be omitted.

3. Given the `SampleClass`, what is the output of this code segment?

   ```java
   SampleClass s = new SampleClass();
   s.sampleMethod(4.4, 4);
   public class SampleClass {
      public void sampleMethod(int a, double b){
         System.out.println("Method 1");
      }
      public void sampleMethod(double b, int a){
         System.out.println("Method 2");
      }
   }
   ```

   A. `Method 1`
   B. `Method 2`

   C. Method 1
       Method 2
   D. Method 2
       Method 1
   E. Compiler error

4. Which of the following methods returns a `float` and accepts an `int` as a parameter?
   A. `public void method1(int var1, float var2) {/*Method Body*/}`
   B. `public int method2(float var1) {/*Method Body*/}`
   C. `public float method3(int var1) {/*Method Body*/}`
   D. `public float, int method4() {/*Method Body*/}`

5. You want to create a method that takes in three character parameters and returns a string. Which declaration is valid?
   A. `public void doMethod (char a, char b, char c) {String s = null;`
       `return s;}`
   B. `public String doMethod (Char a, Char b, Char c) {String s = null;`
       `return s;}`
   C. `public String doMethod (char a, char b, char c) {String s = null;`
       `return s;}`
   D. `public string doMethod (char a, char b, char c) {String s = null;`
       `return s;}`

Pass Objects by Reference and Value

6. Given the class `FloatNumber` and method `addHalf`, what is the output if the following code segment is executed?

```
public class FloatNumber {
  float number;
  public FloatNumber(float number) {
    this.number = number;
  }
  float getNumber() {
    return number;
  }
  void setNumber(float number) {
    this.number = number;
  }
}
```

```
void addHalf(FloatNumber value) {
   value.setNumber(value.getNumber() + (value.getNumber()/2f));
}

/* CODE SEGMENT */
FloatNumber value = new FloatNumber(1f);
addHalf(value);
System.out.println("value = " + value.getNumber());
```

A. value = 1

B. value = 1.5

C. value = 2

D. value = 0

7. Objects are passed by _____.

   A. value

   B. sum

   C. reference

   D. pointer

8. Primitives are passed by _____.

   A. value

   B. sum

   C. reference

   D. pointer

9. What is the value of the variable number when the following code segment is finished?

   Code segment:

   ```
   int number = 7;
   sampleMethod(number);
   ```

   Supporting method:

   ```
   public void sampleMethod(int i){
      i++;
   }
   ```

   A. 0

   B. 1

   C. 7

D. 8

E. A compiler error occurs.

F. A runtime error occurs.

Understand Variable Scope

10. You need to create a class to store information about books contained in a library. What variable scope is best suited for the variable that will store the title of a book?

A. Local variable

B. Static variable

C. Global variable

D. Method parameter

E. Instance variable

11. Given the `SampleClass`, when the following code segment is executed, what is the value of the instance variable `size`?

```
SampleClass sampleClass = new SampleClass(5);
public class SampleClass {
    private int size;
    public SampleClass(int size) {
        size = size;
    }
}
```

A. 0

B. 1

C. 5

D. Compiler error

E. Runtime error

12. What type of variable would be used to store the state of an object?

A. Local variable

B. Method parameter

C. Instance variable

D. Object variable

Create and Use Constructors

13. Given the `SampleClass`, what is the output of this code segment?

```
SampleClass sampleClass = new SampleClass();
public class SampleClass {
    private int size;
    private int priority;

    public SampleClass(){
        super();
        System.out.println("Using default values");
    }

    public SampleClass(int size) {
        this.size = size;
        System.out.println("Setting size");
    }

    public SampleClass(int priority){
        this.priority = priority;
        System.out.println("Setting priority");
    }
}
```

   A. `Using default values`

   B. `Setting size`

   C. `Setting priority`

   D. Compiler error

14. What constructor is equivalent to the one listed here?

```
public SampleConstructor() {
    System.out.println("SampleConstructor");
}
```

   A.
```
public SampleConstructor() {
    this();
    System.out.println("SampleConstructor");
}
```

   B.
```
public SampleConstructor() {
    super();
    System.out.println("SampleConstructor");
}
```

C.
```
public SampleConstructor() {
    this.SampleConstructor();
    System.out.println("SampleConstructor");
}
```

D.
```
public SampleConstructor() {
    super.SampleConstructor();
    System.out.println("SampleConstructor");
}
```

E. None of the above

15. If a constructor does not include an access modifier, which modifier will it use by default?

   A. A constructor that does not include an access modifier will always be declared as `public`.

   B. A constructor that does not include an access modifier will make use of the same access modifier that is used for its class.

   C. A compilation error will occur if a constructor does not include an access modifier.

   D. A constructor that does not include an access modifier will have package-private access.

Use the this and super Keywords

16. Given the `SampleClass`, what is the output of this code segment?

```
SampleClass sampleClass = new SampleClass();
public class SampleClass {
    private int size;

    public SampleClass(){
        this(1);
        System.out.println("Using default values");
    }

    public SampleClass(int size) {
        this.size = size;
        System.out.println("Setting size");
    }
}
```

   A. `Using default values`

   B. `Setting size`

   C. `Using default values Setting size`

   D. `Setting size Using default values`

   E. Compiler error

17. What is the effect of the following line of code?

```
super()
```

A. The method that is overridden by the current method is called.
B. The parent class's constructor is called.
C. The current class's constructor is called.
D. The child class's constructor is called.
E. The current method is recursively called.

Create Static Methods and Instance Variables

18. Given the `SampleClass`, what is the output of this code segment?

```
SampleClass s = new SampleClass();
SampleClass.sampleMethodOne();
public class SampleClass {
    public static void sampleMethodOne(){
        sampleMethodTwo();
        System.out.println("sampleMethodOne");
    }

    public void sampleMethodTwo(){
        System.out.println("sampleMethodTwo");
    }
}
```

A. sampleMethodOne
B. sampleMethodTwo
C. sampleMethodOne
   sampleMethodTwo
D. sampleMethodTwo
   sampleMethodOne
E. Compiler error

19. Given the `SampleClass`, what is the value of `currentCount` for the instance of object x after the code segment had be executed?

```
SampleClass x = new SampleClass();
SampleClass y = new SampleClass();
x.increaseCount();
public class SampleClass {
    private static int currentCount=0;

    public SampleClass(){
        currentCount++;
    }

    public void increaseCount(){
        currentCount++;
    }
}
```

   A. 0
   B. 1
   C. 2
   D. 3
   E. Compiler error
   F. Runtime error

20. Static methods have access to which of the following? (Choose all that apply.)

   A. Static variables
   B. Instance variables
   C. Standard methods
   D. Static methods
   E. None of the above

SELF TEST ANSWERS

Create and Use Methods

1. A method needs to be created that accepts an array of `floats` as an argument and does not return any variables. The method should be called `setPoints`. Which of the following method declarations is correct?

   A. `setPoints(float[] points) {...}`
   B. `void setPoints(float points) {...}`
   C. `void setPoints(float[] points) {...}`
   D. `float setPoints(float[] points) {...}`

   > **Answer:**
   >
   > ☑ **C.** `void` must be used for methods that do not return any data.
   > ☒ **A, B,** and **D** are incorrect. **A** is incorrect because it is missing the return type. If the method is not going to return a variable, it still must use `void`. **B** is incorrect because it does not have an array of `floats` as a parameter. **D** is incorrect because it uses the incorrect return type.

2. When the `void` keyword is used, which of the following statements are true? (Choose all that apply.)

   A. A `return` statement with a value following it must be used.
   B. A `return` statement with a value following it can optionally be used.
   C. A `return` statement with a value following it should never be used.
   D. A `return` statement by itself must be used.
   E. A `return` statement by itself can optionally be used.
   F. A `return` statement by itself can never be used.
   G. A `return` statement must be omitted.
   H. A `return` statement can optionally be omitted.
   I. A `return` statement should never be omitted.

Answer:

☑ **C, E, and H**. When `void` is used, it indicates that there is no returned data from the method. **C** is correct because it is not valid to return any data. **E** is correct because it is valid to optionally use a `return` by itself. **H** is correct because the `return` statement can also be optionally omitted.

☒ **A, B, D, F, G**, and **I** are incorrect. **A** and **B** are incorrect since the `void` keyword means you cannot return a value. **D, F, G**, and **I** are incorrect because the `return` statement is optional when `void` is used.

3. Given the `SampleClass`, what is the output of this code segment?

```
SampleClass s = new SampleClass();
s.sampleMethod(4.4, 4);
public class SampleClass {
    public void sampleMethod(int a, double b){
        System.out.println("Method 1");
    }
    public void sampleMethod(double b, int a){
        System.out.println("Method 2");
    }
}
```

A. Method 1

B. Method 2

C. Method 1
   Method 2

D. Method 2
   Method 1

E. Compiler error

Answer:

☑ **B**. This is an example of a class with an overloaded method. Since it passes `double` and `int` primitives as parameters, it will call the second method, which matches these data types.

☒ **A, C, D**, and **E** are incorrect. **A** is incorrect because `Method 1` is printed from a method with the signature of `sampleMethod(int a, double b)`. The correct signature is `sampleMethod(double b, int a)`. It is important to notice the order of the parameters. **C** and **D** are incorrect because overloading a method does not result in two methods being called. **E** is incorrect because there is no compiler error.

4. Which of the following methods returns a `float` and accepts an `int` as a parameter?
  A. `public void method1(int var1, float var2) {/*Method Body*/}`
  B. `public int method2(float var1) {/*Method Body*/}`
  C. `public float method3(int var1) {/*Method Body*/}`
  D. `public float, int method4() {/*Method Body*/}`

Answer:

☑ **C.** The parts of a method are `<Access Modifier> <Return Type> <Method Identifier> (<Parameter List>){<Body>}`, and answer **C**, `public float method3(int var1) {/*Method Body*/}`, includes these parts.
☒ **A, B,** and **D** are incorrect. **A** is incorrect because it has no return type. **B** is incorrect because it returns an `int` and uses a `float` as a parameter. **D** is incorrect because it is invalid Java code and will cause a compiler error.

5. You want to create a method that takes in three character parameters and returns a string. Which declaration is valid?
  A. `public void doMethod (char a, char b, char c) {String s = null; return s;}`
  B. `public String doMethod (Char a, Char b, Char c) {String s = null; return s;}`
  C. `public String doMethod (char a, char b, char c) {String s = null; return s;}`
  D. `public string doMethod (char a, char b, char c) {String s = null; return s;}`

Answer:

☑ **C.** This is a perfectly formed method declaration.
☒ **A, B,** and **D** are incorrect. **A** is incorrect because the declaration states that no value (`void`) is to be returned, but a string is. **B** is incorrect because the wrapper class for character is `Character` and not `Char`. **D** is incorrect because the return type of `String` does not start with a capital letter as it should. That is, "`public string doMethod`" should read "`public String doMethod`".

Pass Objects by Reference and Value

6. Given the class `FloatNumber` and method `addHalf`, what is the output if the following code segment is executed?

```java
public class FloatNumber {
   float number;
   public FloatNumber(float number) {
      this.number = number;
   }
   float getNumber() {
      return number;
   }
   void setNumber(float number) {
      this.number = number;
   }
}

void addHalf(FloatNumber value) {
   value.setNumber(value.getNumber() + (value.getNumber()/2f));
}

/* CODE SEGMENT */
FloatNumber value = new FloatNumber(1f);
addHalf(value);
System.out.println("value = " + value.getNumber());
```

A. value = 1

B. value = 1.5

C. value = 2

D. value = 0

Answer:

☑ **B.** The `FloatNumber` object is passed by reference. Therefore, when the method changes its value, this change is still present when the code returns to the original calling code segment.

☒ **A, C**, and **D** are incorrect. **A** is incorrect because the `FloatNumber` is passed by reference. If it were a primitive `float` this would be the correct answer. **C** and **D** are incorrect, regardless if the variable is passed by reference or value.

7. Objects are passed by _____.
   A. value
   B. sum
   C. reference
   D. pointer

Answer:
☑ **C.** Objects are always passed by reference.
☒ **A, B,** and **D** are incorrect. **A** is incorrect because primitives are passed only by value. **B** is incorrect because "sum" is not a real term. **D** is incorrect because Java does not use the term "pointer."

8. Primitives are passed by _____.
   A. value
   B. sum
   C. reference
   D. pointer

Answer:
☑ **A.** Primitives are always passed by value.
☒ **B, C,** and **D** are incorrect. **B** is incorrect because "sum" is not a real term. **C** is incorrect because objects are passed only by reference. **D** is incorrect because Java does not use the term "pointer."

9. What is the value of the variable `number` when the following code segment is finished?

Code segment:

```
int number = 7;
sampleMethod(number);
```

Supporting method:

```
public void sampleMethod(int i){
   i++;
}
```

A. 0

B. 1

C. 7

D. 8

E. A compiler error occurs.

F. A runtime error occurs.

Answer:

☑   **C.** Because primitives are passed by value, a copy of the data is sent to the method. Any changes the method makes on the data does not affect the original variable since a copy was made.

☒   **A, B, D, E,** and **F** are incorrect. **A, B,** and **D** are all incorrect values. **E** and **F** are incorrect because this will not produce any errors.

Understand Variable Scope

10.   You need to create a class to store information about books contained in a library. What variable scope is best suited for the variable that will store the title of a book?

A.   Local variable

B.   Static variable

C.   Global variable

D.   Method parameter

E.   Instance variable

Answer:

☑   **E.** In a class that stores information about books, you would want to store the title of the book in a variable that will remain in scope for the life of the object.

☒   **A, B, C,** and **D** are incorrect. **A** is incorrect because a local variable is best suited for data that will be used for only a short amount of time. **B** is incorrect because a static or class variable is best suited for data that all instances of the class would need to access. **C** is incorrect since global variables are discouraged in Java and would not make much sense in this situation. **D** is incorrect since it can only be used with methods.

11. Given the `SampleClass`, when the following code segment is executed, what is the value of the instance variable `size`?

```
SampleClass sampleClass = new SampleClass(5);
public class SampleClass {
    private int size;
    public SampleClass(int size) {
        size = size;
    }
}
```

A. 0

B. 1

C. 5

D. Compiler error

E. Runtime error

Answer:

☑ **A.** The instance variable is hidden with the parameter since they both have the same name. The instance variable is 0 because that is the default value assigned to instance variables.

☒ **B, C, D,** and **E** are incorrect. **B** is incorrect because the instance variable is set to 0, and not 1, by default. **C** is incorrect because to set `size` to 5, `this.size = size;` would have to be used. **D** and **E** are incorrect because this code is valid.

12. What type of variable would be used to store the state of an object?

A. Local variable

B. Method parameter

C. Instance variable

D. Object variable

Answer:

☑ **C.** Instance variables retain their value for the life of the object.

☒ **A, B,** and **D** are incorrect. **A** is incorrect because a local variable is used for temporary items and stays in scope only until the block of code it is declared in is exited. **B** is incorrect because method parameters are the variables passed to a method as arguments. They are in scope only for that method. **D** is incorrect because the object variable does not exist.

Create and Use Constructors

13. Given the `SampleClass`, what is the output of this code segment?

```
SampleClass sampleClass = new SampleClass();
public class SampleClass {
    private int size;
    private int priority;

    public SampleClass(){
        super();
        System.out.println("Using default values");
    }

    public SampleClass(int size) {
        this.size = size;
        System.out.println("Setting size");
    }

    public SampleClass(int priority){
        this.priority = priority;
        System.out.println("Setting priority");
    }
}
```

A. Using default values
B. Setting size
C. Setting priority
D. Compiler error

Answer:

☑ **D**. This would generate a compiler error because you cannot overload a constructor or method and have the same data types for the parameters.

☒ **A**, **B**, and **C** are incorrect. **A** is incorrect; however, if this were valid code, it would be the correct answer. **B** and **C** are incorrect; even if these were valid, they do not represent the flow of execution of the code segment.

14. What constructor is equivalent to the one listed here?

```
public SampleConstructor() {
    System.out.println("SampleConstructor");
}
```

A. ```
public SampleConstructor() {
    this();
    System.out.println("SampleConstructor");
}
```

B. ```
public SampleConstructor() {
    super();
    System.out.println("SampleConstructor");
}
```

C. ```
public SampleConstructor() {
    this.SampleConstructor();
    System.out.println("SampleConstructor");
}
```

D. ```
public SampleConstructor() {
    super.SampleConstructor();
    System.out.println("SampleConstructor");
}
```

E. None of the above

Answer:

☑ **B**. If `super` is not called on the first line of a constructor, the compiler will automatically add it for you.

☒ **A, C, D**, and **E** are incorrect. **A** is incorrect because `this()` calls a constructor of the current class. **C** and **D** are not valid uses of `super` or `this`. **E** is incorrect because answer **B** is correct.

15. If a constructor does not include an access modifier, which modifier will it use by default?

A. A constructor that does not include an access modifier will always be declared as `public`.

B. A constructor that does not include an access modifier will make use of the same access modifier that is used for its class.

C. A compilation error will occur if a constructor does not include an access modifier.

D. A constructor that does not include an access modifier will have package-private access.

Answer:

☑ **D.** A constructor will behave the same way a method behaves. If no access modifier is provided, it will default to package-private. A constructor with package-private access can only be called from other classes in the same package.

☒ **A, B,** and **C** are incorrect. **A** is incorrect because constructors that do not include an access modifier are not always declared as `public`; they are declared the same as their class. **B** is incorrect because a constructor works like a standard method and will be package-private if no modifiers are present. **C** is incorrect because a compilation error will not occur if a constructor does not have an access modifier.

Use the this and super Keywords

16. Given the `SampleClass`, what is the output of this code segment?

```
SampleClass sampleClass = new SampleClass();
public class SampleClass {
    private int size;

    public SampleClass(){
        this(1);
        System.out.println("Using default values");
    }

    public SampleClass(int size) {
        this.size = size;
        System.out.println("Setting size");
    }
}
```

A. `Using default values`
B. `Setting size`
C. `Using default values Setting size`
D. `Setting size Using default values`
E. Compiler error

Answer:

☑ **D**. The first constructor is called. It uses `this(1);` to call the second constructor. The second constructor prints out its statement and then returns to the first constructor, where it prints out its statement.

☒ **A, B, C**, and **E** are incorrect. **A, B**, and **C** are incorrect because they do not represent the correct execution of the code segment. **E** is incorrect because this is valid code.

17. What is the effect of the following line of code?

```
super()
```

A. The method that is overridden by the current method is called.
B. The parent class's constructor is called.
C. The current class's constructor is called.
D. The child class's constructor is called.
E. The current method is recursively called.

Answer:

☑ **B**. The `super` keyword in this case is used to call the parent class's constructor. This must be done from the first line of a constructor in the current class.

☒ **A, C, D**, and **E** are incorrect. **A** is incorrect because to refer to an overridden method, `super` and the method identifier must be used. **C** is incorrect because `this()` would be used to call a correct class's constructor. **D** is incorrect since it is impossible to refer to a child class's methods. **E** is incorrect because `super` has nothing to do with recursion.

Create Static Methods and Instance Variables

18. Given the `SampleClass`, what is the output of this code segment?

```
SampleClass s = new SampleClass();
SampleClass.sampleMethodOne();
public class SampleClass {
    public static void sampleMethodOne(){
        sampleMethodTwo();
        System.out.println("sampleMethodOne");
    }
```

```
    public void sampleMethodTwo(){
        System.out.println("sampleMethodTwo");
    }
}
```

A. sampleMethodOne

B. sampleMethodTwo

C. sampleMethodOne
   sampleMethodTwo

D. sampleMethodTwo
   sampleMethodOne

E. Compiler error

Answer:

☑ **E.** The method `sampleMethodOne` is a static method. This method is not able to call other standard methods; therefore, this will generate a compiler error when it is called.

☒ **A, B, C,** and **D** are incorrect. **A, B,** and **C** are incorrect because the code has a compiler error. **D** is incorrect because of the compiler error; however, it would be correct if `sampleMethodOne` was not static and this was valid code.

19. Given the `SampleClass`, what is the value of `currentCount` for the instance of object x after the code segment had been executed?

```
SampleClass x = new SampleClass();
SampleClass y = new SampleClass();
x.increaseCount();
public class SampleClass {
    private static int currentCount=0;

    public SampleClass(){
        currentCount++;
    }
```

```
        public void increaseCount(){
            currentCount++;
        }
    }
```

A. 0
B. 1
C. 2
D. 3
E. Compiler error
F. Runtime error

Answer:

☑ **D**. The variable `currentCount` is a static variable; therefore, every instance of this class has access to the same variable. The code segment creates two new instances of this class. The constructor increments this variable each time. Finally, the `increaseCount` method is called, which also increments the variable.

☒ **A, B, C, E**, and **F** are incorrect. **A, B**, and **C** are incorrect because `currentCount` is a static variable and the same value is incremented each time an object is created in the `increaseCount` method. **E** and **F** are incorrect because this is valid code.

20. Static methods have access to which of the following? (Choose all that apply.)
A. Static variables
B. Instance variables
C. Standard methods
D. Static methods
E. None of the above

Answer:

☑ **A** and **D**. Static methods can access only static variables and other static methods.

☒ **B, C**, and **E** are incorrect. **B** and **C** are incorrect because static methods cannot access data that is associated with an instance of a class. **E** is incorrect because **A** and **D** are correct answers.

6

Programming with Arrays

CERTIFICATION OBJECTIVES

- Work with Java Arrays
- Work with ArrayList Objects and Their Methods

 Two-Minute Drill

Q&A Self Test

A cornerstone of software development is working with data structures to store and retrieve data. Arrays are one of the most fundamental data structures; in fact, they can be found in nearly every programming language, and Java is no exception. Java inherited arrays from the C language, along with many of its other syntax rules. In addition to standard arrays, Java has an `ArrayList` class that is included in its software development kit. This is a modern approach to standard arrays and follows the principles of object-oriented programming. This chapter will discuss both types of arrays and prepare you for the questions you will encounter on the OCA exam.

CERTIFICATION OBJECTIVE

Work with Java Arrays

Exam Objective   Declare, instantiate, initialize, and use a one-dimensional array
Exam Objective   Declare, instantiate, initialize, and use multi-dimensional array

Java arrays are built into the language to handle multiple pieces of data that are of the same type. They allow the developer to use one variable with one or more indexes to access multiple independent pieces of data. Arrays can be used to store both primitives and objects.

Questions regarding arrays are included throughout the OCA exam. Questions will range from where to use an array, to what type of array to use, how to initialize an array, and how to work with arrays in code. The details of arrays are an important concept for you to understand to achieve success on the OCA exam. This section will review one-dimensional and multi-dimensional arrays.

One-Dimensional Arrays

A Java array is an object that acts as a container by storing a fixed number of the same type values. The values are accessed by using an index. A one-dimensional array uses only a single index. The following is an example of an array of `int` primitives:

```
int[] arrayOfInts = new int[3];
arrayOfInts[0] = 5;
arrayOfInts[1] = 10;
```

FIGURE 6-1

int[ ] arrayOfInts

```
arrayOfInts[2] = 15;
System.out.println("First: " + arrayOfInts[0]
        + " Second: " + arrayOfInts[1]
        + " Third: " + arrayOfInts[2]);
```

Figure 6-1 is a visual representation of this code segment.
This code would produce the following output:

```
First: 5 Second: 10 Third: 15
```

This is a basic example of a one-dimensional array in action. Let's take a closer
look at what happens here before we dig into the details of arrays.

First, the variable `arrayOfInts` is declared. It is declared with the type `int[]`.
The square brackets indicate that this is an array of `int` primitives. Next, it is initialized
with the `new` operator. The `new` operator must be used because all arrays are
considered objects. It is initialized with its type, which is `int`, with the square
brackets to indicate an array and finally a number inside the brackets. The number
is used to assign a size to the array. In this case, it is an array containing three `int`
primitives. The next three lines set a value for each index in the array. Notice that
the first index has a value of `0`. All arrays are zero based and have a first number
index of 0. Finally, the values are accessed and sent to standard output.

Declaring One-Dimensional Arrays

One-dimensional arrays are declared either by using square brackets after the type
or by using the square brackets after the variable name. Both are valid. When the
array is being declared, a number is never placed inside the brackets. An array is
declared the same way for both objects and primitives. Here's an example:

```
/* Valid declaration of object and primitive array */
String[] clockTypes;
int[] alarms;
/*
 * Valid and equivalent to the above declarations
 * This is a less common syntax and is rarely used
 */
String clockTypes[];
int alarms[];
```

Initializing One-Dimensional Arrays

Once an array is declared, it must be initialized. An array can be initialized similarly to how an object is initialized. The new operator is used followed by the type, with square brackets containing the length, or size, of the array. This initialization can be done on the same line as the declaration or on its own line. The following code segment demonstrates this:

```
/*
 * Each of these lines is a valid way to initialize
 * an array with the new operator
 */
String[] clockTypes = new String[3];
String clockTypes[] = new String[3];
clockTypes = new String[4];
/* Even arrays of primitives use the new operator */
int alarms[] = new int[2];
```

Once an array is assigned a size, it cannot be changed without initializing it again. If the declared array contains primitives, then every primitive inside the array is set to 0. An array of objects has each element initially set to null.

It is also possible to initialize an array with all of its values immediately after being declared. This is done by placing the values to be stored in the array in curly brackets. The curly brackets must follow the declaration on the same line. The values in the brackets are separated with commas. This will initialize the array and assign a value to each element in the array. The following code demonstrates this:

```
int[] alarms = {730,900};
String[] clockTypes = {"Wrist Watch","Desk Clock","Wall Clock"};
Clock[] clocks = {new Clock(1100), new Clock(2250)};
```

This example shows the alarms array, containing int primitives, being initialized with two int values. This array now has a length of two and is populated with 730 at index 0 and 900 at index 1. The next line is an array of String objects. This array is initialized with the three strings: "Wrist Watch", "Desk Clock", and "Wall Clock". The array has a length of three. The final example is an object called Clock. This object has a constructor that forms a new object and requires the time to initialize the clock by using an argument. The objects are created inline, and both are stored in the array.

When an array is initialized with curly brackets, it must do so within the same statement as the declaration. Unlike the new operator, an array cannot be initialized with curly brackets on a different line of code.

on the
job

This section has demonstrated how arrays can be declared with square brackets after the variable type or the variable name. In practice, most developers place the square brackets after the variable type because the square brackets describe the type.

Using One-Dimensional Arrays

One-dimensional arrays are very straightforward to use. Once declared and initialized, each element from the array can be accessed by using its corresponding index. Every object or primitive has an index number associated with it. It is important for you to remember that an array with a length of three has the indexes 0, 1, and 2. The first index is always 0.

The next example prints out the string that is stored in the array at index 1:

```
String[] clockTypes = {"Wrist Watch","Desk Clock","Wall Clock"};
System.out.println(clockTypes[1]);
```

The output would be as follows:

```
Desk Clock
```

This array is made up of `String` objects. When the array is used with an index number, it behaves just as a `String` object variable would. For example, the `equalsIgnoreCase()` method from the `String` class can be used like so:

```
if (clockTypes[0].equalsIgnoreCase("Grand Father Clock")({
   System.out.println("It's a grandfather clock!");
}
```

It is also possible to get the length of an array. Arrays are objects in Java. You can access the public `length` field to obtain the length of the array. In the next example, notice that `length` is not a method with open and close parentheses; it is a public field that can be accessed to get the length of the array:

```
System.out.println("length: " + clockTypes.length);
```

The example would produce the following output:

```
length: 3
```

Java has built-in methods for copying the data from one array to another. These methods copy the data and create two independent arrays upon completion. The `arraycopy()` method is a static method that is part of the `System` class. The method signature for `arraycopy()` is shown next:

```
public static void arraycopy(Object src, int srcPos,
     Object dest, int destPos, int length)
```

This method has five parameters. The `src` parameter is the source array, the array from which you intend to copy data. The `srcPos` parameter is the starting position in the array and is where copying starts. The `dest` parameter is the array into which data will be copied. The parameter `destPos` is the starting position of where data will be placed in the array. Finally, the `length` parameter is the number of elements from the array to be copied. When using this method, you must ensure that you do not go outside the bounds of either array. The destination array must also be declared as the same type and initialized.

The following code listing demonstrates part of an array being copied into another array:

```
String[] clockTypes = {"Wrist Watch","Desk Clock","Wall Clock"};
String[] newClockTypes = new String[2];
System.arraycopy(clockTypes, 1, newClockTypes, 0, 2);

for(String s : clockTypes){
    System.out.println(s);
}
System.out.println("------");
for(String s : newClockTypes){
    System.out.println(s);
}
```

In this example, the last two elements from `clockTypes` are copied into `newClockTypes`. Then both are printed to standard output. The two arrays are independent. If values in one are modified, it will not affect the other array. The following is the output of this code segment:

```
Wrist Watch
Desk Clock
Wall Clock
------
Desk Clock
Wall Clock
```

on the job

The `Arrays` *class of the Java utilities package provides sorting, searching, and comparing features for arrays. Static methods of the* `Arrays` *class include* `asList, binarySearch, copyOf, copyOfRange, equals, fill, sort,` *and many other useful methods.*

Multi-Dimensional Arrays

Multi-dimensional arrays have more than one index. A multi-dimensional array with two dimensions, or indexes, is an array of arrays. An array can have three, four, or more dimensions. The Java language specification does not place a limit on the number of dimensions that an array can have. However, the Java virtual machine (JVM) specification does set a practical limit of 256 dimensions.

Here is a complete example of a two-dimensional array. We will go over all of the rules of the arrays in the next few sections.

```
char[][] ticTacToeBoard = new char[3][3];

for(int y=0;y<3;y++){
    for(int x=0;x<3;x++){
        ticTacToeBoard[x][y]='-';
    }
}

ticTacToeBoard[0][0] = 'X';
ticTacToeBoard[1][1] = 'O';
ticTacToeBoard[0][2] = 'X';

for(int y=0;y<3;y++){
  for(int x=0;x<3;x++){
      System.out.print(ticTacToeBoard[x][y]+" ");
  }
  System.out.print("\n");
}
```

This example uses a two-dimensional array to represent a tic-tac-toe board. The array is first declared as char primitives and then initialized to have the size of 3-by-3. The first loop sets each value to a '-' character. Next, the board spaces at 0,0 and 0,2 are set to 'X', and 1,1 is set to 'O'. Finally the board is printed to standard output, resulting in the following output:

```
X - -
- O -
X - -
```

Declaring Multi-Dimensional Arrays

A multi-dimensional array is declared similarly to a one-dimensional array, with additional square brackets for each dimension. Where a one-dimensional array has one square bracket following the type or variable name, a two-dimensional array has two brackets, a three-dimensional array would have three, and so on. Following are some examples of multi-dimensional arrays being declared:

```
//An example of a two-dimensional array being declared both ways
String[][] chessBoard;
String chessBoard[][];
//An example of a three-dimensional array being declared both
ways
int[][][] cube;
int cube[][][];
```

Initializing Multi-Dimensional Arrays

Multi-dimensional arrays can be initialized similarly to one-dimensional arrays. They are either initialized with the new operator or they use curly brackets with the values to be stored in the array:

```
String[][] square = {{"1","2"},{"3","4"}};
String[][] square = new String[2][2];
int[][][] cube = new int[3][3][2];
```

In this example, the curly bracket groups are separated by commas. The values inside the curly brackets represent an array. You can think of multi-dimensional arrays as an array of arrays. This is because the first level is an array that contains an array at each element.

The arrays that are contained do not all have to be the same length. The next code segment demonstrates an array with different sized subarrays. Figure 6-2 shows a visual representation of this array.

```
int[][] oddSizeArray = {{1,2},{1,2,3,4},{1,2,3}};
```

FIGURE 6-2

int[ ][ ]
oddSizeArray

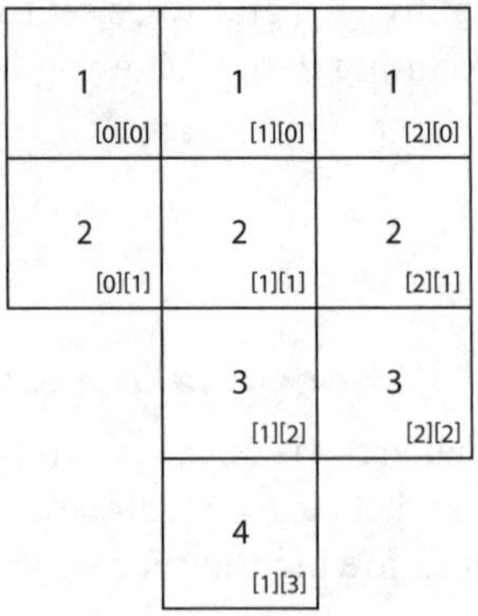

When you use the `new` operator to initialize an array, the size of each dimension does not have to be defined. Because a multi-dimensional array is just an array of arrays, it is okay to define the length of only the first dimension. You can then either assign a preexisting array to that element or use the `new` operator again:

```
int[][][] array3D = new int[2][][];
array3D[0] = new int[5][];
array3D[1] = new int[3][];
array3D[0][0] = new int[7];
array3D[0][1] = new int[2];
array3D[1][0] = new int[4];
```

In this example, `array3D` initializes only the size of the first dimension when it is declared. Then on separate lines, both elements from the first dimension are initialized with another array. And, finally, some elements from the second dimension are initialized with their arrays.

Using Multi-Dimensional Arrays

Multi-dimensional arrays are used similarly to one-dimensional arrays, except that additional dimensions need to be accounted for. When an element is accessed, an index must be provided in square brackets for each dimension:

```
int[][] grid = {{1,2},{3,4}};
System.out.println(grid[0][0] + " " + grid[1][0]);
System.out.println(grid[0][1] + " " + grid[1][1]);
```

It is also possible to assign one of the subarrays to another one-dimensional array. The following example continues with the last example to demonstrate this concept:

```
int[] subGrid = grid[1];
```

INSIDE THE EXAM

Searching for Clues on the Exam

When you're taking the OCA exam, pay close attention to questions containing multi-dimensional arrays. As this section has shown, these arrays can be used in many different ways. Think through the question and try to determine whether the array is valid. If you're in doubt, skip the question. While working on other questions, notice how the exam writers use arrays in these questions.

Work with ArrayList Objects and Their Methods

Exam Objective   Declare and use an ArrayList of a given type

The Java `ArrayList` class is an object-oriented representation of the standard array discussed previously in this chapter. The `ArrayList` class is part of the `java.util` package.

Using the ArrayList Class

The `ArrayList` class can be used to create an object that can store other objects, including enumeration types (enums). An index is used to access the objects inside the `ArrayList`. The `ArrayList` provides additional flexibility over a standard array. It can be dynamically resized and allows for objects to be inserted in the middle of the `ArrayList` while automatically moving other elements to make room. Next is an example of an `ArrayList` in action:

```
Integer integer1 = new Integer(1300);
Integer integer2 = new Integer(2000);
ArrayList<Integer> basicArrayList = new ArrayList<Integer>();
basicArrayList.add(integer1);
basicArrayList.add(integer2);
```

In this example, two `Integer` objects are created: `integer1` and `integer2`. They will be later stored in an `ArrayList`. You should remember that `ArrayList` objects cannot store primitives like basic arrays can. If a primitive is needed, it must be placed into a primitive wrapper object first. If a primitive is added to an `ArrayList`, autoboxing will occur to place it in its wrapper class automatically. Next, the `ArrayList` object `basicArrayList` is created. Notice the `<Integer>` within chevrons—this is a Java generic type indicator. This indicates that the `ArrayList` will be storing `Integer` objects. The compiler will enforce the type declared in the generic. Only objects of that type, or subclasses of it, can be stored in the `ArrayList`. The default constructor is used to create an `ArrayList`. Finally, both objects are added. The default constructor creates an `ArrayList` with ten internal elements. The size of the `ArrayList` is still based on the number of objects in it, and an exception will be thrown if the index is not valid. If the internal size is surpassed, the `ArrayList` is automatically expanded.

The following line of code demonstrates how to access the elements in the `ArrayList`. `ArrayList` indexes are zero based.

```
System.out.println(basicArrayList.get(0)
    + " - " + basicArrayList.get(1));
```

This would result in the following output:

```
1300 - 2000
```

To get the length of an `ArrayList`, the `size()` method is used. The `size()` method returns an `int` that represents the number of elements currently being stored.

```
System.out.println("Size: " + basicArrayList.size());
```

This example would produce the following output:

```
Size: 2
```

When the default constructor is used to create an `ArrayList`, it is given an initial capacity of ten. The capacity is different from the size. As you saw in the preceding example, the `basicArrayList` object used the default constructor and therefore had a capacity of ten. However, the `size()` method returns only the number of elements that it is storing. The `ArrayList` will manage the capacity automatically. When the capacity is exceeded, the `ArrayList` will expand automatically. However, this does incur some overhead. When developing software, if you have a rough idea of the needed capacity, you can set this with the `ArrayList` constructor. This reduces the overhead of the `ArrayList` expanding multiple times. Here is the method signature of this constructor:

```
public ArrayList(int initialCapacity)
```

The capacity of the `ArrayList` can be changed later with the `ensureCapacity()` method. This method increases the size of the `ArrayList` to the argument passed to the method. Here is the `ensureCapacity()` method signature:

```
public void ensureCapacity(int minCapacity)
```

As mentioned, it is possible to add an element into an `ArrayList` at a given index. If the index is in the middle of the `ArrayList`, the current element at that index and everything after it are shifted down by one. Continuing the basicArrayList example, the following code will place an element in the middle of the ArrayList:

```
Integer integer3 = new Integer(900);
basicArrayList.add(1,integer3);
System.out.println(basicArrayList.get(0)
    + " - " + basicArrayList.get(1)
    + " - " + basicArrayList.get(2));
System.out.println("Size: " + basicArrayList.size());
```

A third Integer is created and the add() method is used, which accepts both the index to place the element and the element as arguments. When this code is executed, the following would be displayed:

```
1300 - 900 - 2000
Size: 3
```

Notice that the new Integer, 900, is placed at index one. The size has also been increased by one. The method signature for this add method is shown here:

```
public void add(int index,E element)
```

Objects can be just as easily removed from the ArrayList. When an object is removed, all of the elements after the removed element shift their indexes down by one. The size will also be decreased by one. An element can be removed by referencing its index number or by passing the object to the ArrayList. Here are the two method signatures to remove an object:

```
public E remove(int index)
public boolean remove(Object o)
```

This section covers only the most important methods of the ArrayList class. The bulk of the ArrayList exam questions will focus on these methods. However, it is still a good idea for you to review the Java API for the ArrayList class to get a feel for all of the functionality that this class provides.

on the
ĵob

*The **ArrayList** class belongs to a group of classes called the **collection classes**. These classes all implement the **Collection** interface. As the name implies, the collection classes are used to store data. These classes are some of the most used in the Java language. Every developer should be familiar with most of the classes in this group. This group of classes contains stacks, sets, lists, queues, and arrays. Although **ArrayList** is the only such class on the OCA exam, it is still worthwhile for you to review the Java API for more information on these classes.*

ArrayList vs. Standard Arrays

This chapter has discussed two different valid ways to store data in your software. Which one is the best to use? As with any tool, your best bet is to use the one that fits the job. In most general cases, the `ArrayList` is likely to be easier to work with. It allows for growing and shrinking data sets, allows elements to be added or removed at any valid index, and offers many more methods that make working with `ArrayList` easy.

However, if you are concerned about overhead, using the basic array may be better. If the size of the data is known, then the automatic expanding and shrinking feature of `ArrayList` would not come into play. If primitives are being used, a standard array will be more efficient since they will not be required to be converted to their object wrapper classes.

The following table shows the pros and cons of using `ArrayList`:

Pros	Cons
Automatically resizes when capacity is exceeded.	Cannot store primitives without being in wrapper classes.
Objects can be placed in the middle of the array and it will automatically readjust all other elements.	Extra overhead is required when it is resized.
Objects can be easily removed from anywhere in the array and all other elements will readjust automatically.	Must nest multiple `ArrayLists` in an `ArrayList` to work similar to a standard multi-dimensional array.

The following table shows pros and cons of using standard one-dimensional and multi-dimensional arrays:

Pros	Cons
Can store primitives.	Cannot be resized.
No overhead to access data.	When adding or removing data, the array must be managed manually.
Easy to create multi-dimensional arrays.	

EXERCISE 6-1

Implement an ArrayList and Standard Array

This exercise will help you get more familiar with both the `ArrayList` class and standard arrays.

1. Create a Java project in the IDE of your choice.

2. Find the daily high temperature for the last seven days.

3. Create a standard one-dimensional array and enter each day's temperature into the array. It should contain seven elements when you are done.

4. Create an `ArrayList` and enter the same seven temperatures into it.

5. Use both the standard array and the `ArrayList` and find the average temperature over that time.

6. Print each value to standard output.

7. Ensure that you have calculated the same value from each array type.

CERTIFICATION SUMMARY

This chapter examined how to use standard Java arrays and `ArrayLists`. For the OCA exam, you need to know how to use each array type, how each works, and the semantic details of what is and is not valid. The exam will test you on all three areas in the same question.

Standard Java arrays and their syntax were inherited into the Java language from C. They are a very primitive way of storing multiple values of the same type. They incur low overhead, but changes must be managed manually. Once a size is declared, the array cannot grow. These arrays are able to store both primitive values and objects. It is also easy to create an array with many dimensions.

The `ArrayList` is a Java class that attempts to provide the same functionality as a standard array, but in an object-oriented manner. The `ArrayList` can store only objects, but primitives can be used when placed into their wrapper class first. The `ArrayList` will automatically adjust its size if its capacity is exceeded. It is also possible to add or remove elements from any location in the `ArrayList`. When objects are added or removed, the `ArrayList` will adjust the remaining objects.

The OCA exam will focus equally on using both array types, as well as the proper syntax for both. It is not enough to know how to use a standard array or `ArrayList`. You must also know the details of what is and is not valid.

✓ TWO-MINUTE DRILL

Work with Java Arrays

- ☐ Standard Java arrays are built into the Java language.
- ☐ Standard Java arrays can store both objects and primitives.
- ☐ Standard Java arrays can have one or many dimensions.
- ☐ Standard Java arrays are objects and must be initialized after they are declared.
- ☐ Standard Java arrays can be declared with square brackets after the type or variable name. Example: `int [] myArray` or `int myArray[]`.
- ☐ Standard Java arrays can be initialized with the new operator and their size in square brackets after the type. Example: `int [] myArray = `**`new int[4]`**.
- ☐ Standard Java arrays can be initialized by placing the values that will populate the array in curly brackets. Example: `int [] myArray = `**`{1,2,3,4}`**.
- ☐ Standard Java arrays can be multi-dimensional; each set of square brackets represents a dimension.
- ☐ A three-dimensional array would be declared as `int [] [] [] threeDArray`.
- ☐ Multi-dimensional arrays can declared with the new operator by placing the size of each dimension in square brackets. Example: `int [] [] [] threeDArray = `**`new int[3] [2] [2]`**.
- ☐ Multi-dimensional arrays can be initialized by placing the values that will populate the array in curly brackets. Each dimension is represented by a nested set of curly brackets. Example: `int [] [] [] threeDArray = `**`{{{1,2},{3,4}},{{5,6},{7,8}},{{9,10},{11,12}}}`**.
- ☐ Multi-dimensional arrays do not have to have the same size subarrays. Example: `int [] [] oddSizes = {{1,2,3,4},{3},{6,7}}`.
- ☐ Multi-dimensional arrays do not have to declare the size of every dimension when initialized. Example: `int [] [] [] array5 = new int[3] [] []`.

Work with ArrayList Objects and Their Methods

☐ The `ArrayList` class is an object-orientated representation of a standard Java array.

☐ The `ArrayList` class is part of the `java.util` package.

☐ An `ArrayList` object will automatically resize if its capacity is exceeded.

☐ An `ArrayList` object can have its internal capacity adjusted manually to improve efficiency.

☐ An `ArrayList` object can have elements added at any index in the array and will automatically move the other elements.

☐ An `ArrayList` object can have any element in it removed and will automatically move the other elements.

☐ In most cases, the `ArrayList` is the preferred method of storing data in an array.

SELF TEST

Work with Java Arrays

1. What lines will compile without errors? (Choose all that apply.)

   A. `Object obj = new Object();`
   B. `Object[] obj =  new Object();`
   C. `Object obj[] =  new Object();`
   D. `Object[] obj =  new Object[];`
   E. `Object[] obj =  new Object[3]();`
   F. `Object[] obj =  new Object[7];`
   G. `Object obj[] =  new Object[];`
   H. `Object obj[] =  new Object[3]();`
   I. `Object obj[] =  new Object[7];`
   J. `Object[8] obj =  new Object[];`
   K. `Object[3] obj =  new Object[3]();`
   L. `Object[7] obj =  new Object[7];`
   M. `Object obj[] =  new {new Object(), new Object()};`
   N. `Object obj[] = {new Object(), new Object()};`
   O. `Object obj[] = {new Object[1], new Object[2]};`

2. What is the output of the following code segment?

   ```
   String[] numbers = {"One","Two","Three"};
   System.out.println(numbers[3] + " " + numbers[2] + " " +
       numbers[1]);
   ```

   A. One Two Three
   B. Three Two One
   C. A compile time error will be generated.
   D. A runtime exception will be thrown.

3. What is the output of the following code segment?

   ```
   String[] numbers = {"One","Two","Three"};
   for(String s : numbers){
       System.out.print(s + " ");
   }
   ```

   A. One Two Three

   B. Three Two One

   C. A compile time error will be generated.

   D. A runtime exception will be thrown.

4. What is the output of the following code segment?

```java
int[] testScores = {80,63,99,87,100};
System.out.println("Length: " + testScores.length);
```

   A. Length: 4

   B. Length: 5

   C. Length: 100

   D. A compile time error will be generated.

   E. A runtime exception will be thrown.

5. What is the output of the following code segment?

```java
Integer[] integerArray1 = {new Integer(100),new Integer(1)
    ,new Integer(30),new Integer(50)};
Integer[] integerArray2 = new Integer[2];
integerArray2[0]=new Integer(100);
System.arraycopy(integerArray1, 2, integerArray2, 1, 1);
for(Integer i : integerArray2){
    System.out.print(i + " ");
}
```

   A. 100 1 30 50

   B. 100 1

   C. 100 30

   D. 100 1 30

   E. 600 1

   F. 600 30

   G. 600 1 30

   H. A compile time error will be generated.

   I. A runtime exception will be thrown.

6. What line *will* produce a compiler error?

   A. `double[] [] numbers;`

   B. `double[] [] [] numbers;`

   C. `double[] [] numbers = {{1,2,3},{7,8,9},{4,5,6}};`

D. `double[][] numbers = {{1,2,3},{7,8},{4,5,6,9}};`

E. `double[][][] numbers = new double[7][][];`

F. `double[][][] numbers = new double[][][];`

G. `double[][][] numbers = new double[7][3][2];`

7. What is the value of the variable sum at the end of this code segment?

```
int[][] square = new int[3][3];
for(int i=0;i<3;i++){
    square[i][i] = 5;
}
int sum=0;
for(int i=0;i<3;i++){
    for(int j=0;j<3;j++){
        sum+=square[i][j];
    }
}
```

A. 0

B. 5

C. 10

D. 15

E. 20

F. 25

G. 30

H. 35

I. 40

J. 45

K. 50

L. It will generate a compiler error.

8. The following code segment is valid. True or false?

```
int[][] square = new int[2][];
square[0] = new int[5];
square[1] =new int[3];
```

A. True

B. False

9. Given:

```
int sampleArray[] = new int[3];
sampleArray[1] = 3;
sampleArray[2] = 5;
sampleArray[3] = 7;
int var = sampleArray[1+1];
```

What is the value of the variable `var`?

A. 3

B. 5

C. 7

D. 6

E. 8

F. A compiler error will occur.

G. A runtime error will occur.

10. What is missing from the following multi-dimensional array declaration?

```
int[][] array = int[10][10];
```

A. Curly brackets

B. Parentheses

C. The `new` keyword

D. Nothing is missing.

Work with ArrayList Objects and Their Methods

11. What can be stored in an `ArrayList`? (Choose all that apply.)

A. Primitives

B. Objects

C. Standard arrays

D. Enums

12. What is the value of the `size` variable at the completion of this code segment?

```
ArrayList<Object> sampleArrayList = new ArrayList<Object>();
sampleArrayList.add(new Object());
sampleArrayList.ensureCapacity(15);
sampleArrayList.add(new Object());
int size = sampleArrayList.size();
```

A. 0

B. 1

C. 2

D. 10

E. 15

F. A compile time error will be generated.

G. A runtime exception will be thrown.

13. For standard situations, what is typically the best type of array to use?

A. `ArrayList`

B. One-dimensional array

C. Multi-dimensional array

14. What is the output of the following code segment?

```
ArrayList<String> sampleArrayList = new ArrayList<String>();
sampleArrayList.add("One");
sampleArrayList.add("Two");
sampleArrayList.add(1,"Three");
for(String s : sampleArrayList){
    System.out.print(s + " ");
}
```

A. One Two Three

B. One Three Two

C. Three One Two

D. One Three

E. Three Two

F. A compile time error will be generated.

G. A runtime exception will be thrown.

15. The `ArrayList` class is part of what Java package?

A. `java.lang`

B. `java.util`

C. `javax.tools`

D. `javax.swing`

16. What array type has the most overhead?
   A. One-dimensional array
   B. Multi-dimensional array
   C. `ArrayList`

17. What best describes the result of the following code segment? The `ArrayList` `sampleArrayList` has already been declared and initialized.

```
int i = 63;
sampleArrayList.add(i);
```

   A. The `int` is successfully placed into the `ArrayList`.
   B. The `int` is converted to an `Integer` via autoboxing and then placed into the `ArrayList`.
   C. `null` is placed into the `ArrayList`.
   D. A compile time error will be generated.
   E. A runtime exception will be thrown.

18. Which of the following are interfaces to `ArrayList`? (Choose all that apply.)
   A. `List`
   B. `Map`
   C. `Queue`
   D. `Set`
   E. `RandomAccess`

SELF TEST ANSWERS

Work with Java Arrays

1. What lines will compile without errors? (Choose all that apply.)

   A. `Object obj = new Object();`
   B. `Object[] obj = new Object();`
   C. `Object obj[] = new Object();`
   D. `Object[] obj = new Object[];`
   E. `Object[] obj = new Object[3]();`
   F. `Object[] obj = new Object[7];`
   G. `Object obj[] = new Object[];`
   H. `Object obj[] = new Object[3]();`
   I. `Object obj[] = new Object[7];`
   J. `Object[8] obj = new Object[];`
   K. `Object[3] obj = new Object[3]();`
   L. `Object[7] obj = new Object[7];`
   M. `Object obj[] = new {new Object(), new Object()};`
   N. `Object obj[] = {new Object(), new Object()};`
   O. `Object obj[] = {new Object[1], new Object[2]};`

   Answer:

   ☑ **A, F, I, N,** and **O.** Are all correct ways to declare and initialize an array.

   ☒ **B, C, D, E, G, H, J, K, L,** and **M** are incorrect. **B** and **C** are incorrect because they have `()` instead of `[]` after the type. **D** and **G** are incorrect because they do not assign a size to the array. **E** and **H** are incorrect because the `()` after the `[]` is not the correct syntax. **J** and **L** are incorrect because the size is not assigned when it is declared. **K** is incorrect because the size is in the declaration and the extra `()` after the `[]` is not the correct syntax. **M** is incorrect because the first new operator is being used with the `{}` initialization method.

2. What is the output of the following code segment?

   ```
   String[] numbers = {"One","Two","Three"};
   System.out.println(numbers[3] + " " + numbers[2] + " " + numbers[1]);
   ```

A. `One Two Three`

B. `Three Two One`

C. A compile time error will be generated.

D. A runtime exception will be thrown.

Answer:

☑ **D**. Array indexes start at 0. The `numbers[3]` variable will throw a runtime `ArrayIndexOutOfBoundsException`.

☒ **A**, **B**, and **C** are incorrect. If the indexes were each one number lower, **B** would be the correct answer.

3. What is the output of the following code segment?

```
String[] numbers = {"One","Two","Three"};
for(String s : numbers){
    System.out.print(s + " ");
}
```

A. `One Two Three`

B. `Three Two One`

C. A compile time error will be generated.

D. A runtime exception will be thrown.

Answer:

☑ **A**. The enhanced `for` loop will print out each string in order.

☒ **B**, **C**, and **D** are incorrect. **B** is incorrect because it is in the wrong order. **C** and **D** are incorrect because this code is valid.

4. What is the output of the following code segment?

```
int[] testScores = {80,63,99,87,100};
System.out.println("Length: " + testScores.length);
```

A. `Length: 4`

B. `Length: 5`

C. `Length: 100`

D. A compile time error will be generated.

E. A runtime exception will be thrown.

Answer:

☑ **B.** The length of an array equals the number of elements in the array.

☒ **A, C, D**, and **E** are incorrect. **A** is incorrect because length is not zero based, which the value 4 would imply. **C** is incorrect because the length returns the size of the array, not the last value. **D** and **E** are incorrect because no error or exceptions will be generated.

5. What is the output of the following code segment?

```
Integer[] integerArray1 = {new Integer(100),new Integer(1)
    ,new Integer(30),new Integer(50)};
Integer[] integerArray2 = new Integer[2];
integerArray2[0]=new Integer(100);
System.arraycopy(integerArray1, 2, integerArray2, 1, 1);
for(Integer i : integerArray2){
    System.out.print(i + " ");
}
```

A. 100 1 30 50

B. 100 1

C. 100 30

D. 100 1 30

E. 600 1

F. 600 30

G. 600 1 30

H. A compile time error will be generated.

I. A runtime exception will be thrown.

Answer:

☑ **C.** 100 is added to the array first, and then the 30 is copied into the array with the `arraycopy()` method.

☒ **A, B, D, E, F, G, H**, and **I** are incorrect. Each of these sets of numbers is not what will be output from this code segment.

6. What line *will* produce a compiler error?

A. `double[][] numbers;`

B. `double[][][] numbers;`

```
C.  double[][] numbers = {{1,2,3},{7,8,9},{4,5,6}};
D.  double[][] numbers = {{1,2,3},{7,8},{4,5,6,9}};
E.  double[][][] numbers = new double[7][][];
F.  double[][][] numbers = new double[][][];
G.  double[][][] numbers = new double[7][3][2];
```

Answer:

☑ **F.** When the new operator is used, at least one array dimension in a multi-dimensional array must be given a size.

☒ **A, B, C, D, E**, and **G** are incorrect. These are all valid ways to work with arrays.

7. What is the value of the variable sum at the end of this code segment?

```
int[][] square = new int[3][3];
for(int i=0;i<3;i++){
    square[i][i] = 5;
}
int sum=0;
for(int i=0;i<3;i++){
    for(int j=0;j<3;j++){
        sum+=square[i][j];
    }
}
```

A. 0
B. 5
C. 10
D. 15
E. 20
F. 25
G. 30
H. 35
I. 40
J. 45
K. 50
L. It will generate a compiler error.

Answer:

☑   **D.** All primitive array elements start with a value of 0. Then the first `for` loop sets `square[0][0]`, `square[1][1]`, and `square[2][2]` to 5. All the array elements are summed in the second `for` loop, resulting in the `sum` variable having the value of 15 at the end.

☒   **A, B, C, E, F, G, H, I, J,** and **K** are incorrect. These values are all incorrect results for the `sum` variable. **L** is incorrect because this is valid code that does not produce an error.

8. The following code segment is valid. True or false?

```
int[][] square = new int[2][];
square[0] = new int[5];
square[1] = new int[3];
```

A. True
B. False

Answer:

☑   **A.** The code sample is valid, so the answer is true.

☒   **B** is incorrect because the sample is valid.

9. Given:

```
int sampleArray[] = new int[3];
sampleArray[1] = 3;
sampleArray[2] = 5;
sampleArray[3] = 7;
int var = sampleArray[1+1];
```

What is the value of the variable `var`?

A. 3
B. 5
C. 7
D. 6
E. 8
F. A compiler error will occur.
G. A runtime error will occur.

Answer:

☑   **G.** This will cause a runtime error. This code will throw a `java.lang`
`.ArrayIndexOutOfBoundsException`. Arrays have an index that starts at 0. In this code
segment, the valid indexes would be 0, 1, and 2.
☒   **A, B, C, D, E,** and **F** are incorrect. **A, B, C, D,** and **E** are incorrect because this
code cannot be run without an error. However, if `sampleArray[3]` was changed to
`sampleArray[0]`, **B** would be correct. **F** is incorrect since the code will compile without
any issues; however, some IDEs may flag this as a possible problem.

10. What is missing from the following multi-dimensional array declaration?

```
int[][] array = int[10][10];
```

   A.   Curly brackets
   B.   Parentheses
   C.   The `new` keyword
   D.   Nothing is missing.

Answer:

☑   **C.** The `new` keyword is needed to establish memory allocation.
☒   **A, B,** and **D** are incorrect. **A** is incorrect because for the declaration specified, curly
brackets are not needed. **B** is incorrect because for the declaration specified, parentheses are
not needed. **D** is incorrect because the `new` keyword is missing.

Work with ArrayList Objects and Their Methods

11. What can be stored in an `ArrayList`? (Choose all that apply.)
   A.   Primitives
   B.   Objects
   C.   Standard arrays
   D.   Enums

Answer:

☑ **B, C**, and **D**. Objects, standard arrays, and enums can be stored in an `ArrayList`.
☒ **A** is incorrect. Primitives cannot be stored in an `ArrayList` unless they are placed in their primitive wrapper class.

12. What is the value of the `size` variable at the completion of this code segment?

```
ArrayList<Object> sampleArrayList = new ArrayList<Object>();
sampleArrayList.add(new Object());
sampleArrayList.ensureCapacity(15);
sampleArrayList.add(new Object());
int size = sampleArrayList.size();
```

A. 0
B. 1
C. 2
D. 10
E. 15
F. A compile time error will be generated.
G. A runtime exception will be thrown.

Answer:

☑ **C**. The size of an `ArrayList` is based on the number of objects in it, not its capacity.
☒ **A, B, D, E, F**, and **G** are incorrect because the size of an `ArrayList` is based on the number of objects in it, not its capacity.

13. For standard situations, what is typically the best type of array to use?
A. `ArrayList`
B. One-dimensional array
C. Multi-dimensional array

Answer:

☑ **A.** An `ArrayList` is a modern implementation of an array. It provides more flexibility than standard arrays, and its methods and automatic managing of internal resources will help reduce programming errors.

☒ **B** and **C** are incorrect. Both of these standard Java arrays are less flexible than an `ArrayList`.

14. What is the output of the following code segment?

```
ArrayList<String> sampleArrayList = new ArrayList<String>();
sampleArrayList.add("One");
sampleArrayList.add("Two");
sampleArrayList.add(1,"Three");
for(String s : sampleArrayList){
    System.out.print(s + " ");
}
```

A. One Two Three
B. One Three Two
C. Three One Two
D. One Three
E. Three Two
F. A compile time error will be generated.
G. A runtime exception will be thrown.

Answer:

☑ **B.** The `Three` string is inserted at index 1. Since arrays have indexes starting at 0, an index of 1 places `Three` in the middle of the other two elements.

☒ **A, C, D, E, F,** and **G** are incorrect. **A, C, D,** and **E** are not the correct output for the given code segment. **F** and **G** are incorrect because this is a valid code segment.

15. The `ArrayList` class is part of what Java package?
A. `java.lang`
B. `java.util`
C. `javax.tools`
D. `javax.swing`

Answer:

☑ **B**. The `java.util` package contains the collection classes and many other common Java classes.

☒ **A, C**, and **D** are incorrect. **A** is incorrect because `java.lang` contains many of the fundamental classes that make up Java. **C** is incorrect because `javax.tools` contains Java tools that can be invoked from programs. **D** is incorrect because `javax.swing` contains classes that are used to create graphical interfaces.

16. What array type has the most overhead?
  A. One-dimensional array
  B. Multi-dimensional array
  C. `ArrayList`

Answer:

☑ **C**. `ArrayList` objects have more overhead involved than standard arrays. However, their flexibility often more than makes up for this.

☒ **A** and **B** are incorrect. These are examples of traditional Java arrays. They both have less overhead than an `ArrayList` and therefore are incorrect answers for this question.

17. What best describes the result of the following code segment? The `ArrayList` `sampleArrayList` has already been declared and initialized.

```
int i = 63;
sampleArrayList.add(i);
```

  A. The `int` is successfully placed into the `ArrayList`.
  B. The `int` is converted to an `Integer` via autoboxing and then placed into the `ArrayList`.
  C. `null` is placed into the `ArrayList`.
  D. A compile time error will be generated.
  E. A runtime exception will be thrown.

Answer:

☑ **B.** Primitives cannot be stored in an `ArrayList`. However, if they are placed into their primitive wrapper class, they can be stored. Java will automatically make that conversion via its autoboxing feature if a primitive is placed into an `ArrayList`.

☒ **A, C, D,** and **E** are incorrect. **A** is incorrect because an `int` cannot be directly placed into an `ArrayList`. **C** is incorrect because `null` is not placed into the `ArrayList`. **D** and **E** are incorrect because this is valid code.

18. Which of the following are interfaces to `ArrayList`? (Choose all that apply.)

A. `List`

B. `Map`

C. `Queue`

D. `Set`

E. `RandomAccess`

Answer:

☑ **A** and **E.** `List` and `RandomAccess` are interfaces to `ArrayList`.

☒ **B, C,** and **D** are incorrect. **B** is incorrect because `Map` is not an interface to `ArrayList`. **C** is incorrect because `Queue` is not an interface to `ArrayList`. **D** is incorrect because `Set` is not an interface to `ArrayList`.

7
Understanding Class Inheritance

- Implement and Use Inheritance and Class Types
- Understand Encapsulation Principles
- Advanced Use of Classes with Inheritance and Encapsulation

✓   Two-Minute Drill

Q&A   Self Test

I nheritance is a core feature of object-orientated programming languages. It allows for better architected software through code reuse, encapsulation, and data protection. It is critical that you understand this fundamental concept for the OCA exam. As a professional developer, you will be required to use inheritance daily in your own code and while interacting with existing code and frameworks. This chapter will cover the important theory of inheritance and demonstrate it with practical examples.

Implement and Use Inheritance and Class Types

Exam Objective *Describe inheritance and its benefits*
Exam Objective *Use abstract classes and interfaces*

Inheritance is a fundamental concept of the Java language that allows specific classes to inherit the methods and instance variables of more general classes. This enables you to create code that is maintainable and emphasizes code reuse. You will need to have a thorough understanding of these topics for the exam.

This section also examines the differences between concrete classes and abstract classes. *Concrete* classes are basic normal classes, whereas *abstract* classes are tied to inheritance. The OCA exam will surely include a few questions for which you will need to understand what type of class is being used.

Finally, interfaces will be discussed. In short, an *interface* allows the developer to specify an external public interface to a class. Any class that implements or uses this interface must abide by the specifications outlined in the interface.

This section is about inheritance and the details of how inheritance works. This concept will not only be a major part of the OCA exam, but is also a very important concept to understand as a developer. The following topics will be covered in this chapter:

- Inheritance
- Overriding methods
- Abstract classes
- Interfaces
- Advanced concepts of inheritance

Inheritance

Inheritance allows a developer to create general classes that can be used as the foundation for multiple specific classes. For example, a program may be required to have classes that represent animals. The animals that must be represented are dogs, cats, and horses. All of these animal classes share some common elements. In this simple example, each animal would have a `weight`, `age`, and `color` instance variable. Each animal class would also have methods that allow it to do such things as eat, rest, and move. These methods could be called `eat()`, `rest()`, and `move(int direction)`.

This can be implemented without inheritance by creating a class for each animal type and then defining each of the methods. This implementation approach will work, but it has a few drawbacks. Since each type of animal eats, rests, and moves very similarly, there will be a lot of duplicated code between each class. Duplicated code makes a program hard to maintain. If a bug is found in one class, the developer must remember to find it in every other class that has a copy of that code. The same problem exists for adding features to the duplicated code. It becomes very easy for code that *should* perform the same to slowly start performing differently as the code goes through the development and maintenance process. Another disadvantage of this approach is that polymorphism cannot be used. *Polymorphism* is a technique that allows a specific object, such as a dog object, to be referred to in code as its more general parent animal. (Polymorphism will be covered in detail in Chapter 8.) Because this approach does not use inheritance, polymorphism is not possible. The following is an example of each animal class implemented in this approach. The details of the class are represented as comments to explain what functionality would be present if implemented.

```java
public class Dog1 {
    int weight;
    int age;
    String hairColor;

    public void eat(){ /* Eat food by chewing */ }

    public void rest(){ /* Rest */ }

    public void move(int direction)
        { /* Walk in the direction given as a parameter */ }

    public void bark() { /* Bark */ }
}
```

```
public class Cat1 {
   int weight;
   int age;
   String hairColor;

   public void eat(){ /* Eat food by chewing */ }

   public void rest(){ /* Rest */ }

   public void move(int direction)
        { /* Walk in the direction given as a parameter */ }

   public void meow() { /* Meow */ }
}

public class Horse1 {

   int weight;
   int age;
   String hairColor;

   public void eat(){ /* Eat food by chewing */ }

   public void rest(){ /* rest */ }

   public void move(int direction)
        { /* Walk in the direction given as a parameter */ }

   public void neigh() { /* Neigh */ }
}
```

The first implementation of these animals is to create a unique class for each
one. Each of the preceding classes has no relationship to the other. It is easy to see
that the classes are all very similar and code is duplicated among them. In fact, all
the methods are the same except the bark(), meow(), and neigh() methods.
Although there is no explicit relationship defined in the code, it is easy to infer that
all three classes are related.

The same example can be better implemented by using inheritance. In the
next simple example, three of the four methods that need to be implemented are
common to each different animal. A dog, cat, and horse all eat, rest, and move in
similar fashion. This common functionality can be placed in a general Animal
class that defines all the general methods and instance variables that make up an
animal. When the developer creates more specific types of animals such as dogs,

cats, or horses, he or she can use the `Animal` class as a base, or *superclass*. The more specific classes will inherit all of the nonprivate methods and instance variables from the base `Animal` class. A class is inherited when it is extended. It is important to remember that a class can extend only one class. It is invalid to inherit multiple classes in one class. However, a class can inherit a class that then inherits another class, and so on. The `extends` keyword is used in the class signature line. The following is an example of the same animals being implemented using inheritance:

```
public class Animal {
    int weight;
    int age;
    String hairColor;

    public void eat(){ /* Eat food by chewing */ }

    public void rest(){ /* Rest */ }

    public void move(int direction)
        { /* Walk in the direction given as a parameter */ }
}

public class Dog2 extends Animal{
    public void bark() { /* Bark */ }
}

public class Cat2 extends Animal{
    public void meow() { /* Meow */ }
}

public class Horse2 extends Animal{
    public void neigh() { /* Neigh */ }
}
```

This example creates `Dog2`, `Cat2`, and `Horse2` classes that are functionally the same as the first example. Each one of these classes extends, or inherits, the Animal class. The `Animal` class is used as their base, or superclass. The specific classes inherit all of the methods and instance variables from the `Animal` class and are then permitted to add specific methods and variables that the particular class may need. In this example, each class added a method to make the noise of the

Saying that class X extends class Y is the same as saying that class X inherits class Y.

animal. You may add as many instance variables or methods as needed to the class or use only those provided from the superclass.

When a class extends another class, any nonprivate methods that are contained in the superclass are accessible from the subclass. Later in this chapter, in the section "Understand Encapsulation Principles," you'll learn more about the four Java access modifiers; for now, assume that all of the examples use public methods. They can be invoked in the same manner as the methods implemented in the subclass. The following example demonstrates how the Dog2 class can be used:

```
Dog2 dog = new Dog2();
dog.bark();
dog.eat();
```

In this example, a Dog2 object named dog is created. Then the bark() and eat() methods are called. Notice that both methods can be called in the same manner, even though only the bark() method is implemented in the Dog2 class. This is because any Dog2 object inherits all of the nonprivate methods in the Animal class.

Overriding Methods

Inheriting, or extending, a class is a very good approach for factoring out common functionality between classes. Specific classes extending more general classes allow code to be reused in a project. As stated previously, this helps keep the project more maintainable and less prone to bugs as the development cycle progresses.

The problem with this approach, however, is that the subclass that inherits the methods of the superclass is sometimes slightly different. For example, if a Fish class extends the Animal class, the move() method would not work since it is implemented by code that walks—and a fish needs to swim. A class that extends another class may override any inherited method. This is done by defining another method called move() with the same arguments and return type. When the move() method is invoked, the one that is implemented in the Fish class will be used. A class may override all, none, or just some of the methods it inherits from a parent class. The following is an example of the Fish class extending the Animal class and then overriding the move() method:

```
public class Fish extends Animal {
  public void move(int direction)
      { /* Swim in the direction given as a parameter */ }
}
```

Notice that the move() method signature is the same as in the Animal class. However, the move() method in the Fish class is overriding the move() method in the Animal class. When a Fish object is created and the move() method is called, the code that is located in the Fish class will be executed. To override a method, the method signatures, which is all of the parameters and return type, must be identical.

When a subclass overrides a method, it has the option of calling the method that is being overridden. This can be achieved by using the super keyword. The super keyword works just like the this keyword, but instead of referring to the current class, super refers to the superclass. When super is used, it must pass the correct arguments to the parent method. The following is an example of super being used in the Horse3 class. Because horses normally rest standing, the Horse2 class from earlier can be further modified to put the horse in a standing position before it performs the rest() method.

```
public class Horse3 extends Animal{
  public void rest(){
    /* Stand before rest */
    super.rest();
  }

  public void neigh() { /* Neigh */ }
}
```

When a Horse3 object has its rest() method called, it will execute the code inside the rest() method of the Horse3 class. This is because the rest() method overrides the rest() method in the Animal class. The Horse3's rest() method makes the horse stand and then uses super to call the rest() method in the Animal class.

Abstract Classes

So far, all the examples presented use concrete classes. A *concrete class* is a regular class that can be instantiated. Java has another class type called an *abstract class*, which is different from a concrete class because it cannot be instantiated and must be extended. An abstract class may contain *abstract methods*, or methods that are not implemented. They have a valid method signature but must be overridden and implemented in the concrete class that extends the abstract class. However, an abstract class can extend another abstract class without implementing its methods. Abstract classes can have instance variables that may be used by concrete classes that extend the abstract class. The following is an example of an abstract class:

```
public abstract class MusicPlayer {
  public abstract void play();

  public abstract void stop();

  public void changeVolume(int volumeLevel)
    { /* Set volume to volumeLevel */}
}
```

This example is an abstract class for a music player. This is intended to be the base class for different music-playing devices such as MP3 players or CD players. Notice how the class is defined: the keyword abstract is used to indicate that this is an abstract class. This class provides some functionality with the changeVolume() method. It also contains two abstract methods. An abstract method can exist only in an abstract class. The abstract keyword is used to mark a method as such. Every abstract method must be implemented in the concrete subclass that extends it.

An abstract class can extend other abstract classes. Abstract classes are not required to implement the methods of an abstract superclass. However, all of these methods must be implemented by the first concrete subclass. The purpose of an abstract method is to define the required functionality that any subclass must have. In this case, any music player must be able to play and stop. The functionality cannot be implemented in the MusicPlayer class because it is different from player to player. The following example shows two classes extending the MusicPlayer class:

```
public class MP3Player extends MusicPlayer{

  @Override
  public void play() { /* Start decoding and playing MP3 */ }
  @Override
  public void stop() { /* Stop decoding and playing MP3 */ }
}

public class CDPlayer extends MusicPlayer {

  @Override
  public void play() { /* Start reading and playing disc */ }
  @Override
  public void stop() { /* Stop reading disc and playing disc */ }
}
```

The MP3Player and CDPlayer classes are both types of music players. By extending the MusicPlayer class, they are required to implement the play() and stop() methods by overriding the abstract classes in the base class.

on the
ⓙob

The @Override and @Implements annotations provide a way for the Java compiler to check that the annotated method is truly doing what the developer intends. @Override should be used when a method is overriding, and therefore hiding, a method in a superclass. The @Implements annotation is used when a method from an interface is implemented.

Interfaces

Interfaces are used in the Java language to define a required set of functionalities for the classes that implement the interface. Unlike extending base classes, a class is free to implement as many interfaces as needed. An interface can be thought of as an abstract class with all abstract methods.

When a concrete class implements an interface, it is required to implement all of the methods defined in the interface. An abstract class is not required to implement the interface methods, but the concrete class that extends it is still responsible to provide the functionality that the interface defines. Interfaces are used to create a standard public interface for similar items. This enables code to be more modular.

The interface keyword is used to create an interface in the next example:

```
public interface Phone {
  public void dialNumber(int number);

  public boolean isCallInProgress();
}
```

This example is a very basic interface for a phone.

The next example demonstrates this interface being implemented by a cell phone class and a landline phone. The keyword implements is used to implement an interface.

```
public class LandlinePhone implements Phone{
  private boolean callInProgress;

  public void dialNumber(int number)
    { /* Dial number via wired network */}

  public boolean isCallInProgress() { return callInProgress; }
```

```
   }

   public class CellPhone implements Phone{
     private boolean callInProgress;

     public void dialNumber(int number)
         { /* Dial number via cell network */ }

     public boolean isCallInProgress() { return callInProgress; }
   }
```

When an interface is implemented, all of its methods must then be implemented in that class. It is possible to implement multiple interfaces. When more than one interface is being used, they are separated in a comma-delimited list. When multiple interfaces are used, all of the methods defined in each one must be implemented. Any unimplemented methods will cause the compiler to generate errors. The following is an example of a class implementing two interfaces:

```
   public class VideoPhone implements Phone, VideoPlayer{
       . . .
   }
```

The big advantage of using interfaces is that any class that uses the same interface will have the same public methods, as shown in Figure 7-1. This means that the CellPhone class shown earlier could be used instead of LandlinePhone. Changing between these classes should not require any code change other than the type declared. This gets close to the idea of polymorphism and will be covered in detail in Chapter 8.

FIGURE 7-1   Implementation of the Phone interface

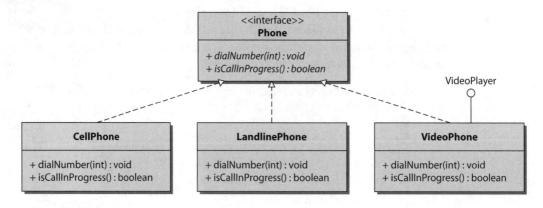

Advanced Concepts of Inheritance

The last few sections discussed the basic cases of inheritance—one concrete class extending another concrete class, abstract class, or implementing interfaces. However, it is possible and common to have many levels of inheritance. In fact, every class in the Java language inherits from the base class Object. This includes the classes built by developers.

The use of Object as a base class is implied and does not have to be explicitly extended with the extends keyword. This means that in the preceding examples where a class was inherited, there were really two levels of inheritance. Looking back at the animal example, the Dog2 class extended the Animal class, and the Animal class extended the Object class. This means that the Dog2 class gained all of the functionality of both classes. If a class overrides the methods of another, the new method is then passed down the inheritance chain. The inheritance chain can continue as long as it is applicable to the application, meaning class A can extend class B, which extends C, which extends D, and so forth. The classes can be a mixture of abstract and concrete. The classes are also able to implement any interfaces required.

Interfaces may also extend other interfaces. When an interface extends another interface, it gains all of the defined methods of the extended interface. Unlike a class, an interface may extend multiple interfaces. This is achieved by using the extends keyword, followed by a comma-delimited list of interfaces.

The diagram in Figure 7-2 represents a possible inheritance tree. At the bottom of this tree is the concrete class SportsCar. This class extends the abstract class

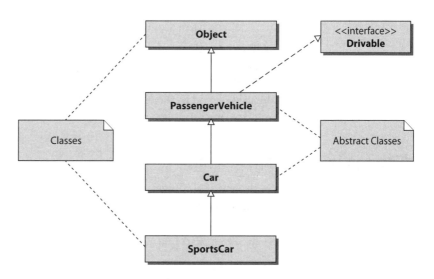

FIGURE 7-2

An example of an inheritance tree

Car. The Car class extends the PassengerVehicle class, which extends the base Object class. The PassengerVehicle class also implements the Drivable interface.

In an example like this, the SportsCar class has access to all the visible methods and instance variables in both the PassengerVehicle class and the Car class. The SportsCar class must also implement any methods that were abstract and unimplemented, including those required by the Drivable interface.

CERTIFICATION OBJECTIVE

Understand Encapsulation Principles

Exam Objective   Apply access modifiers
Exam Objective   Apply encapsulation principles to a class

Encapsulation is the concept of storing data together with methods that operate on that data. Objects are used as the container for the data and code. This section discusses the principles of encapsulation and how it should be applied by a developer.

Encapsulation allows for data and method hiding. This concept is called *information hiding*. Information hiding makes it possible to expose a public interface while hiding the implementation details. Finally, this section will explore the JavaBean conventions for creating getter and setter methods. These are the methods used to read and modify properties of a Java object.

This section will expose the reader to some good basic design principles that should be used with the Java language. The OCA exam will require an understanding of these principles. These conventions will be used on the exam even when the question is not directly related to them. Learning these concepts thoroughly will help you in understanding many exam questions.

Good Design with Encapsulation

The fundamental theory of an object-oriented language is that software is designed by creating discrete objects that interact to make up the functionality of the application. Encapsulation is the concept of storing similar data and methods together in discrete classes. In many non–object-oriented languages, there is no association between where the data is and where the code is. This can increase the complexity of maintaining the code, because often the variables that the code is using are spread apart over the code base. Bugs in the code can be hard to find and resolve due to different remote procedures using the same variables.

Encapsulation tries to solve these problems. It lets you create code that is easier to read and maintain by allowing you to group related variables and methods together in classes. Object-oriented software is very modular, and encapsulation is used for creating these modules.

A well-encapsulated class has a single clear purpose. This class should contain only the methods and variables that are needed to fulfill its purpose. For example, if a class was intended to represent a television, it should contain variables such as `currentChannel`, `volume`, and `isPoweredOn`. A `Television` class would also have methods such as `setChannel(int channel)` or `setVolume(int volume)`. These variables and methods are all related. They are specific to the properties and actions needed to create a `Television` class. The `Television` class would not contain methods such as `playBluray()`; this should be contained in a separate `Bluray` class.

Encapsulation is about creating well-defined classes that have a clear purpose. These classes contain all the data and methods needed to perform their intended functions.

Encapsulation is defined slightly differently depending on the source. Sometimes the definition indicates that encapsulation is solely about storing related data and methods together in a class. Other places define encapsulation as also including information hiding of the implementation details. We will be using the first, more pure definition of encapsulation.

Access Modifiers

Access modifiers are keywords that define what can access methods and instance variables. The three access modifiers are `private`, `protected`, and `public`. These all change the default level of access. The default access level does not use a keyword and is assigned to a method or instance variable when neither `private`, `protected`, nor `public` is used, and the area is left blank. Access modifiers are an important concept in object-oriented languages. They allow the implementation details to be hidden in a class. The developer can choose specifically what parts of a class are accessible to other objects.

The OCA exam will focus on the different effects that each modifier has. The topics listed next will be covered in the following subsections:

- The access modifiers
- Information hiding
- Exposing object functionality

The Access Modifiers

As mentioned, Java uses three access modifiers: `private`, `protected`, and `public`. There is also the default access level, which is known as *package-private*. Each access level has different restrictions that allow or deny classes access to methods or instance variables. Access modifiers are also used when defining a class. This is beyond the scope of the OCA, so you can just assume all classes are `public`. The Java compiler will produce errors if a restricted method or instance variable is accessed by code that is unauthorized.

The `private` access modifier is the most restrictive and most commonly used access modifier. Any method or instance variable that is marked as `private` can be accessed only by other methods in the same class. Subclasses cannot access instance variables or methods that are `private`. The following is an example of the `private` keyword in use:

```
private int numberOfPoints;
private int calculateAverage() { … }
```

The default access level is the second most restrictive. It is often referred to as *package-private*. This access level allows access to its methods and instance variables from code that is in the same package. The default access level does not have a keyword to indicate it is in use. A method or instance variable is set to default when an access modifier is omitted. The following is an example of this access level in use:

```
int maxSpeed;
float calculateAcceleration() { … }
```

The `protected` access modifier is the third most restrictive. It is the same as the default access level but adds the ability of subclasses outside of the package to access its methods or instance variables. This means the methods that can access this data must either be in the same package (same as default) or be in a subclass of the class that contains the protected data. Remember that a subclass is a class that extends another class. The following is an example of the use of the `protected` access modifier:

```
protected boolean active;
protected char getFirstChar() { … }
```

The final access modifier is `public`. This is the least restrictive and second most common access modifier. The `public` access modifier provides no restriction to what can access its methods and instance variables. Any method can access a `public` method or instance variable regardless of which package it is contained in or which superclass it extends. An item marked as `public` is accessible to the world. The following is an example of using the `public` access modifier:

```
public int streetAddress;
public int findZipCode(){ … };
```

Information Hiding

Information hiding is the concept of hiding the implementation details of a class. Information hiding is achieved by using restrictive access modifiers. By hiding data, the developer can control how the data is accessed.

Instance variables are used to store the state of an object. If outside objects were able to access an object's entire set of instance variables, the risk of introducing bugs would be increased. A developer may create a new class that incorrectly tries to use the internal features of another class. Even if this approach works at first, it requires that the class's internal data structure not change. This concept also applies to methods. Not all methods need to be accessible by external classes. Often, a class will be composed of more methods used internally to perform tasks rather than methods designed for external objects.

SCENARIO & SOLUTION

You need to make an instance variable available only to the class in which it is declared. What access modifier would you use?	Use the `private` access modifier.
You need to make a method available only to other methods in the same package or a subclass of the class in which it is defined. What access modifier would you use?	Use the `protected` access modifier.
You need to make a method that is available to any other method in the application. What access modifier would you use?	Use the `public` access modifier.
You need to make an instance variable that is available only to other objects in the same package. What access modifier would you use?	Use the *package-private* modifier (default).

A benefit of hiding data can be seen in this scenario: A class contains an instance variable that must be between a certain range. An outside object may set this variable and disregard the proper range. To prevent this, the variable can be marked private and a public method can be used to set it. This method would contain code that would change its value only if the new value were valid.

When you're working on a project, a general rule is that every method and instance variable should use the most restrictive access modifier possible. This promotes good encapsulated design by protecting data and helps reduce the areas in which bugs can be inadvertently introduced.

Exposing Object Functionality

Once all of your internal implementation details are hidden, the class must have a set of public methods that expose its functionality to other objects. In most classes, all of the instance variables will use the private access modifier. The public methods should be the only required methods that other classes need to use this class. Any method used internally and not required by external classes should not be public.

Methods that are public can be compared to controls on the inside of a car. Only a few exist, but they allow the car to be driven. However, inside the car are many wires and mechanical controls that should not be altered and do not need to be altered to drive the car. These controls are like public methods, while the inside components are like private methods and instance variables.

Earlier in this chapter, interfaces were discussed. If a class implements an interface, it is required to implement each method in the interface as a public method. They are called "interfaces" because they represent the interface that other classes must use to work with this class. The public methods of any class can be thought of as an interface for the class. External objects have no knowledge of the underlying details of the class. They can see and use only the public interface that an object presents to them.

Setters and Getters

Setters and *getters* are the final concept of information hiding and encapsulation. As was discussed previously, it is good design to make all instance variables private. This means external classes have no way to access these variables. Sometimes an external object may need to read one of these variables to determine its state, or it may have to set the value. To achieve this, a public method is created for the variable, both to get and set the value. These are called *getters* and *setters*. They can be as simple as one line that only sets or returns a value.

The following example is a class that has one instance variable and a setter and getter:

```java
public class ScoreBoard {
  private int score;

  public int getScore() {
    return this.score;
  }

  public void setScore(int score) {
    this.score = score;
  }
}
```

Notice in this example a `private` instance variable named `score`. The two methods that are present are a getter and setter for the variable `score`. In this case, the class is giving read and write access to the variable via the methods. In some cases, a class may give only one or the other. The getter and setter in this example are simple and only set or return the value. However, if the class had to perform an action every time the `score` variable was changed, it could be done from the setter. For example, each time the score is changed, the class must record it to a log. This can be done in the setter. This is the benefit of keeping instance variables private. It gives control to the class as to how its instance variables are accessed.

Getters and setters are the standard way of creating access to a class's instance variables. When developers are working with a class, they expect to find getters and setters. They also expect the JavaBeans naming convention to be followed. When creating a getter, the name should start with a lowercase `get`, followed by the variable name with no spaces and the first letter capitalized. The one exception to this is when a `boolean` value is returned. In this case, instead of using `get`, `is` is used with the same rules being applied to the variable name. When creating a setter, a similar convention should be followed. A setter should start with the word `set`, followed by the variable name with the first letter capitalized.

Variable Type and Name	Getter and Setter Names
`int boatNumber`	`public int getBoatNumber()` `public void setBoatNumber(int boatNumber)`
`boolean boatRunning`	`public boolean isBoatRunning()` `public void setBoatRunning(boolean boatRunning)`
`Object position`	`public Object getPosition()` `public void setPosition(Object position)`

CERTIFICATION OBJECTIVE

Advanced Use of Classes with Inheritance and Encapsulation

Exam Objective 2.3   Know how to read or write to object fields

This section will conclude the chapter by revisiting all of the concepts that have been discussed and demonstrating them with code examples. Each example will be followed by a detailed explanation of what is being highlighted and how it works. Pay close attention to the examples. They should help reinforce all of the concepts already covered.

Java Access Modifiers Example

The following example is a class implemented with its implementation details hidden. It uses public methods to expose an interface, as well as getters and setters to allow access to its instance variables.

```java
public class PhoneBookEntry {
  private String name = "";
  private int phoneNumber = 0;
  private long lastUpdate = 0;

  public String getName() {
    return name;
  }

  public void setNameNumber(String name,int phoneNumber) {
    this.name = name;
    this.phoneNumber = phoneNumber;
    lastUpdate = System.currentTimeMillis();
  }

  public int getPhoneNumber() {
    return phoneNumber;
  }

  public void setPhoneNumber(int phoneNumber) {
```

```
      this.phoneNumber = phoneNumber;
      lastUpdate = System.currentTimeMillis();
    }
}
```

This example is a well-encapsulated class. It is a class that represents a basic phone book entry. It can store a name and a phone number. It also uses an instance variable to track the last time it was updated. All of the instance variables use the `private` access modifier. This means external classes are unable to read or modify them. It then uses getters and setters to modify the instance variables. In this example, there is no setter to set the `name` instance variable. To set the `name` instance variable, the object must also set the `phoneNumber` variable. This ensures that there is never a name without a phone number. If the instance variables were public, this class could not prevent another class from setting a name without a number.

This example also uses its setters to update the `lastUpdate` variable. This variable is used to track the last time this class had its information updated. By using the getters and setters, the class can guarantee that any time an external object updates a field via a setter, the `lastUpdate` variable will also be updated. The details of how `lastUpdate` becomes updated are invisible to external objects.

Inheritance with Concrete Classes Examples

A concrete class is the standard Java class. All of its methods are implemented and it can be instantiated. The following example uses a `Bicycle` class. The base class represents a basic bicycle. Another class represents a ten-speed bicycle. It is called `TenSpeedBicycle` and extends the `Bicycle` class. The `TenSpeedBicycle` class is able to inherit some of its functionality while overriding the parts of the base class that need to behave differently. The `TenSpeedBicycle` class has the ability to change its gear ratio in addition to what the `Bicycle` class can do.

```
public class Bicycle {
  private float wheelRPM;
  private int degreeOfTurn;

  public void pedalRPM(float pedalRPM){
    float gearRatio = 2f;
    this.wheelRPM = pedalRPM * gearRatio;
  }

  public void setDegreeOfTurn(int degreeOfTurn){
```

```
      this.degreeOfTurn = degreeOfTurn;
   }

   public float getWheelRPM() {
      return this.wheelRPM;
   }

   public int getDegreeOfTurn() {
      return this.degreeOfTurn;
   }
}
```

The `Bicycle` class is a concrete class and, therefore, can be instantiated. It represents a basic bicycle. It has two instance variables: `wheelRPM`, which is used to store the RPM of the wheels, and `degreeOfTurn`, which is used to store the degree the handlebars are turned. Each variable has a getter, and `degreeOfTurn` has a setter. The `wheelRPM` variable is set with the method `pedalRPM(float pedalRPM)`. This accepts an argument that contains the RPM of the pedals and then multiplies that by a set gear ratio to find and set the `wheelRPM` variable.

The next example is the `TenSpeedBicycle` class. It extends the `Bicycle` class:

```
public class TenSpeedBicycle extends Bicycle {
   private float gearRatio = 2f;
   private float wheelRPM;

   public void setGearRatio(float gearRatio) {
      this.gearRatio = gearRatio;
   }

   public void pedalRPM(float pedalRPM) {
      this.wheelRPM = pedalRPM * gearRatio;
   }

   public float getWheelRPM() {
      return this.wheelRPM;
   }
}
```

The `TenSpeedBicycle` class represents a bicycle that has ten different possible gear ratios. The regular `Bicycle` class cannot be used, because it has a fixed gear ratio. The `TenSpeedBicycle` class adds a method and instance variable so a gear ratio can be set. It also overrides the `wheelRPM` variable. This must be done because the `Bicycle` class has no setter to set that variable directly. The `TenSpeedBicycle` class also overrides the `pedalRPM(float pedalRPM)` method. In the `Bicycle` class version of this method, the gear ratio was fixed. In the newer version, it uses the gear ratio that can be set. To retrieve the `wheelRPM` variable, the getter must also be overridden. This is because the original version of this method can return only the instance variable that is in its same class.

The next segment of code demonstrates both classes in use.

```
public class Main {
  public static void main(String[] args) {
    System.out.println("Starting...");
    System.out.println("Creating a bicycle...");
    Bicycle b = new Bicycle();
    b.setDegreeOfTurn(0);
    b.pedalRPM(50);
    System.out.println("Turning: " + b.getDegreeOfTurn());
    System.out.println("Wheel RPM: " + b.getWheelRPM());
    System.out.println("Creating a 10 speed bicycle...");
    TenSpeedBicycle tb = new TenSpeedBicycle();
    tb.setDegreeOfTurn(10);
    tb.setGearRatio(3f);
    tb.pedalRPM(40);
    System.out.println("Turning: " + tb.getDegreeOfTurn());
    System.out.println("Wheel RPM: " + tb.getWheelRPM());
  }
}
```

This code prints information to standard output for each step it takes. First, it creates a `Bicycle` object. It then sets the degree of turn to 0 and the pedal RPM to 50. The code then prints out the degree of turn, which will be 0, and the wheel RPM, which will be 100, since the gear ratio is 2 (2 × 50). Next, a `TenSpeedBicycle` object is created. This object has its degree of turn set to 10, its gear ratio set to 3, and its pedal RPM set to 40. Finally, this object prints out its degree of turn, which is 10, and its wheel RPM, which is 120 (3 × 40). Notice that the `TenSpeedBicycle` object's `getDegreeOfTurn()` and `setDegreeOfTurn()` were inherited from the base class `Bicycle`.

This is the output of the program after it was compiled and run:

```
Starting...
Creating a bicycle...
Turning: 0
Wheel RPM: 100.0
Creating a 10 speed bicycle...
Turning: 10
Wheel RPM: 120.0
```

FIGURE 7-3

Basic inheritance

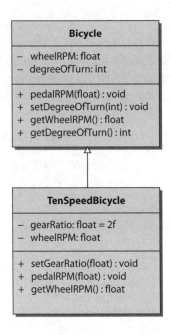

This example shows most of the basic concepts of inheritance, as you can see in Figure 7-3.

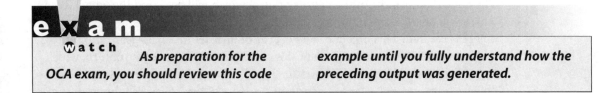

e x a m

ⓦ a t c h

As preparation for the OCA exam, you should review this code *example until you fully understand how the preceding output was generated.*

Inheritance with Abstract Classes Examples

This example will demonstrate an abstract class, a Java class that cannot be instantiated. Another concrete class must extend it. An abstract class may contain both concrete methods that have implementations and abstract methods that must be implemented by the subclass.

This example creates a plant simulator. It has a `Plant` abstract class that is extended by a `MapleTree` class and `Tulip` class. The `Plant` class is a good abstract class, because a plant is an abstract, or general, thing. Plants all share some characteristics that can be placed in this class. Each specific class can then contain the implementation details. The following code segment is the abstract Plant class:

```
public abstract class Plant {
  private int age=0;
  private int height=0;

  public int getAge() {
    return age;
  }

  public void addYearToAge() {
    age++;
  }

  public int getHeight() {
    return height;
  }

  public void setHeight(int height) {
    this.height = height;
  }

  abstract public void doSpring();
  abstract public void doSummer();
  abstract public void doFall();
  abstract public void doWinter();
}
```

This abstract class offers a very simplistic view of what represents a plant. It contains two instance variables that every type of plant would use: age and height. There is both a getter and setter for height and a getter for age. The age instance variable has a method that is used to increment it each year.

The Plant class has four abstract methods. Each of these methods represents the actions that a plant must take during the specified season. These actions are specific to the type of plant and, therefore, cannot be generalized. Having them declared in the abstract Plant class guarantees that any class that extends the Plant class must implement them.

The next class is the MapleTree class:

```
public class MapleTree extends Plant {
  private static final int AMOUNT_TO_GROW_IN_ONE_GROWING_SEASON = 2;
```

```
/*
 * A tree grows upwards a certain number of feet a year.
 * A tree does not die down to ground level during the winter.
 */
  private void grow() {
    int currentHeight = getHeight();
    setHeight(currentHeight + AMOUNT_TO_GROW_IN_ONE_GROWING_SEASON);
  }

  public void doSpring() {
    grow();
    addYearToAge();
    System.out.println("Spring: The maple tree is starting to grow " +
        "leaves and new branches");
    System.out.println("\tCurrent Age: " + getAge() + " " +
        "Current Height: " + getHeight());
  }

  public void doSummer() {
    grow();
    System.out.println("Summer: The maple tree is continuing to grow");
    System.out.println("\tCurrent Age: " + getAge() + " " +
        "Current Height: " + getHeight());
  }

  public void doFall() {
    System.out.println("Fall:   The maple tree has stopped growing" +
        " and is losing its leaves");
    System.out.println("\tCurrent Age: " + getAge() + " " +
        "Current Height: " + getHeight());
  }

  public void doWinter() {
    System.out.println("Winter: The maple tree is dormant");
    System.out.println("\tCurrent Age: " + getAge() + " " +
        "Current Height: " + getHeight());
  }
}
```

The MapleTree class extends the Plant class and is used as a simple representation of a maple tree. Because the Plant class is abstract, the MapleTree class must implement all of its abstract methods. The MapleTree class contains one variable named AMOUNT_TO_GROW_IN_ONE_GROWING_SEASON. This variable is marked as private static final int. This is how Java declares a constant. These details are beyond the scope of the OCA exam. Just consider this a constant that is a primitive int and is private. This variable is used to set the amount of growth that a maple tree completes during a growing season.

The MapleTree class contains a method to grow, called grow(). This method is used to add the new height to the current height. The next four methods are all methods that are required to be implemented. These abstract methods are declared in the Plant class, with each one representing a different season. When they are invoked, they perform any required action that is needed for that season and then print two lines to standard output. The first line of text states what season it is and what the maple tree is doing. The next line displays the values of the age and height variables.

The next class is the Tulip class:

```
public class Tulip extends Plant {
  private static final int AMOUNT_TO_GROW_IN_ONE_GROWING_SEASON = 1;

/*
 * A tulip grows each year to the same height. During
 * the winter they die down to ground level.
 */
  private void grow() {
    int currentHeight = getHeight();
    setHeight(currentHeight + AMOUNT_TO_GROW_IN_ONE_GROWING_SEASON);
  }

  private void dieDownForWinter(){
    setHeight(0);
  }

  public void doSpring() {
    grow();
    addYearToAge();
    System.out.println("Spring: The tulip is starting to grow " +
        "up from the ground");
    System.out.println("\tCurrent Age: " + getAge() + " " +
        "Current Height: " + getHeight());
  }

  public void doSummer() {
    System.out.println("Summer: The tulip has stopped growing " +
        "and is flowering");
    System.out.println("\tCurrent Age: " + getAge() + " " +
        "Current Height: " + getHeight());
  }
```

```
   public void doFall() {
     System.out.println("Fall:    The tulip begins to wilt");
     System.out.println("\tCurrent Age: " + getAge() + " " +
        "Current Height: " + getHeight());
   }

   public void doWinter() {
     dieDownForWinter();
     System.out.println("Winter: The tulip is dormant underground");
     System.out.println("\tCurrent Age: " + getAge() + " " +
        "Current Height: " + getHeight());
   }
 }
```

The `Tulip` class is intended to represent a tulip. It extends the `Plant` class and, therefore, must also implement all its abstract methods. Like the `MapleTree` class, the `Tulip` class also has a constant that is used to store the amount of growth per growing season.

The `Tulip` class has two private methods: a `grow()` method that is like the one present in the `MapleTree` class, and a `dieDownForWinter()` method that is used to reset the `height` to `0` when the tulip loses all of its leaves during the winter.

The last four methods in the class are the abstract methods from the `Plant` class. Each season method performs the needed actions first, such as grow, die down, or age. It then prints to standard output a message about what it is doing and what season it is. The second line of text contains the values of the `age` and `height` variables.

The final code segment is the `main()` method that uses both the `Tulip` and `MapleTree` classes:

```
public class Simulator{
  public static void main(String[] args) {
    System.out.println("Creating a maple tree and tulip...");
    MapleTree mapleTree = new MapleTree();
    Tulip tulip = new Tulip();
    System.out.println("Entering a loop to simulate 3 years");
    for (int i = 0; i < 3; i++) {
      mapleTree.doSpring();
      tulip.doSpring();
      mapleTree.doSummer();
      tulip.doSummer();
      mapleTree.doFall();
      tulip.doFall();
```

```
        mapleTree.doWinter();
        tulip.doWinter();
    }
  }
}
```

First, an object of each type is created. Then a `for` loop invokes the methods for all four seasons for each object. This loop represents a simple simulation program. Each time through the loop represents one year. Both objects age and grow from year to year.

When the preceding code is executed, it will produce the output shown next:

```
Creating a maple tree and tulip...
Entering a loop to simulate 3 years
Spring: The maple tree is starting to grow leaves and new branches
        Current Age: 1 Current Height: 2
Spring: The tulip is starting to grow up from the ground
        Current Age: 1 Current Height: 1
Summer: The maple tree is continuing to grow
        Current Age: 1 Current Height: 4
Summer: The tulip has stopped growing and is flowering
        Current Age: 1 Current Height: 1
Fall:   The maple tree has stopped growing and is losing its leaves
        Current Age: 1 Current Height: 4
Fall:   The tulip begins to wilt
        Current Age: 1 Current Height: 1
Winter: The maple tree is dormant
        Current Age: 1 Current Height: 4
Winter: The tulip is dormant underground
        Current Age: 1 Current Height: 0
Spring: The maple tree is starting to grow leaves and new branches
        Current Age: 2 Current Height: 6
Spring: The tulip is starting to grow up from the ground
        Current Age: 2 Current Height: 1
Summer: The maple tree is continuing to grow
        Current Age: 2 Current Height: 8
Summer: The tulip has stopped growing and is flowering
        Current Age: 2 Current Height: 1
Fall:   The maple tree has stopped growing and is losing its leaves
        Current Age: 2 Current Height: 8
Fall:   The tulip begins to wilt
        Current Age: 2 Current Height: 1
Winter: The maple tree is dormant
        Current Age: 2 Current Height: 8
Winter: The tulip is dormant underground
```

```
                Current Age: 2 Current Height: 0
   Spring: The maple tree is starting to grow leaves and new branches
                Current Age: 3 Current Height: 10
   Spring: The tulip is starting to grow up from the ground
                Current Age: 3 Current Height: 1
   Summer: The maple tree is continuing to grow
                Current Age: 3 Current Height: 12
   Summer: The tulip has stopped growing and is flowering
                Current Age: 3 Current Height: 1
   Fall:   The maple tree has stopped growing and is losing its leaves
                Current Age: 3 Current Height: 12
   Fall:   The tulip begins to wilt
                Current Age: 3 Current Height: 1
   Winter: The maple tree is dormant
                Current Age: 3 Current Height: 12
   Winter: The tulip is dormant underground
                Current Age: 3 Current Height: 0
```

Notice how the maple tree continues to grow each year. The tulip, however, must regrow each year. Both the Tulip and the MapleTree objects have access to the getAge() and getHeight() methods that were implemented in the abstract Plant class. Review the code and the output thoroughly. Your understanding of the examples in this section will better prepare you for the OCA exam.

EXERCISE 7-1

Add Functionality to the Plant Simulator

This exercise will use the previous plant simulator and add new functionality to it.

1. Copy the plant simulator into the text editor or IDE of your choice.

2. Compile and run the example to ensure that the code has been copied correctly.

3. Add a new class called Rose that will represent a rose. Use the Plant base class and implement all of the required methods.

4. Add your new class into the simulator and run the application.

Interface Example

This final example involves interfaces. An *interface* is a public set of methods that must be implemented by the class that uses the interface. By using an interface, a class is declaring that it implements the functionality defined by the interface. New for Java 8 is the ability to define default methods and static methods in an interface. Default methods are fully implemented methods that will be used if the method is not defined in the class that is using the interface. Static methods are methods that belong to the interface and are useful for helper and utility methods.

This example includes two interfaces. One is called `Printer` and provides a public interface that printers should implement. Any class that implements `Printer` can be said to have the ability to print. The other interface in this example is `Fax`. It provides the public interface for a faxing capability. Finally, this example has a class that implements both interfaces. This class represents an all-in-one printer/fax machine. The class is called `PrinterFaxCombo`.

In this simple example, the printer can do two things: it can print a file with the `printFile(File f)` method, and it can check the ink levels with the `getInkLevel()` method. Notice that the `getInkLevel()` method has a default implementation defined.

```
public interface Printer {
  public void printFile(File f);
  default public int getInkLevel(){
    return 0;
  }
}
```

The next interface is for a fax machine. This simple fax machine can send a file with the `sendFax(File f,int number)` method or return a fax as an `Object` with the `getReceivedFaxes()` method.

```
public interface Fax {
  public void sendFax(File f,int number);
  public Object getReceivedFaxes();
}
```

The following is the `PrinterFaxCombo` class. This class implements both interfaces.

```
public class PrinterFaxCombo implements Fax, Printer{
  private Object incomingFax;
  private int inkLevel;

  public void sendFax(File f, int number) {
    dialNumber(number);
    faxFile(f);
  }
```

```
public Object getReceivedFaxes() {
  return incomingFax;
}

public void printFile(File f) {
  sendFileToPrinter(f);
}

public int getInkLevel() {
  return inkLevel;
}

private boolean dialNumber(int number){
  boolean success = true;
  /* Dial number set success to false if it is not successful */
  return success;
}

private void faxFile(File f){
  /* Send the File f as a fax */
}

private void sendFileToPrinter(File f){
  /* Print the File f */
}

/*
 * This class would contain many more methods to
 * implement all of this functionality.
 */
}
```

The `PrinterFaxCombo` class is a simplistic version of a printer that can also fax. The class is not fully implemented, but the comments in the empty methods should explain the purpose of each method. The important point of this example is that this class implements both the `Printer` and `Fax` interfaces. By implementing the interfaces, the `PrinterFaxCombo` class is obligated to implement each method they contain that does not have a default implementation. Implementing interfaces allows an external object to know that this class provides the functionality of a printer and fax machine. Every class that implements the `Printer` interface provides printing functionality and has the same public interface. This creates modular code and allows easy swapping in and out of different classes based on the needs of the application. Interfaces also allow for polymorphism, which will be discussed in detail in Chapter 8.

CERTIFICATION SUMMARY

This chapter has been about class inheritance and encapsulation. *Inheritance* is an important concept in Java. It is the term used to describe one class gaining the methods and instance variables of a parent class. This allows a developer to find commonality between classes and create a general parent class that each specific class can extend, or inherit, to then gain common functionality. This promotes code reuse.

Concrete classes and abstract classes are both able to be extended to create subclasses. The class that is extended is then considered the superclass, or base class. A class may extend only one class. Concrete classes are the standard class type with each method implemented. A class that extends a concrete class gains all of its visible methods. Abstract classes must be extended and cannot be instantiated in code. They contain a mixture of implemented and abstract, or unimplemented, methods. When an abstract class is extended, all of its abstract methods must be implemented by the concrete subclass.

Interfaces are a set of primarily unimplemented methods. When a class implements an interface, that class must then implement each method that is in the interface with the exception of methods that already contain a default implantation. Interfaces are used to define a predetermined set of exposed methods. Classes may implement as many interfaces as they need as long as all methods are then implemented in that class.

Next, Java access modifiers were discussed. The `public`, `private`, `protected`, and default access modifiers are used to prefix a method or instance variable. The `public` access modifier allows any code to access the method or instance variable that it prefixes. The `private` access modifier allows code only within its own class to access the method or instance variable. The default, or package-private, modifier restricts access only to classes in the same package. The `protected` modifier allows any class in the same package, or in a subclass, to have access.

Another major concept covered in this chapter was encapsulation. Encapsulation is the design concept of storing related code and variables together. It can also lead to the practice of information hiding, which allows access to a class only through a public interface while hiding the rest of the implementation details. A public interface is created by the methods that have the `public` access modifier. Implementation details should be hidden by using the `private`, `protected`, or default access modifier. Getters and setters are normally used to access the hidden data. A getter is a simple method that returns an instance variable, and a setter is a method that sets an instance variable to the value passed to it as an argument.

This chapter concluded with code examples. These examples are important for you to understand because the OCA exam will have questions based on a given code segment.

TWO-MINUTE DRILL

Implement and Use Inheritance and Class Type

☐ Inheritance is used to place common code in a base class.

☐ Inheritance makes code more modular and easier to maintain.

☐ The `extends` keyword is used for a class to extend or inherit another class, or for an interface to extend or inherit another interface.

☐ When a class inherits another class, it gains access to all of its `public` and `protected` methods and instance variables. If the two classes are in the same package, it also gains access to any methods or instance variables that have the default, or package-private, access.

☐ The class that is being inherited is called the base class or superclass.

☐ The class that gains the functionality is called the subclass.

☐ A method in a superclass can be overridden by the subclass having a method with an identical signature.

☐ The `super` keyword can be used to access the overridden method.

☐ A class can extend only one other class.

☐ A concrete class can be instantiated; all of its methods must have been implemented.

☐ An abstract class cannot be instantiated. It must be extended and may or may not contain abstract methods.

☐ When a concrete class extends an abstract class, all of the abstract methods must be implemented.

☐ An interface is used to define a public interface that a class must have.

☐ The keyword `implements` is used to implement an interface.

☐ A class may implement multiple interfaces by using a comma-delimited list.

☐ A class that implements an interface must implement all of the methods contained in the interface that do not have a default implementation defined.

Understand Encapsulation Principles

☐ Access modifiers can be used to restrict access to methods and instance variables.

☐ The `public` access modifier allows any class to access the public method or instance variable.

☐ The `protected` access modifier allows classes that are in the same package or are a subclass to have access to the method or instance variable.

☐ The default, or package-private, access allows classes that are in the same package to access the method or instance variable.

☐ The `private` access modifier allows only methods in the same class to access the private method or instance variable.

☐ Information hiding is the concept of using restrictive access modifiers to hide the implementation details of a class.

☐ Both getters and setters should follow the JavaBeans naming convention. They should start with `get`, `set`, or `is`, followed by the variable name, starting with a capital letter.

Advanced Use of Classes with Inheritance and Encapsulation

☐ When creating methods or instance variables, the most restrictive access modifier possible should be used.

☐ A getter is used to access private instance variables.

☐ A setter is used to set private instance variables.

SELF TEST

Implement and Use Inheritance and Class Type

1. What contains methods and instance variables and can be instantiated?
   A. Concrete class
   B. Abstract class
   C. Java class
   D. Interface

2. What is used to define a public interface?
   A. Concrete class
   B. Abstract class
   C. Java class
   D. Interface

3. What can contain unimplemented methods and instance variables and cannot be instantiated?
   A. Concrete class
   B. Abstract class
   C. Java class

4. Inheritance provides which of the following? (Choose all that apply.)
   A. Allows faster execution times since methods can inherit processor time from superclasses
   B. Allows developers to place general code in a class that more specialized classes can gain through inheritance
   C. Promotes code reuse
   D. Is an automated process to transfer old code to the latest Java version

5. A class being inherited is referred to by what name? (Choose all that apply.)
   A. Subclass
   B. Superclass
   C. Base class
   D. Super duper class

6. Must an abstract class implement all of the abstract methods inherited from another abstract class?

   A. Yes.

   B. No, but it must implement at least one method.

   C. No; it does not have to implement any methods.

   D. No, but it must implement any methods that are defined in its immediate superclass.

7. Which keyword can be used to access overridden methods?

   A. `super`

   B. `transient`

   C. `top`

   D. `upper`

8. If class A extends class B, what terms can be used to describe class A? (Choose all that apply.)

   A. Subclass

   B. Superclass

   C. Base class

   D. Parent class

   E. Child class

Understand Encapsulation Principles

Refer to this class for the following two questions.

```
public class Account {
   private int money;

   public int getMoney() {
      return this.money;
   }

   public void setMoney(int money) {
      this.money = money;
   }
}
```

9. In the code segment, what is the method `getMoney()` considered?

   A. Get method

   B. Access method

   C. Getter method

   D. Instance variable method

10. In the code segment, what is the method `setMoney(int money)` considered?
    A. Set method
    B. Access method
    C. Setter method
    D. Instance variable method

11. Which of the following defines information hiding?
    A. Information hiding is about hiding as much detail about your class as possible so others can't steal it.
    B. Information hiding is about hiding implementation details and protecting variables from being used the wrong way.
    C. Information hiding is used to obscure the interworking of your class so external classes must use the public interface.

12. What access modifier is used to make the instance variable or method available only to the class in which it is defined?
    A. `public`
    B. `private`
    C. `protected`
    D. package-private (default)

13. What access modifier is used for methods that were defined in an interface?
    A. `public`
    B. `private`
    C. `protected`
    D. package-private (default)

14. Unless there is a particular reason not to use it, what access modifier, if any, should be used on all instance variables?
    A. `public`
    B. `private`
    C. `protected`
    D. package-private (default)

15. The `private` and `protected` access modifiers can be used with which entities? (Choose all that apply.)
    A. Classes
    B. Interfaces
    C. Constructors
    D. Methods
    E. Data members

Advanced Use of Classes with Inheritance and Encapsulation

16. What is the proper signature for class X if it inherits class Z?

   A. `public class X inherits Z{ … }`

   B. `public class X extends Z{ … }`

   C. `public class X implements Z{ … }`

17. How many classes can a class extend directly?

   A. Zero

   B. One

   C. Two

   D. As many as it needs

18. How many interfaces can a class implement directly?

   A. Zero

   B. One

   C. Two

   D. As many as it needs

19. Consider the following UML illustration for assistance with this question:

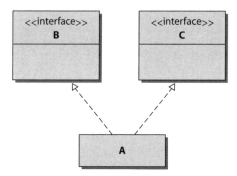

   What is the proper signature for class A if it implements interfaces B and C?

   A. `public class A implements B, implements C{ … }`

   B. `public class A implements B, C{ … }`

   C. `public class A interface B, interface C{ … }`

   D. `public class A interface B, C{ … }`

   E. `public class A extends B, C{ … }`

20. Consider the following UML illustration for assistance with this question:

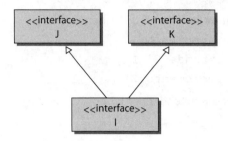

What is the proper signature for interface I to inherit interfaces J and K?

A. `public interface I extends J, K{ … }`
B. `public interface I implements J, K{ … }`
C. `public interface I implements J, implements K{ … }`
D. `public interface I interface J, K{ … }`

SELF TEST ANSWERS

Implement and Use Inheritance and Class Type

1. What contains methods and instance variables and can be instantiated?
   A. Concrete class
   B. Abstract class
   C. Java class
   D. Interface

   Answer:

   ☑ **A**. A concrete class is the standard Java class that is used to create objects.
   ☒ **B, C**, and **D** are incorrect. **B** is incorrect because an abstract class cannot be instantiated. **C** is incorrect because a Java class is a made-up term. **D** is incorrect because an interface cannot be instantiated.

2. What is used to define a public interface?
   A. Concrete class
   B. Abstract class
   C. Java class
   D. Interface

   Answer:

   ☑ **D**. An interface is used to define a public list of methods that must be implemented by the class. This represents a public interface.
   ☒ **A, B**, and **C** are incorrect. **A** is incorrect because a concrete class is used to build objects. **B** is incorrect because abstract classes are used to define abstract methods for other classes to override. **C** is incorrect because a Java class is a made-up term.

3. What can contain unimplemented methods and instance variables and cannot be instantiated?
   A. Concrete class
   B. Abstract class
   C. Java class

Answer:

☑ **B**. An abstract class must always be extended; it cannot be instantiated to create an object. It can contain implemented and unimplemented methods.

☒ **A** and **C** are incorrect. **A** is incorrect because a concrete class is not able to have any unimplemented methods. **C** is incorrect because a Java class is a made-up term.

4. Inheritance provides which of the following? (Choose all that apply.)
   A. Allows faster execution times since methods can inherit processor time from superclasses
   B. Allows developers to place general code in a class that more specialized classes can gain through inheritance
   C. Promotes code reuse
   D. Is an automated process to transfer old code to the latest Java version

Answer:

☑ **B** and **C**. Both statements are true about inheritance.

☒ **A** and **D** are incorrect. **A** is incorrect because inheritance has no effect on processor scheduling. **D** is incorrect because inheritance has no relationship to the Java version.

5. A class being inherited is referred to by what name? (Choose all that apply.)
   A. Subclass
   B. Superclass
   C. Base class
   D. Super duper class

Answer:

☑ **B** and **C**. The class that is inherited is the superclass or base class in reference to the class that extends it.

☒ **A** and **D** are incorrect. **A** is incorrect because the subclass is the class that inherits from another. **D** is incorrect because this is a made-up term.

6. Must an abstract class implement all of the abstract methods inherited from another abstract class?

   A. Yes.
   B. No, but it must implement at least one method.
   C. No; it does not have to implement any methods.
   D. No, but it must implement any methods that are defined in its immediate superclass.

   Answer:

   ☑ **C.** An abstract class does not have to implement all of the abstract methods inherited from another abstract class because it is also abstract.
   ☒ **A, B,** and **D** are incorrect. A concrete class must implement all of the methods.

7. Which keyword can be used to access overridden methods?

   A. `super`
   B. `transient`
   C. `top`
   D. `upper`

   Answer:

   ☑ **A.** The `super` keyword can be used to access overridden methods.
   ☒ **B, C,** and **D** are incorrect. **B** is incorrect because the `transient` keyword is used when serializing objects. **C** is incorrect because there is no `top` keyword. **D** is incorrect because there is no `upper` keyword.

8. If class A extends class B, what terms can be used to describe class A? (Choose all that apply.)

   A. Subclass
   B. Superclass
   C. Base class
   D. Parent class
   E. Child class

> Answer:
>
> ☑ **A** and **E**. A class that gains the functionality of other classes is called either a subclass or child class.
>
> ☒ **B, C**, and **D** are incorrect. Superclass, base class, and parent class are all terms to describe the class that is being inherited.

Understand Encapsulation Principles

Refer to this class for the following two questions.

```
public class Account {
  private int money;

  public int getMoney() {
    return this.money;
  }

  public void setMoney(int money) {
    this.money = money;
  }
}
```

9. In the code segment, what is the method getMoney() considered?
   A. Get method
   B. Access method
   C. Getter method
   D. Instance variable method

> Answer:
>
> ☑ **C**. This is a getter. Getters are used to retrieve a private instance variable. The name of a getter method is always get followed by the variable name with a capital letter. If the variable is a boolean, the get is replaced with is.
>
> ☒ **A, B**, and **D** are incorrect. None of these answers is a typical Java term.

10. In the code segment, what is the method `setMoney(int money)` considered?
  A. Set method
  B. Access method
  C. Setter method
  D. Instance variable method

Answer:

☑ **C.** This is a setter. Setters are used to set a `private` instance variable. The name of a setter method is always `set`, followed by the variable name with a capital letter. They take one argument and use this to set the variable.
☒ **A, B,** and **D** are incorrect. None of these answers is a typical Java term.

11. Which of the following defines information hiding?
  A. Information hiding is about hiding as much detail about your class as possible so others can't steal it.
  B. Information hiding is about hiding implementation details and protecting variables from being used the wrong way.
  C. Information hiding is used to obscure the interworking of your class so external classes must use the public interface.

Answer:

☑ **B.** Good class design hides as many methods and instance variables as possible. This is done by using the `private` access modifier. This is so external objects do not try to interact with the object in ways the developer has not intended. Hiding information makes code easier to maintain and more modular.
☒ **A** and **C** are incorrect. **A** is incorrect because information hiding has nothing to do with protecting your code from others. **C** is incorrect because access modifiers should be used to force external classes to use the proper public interface.

12. What access modifier is used to make the instance variable or method available only to the class in which it is defined?
  A. `public`
  B. `private`
  C. `protected`
  D. package-private (default)

Answer:

☑ **B.** The `private` access modifier is used to allow only the methods in the class to access the method or instance variable.

☒ **A, C,** and **D** are incorrect. **A** is incorrect because `public` would make the instance variable available to every class. **C** is incorrect because `protected` would make the instance variable available to any subclass or class in the same package. **D** is incorrect because package-private, or the default access level, would make the instance variable available to any other class in the same package.

13. What access modifier is used for methods that were defined in an interface?
    A. `public`
    B. `private`
    C. `protected`
    D. package-private (default)

Answer:

☑ **A.** The `public` access modifier is used when implementing methods from an interface. Furthermore, the Java Language Specification states that it is permitted, but discouraged as a matter of style, to redundantly specify the public and/or abstract modifier for a method declared in an interface.

☒ **B, C,** and **D** are incorrect. All three of these are incorrect because they limit the accessibility of the method and therefore would not be appropriate for an interface.

14. Unless there is a particular reason not to use it, what access modifier, if any, should be used on all instance variables?
    A. `public`
    B. `private`
    C. `protected`
    D. package-private (default)

Answer:

☑ **B.** Instance variables should have the most restrictive modifier compatible with their intended use. The `private` modifier is the most restrictive and therefore the correct answer.

☒ **A, C,** and **D** are incorrect. All of these access modifiers, including the default access level, are less restrictive than `private`.

15. The `private` and `protected` access modifiers can be used with which entities? (Choose all that apply.)
- A. Classes
- B. Interfaces
- C. Constructors
- D. Methods
- E. Data members

Answer:

☑ **C, D**, and **E.** The `private` and `protected` access modifiers can be used with constructors, methods, data members, and inner classes.

☒ **A** and **B** are incorrect. The `private` and `protected` access modifiers cannot be used with classes and interfaces.

Advanced Use of Classes with Inheritance and Encapsulation

16. What is the proper signature for class X if it inherits class Z?
- A. `public class X inherits Z{ ... }`
- B. `public class X extends Z{ ... }`
- C. `public class X implements Z{ ... }`

Answer:

☑ **B.** The `extends` keyword is used to inherit a class.

☒ **A** and **C** are incorrect. **A** is incorrect because `inherits` is not a valid Java keyword. **C** is incorrect because the `implements` keyword is used for interfaces, not classes.

17. How many classes can a class extend directly?
- A. Zero
- B. One
- C. Two
- D. As many as it needs

Answer:

☑ **B**. A class can extend only one other class. However, it is possible to have one class extend a class that extends another class, and so on.

☒ **A**, **C**, and **D** are incorrect.

18. How many interfaces can a class implement directly?

A. Zero

B. One

C. Two

D. As many as it needs

Answer:

☑ **D**. A class can implement as many interfaces as it needs.

☒ **A**, **B**, and **C** are incorrect.

19. Consider the following UML illustration for assistance with this question:

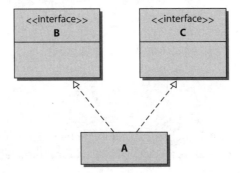

What is the proper signature for class A if it implements interfaces B and C?

A. `public class A implements B, implements C{ … }`

B. `public class A implements B, C{ … }`

C. `public class A interface B, interface C{ … }`

D. `public class A interface B, C{ … }`

E. `public class A extends B, C{ … }`

Answer:

☑ **B.** A class uses the keyword `implements` to implement an interface. To implement multiple interfaces, the interface names should appear in a comma-delimited list after the keyword `implements`.

☒ **A, C, D,** and **E** are incorrect. **A** is incorrect because the `implements` keyword should not be included more than once. **C** is incorrect because the `implements` keyword should be used instead of `interface`, and it should be used only once. **D** is incorrect because `implements` should be used instead of `interface`. **E** is incorrect because `extends` is used for classes, not interfaces; `implements` should be used instead.

20. Consider the following UML illustration for assistance with this question:

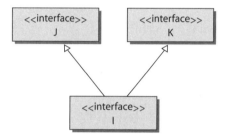

What is the proper signature for interface I to inherit interfaces J and K?
A. `public interface I extends J, K{ … }`
B. `public interface I implements J, K{ … }`
C. `public interface I implements J, implements K{ … }`
D. `public interface I interface J, K{ … }`

Answer:

☑ **A.** An interface can also inherit other interfaces. Unlike classes, interfaces can inherit or extend as many other interfaces as needed. An interface uses the keyword `extends`, followed by a comma-delimited list of all the other interfaces it wants to extend.

☒ **B, C,** and **D** are incorrect. **B** is incorrect because only classes implement interfaces. An interface `extends` other interfaces. **C** is incorrect because `extends` should be used, and only once. **D** is incorrect because the `interface` keyword is not used correctly.

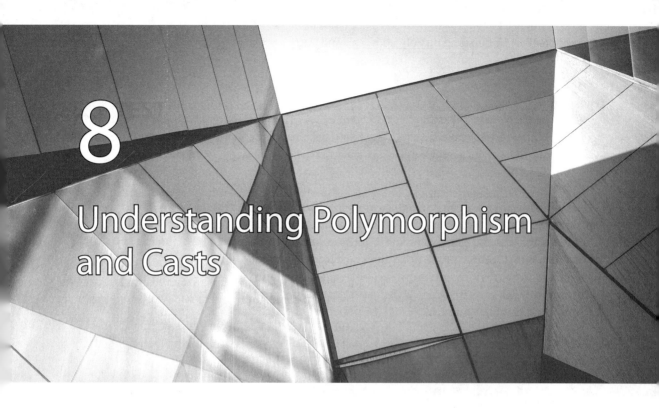

8

Understanding Polymorphism and Casts

CERTIFICATION OBJECTIVES

- Understand Polymorphism

- Understand Casting

 Two-Minute Drill

Q&A Self Test

T he OCA exam will expect you to have a firm understanding of what polymorphism is and when it should be used. The exam will present scenarios using polymorphism in correct and incorrect ways.

Casting will also be covered on the OCA exam. On the surface, casting looks similar to polymorphism; however, it is very different. The OCA exam is likely to ask questions that require you to have a solid understanding of when and how casting can be used.

At the conclusion of this chapter you should understand how to manipulate the type of an object using either polymorphism or casting. You should also know when each is needed or not needed. These are core concepts that will be asked directly on the OCA exam.

CERTIFICATION OBJECTIVE

Understand Polymorphism

Exam Objective   Develop code that demonstrates the use of polymorphism, including overriding and object type versus reference type

Polymorphism is a fundamental aspect of object-oriented programming languages, including Java. Polymorphism allows the developer to write generic code that is flexible and that allows for easier code reuse, another fundamental object-oriented principle.

Concepts of Polymorphism

The word *polymorphism* comes from the Greeks and roughly means "many forms." In Java, polymorphism means that one object can take the form or place of an object of a different type. Polymorphism can exist when one class inherits another. It can also exist when a class implements an interface. This section will describe how polymorphism can apply in both cases. Finally, this section will demonstrate what polymorphism looks like in Java code.

The following topics will be discussed:

- Polymorphism via class inheritance
- Polymorphism via implementing interfaces
- Polymorphism in code

Polymorphism via Class Inheritance

A more specific object can polymorphically take the place of a more general object. You'll recall that you can extend one object to create a more specific object that inherits the original object's functionality in addition to the new functionality. For example, suppose a method requires a Human object. When the Child and Adult classes extend the Human class, they would each inherit all of the functionality of Human, plus all the more specific functionality of their specific classes. The Child and Adult objects are guaranteed to inherit all of the methods of the Human object. Therefore, both the Child and Adult objects would satisfy any operation that required a Human object. To continue the example further, suppose the Shannon and Colleen classes each extend the Adult class. Each of the objects created from the Shannon and Colleen classes would inherit the functionality of the more general Adult and Human classes and could therefore be used anywhere a Human or Adult object is required.

Polymorphism utilizes the *is-a* relationship. In Figure 8-1, the Child object *is-a* Human object, and the Adult object *is-a* Human object. Both Child and Adult are specific types of a Human object. Furthermore, the Shannon object *is-an* Adult object and *is-a* Human object. This is also true for the Colleen object.

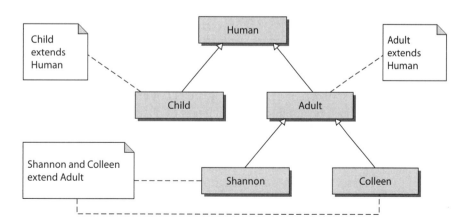

FIGURE 8-1

Polymorphic objects

The Shannon object is not only a more specific type of Adult object, but it's also a more specific type of Human object. Any subclass object is a more specific type of its parent object. The *is-a* relationship is created when an object inherits, or extends, another. Any object that extends another object can be said to have an *is-a* relationship to the object that it extends. Any object that has an *is-a* relationship with another can polymorphically be used as that object.

When an object is polymorphically acting as another object, the more specific object is restricted to using only the public interface of the more general object. In the preceding example, when the Adult object is used as a Human object, only the methods that are available in the Human class can be used. This is because the Java code that is using the Adult object as a Human object has no knowledge that this Human object is really an Adult object. This is the benefit of polymorphism. The Java code does not always have to be aware of the specifics of an object. If a general object meets the needs of a method, Java does not care whether the object is general or specific. The only requirement is that the object has an *is-a* relationship with the object that the method requires.

This relationship is unidirectional, so the more specific object can take the place of a general object, but not vice versa. For example, if an Adult object were needed, a more general Human object would not be able to provide all of the functionality of an Adult object.

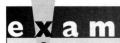

Polymorphism via Implementing Interfaces

The application of polymorphism is not limited to class inheritance. Polymorphism can also be applied to the objects of classes that implement interfaces. When a class implements an interface, it is then required to implement all of the methods that the interface contains. By doing this, the class is guaranteed to have the functionality that the interface defines. This allows the objects created from these classes to be treated as instances of the interface.

An interface called Display, for example, can be used for classes that have the ability to display text on a screen. This interface contains two methods:

One method is used to display text, and the second is used to get the text that is currently being displayed. Any class that implements this interface is declaring to other objects that it has the functionality of a `Display`. By implementing this interface, the class is then required to implement every method that the interface contains. Since the object was created from a class that implements the `Display` interface, it is guaranteed to have the functionality of a display. The object has an *is-a* relationship with `Display`. This object can now masquerade as an object of the `Display` type. An object can polymorphically act as any interface that its class or any superclass implements.

Polymorphism and interfaces are very powerful tools. They are used extensively on large projects. As a professional developer, you'll find it helpful to study design patterns to look for common reusable software designs that make use of the concepts in this chapter. A good developer not only understands all of the basic concepts, but also knows how best to use them.

Polymorphism in Code

When one specific object can be used as another general object polymorphically, the specific object can be used in place of the more general one without being cast. For example (see Figure 8-2), if class `TypeC` extends `TypeB`, and `TypeB` extends

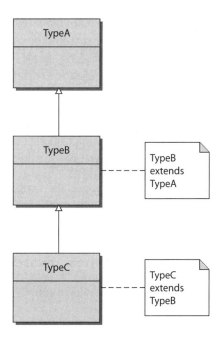

FIGURE 8-2

TypeA, TypeB, and TypeC

`TypeA`, any time an object type of `TypeA` or `TypeB` is needed, `TypeC` can be used. The following code segment shows an example of this:

```
TypeA var1 = new TypeA();
TypeA var2 = new TypeB();
TypeA var3 = new TypeC();

TypeB var4 = new TypeB();
TypeB var5 = new TypeC();

TypeC var6 = new TypeC();
```

In this example, any subclass can be used interchangeably with its superclass. The variable `var3` is declared as a `TypeA` object but is initialized with a new `TypeC` object. Even though `var3` is really a `TypeC` object, it will be treated as a `TypeA` object anywhere `var3` is referenced. This is okay because the `TypeC` object has inherited all of the functionality of the `TypeA` and `TypeB` objects. However, since `var3` was declared as `TypeA`, it can now be treated only as an object of this type. If `TypeC` objects have additional methods that are not part of the `TypeA` class, these methods would be unavailable.

More commonly, polymorphism will be used for method arguments. This allows a method to be written more abstractly and therefore more flexible. For instance, a method may be required to accept a type of animal object as its argument and use it to determine whether the animal is hungry. In this scenario, there is no benefit in creating a method that would accept a `Penguin` object and another that accepts a `PolarBear` object. Instead, it would be a better design to create one single method that accepts an `Animal` class. The state of hunger is general to the `Animal` class. The `Animal` class is a superclass for both the `Penguin` class and `PolarBear` class.

These basic examples are provided to help you understand the concepts of polymorphism. Keep in mind that they are described at a very high level here. This chapter will later offer more examples that show polymorphism in greater depth.

Programming to an Interface

"Programming to an interface" is the concept that code should interact based on a defined set of functionality instead of an explicitly defined object type. In other words, it is better for the public interfaces of objects to use data types that are defined as interfaces as opposed to a particular class when possible. When an object is implementing an interface, it is declaring that it has a certain set of functionalities. Many different classes can implement the same interface and provide its functionality. When a method uses an interface as its argument type, it allows any object, regardless of its type, to be used as long as it implements the interface. This allows the code to be more abstract and flexible and also promotes code reuse. Programming to an interface is also known as "design by contract."

Practical Examples of Polymorphism

The first section in this chapter approached polymorphism from a theoretical viewpoint; this section will look at coding examples. These examples are important for you to understand, and if you review them carefully, they should give you a clear understanding of the concepts presented in the earlier section.

The first example will demonstrate how polymorphism can be applied when a class extends another. There is no difference between the use of concrete and abstract classes. The next example demonstrates the use of polymorphism when interfaces are used. These examples will help reinforce the concepts covered in this chapter. The OCA exam will require that you know how to use polymorphism. Understanding these examples will better prepare you for the polymorphism questions on the test.

Examples of Polymorphism via Class Inheritance

The following example is intended to demonstrate the use of polymorphism with class inheritance. This example has three classes. Two classes are used to represent phones. The Phone class is intended to be a simple representation of a standard phone. This class has a method to dial a number and return to the state of whether the phone is ringing or not. The second class represents a smart phone and is appropriately named SmartPhone. The SmartPhone class extends the Phone class. This class adds the functionality of being able to send and receive e-mails. The final class is named Tester and is used as a driver to test both phone classes and demonstrate polymorphism in action. The phone classes are simple representations, and most of their functionality is not implemented. Instead, it is noted as comments regarding its intended purposes. The following is the Phone class:

```
public class Phone {

    public void callNumber(long number) {
        System.out.println("Phone: Calling number " + number);
        /* Logic to dial number and maintain connection. */
    }

    public boolean isRinging() {
        System.out.println("Phone: Checking if phone is ringing");
        boolean ringing = false;
        /* Check if the phone is ringing and set the ringing variable */
        return ringing;
    }
}
```

The Phone class is a simple class used for a normal phone with basic features. The class has a callNumber() method that is used to call the number that is passed as an argument. The isRinging() method is used to determine whether the phone is currently ringing. This class prints to standard output its class name and what action it is performing as it enters each method. The Phone class is the base class for the SmartPhone class. The SmartPhone class is listed next:

```
public class SmartPhone extends Phone {

    public void sendEmail(String message, String address) {
        System.out.println("SmartPhone: Sending Email");
        /* Logic to send email message */
    }

    public String retrieveEmail() {
        System.out.println("SmartPhone: Retrieving Email");
        String messages = new String();
        /* Return a String containing all of the messages*/
        return messages;
    }

    public boolean isRinging() {
        System.out.println("SmartPhone: Checking if phone is ringing");
        boolean ringing = false;
        /* Check for email activity and only continue when there is none. */
        /* Check if the phone is ringing and set the ringing variable */
        return ringing;
    }
}
```

The SmartPhone class represents a smart phone. This class extends the Phone class and therefore inherits its functionality. The SmartPhone class has a sendEmail() method that is used to send an e-mail message. It has a retrieveEmail() method that will return a String for any messages that have not yet been retrieved. This class also has an isRinging() method that overrides the isRinging() method from the superclass Phone. Similar to the Phone class, the SmartPhone class prints to standard output the class name and function that it will perform each time it enters a method.

The final class is named Tester. The class has the main() method for the demonstration program. This class exercises all of the methods in the Phone and SmartPhone classes.

```java
public class Tester {
  public static void main(String[] args) {
    new Tester();
  }

  public Tester() {
    Phone landLinePhone = new Phone();
    SmartPhone smartPhone = new SmartPhone();
    System.out.println("About to test a land line phone " +
      "as a phone...");
    testPhone(landLinePhone);
    System.out.println("\nAbout to test a smart phone " +
      "as a phone...");
    testPhone(smartPhone);
    System.out.println("\nAbout to test a smart phone " +
      "as a smart phone...");
    testSmartPhone(smartPhone);
  }

  private void testPhone(Phone phone) {
    phone.callNumber(5559869447L);
    phone.isRinging();
  }

  private void testSmartPhone(SmartPhone phone) {
    phone.sendEmail("Hi","edward@ocajexam.com");
    phone.retrieveEmail();
  }
}
```

The main() method kicks off the program by creating a Tester object and therefore calling Tester() the constructor. The constructor is used to call each test method. In between each method call, it prints a line to standard output that indicates what the program is doing. The testPhone() method is used to test each method of the Phone class. It accepts a Phone object as an argument. The final method is the testSmartPhone() method. This method tests each method of the SmartPhone class.

The Tester() constructor starts by creating two local variables. The first is called landLinePhone and is a Phone object. The second is called smartPhone and is a SmartPhone object. The constructor then displays a message and calls the testPhone() method with the landLinePhone variable as an argument.

Next, the constructor displays another message and again calls the testPhone() method. The smartPhone variable is used as the argument. The testPhone() method requires a Phone object as its argument, but the example has used a SmartPhone object instead. This is polymorphism. A smart phone is a more specific type of phone. A smart phone can do everything a landline phone can and more. This is represented in the SmartPhone class by it extending Phone. Notice that the testPhone() method is expecting a Phone object as an argument. It is perfectly acceptable if it gets a more specific type of phone. However, any additional method of the more specific class cannot be utilized. Since this method is designed for a Phone object as an argument, it can use only methods declared in the Phone class.

Finally, the constructor displays another status message and calls the testSmartPhone() method. This method exercises the methods declared in the SmartPhone object. Since polymorphism is unidirectional, the testSmartPhone() method cannot be called with a Phone object as its argument. The following output would be generated by this program:

```
About to test a land line phone as a phone...
Phone: Calling number 5559869447
Phone: Checking if phone is ringing

About to test a smart phone as a phone...
Phone: Calling number 5559869447
SmartPhone: Checking if phone is ringing

About to test a smart phone as a smart phone...
SmartPhone: Sending Email
SmartPhone: Retrieving Email
```

When the landLinePhone variable is used with the testPhone() method, the output is simply generated from the Phone class since it is a Phone object. When the smartPhone variable is used with the testPhone() method, the flow of execution is more complex. Because the SmartPhone class extends the Phone class, the SmartPhone class inherits both the callNumber() and isRinging()

methods. However, the SmartPhone class overrides the isRinging() method with its own. When the callNumber() method is invoked on a SmartPhone object, the method in the Phone class is used since it is not overridden. However, when the isRinging() method is called, the method in the SmartPhone class is used. This follows the basic rule of inheritance and overriding methods.

Examples of Polymorphism via Implementing Interfaces

This example will focus on an object's ability to behave polymorphically as an interface that its class implements. This allows objects that may be radically different, but share some common functionality, to be treated similarly. The common functionality is defined in an interface that each class must implement.

This example is composed of three classes and one interface. There is a Tester class to test the program. The other two classes are objects representing a goat and his home (that is, his shelter). Both in this program and conceptually, the objects are very different. A goat is a living animal and a goat shelter is an inanimate item. However, they both share a common ability. Both the Goat class and the GoatShelter class can describe themselves. This functionality has been reflected in the fact that they both implement the Describable interface. Classes that implement this interface are then required to implement the getDescription() method. Here is the Describable interface:

```
public interface Describable {
  public String getDescription();
}
```

This interface has only one method. The getDescription() method is used to return a description about the object. Any class that implements this interface is stating it has a method that can be used to get its description. The Goat class is shown next.

```
public class Goat implements Describable {

  private String description;

  public Goat(String name){
    description = "A goat named " + name;
  }

  public String getDescription() {
    return description;
  }
  /*
```

```
   * Implement other methods for a goat
   */
}
```

The Goat class is a simple class that can be used to represent a goat. This class implements the Describable interface and therefore is required to implement the getDescription() method. The constructor of the Goat class has one parameter that it uses to place the name of the goat in the description string. The next class in this example is the GoatShelter class. It is listed next:

```
public class GoatShelter implements Describable {

  private String description;
  private int height;
  private int width;
  private int length;

  public GoatShelter (int height, int width, int length) {
    this.height = height;
    this.width = width;
    this.length = length;
    this.description = "A goat shelter that is " + height + " high, "
      + length + " long and " + width + " wide ";
  }

  public String getDescription() {
    return description;
  }
  /*
   * Implement other methods for a goat shelter
   */
}
```

The GoatShelter class is designed generally to model a box. Its constructor requires that the dimensions of the box be used as arguments. The constructor also creates the description text that is returned in the getDescription() method. Similar to the Goat class, the GoatShelter class also implements the Describable interface. The final class is the Tester class. This class is used to demonstrate the concept of polymorphism with interfaces.

```
public class Tester {

  public static void main(String[] args) {
    new Tester();
```

```
    }

    public Tester() {
      Goat goat = new Goat("Bob");
      GoatShelter goatShelter = new GoatShelter (4, 4, 6);
      System.out.println(description(goat));
      System.out.println(description(goatShelter));
    }

    private String description(Describable d){
      return d.getDescription();
    }
}
```

The Tester class contains the main() method that starts the execution of the program. This calls the Tester() constructor, where a Goat object and GoatShelter object are both created. The description() method is then used to print to standard output the description of each object. The description() method requires a Describable object. It is impossible to have a true Describable object since it is an interface. However, classes that implement this interface are declaring that they have the functionality of Describable. These objects can then polymorphically act as if they were of type Describable. The following is the output of this program:

```
A goat named Bob
A goat shelter that is 4 high, 4 long and 6 wide
```

INSIDE THE EXAM

Unidirectional Polymorphism

The OCA exam may try to present the test taker with a polymorphism question in which the more general object behaves as the more specific one. Remember that polymorphism works in only one direction. Only specific objects can behave as more general ones.

Add Functionality to the Describable Example

This exercise will use the preceding example. The goal of the exercise is to compile and run the example and add a class that implements the Describable interface.

1. Copy the example into the text editor or IDE of your choice.
2. Compile and run the example to ensure the code has been copied correctly.
3. Add a new class that implements the Describable interface.
4. Compile and run the application.

Examples of Programming to an Interface

This example will demonstrate the concept of programming to an interface. This concept allows a developer to define the functionality that is required instead of defining an actual object type. This creates more flexible code that adheres to the object-oriented design principle of creating reusable code.

Suppose a developer creates a class that is used for creating log files. This class is responsible for creating and managing the log file on the file system, and then appending the log messages to it. This class is called Logger. The Logger class has a method called appendToLog() that accepts one object as an argument and then appends a message about it in the log.

The developer could overload this method with every possible data type that the program uses. Although this would work, it would be very inefficient. Suppose the program-to-an-interface concept is used instead, and the developer creates an interface that defines the required method for a logable class. This interface is called Logable. The appendToLog() method then uses the Logable interface as its argument. Any class that requires logging could implement this interface and then be used polymorphically with the appendToLog() method.

The following is the Logable interface:

```
public interface Logable {
  public String getInitInfo();
  public String getLogableEvent();
}
```

The Logable interface is a basic interface that defines the methods required to work with the appendToLog() method in the Logger class. The appendToLog()

method is not concerned with the details of an object other than what pertains to logging. By using this interface, the developer has defined a functionality requirement as opposed to a strict object data type. This is what is meant by the phrase "programming to an interface."

The Logger class is displayed next:

```java
import java.io.BufferedWriter;
import java.io.FileWriter;
import java.io.IOException;

public class Logger {

  private BufferedWriter out;

  public Logger() throws IOException {
    out = new BufferedWriter(new FileWriter("logfile.txt"));
  }

  public void appendToLog(Logable logable) throws IOException {
    out.write("Object history: " + logable.getInitInfo());
    out.newLine();
    out.write("Object log event: " + logable.getLogableEvent());
    out.newLine();
  }

  public void close() throws IOException {
    out.flush();
    out.close();
  }
}
```

The Logger class creates a BufferedWriter, which is a means to write to a file. (This is beyond the scope of this chapter and therefore will not be discussed.) The appendToLog() method is used to write to the log file. This class uses the Logable interface to remain flexible. This method will work with any other class that implements this interface and will follow the program-to-an-interface concept.

The next class is the NetworkConnection class. This class implements the Logable interface.

```java
public class NetworkConnection implements Logable {

  private long createdTimestamp;
  private String currentLogMessage;
```

```
public NetworkConnection() {
  createdTimestamp = System.currentTimeMillis();
  currentLogMessage = "Initialized";
}

public void connect(){
  /*
   * Established connection
   */
  currentLogMessage = "Connected at " + System.currentTimeMillis();
}

public String getInitInfo() {
  return "NetworkConnection object created " + createdTimestamp;
}

public String getLogableEvent() {
  return currentLogMessage;
}
}
```

This class implements the Logable interface and all of the methods required for it. When this class is polymorphically behaving as the Logable data type, the code being used does not care about the implementation details of the class. As long as the class implements the Logable interface, it is free to choose how the methods are implemented.

The SystemStatus class is the other class that uses the Logable interface.

```
public class SystemStatus implements Logable {

  private long createdTimestamp;

  public SystemStatus() {
    createdTimestamp = System.currentTimeMillis();
  }

  private int getStatus(){
    if(System.currentTimeMillis() - createdTimestamp > 1000){
      return 1;
    }
    else{
      return -1;
    }
  }
}
```

```
public String getInitInfo() {
  return "SystemStatus object created " + createdTimestamp;
}

public String getLogableEvent() {
  return String.valueOf("Status: "+getStatus());
}
}
```

The SystemStatus class's only similarity to the NetworkConnection class is that they both implement the Logable interface. This class chooses to implement the required getInitInfo() and getLogableEvent() methods in a different manner than the NetworkConnection class.

The final class is the Tester class. This is a simple class that demonstrates all of the preceding classes and interface in action.

```
public class Tester {

  public static void main(String[] args) throws Exception {
    new Tester();
  }

  public Tester() throws Exception {
    Logger logger = new Logger();
    SystemStatus systemStatus = new SystemStatus();
    NetworkConnection networkConnection = new NetworkConnec-
tion();
    logger.appendToLog(systemStatus);
    logger.appendToLog(networkConnection);
    networkConnection.connect();
    Thread.sleep(2000);
    logger.appendToLog(systemStatus);
    logger.appendToLog(networkConnection);
    logger.close();
  }
}
```

The Tester class does all of its work in its constructor. The class creates a new Logger object called logger. It then creates a SystemStatus object named systemStatus and a NetworkConnection object named networkConnection. It then uses the appendToLog() method from the Logger object. This method uses the Logable object as a parameter. Because both the SystemStatus and NetworkConnection classes implement this interface, their objects can be used polymorphically with this method. The following text is written to the log file:

```
Object history: SystemStatus object created 1238811437373
Object log event: Status: -1
Object history: NetworkConnection object created 1238811437374
Object log event: Initialized
Object history: SystemStatus object created 1238811437373
Object log event: Status: 1
Object history: NetworkConnection object created 1238811437374
Object log event: Connected at 1238811437374
```

CERTIFICATION OBJECTIVE

Understand Casting

Exam Objective   Determine when casting is necessary

So far, this chapter has discussed how to use a more specific object in place of a general one. Polymorphism allows for any subclass to fill in for its superclass. You saw that no special conversion is needed to do this. We are now going to look at the opposite situation. How can you take an object that is general and make it more specific? *Casting* will allow you to convert an object back to its original runtime type or any of its superclasses.

When Casting Is Needed

Polymorphism allows an object to be used as a more general object without the need to add new syntax. However, casting must be used when an object is to be used as a more detailed type or when converting a primitive to a type that will cause data to be lost. Polymorphism can occur without interaction because there is no possibility of incompatible data. When there is the chance of incompatible data types, the Java compiler requires the developer to declare formally their intention to use a variable as a different type.

Casting must occur when the primitive double is used as a `float` or a `HashMap` object is used as a `LinkedHashMap` object. This section will look at each case and explain when it is possible to convert the object or primitive and why you might need to do so.

The Java syntax to cast an object or primitive is relatively simple. To cast an object or primitive, place the type before it in parentheses. In the next example, detailedScore is declared as a double. It is then assigned to a float. For this code to be valid and compile, detailedScore must be cast to a float. The cast is performed by placing (float) in front of the double, detailedScore. This tells the compiler to treat detailedScore as a float and allow it to be assigned the variable score, which is declared as a float.

```
double detailedScore = 1.2;
float score = (float)detailedScore;
```

Casting Primitives

Primitives need to be explicitly cast when the conversion will potentially result in the loss of precision. If there is no potential for precision loss, the compiler will automatically cast the primitive. Precision is lost when a larger primitive is cast to a smaller primitive. Precision can also be lost when a primitive with a floating-point decimal is cast to a whole number primitive type. For example, an int is a 32-bit signed two's complement integer and has a minimum value of −2,147,483,648 and a maximum value of 2,147,483,647 (inclusive). A byte is an 8-bit signed two's complement integer with a minimum value of −128 and a maximum value of 127 (inclusive). If an int that was storing the value 1236 were cast to a byte, there would be a loss of precision, because a byte cannot store a value as large as 1236.

So, if a byte cannot store a large int, but the compiler will allow you to cast the int into a byte, what happens at runtime? At runtime, the Java virtual machine (JVM) will truncate the bits from the int. In the cast of an int with the value of 1236, the JVM would truncate it to a byte with the value of −44. The following code will output Byte: -44:

```
int i = 1236;
byte b = (byte) i;
System.out.println("Byte: "+b);
```

To understand where the value −44 comes from, you need to look at the binary representation of the numbers. In the following example, the number *1236* is displayed as a 32-bit binary number. The number *−44* is displayed as an 8-bit binary number. Remember that the most significant bit is used as a signed byte.

```
1236 = 0000 0000 0000 0000 0000 0100 1101 0100
 -44  =                               1101 0100
```

TABLE 8-1 Primitive Casting

Starting Primitive Type	Finished Primitive Type						
		byte	short	char	int	long	float	double
byte		Safe Conversion	Explicit Cast	Safe Conversion	Safe Conversion	Safe Conversion	Safe Conversion
short	Explicit Cast Precision Lost		Explicit Cast Sign Lost	Safe Conversion	Safe Conversion	Safe Conversion	Safe Conversion
char	Explicit Cast Precision Lost	Explicit Cast Sign Added		Safe Conversion	Safe Conversion	Safe Conversion	Safe Conversion
int	Explicit Cast Precision Lost	Explicit Cast Precision Lost	Explicit Cast Precision Lost		Safe Conversion	Safe Conversion	Safe Conversion
long	Explicit Cast Precision Lost	Explicit Cast Precision Lost	Explicit Cast Precision Lost	Explicit Cast Precision Lost		Explicit Cast Precision Lost	Safe Conversion
float	Explicit Cast Precision Lost	Explicit Cast Precision Lost	Explicit Cast Precision Lost	Explicit Cast Precision Lost	Explicit Cast Precision Lost		Safe Conversion
double	Explicit Cast Precision Lost	Explicit Cast Precision Lost	Explicit Cast Precision Lost	Explicit Cast Precision Lost	Explicit Cast Precision Lost	Explicit Cast Precision Lost	

It is easy to see that the 24 most significant bits are being truncated from the `int`. The negative signed value is due to the most significant bit of the byte being a 1.

A cast is also required to convert a floating-point decimal number such as a `float` or `double` to a primitive whole number. The decimal value of the number is truncated. For example, the value of 5.7 would be truncated to 5. Rounding the number is not a consideration. Once the decimal value is removed, bits are truncated from the most significant bit onward until it is the proper new size.

Casting Between Primitives and Objects

Since the introduction of Java 5.0, it is possible to cast primitives to and from their object wrapper classes. Not only has Java made it easy to make these basic conversions, but it will also automatically do the casting with autoboxing and auto unboxing. Autoboxing and unboxing allow a primitive to be used interchangeably as its object wrapper class. The proper conversion is done automatically. The following code segment will demonstrate different ways of making an `Integer` object from an `int`:

```
int i = 8;
Integer obj1 = new Integer(i);
Integer obj2 = (Integer)i;
Integer obj3 = i;
Float obj4 = 5.7f;
//Below is invalid
Integer obj5 = obj4;
```

In this code segment, a primitive `int` named `i` is created and set to 8. This variable is then used to create three `Integer` objects. The object `obj1` is created using the method that was required prior to Java 5.0. It uses the `Integer` class's constructor to instantiate a new object. This line of code demonstrates the basic way to instantiate an object and does not demonstrate any casting. Next, the `obj2` variable is set by casting a primitive `int` to an `Integer` object. Although this syntax is valid, it is rarely used. The `obj3` object is set by using only the primitive `i`. No cast is used in this case. However, the autoboxing feature of Java performs the cast for you. Most developers will use the autoboxing and unboxing method to move between primitives and their wrapper class. A `Float` object is also created. Autoboxing is used to convert the `5.7f` value to a `Float` object. Finally, an invalid example is shown. Unlike a primitive where a `float` will be automatically truncated to fit into an `int`, a `Float` object will not automatically truncate to fit into an `Integer` object. This line of code would produce compiler warnings and throw a runtime exception. It is important to remember that you do not have to cast explicitly when writing the code, because a cast will be done for you automatically.

INSIDE THE EXAM

Hidden Casting

Be on the lookout for hidden casting. The Java compiler does not require you to cast explicitly between a primitive and its corresponding wrapper classes. However, a cast is still happening automatically as a convenience.

Casting Objects

An object can polymorphically become any object that is its superclass. Once an object is assigned a more general type, it can no longer access its more specific features. An object has to be cast back into its original runtime type to use these methods. It is important to ensure that the object to be cast was instantiated as that object or an object that inherited it. A runtime exception will be thrown if an object is incorrectly cast. Following are three example classes:

```
public class ClassA {

  public String whoAmI(){
    return "ClassA";
  }

  public String specialClassAMethod(){
    return "ClassA only method";
  }
}
public class ClassB extends ClassA{

  public String whoAmI(){
    return "ClassB";
  }

  public String specialClassBMethod(){
    return "ClassB only method";
  }
}
```

ClassA in the example is a basic class with two methods: one method returns a string with its class name, and the other represents a unique method that only ClassA contains. ClassB extends ClassA. It overrides the whoAmI method with its own functionality. It also contains a method that is unique to itself, specialClassBMethod.

The following code segment creates a ClassB object named obj1. It then creates a ClassA object, obj2. This object is initialized with a new ClassB object. This is valid because a ClassB object can polymorphically act as a ClassA object since ClassB extends ClassA. Finally a second ClassA object is created and initialized with a new ClassA object.

```
ClassB obj1 = new ClassB();
ClassA obj2 = new ClassB();;
ClassA obj3 = new ClassA();
```

```
System.out.println("obj1: " + obj1.whoAmI());
System.out.println("obj2: " + obj2.whoAmI());
System.out.println("obj3: " + obj3.whoAmI());
```

The following is the output when the preceding code is executed:

```
obj1: ClassB
obj2: ClassB
obj3: ClassA
```

The `obj2` object is assigned the type of `ClassA` but is initialized with a `ClassB` object. This object retains all of the functionality of a `ClassB` object. This can be seen when the string from `obj2.whoAmI()` method is printed. However, since this object is assigned the type `ClassA`, it can be treated only as a `ClassA` object. For example, the following line of code would not compile:

```
System.out.println("obj2: " + obj2.specialClassBMethod());
```

Even though `obj2` was created as a `ClassB` object, it was assigned the `ClassA` type and therefore can be treated only as a `ClassA` object. To be able to access the functionality that `ClassB` provides, the object would have to be cast to the `ClassB` type. The next example demonstrates `obj2` being cast into a `ClassB` object:

```
ClassB obj4 = (ClassB)obj2;
System.out.println("obj4: " + obj4.specialClassBMethod());
```

It is also possible to cast the object inline. This shorthand syntax would be as follows:

```
System.out.println("obj2: " + ((ClassB)obj2).specialClassBMethod());
```

It is important that you understand that `obj3` cannot be cast to a `ClassB` object. You can cast to an object type successfully only if the object was instantiated as it or as one of its subclasses. If it were cast to `ClassB`, a runtime exception would be thrown.

exam
watch

When you're taking the OCA exam, remember that you have to cast objects only when you are going down the inheritance chain—that is, superclass to subclass. It is also important that you understand that the object at one point must have been the object that is being cast to, or a subclass of it.

When casting an object, you should always check whether the object can be cast without generating an exception. To check whether an object is the proper type, use the Java `instanceof` *operator. This operator can be used in an* `if` *statement to determine whether object A is an instance of object B.*

```
if(obj2 instanceof ClassB){
   /*Do cast*/
}
```

CERTIFICATION SUMMARY

Polymorphism is a fundamental concept of any object-oriented programming language. This chapter has discussed the fundamental concepts of polymorphism and then demonstrated these concepts through examples.

The first part of this chapter defined polymorphism. Polymorphism is a tool that can be used to create more reliable code and produce it faster. Polymorphism allows you to treat a specific object as if it were a more general object. In other words, a class's object can masquerade as any object that the class uses to derive itself. The benefit is that applications can be written more abstractly. A common form of polymorphism is between classes that extend other classes. A class's object can be treated as any object that it extends, and this includes both concrete and abstract classes. Polymorphism also allows an object to be treated as any interface that it implements.

Polymorphism is most commonly used for method arguments. Often, a method will require only a general object. A more specific object can be used, however, since it will provide all of the functionality of the general object. You can think of the *is-a* relationship to help you understand polymorphism. For example, a specific object such as `Blue` *is-a* `Color`. So `Blue` is a specific object and extends the `Color` object.

This chapter then covered the benefits of programming to an interface. Programming to an interface allows the developer to specify the capabilities or behaviors that are expected, instead of strictly defining an expected object type. This allows the code to be more abstract and flexible. This is an example of polymorphism in use. Programming to an interface requires that an object polymorphically act as the interface it implements.

The chapter then used coding examples to clarify polymorphism and programming to an interface. These examples highlighted the important concepts discussed in theory in this chapter.

Finally, casting was examined. Casting is often used with polymorphism to return an object back to its original level of detail. It is important that you learn how to use casting correctly. Improper use can lead to unstable and difficult-to-maintain code that often crashes.

TWO-MINUTE DRILL

Understand Polymorphism

- ☐ Polymorphism is a fundamental concept of object-oriented languages, including Java.
- ☐ Polymorphism stimulates code reuse.
- ☐ Polymorphism allows one object to act as either one of its superclasses or as an interface that it implements.
- ☐ In an *is-a* relationship, the subclass object (the more specific object) "is-a" superclass object (the more general object).
- ☐ Polymorphism is unidirectional. More specific objects can act polymorphically only as more general objects.
- ☐ By implementing an interface, an object is declaring it has the functionality defined in the interface. This allows that object to act polymorphically as the interface.
- ☐ Programming to an interface is the concept in which the developer defines the required functionality instead of defining strict object data types. This allows other developers to interact with the code using any object they choose as long as it implements the required interfaces.
- ☐ An object can be used interchangeably with any of its superclasses without the need to be cast.
- ☐ An object can be used interchangeably with any interface that it implements without the need to be cast.
- ☐ When a more specific object is polymorphically used as a general object, the more specific functionality is not available.
- ☐ Polymorphism is commonly used for method arguments.

Understand Casting

- ☐ Casting is needed to convert an object back to a more detailed object in its inheritance chain.
- ☐ If you cast an object to an invalid type, a runtime exception will be thrown.
- ☐ To cast an object, you place the class name in front of it in parentheses.

☐ You must cast a primitive to another primitive type if there is the possibility that precision will be lost.

☐ Casting is not needed when going from a primitive to its wrapper class. Java's autoboxing/unboxing feature will do this automatically.

☐ Objects need to be cast when they move down the inheritance chain—that is, from a superclass to a subclass. Polymorphism allows objects to become more general.

SELF TEST

Understand Polymorphism

1. Which statement is true about the term *polymorphism*?
   A. It is a Latin word that roughly means "changeable."
   B. It is a Greek word that roughly means "many forms."
   C. It is an Old English word that roughly means "insectlike."
   D. It is a new technical term that means "Java object."

2. What type of object can polymorphically behave as another?
   A. An object can act as any subclass of the class it was created from.
   B. An object can act as any superclass of the class it was created from.
   C. An object can act as any other abstract class.

3. Polymorphism helps to facilitate which of the following? (Choose all that apply.)
   A. Highly optimized code
   B. Code reuse
   C. Code obfuscation
   D. Code that is generic and flexible

4. What is a correct *is-a* relationship?
   A. A specific object *is-a* more generic one.
   B. A generic object *is-a* more specific one.
   C. A null reference *is-an* object.

5. Which of the following statements explains why an object can polymorphically behave as an interface?
   A. By implementing the interface, the object is required to have all of the functionality that the interface represents.
   B. By implementing the interface, the object inherits all the required methods it defines.
   C. An object can behave as an interface because interfaces do not have a strict expected behavior and therefore any object can act as an interface.

6. What does it mean if a developer is programming to an interface?
   A. The developer is implementing an interface for the class he or she is working on.
   B. The developer was given a set of interfaces he or she must implement.
   C. The developer is defining the functionality instead of strict object types as much as possible.

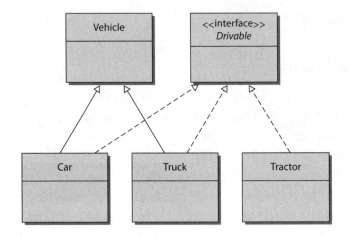

FIGURE 8-3

UML for
questions 7–12

The following code example will be referenced in questions 7 through 12. Afterward, see Figure 8-3.

The `Drivable` interface:

```
public interface Drivable {
/*
 * Drivable definitions
 */
}
```

The `Tractor` class:

```
public class Tractor implements Drivable{
/*
 * Tractor functionality
 */
}
```

The `Vehicle` class:

```
public class Vehicle {
/*
 * Vehicle functionality
 */
}
```

The Car class:

```
public class Car extends Vehicle implements Drivable{
/*
 * Car functionality
 */
}
```

The Truck class:

```
public class Truck extends Vehicle implements Drivable{
/*
 * Truck functionality
 */
}
```

7. Given the preceding classes and interface, would the following code segment produce errors when compiled?

```
Car car = new Car();
Vehicle vehicle = car;
```

A. No errors would be produced.

B. This code would result in compile errors.

8. Given the preceding classes and interface, would the following code segment produce errors when compiled?

```
Truck truck = new Truck();
Drivable drivable = truck;
```

A. No errors would be produced.

B. This code would result in compile errors.

9. Given the preceding classes and interface, would the following code segment produce errors when compiled?

```
Tractor tractor = new Tractor();
Vehicle vehicle = tractor;
```

A. No errors would be produced.

B. This code would result in compile errors.

10. Given the preceding classes and interface, would the following code segment produce errors when compiled?

```
Drivable drivable = new Drivable();
Truck truck = drivable;
```

A. No errors would be produced.

B. This code would result in compile errors.

11. Given the preceding classes and interface, would the following code segment produce errors when compiled?

    ```
    Vehicle vehicle = new Vehicle();
    Object o = vehicle;
    ```

    A. No errors would be produced.

    B. This code would result in compile errors.

12. Given the preceding classes and interface, would the following code segment produce errors when compiled?

    ```
    Truck truck = new Truck();
    Object o = truck;
    ```

    A. No errors would be produced.

    B. This code would result in compile errors.

Understand Casting

13. In what cases is casting needed? (Choose all that apply.)

    A. Going from a superclass to subclass

    B. Going from a subclass to superclass

    C. Using an `int` as a `double`

    D. Using a `float` as a `long`

14. Why must the a variable be cast?

    A. So future developers understand the intended use of the variable

    B. To tell the compiler that the data conversion is safe to make

    C. Because it was used polymorphically before

15. What would cause an exception to be thrown from a cast?

    A. If precision is lost due to the cast

    B. If the object is cast to a superclass of its current type

    C. If the object was never instantiated as the object that it is being cast to or one of its subclasses

    D. If the object being cast is null

SELF TEST ANSWERS

Understand Polymorphism

1. Which statement is true about the term *polymorphism*?
   A. It is a Latin word that roughly means "changeable."
   B. It is a Greek word that roughly means "many forms."
   C. It is an Old English word that roughly means "insectlike."
   D. It is a new technical term that means "Java object."

> Answer:
>
> ☑ **B.** The word *polymorphism* comes from the Greeks and means "many forms."
> ☒ **A**, **C**, and **D** are incorrect.

2. What type of object can polymorphically behave as another?
   A. An object can act as any subclass of the class it was created from.
   B. An object can act as any superclass of the class it was created from.
   C. An object can act as any other abstract class.

> Answer:
>
> ☑ **B.** An object inherits all of the functionality of its superclasses and can therefore polymorphically behave as they do.
> ☒ **A** and **C** are incorrect. **A** is incorrect because an object cannot behave as its subclass since this class is more specific and contains functionality that is not present in the superclass. **C** is incorrect because there needs to be an *is-a* relationship between the classes. This answer does not mention what the relationship is.

3. Polymorphism helps to facilitate which of the following? (Choose all that apply.)
   A. Highly optimized code
   B. Code reuse
   C. Code obfuscation
   D. Code that is generic and flexible

Answer:

☑ **B** and **D**. Polymorphism aids in creating reusable code, because it allows the code to be written more abstractly, thus **B** is correct. Similar to **B**, polymorphism allows the code to be generic by using generic data types that any more specific object can fulfill. Thus, **D** is also correct.

☒ **A** and **C** are incorrect. **A** is incorrect because polymorphism has no effect on the level of optimization of the code. **C** is incorrect because obfuscated code (code that is intentionally difficult to read) is not related to polymorphism.

4. What is a correct *is-a* relationship?
    A. A specific object *is-a* more generic one.
    B. A generic object *is-a* more specific one.
    C. A null reference *is-an* object.

Answer:

☑ **A**. A more specific object can be considered to be a more generic one. This is the fundamental principle of polymorphism.

☒ **B** and **C** are incorrect. **B** is incorrect because generic objects do not have all of the functionality of more specific ones and therefore do not possess an *is-a* relationship with the specific objects. **C** is incorrect because a null reference has no effect on its relationship with other objects.

5. Which of the following statements explains why an object can polymorphically behave as an interface?
    A. By implementing the interface, the object is required to have all of the functionality that the interface represents.
    B. By implementing the interface, the object inherits all the required methods it defines.
    C. An object can behave as an interface because interfaces do not have a strict expected behavior and therefore any object can act as an interface.

Answer:

☑ **A.** When a class implements an interface, it is then required to implement all the methods the interface contains. This gives the class the functionality defined in the interface and therefore allows this class to behave as the interface.

☒ **B** and **C** are incorrect. **B** is incorrect because nothing is inherited when an interface is implemented. **C** is incorrect because each interface has a strict behavior expected of it. This is represented by the methods that must be implemented.

6. What does it mean if a developer is programming to an interface?
   A. The developer is implementing an interface for the class he or she is working on.
   B. The developer was given a set of interfaces he or she must implement.
   C. The developer is defining the functionality instead of strict object types as much as possible.

Answer:

☑ **C.** Programming to an interface means that a developer is defining functionality instead of object data types. Any object can then implement the required interface and be used. If an interface were not used, only objects of the specific defined data type would be usable.

☒ **A** and **B** are incorrect. **A** is incorrect because programming to an interface is a larger concept than just implementing one interface in one class. **B** is incorrect because in this situation the developer is just implementing a group of interfaces that have been predetermined.

The following code example will be referenced in questions 7 through 12.

FIGURE 8-3

UML for
questions 7–12

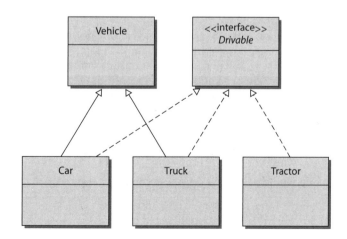

The `Drivable` interface:

```
public interface Drivable {
/*
 * Drivable definitions
 */
}
```

The `Tractor` class:

```
public class Tractor implements Drivable{
/*
 * Tractor functionality
 */
}
```

The `Vehicle` class:

```
public class Vehicle {
/*
 * Vehicle functionality
 */
}
```

The `Car` class:

```
public class Car extends Vehicle implements Drivable{
/*
 * Car functionality
 */
}
```

The `Truck` class:

```
public class Truck extends Vehicle implements Drivable{
/*
 * Truck functionality
 */
}
```

7. Given the preceding classes and interface, would the following code segment produce errors when compiled?

```
Car car = new Car();
Vehicle vehicle = car;
```

A. No errors would be produced.

B. This code would result in compile errors.

Answer:

☑ **A**. No errors would be produced because the `Car` class extends the `Vehicle` class and therefore can be used as a `Vehicle` object.

☒ **B** is incorrect.

8. Given the preceding classes and interface, would the following code segment produce errors when compiled?

```
Truck truck = new Truck();
Drivable drivable = truck;
```

A. No errors would be produced.

B. This code would result in compile errors.

Answer:

☑ **A**. No errors would be produced because the `Truck` class implements the `Drivable` interface and therefore can be used as a `Drivable` object.

☒ **B** is incorrect.

9. Given the preceding classes and interface, would the following code segment produce errors when compiled?

```
Tractor tractor = new Tractor();
Vehicle vehicle = tractor;
```

A. No errors would be produced.

B. This code would result in compile errors.

Answer:

☑ **B**. This code would result in compile errors because the `Vehicle` class is not a superclass for the `Tractor` class.

☒ **A** is incorrect.

10. Given the preceding classes and interface, would the following code segment produce errors when compiled?

    ```
    Drivable drivable = new Drivable();
    Truck truck = drivable;
    ```

    A. No errors would be produced.
    B. This code would result in compile errors.

    Answer:

    ☑ **B.** This code would result in compile errors because the `Drivable` interface cannot be instantiated since it is an interface.
    ☒ **A** is incorrect.

11. Given the preceding classes and interface, would the following code segment produce errors when compiled?

    ```
    Vehicle vehicle = new Vehicle();
    Object o = vehicle;
    ```

    A. No errors would be produced.
    B. This code would result in compile errors.

    Answer:

    ☑ **A.** No errors would be produced because the `Vehicle` class is concrete, and the `Object` class is the superclass for every Java object.
    ☒ **B** is incorrect.

12. Given the preceding classes and interface, would the following code segment produce errors when compiled?

    ```
    Truck truck = new Truck();
    Object o = truck;
    ```

    A. No errors would be produced.
    B. This code would result in compile errors.

Answer:

☑ **A.** No errors would be produced because the `Object` class is the superclass for all Java objects.

☒ **B** is incorrect.

Understand Casting

13. In what cases is casting needed? (Choose all that apply.)

    A. Going from a superclass to subclass

    B. Going from a subclass to superclass

    C. Using an `int` as a `double`

    D. Using a `float` as a `long`

Answer:

☑ **A** and **D.** **A** is correct because a cast is always needed to go down the inheritance chain. **D** is correct because a `long` is not a floating-point number; precision will be lost and therefore it requires a cast.

☒ **B** and **C** are incorrect. **B** is incorrect because polymorphism occurs when going from a subclass to a superclass. **C** is incorrect because no precision is lost when using an `int` as a `double`, so no cast is needed.

14. Why must the a variable be cast?

    A. So future developers understand the intended use of the variable

    B. To tell the compiler that the data conversion is safe to make

    C. Because it was used polymorphically before

Answer:

☑ **B.** If there is a possibility of incompatible data, a cast must be used.

☒ **A** and **C** are incorrect. **A** is incorrect, even though it is helpful for developers—that is not its sole purpose. **C** is incorrect because polymorphism does not change when a variable needs to be cast.

15. What would cause an exception to be thrown from a cast?

  A. If precision is lost due to the cast

  B. If the object is cast to a superclass of its current type

  C. If the object was never instantiated as the object that it is being cast to or one of its subclasses

  D. If the object being cast is null

Answer:

☑ **C.** If the object was not instantiated with the level of detail it is being cast to, it will cause a runtime exception.

☒ **A, B,** and **D** are incorrect. **A** is incorrect because if precision is lost between primitive types, there is no exception. **B** is an example of polymorphism. A cast can be done but is not needed. **D** is incorrect because a null reference can be cast. This will not cause an exception. However, if the cast is to an invalid type, the compiler will produce an error.

9

Handling Exceptions

"Throw and catch." Once that phrase makes sense to you, you'll know that you understand exception handling in Java. Throughout this chapter, we will explore the primary focus of exception handling in Java by throwing exceptions and handling them where appropriate. We'll discuss the different types of exceptions, when and how to handle them, as well as how to recognize common checked exceptions, unchecked exceptions, and errors. By the end of the chapter, you should know enough about exception handling in Java to score well on the exceptions-related questions when you sit the exam. Good luck!

CERTIFICATION OBJECTIVE

Understand the Rationale and Types of Exceptions

Exam Objective   *Describe the advantages of exception handling*
Exam Objective   *Differentiate among checked exceptions, unchecked exceptions, and errors*

The Java Language Specification provides the following definition for a software exception: "When a program violates the semantic constraints of the Java programming language, the Java virtual machine signals this error to the program as an exception."

Exceptions are used in Java to handle events that affect the normal flow of the application's execution. These events can result from coding errors or issues with the resources in place. For portability and robustness, Java aims to manage exceptions in a predictable way, by throwing and catching exceptions that have been or will be grouped in logical, sensible ways. We'll explore the exception hierarchy in Java and the different types of exceptions.

The following topics will be covered:

- Advantages of exceptions
- Exception hierarchy in Java
- Checked exceptions
- Unchecked exceptions
- Errors

Advantages of Exceptions

Java exceptions provide three main advantages to writing and maintaining code. The first advantage is the separation of error-handling code from the main code of a program. The use of try-catch blocks allows a block of code to be executed without having to explicitly check each possible statement for errors. Instead, the statements can be grouped together, and any error will generate an exception that can be caught in a different section of code. This makes code much easier to read and maintain.

Exceptions provide a means to propagate errors up the call stack—the second advantage. Oftentimes, the code that may be best suited for handling the error condition is a method higher up in the call stack. Java allows exceptions to be thrown up the chain. Exceptions allow this to occur in a consistent and organized manor.

Another advantage of Java exception handling is the ability to group like exceptions together. Since exceptions are Java objects, the grouping is done via class hierarchy. For example, the `IOException` is one of the most common exceptions a developer will encounter. More specific exceptions will extend it. The `FileNotFoundException` is a subclass of `IOException`. When handling exceptions, a developer can catch the more generic `IOException` or target specific exceptions such as the `FileNotFoundException`.

Exception Hierarchy in Java

An exception in Java is defined by an instance of the class `Throwable`. `Exception` classes include the class `Throwable` and all of its subclasses. Figure 9-1 depicts the `Exception` class's hierarchy.

In the hierarchy, the two direct subclasses to `Throwable` are `Exception` and `Error`. Another important subclass is `RuntimeException`, which is a direct subclass to the `Exception` class. Runtime exceptions and errors are not checked. All of the other exceptions are checked. Let's take a look at each category.

Checked Exceptions

Checked exceptions are checked by the compiler at compile time. Checked exceptions must be caught by a `catch` block or the thread will terminate, and so will the application if it is the only thread. The application will not terminate if you have started nondaemon threads. A handler can actually be registered to catch

FIGURE 9-1

Exception
handling class
hierarchy

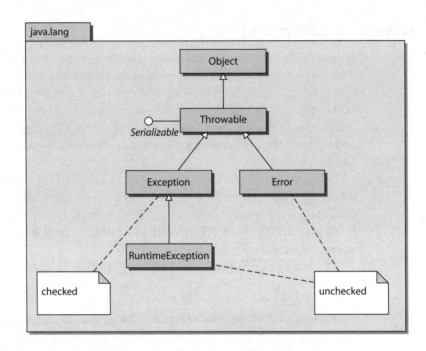

the exception in a multithreaded application. The following code demonstrates an application throwing an uncaught exception, but continuing to run because of the existence of other threads:

```java
public class CEExample implements Runnable {
  public static void main(String args[]) throws IOException {
    Thread thrd = new Thread(new CEExample());
    thrd.start();
    try {
      Thread.sleep(5000);
    } catch (InterruptedException ie) {
      ie.printStackTrace();
    }
    throw new IOException("Oops");
  }
  public void run() {
    while (true) {
      try {
        Thread.sleep(5000);
```

```
        } catch (InterruptedException ie) {
          ie.printStackTrace();
        }
        System.out.println("Alive!");
      }
    }
  }
```

Unchecked Exceptions

Unchecked exceptions are checked at runtime, rather than at compile time. Unchecked exceptions are all subclasses to the RuntimeException class, including RuntimeException itself. Unchecked exceptions and Errors do not need to be caught. More specifically, you should code your application with the assumption that unchecked exceptions would not be encountered; this is why you do not need to waste your efforts trying to catch and manage them, as these exceptions should rarely occur. Most runtime exceptions occur due to programming mistakes.

on the
Öob

Oracle provides excellent online coverage of exceptions through the Java Tutorial, "Lesson: Exceptions." The section "Unchecked Exceptions - The Controversy" is of particular interest and is worth review.

(Unchecked) Errors

Errors are unchecked exceptions that represent extreme conditions and will typically cause your application to fail. Most errors are unrecoverable external errors. Errors shouldn't be handled, but they can be.

EXERCISE 9-1

Determining When to Use Assertions in Place of Exceptions

This chapter does not cover assertions because assertions are not covered on the exam. But you should know when to use them. Do a little research and determine when assertions should be used in place of traditional exception handling.

Understand the Nature of Exceptions

Exam Objective   Create and invoke a method that throws an exception

Creating, throwing, and propagating exceptions is easier than it seems. In this section, we'll take a quick look at throwing exceptions; in the next section, we'll look further into catching them.

The following topics will be covered:

- Defining exceptions
- Throwing exceptions
- Propagating exceptions

Defining Exceptions

Exceptions in Java should have a no argument constructor and a constructor with a single `String` argument, as shown in the upcoming code sample. These guidelines are provided by convention and should be followed. To reinforce this point and provide a reference to the convention, *Murach's Java Programming, 4th Edition*, by Joel Murach (Mike Murach & Associates, 2011) states the following: "By convention, all exception classes should have a default constructor that doesn't accept any arguments and another constructor that accepts a string argument." The following example demonstrates a custom exception called `RecordException`:

```
public class RecordException extends Exception {
    public RecordException() {
        super();
    }
    public RecordException(String s) {
        super(s);
    }
}
```

This example demonstrates the creation of a checked exception as it is directly inherited from the `Exception` class. This `Exception` class could easily be made an unchecked exception by inheriting from the `RuntimeException` class.

All `Exception` subclass names should end with `Exception`—for example, `SQLException` and `NumberFormatException`. All `Error` subclass names should end with `Error`—for example, `VirtualMachineError` and `OutOfMemoryError`.

Throwing Exceptions

Methods use the `throw` statement to throw exceptions in Java. Only objects of the type or subtype of class `Throwable` can be thrown. Here is a valid `throw` statement:

```
throw new IllegalStateException();
```

An error will occur if the application attempts to throw an object that is not an instance of `Throwable`:

```
throw new String(); // Must be subtype of Throwable
```

This statement will invoke a compilation error and will also result in the following error message if executed:

```
$ Exception in thread "main" java.lang.RuntimeException:

  Uncompilable source code - incompatible types
  required: java.lang.Throwable
  found:    java.lang.String
      at thrower.Thrower.main(Thrower.java:10)
```

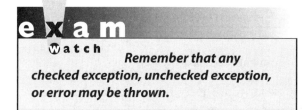

Propagating Exceptions

Exceptions can be propagated all the way up to the main method. If the main method does not handle the exception, it will be thrown to the Java virtual machine (JVM) and the application may be terminated. When an application throws an exception, the method that contains the exception must catch the exception or send it to the calling method, or else the application will end. To send an exception to the calling method, you must include the `throws` keyword in the method declaration along with the exception name to be thrown. This is demonstrated in the following code:

```
import java.io.IOException;
public class Thrower {
  public static void main(String[] args) {
    Thrower t = new Thrower();
```

```
      try {
        t.throw1();
      } catch (IOException ex) {
        System.out.println("An IOException has occurred");
      }
    }
    public void throw1() throws IOException {
      throw2();
    }
    public void throw2() throws IOException {
      throw3();
    }
    public void throw3() throws IOException {
      throw4();
    }
    public void throw4() throws IOException {
      throw new IOException();
    }
  }
```

on the ()ob

A best practice is to use a logging API in conjunction with the items being caught in your catch statements. Take a look at your current projects. If the projects are littered with print statements (directed to standard output), especially in the catch *clauses, consider doing some refactoring to leverage off of the logging APIs.*

EXERCISE 9-2

Creating a Custom Exception Class

In this exercise, you will create a custom checked Exception class.

1. Determine a name and purpose for your checked Exception class.

2. Create a new class that inherits from the Exception class.

3. Create a no-argument constructor that calls super().

4. Create a constructor with a single string argument that calls super(s).

5. Develop code that will throw the exception.

6. Develop code that will catch the exception.

Alter the Program Flow

Exam Objective   *Create a try-catch block and determine how exceptions alter normal program flow*

When code that is in scope of a `try` clause throws an exception, the exception will be evaluated by the associated `catch` clauses. Various statements work in conjunction with the `try` clause. We'll take a look at each one.

The following topics will be covered in these pages:

■ The `try-catch` statement

■ The `try-finally` statement

■ The `try-catch-finally` statement

■ The `try-with-resources` statement

■ The `multi-catch` clause

The try-catch Statement

The `try-catch` statement contains code to "catch" thrown exceptions from within the `try` block, either explicitly or propagated up through method calls. In a `try` clause, the code within its block is attempting (trying) to complete without encountering any exceptions. If an exception is thrown, all statements after the exception in the `try` block will not be executed. This is demonstrated in the following code:

```
try {
  System.out.print("What's up!");
  throw new ArithmeticException();
  System.out.print(", Hello!"); // code never reached
  System.out.print(", Hi there! "); // code never reached
} catch (ArithmeticException ae) {
  System.out.print(", Howdy! ");
  ae.printStackTrace();
}
$ What's up!, Howdy!
```

Always begin with the subclasses when ordering the `catch` clauses to catch exceptions. This necessary design (coding implementation) is illustrated in the next example:

```java
public void demonstrateTryCatch() {
  try {
    throw new NumberFormatException();
  } catch (NumberFormatException nfe) {  // Exception is caught here
    nfe.printStackTrace();
  } catch (IllegalArgumentException iae) {
    iae.printStackTrace();
  } catch (RuntimeException re) {
    re.printStackTrace();
  } catch (Exception e) {
    e.printStackTrace();
  }
}
```

`NumberFormatException` is on the bottom of the hierarchy and is a subclass to `IllegalArgumentException`. `IllegalArgumentException` is a subclass to `RuntimeException`, and `RuntimeException` is a subclass to `Exception`. Therefore, the order of the `catch` clauses is relative to this order: `NumberFormatException`, `IllegalArgumentException`, `RuntimeException`, and `Exception`.

on the **!** **()** o b

In the real world, it is not a best practice to catch `RuntimeException` or the `Exception` classes themselves. That is, you should catch their subclasses as appropriate to your code.

You have several options when you're printing data relative to an exception being caught, such as using the `getMessage`, `toString`, and `printStackTrace` methods. The `getMessage` method returns a detailed message about the exception. The `toString` method returns detailed messages about the exception and a class name. The `printStackTrace` method prints a detailed message, the class name, and a stack trace. These methods are demonstrated in the following code:

```java
public void demonstrateTryCatch() {
  try {
    int result = (3 / 0); // throws ArithmeticException
  } catch (ArithmeticException ae) {
    System.out.println(ae.getMessage());
    System.out.println(ae.toString());
    ae.printStackTrace();
  }
}
```

They result in this output:

```
$ / by zero (divide by zero)
$ java.lang.ArithmeticException: / by zero
$ java.lang.ArithmeticException: / by zero
$        at com.ocajexam.exceptions_tester.TryStatements.demonstrateTryCatch
  (TryStatements.java:20)
         at com.ocajexam.exceptions_tester.Main.main(Main.java:26)
```

The catch clause should never be empty. This is considered *silencing* an exception and is not a good practice. A catch clause should either log a message, print the stack trace, or provide some sort of notification to the consumer (developer, user, and so on) of the application that an error has occurred. Here's an example:

```
public void demonstrateTryCatch() {
  try {
     throw new NumberFormatException();
  } catch (NumberFormatException nfe) {
     // This catch clause should not be empty
  }
}
```

When exceptions are being caught, if the Exception class is not found, the system will look for the superclass of the exception being thrown. In the following example, IllegalArgumentException is the superclass of NumberFormatException, so it will catch the exception being thrown:

```
public void demonstrateTryCatch() {
  try {
     throw new NumberFormatException();
  } catch (IllegalArgumentException iae) {
     iae.printStackTrace();
  }
}
```

In the preceding examples, you'll notice a common naming convention for the exception parameters. It is customary to use the first letter of each word in the Exception class for the parameter name. For example, for ClassCastException, the parameter name would be cce.

The try-finally Statement

In the try-finally statement, the finally clause is always executed after the try clause has completed, unless, of course, the application is terminated prior to the try clause finishing up.

The following example demonstrates the `try-finally` statement:

```
public void demonstrateTryFinally() {
  try {
    System.out.print("Jab");
  } finally {
    System.out.println(" and Roundhouse ");
  }
}
```

The resultant output of running the `demonstrateTryFinally` method is as follows:

```
$ Jab and Roundhouse
```

The following example demonstrates a `try-finally` statement in which the `try` clause exits prematurely with a call to `System.exit`:

```
public void demonstrateTryFinally() {
  try {
    System.out.print("Jab");
    System.exit(0);
  } finally {
    System.out.println(" and Roundhouse ");
  }
}
```

The resultant output of running the `demonstrateTryFinally` method in this scenario is as follows:

```
$ Jab
```

Note that if an unchecked exception is thrown in a `try` block, the `finally` method will be invoked, as shown next. Because the unchecked exception is not caught, the application terminates, but only *after* the `finally` statement completes.

```
public class Example {
  public static void main(String[] args) {
    System.out.print("Bread");
    try {
      throw new NumberFormatException(); //unchecked exception
    } finally {
      System.out.print(" and "); // this gets executed!
    }
    System.out.println(" butter"); // this statement is not reached
  }
}
```

Because of the termination of the application after completion of the `finally` statement, but before the end of the program, we do not get our butter:

```
$ Bread and
```

The try-catch-finally Statement

The `try-catch-finally` statement is exactly what it appears to be—a `try-catch` statement with a `finally` clause attached. The `finally` clause will execute after the `try-catch` portion of the statement, unless the application is terminated prior to the entry point of the `finally` clause.

The try-with-resources Statement

The `try-with-resources` statement provides the capability of declaring resources that must be closed when they are no longer needed. These resources must implement the `AutoCloseable` interface. Prior to Java SE 7, these resources were typically closed in the `finally` clause. With version 7, the resources are automatically closed at the end of the `try-with-resources` statement—that is, if an exception is thrown or if the code block reaches its end, the resource is closed.

The Javadoc documentation for `AutoCloseable` (http://docs.oracle.com/javase/8/docs/api/java/lang/AutoCloseable.html) calls out all of the classes that can be used with the `try-with-resources` statement. The following classes here implement `AutoCloseable`; they give you the big picture of the wide and possible usages of resources for the `try-with-resources` statement:

AbstractInterruptibleChannel	AbstractSelectableChannel	AbstractSelector
AsynchronousFileChannel	AsynchronousServerSocketChannel	AsynchronousSocketChannel
AudioInputStream	BufferedInputStream	BufferedOutputStream
BufferedReader	BufferedWriter	ByteArrayInputStream
ByteArrayOutputStream	CharArrayReader	CharArrayWriter
CheckedInputStream	CheckedOutputStream	CipherInputStream
CipherOutputStream	DatagramChannel	DatagramSocket
DataInputStream	DataOutputStream	DeflaterInputStream
DeflaterOutputStream	DigestInputStream	DigestOutputStream
FileCacheImageInputStream	FileCacheImageOutputStream	FileChannel
FileImageInputStream	FileImageOutputStream	FileInputStream
FileLock	FileOutputStream	FileReader
FileSystem	FileWriter	FilterInputStream

(continued)

FilterOutputStream	FilterReader	FilterWriter
Formatter	ForwardingJavaFileManager	GZIPInputStream
GZIPOutputStream	ImageInputStreamImpl	ImageOutputStreamImpl
InflaterInputStream	InflaterOutputStream	InputStream
InputStream	InputStream	InputStreamReader
JarFile	JarInputStream	JarOutputStream
LineNumberInputStream	LineNumberReader	LogStream
MemoryCacheImageInputStream	MemoryCacheImageOutputStream	MLet
MulticastSocket	ObjectInputStream	ObjectOutputStream
OutputStream	OutputStream	OutputStream
OutputStreamWriter	Pipe.SinkChannel	Pipe.SourceChannel
PipedInputStream	PipedOutputStream	PipedReader
PipedWriter	PrintStream	PrintWriter
PrivateMLet	ProgressMonitorInputStream	PushbackInputStream
PushbackReader	RandomAccessFile	Reader
RMIConnectionImpl	RMIConnectionImpl_Stub	RMIConnector
RMIIIOPServerImpl	RMIJRMPServerImpl	RMIServerImpl
Scanner	SelectableChannel	Selector
SequenceInputStream	ServerSocket	ServerSocketChannel
Socket	SocketChannel	SSLServerSocket
SSLSocket	StringBufferInputStream	StringReader
StringWriter	URLClassLoader	Writer
XMLDecoder	XMLEncoder	ZipFile
ZipInputStream	ZipOutputStream	

Now let's compare some code. Here is the legacy `try-catch-finally` code performing the `close` method explicitly in the `finally` statement:

```
public void demonstrateTryWithResources() {
  Scanner sc = new Scanner(System.in);
  try {
    System.out.print("Number of apples: ");
    int apples = sc.nextInt();
    System.out.print("Number of oranges: ");
    int oranges = sc.nextInt();
    System.out.println("Pieces of Fruit: " + (apples + oranges));
  } catch (InputMismatchException ime) {
    ime.printStackTrace();
  } finally {
    sc.close();
  }
}
```

Now let's refactor this code into a `try-with-resources` statement, where the `close` method will be called implicitly. Notice two changes: the first is the `Scanner` declaration as an argument in the `try` clause, and the second is the removal of the `finally` clause.

```
public void demonstrateTryWithResources() {
  try (Scanner sc = new Scanner(System.in)) {
    System.out.print("Number of apples: ");
    int apples = sc.nextInt();
    System.out.print("Number of oranges: ");
    int oranges = sc.nextInt();
    System.out.println("Pieces of Fruit: " + (apples + oranges));
  } catch (InputMismatchException ime) {
    ime.printStackTrace();
  }
}
```

The multi-catch Clause

The `multi-catch` clause allows for multiple exception arguments in one `catch` clause. Examine the following code segment:

```
...
} catch (ArrayIndexOutOfBoundsException aioobe) {
} catch (NullPointerException nbe) {}
...
```

These two `catch` clauses can be refactored into one `multi-catch` clause using the appropriate syntax:

```
catch (exceptionTypeA | exceptionTypeB [| ExceptionTypeX] ... e ) { }
```

An example of `multi-catch` is shown in the following `demonstrateMultiCatch` method:

```
public void demonstrateMultiCatch2() {
  try {
    Random random = new Random();
    int i = random.nextInt(2);
    if (i == 0) {
      throw new ArrayIndexOutOfBoundsException();
    } else {
      throw new NullPointerException();
    }
```

```
    } catch (ArrayIndexOutOfBoundsException | NullPointerException e) {
      e.printStackTrace();
    }
  }
```

The left margin of the NetBeans source editor will provide hints that encourage the automated refactoring of multiple related `catch` *statements to a* `multi-catch` *statement. You can search for "Seven NetBeans Hints for Modernizing Java Code" on the Web to find more information.*

EXERCISE 9-3

Using NetBeans Code Templates for Exception Handling Elements

The NetBeans integrated development environment (IDE) includes a nice feature called *code templates*. Code templates are abbreviated strings that expand into fuller strings or blocks of code. There are currently six related code templates for exception handling. This exercise has you using them all:

   1. Make use of the `ca` code template.

   2. Make use of the `fy` code template.

   3. Make use of the `th` code template.

   4. Make use of the `tw` code template.

   5. Make use of the `twn` code template.

   6. Make use of the `trycatch` code template.

CERTIFICATION OBJECTIVE

Recognize Common Exceptions

Exam Objective   Recognize common Exception classes (such as NullPointerException, ArithmeticException, ArrayIndexOutOfBoundsException, ClassCastException)

This objective is pretty much a review, because we've already discussed the differences between exception types. To help you grasp the specifics of the most common exceptions, let's take a look at the class hierarchies in some diagrams and produce some unchecked exceptions.

Common Checked Exceptions

Common checked exceptions include the following:

CloneNotSupportedException	ClassNotFoundException
NoSuchMethodException	IOException
FileNotFoundException	SQLException
InterruptedIOException	FontFormatException

These exceptions are shown in Figure 9-2 and are detailed in the following sections.

CloneNotSupportedException

The CloneNotSupportedException is thrown when the clone method is called by an object that cannot be cloned. Deep copy cannot be generated. Deep copying (for example, deep cloning) is when a cloned object makes an exact duplicate of an object's state. (To learn more about deep copies [and shallow copies] read "Deep Copy and Shallow Copy" from JusForTechies [www.jusfortechies.com/java/core-java/deepcopy_and_shallowcopy.php].)

FIGURE 9-2   Common checked exceptions

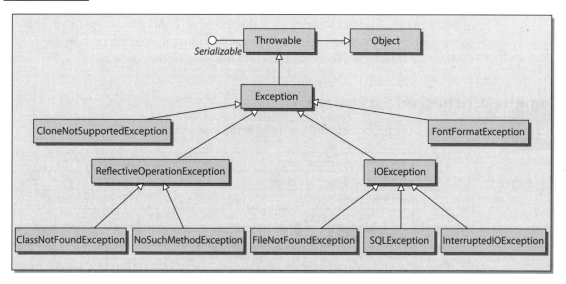

ClassNotFoundException

The `ClassNotFoundException` is thrown when a class cannot be loaded because of a failure to locate its definition.

NoSuchMethodException

The `NoSuchMethodException` is thrown when a called method is unable to be located. For example, a `NoSuchMethodException` would occur if you tried to use reflection and attempted to invoke a method that did not exist.

FileNotFoundException

The `FileNotFoundException` is thrown with an attempt to open a file that cannot be found.

IOException

The `IOException` is thrown when a failed input/output operation occurs.

SQLException

The `SQLException` is thrown when a database or SQL statement error occurs.

InterruptedIOException

The `InterruptedIOException` is thrown when a thread is interrupted. This class has a `bytesTransferred` field that provides information on how many bytes were transferred successfully before the interruption occurred.

Common Unchecked Exceptions

Common unchecked exceptions include the following:

`IllegalArgumentException`	`NumberFormatException`
`ArrayIndexOutOfBoundsException`	`IndexOutOfBoundsException`
`NullPointerException`	`IllegalStateException`
`IllegalStateException`	`ClassCastException`
`ArithmeticException`	

These exceptions are visualized in Figure 9-3 and are detailed in the following sections with examples.

FIGURE 9-3   Common unchecked exceptions

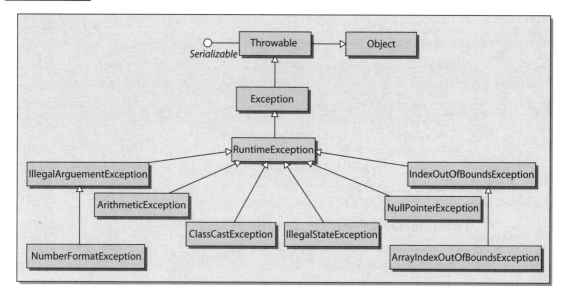

The IllegalArgumentException Class

The IllegalArgumentException of the java.nio.file package is thrown when a method has been passed an illegal or inappropriate argument.

Here's an example:

```
public void forceIllegalArgumentException() {
  PageFormat   path = new PageFormat();
  path.setOrientation(3); // IllegalArgumentException
}
```

The NumberFormatException Class

The NumberFormatException is thrown when the application has attempted to convert a string to one of the numeric types with the wrong format.

Here's an example:

```
public void forceNumberFormatException() {
  Double.parseDouble("2.1");
  Double.parseDouble("INVALID");  // NumberFormatException
}
```

The ArrayIndexOutOfBoundsException Class

The `ArrayIndexOutOfBoundsException` is thrown when an array has been accessed with an illegal index that is either less than, equal to, or greater than the size of the array.

Here's an example:

```
public void forceArrayIndexOutOfBoundsException() {
   Float[][] num = new Float[3][3];
   num[2][0] = (float)1.0;
   num[2][1] = (float)2.0;
   System.out.println(num[2][2]);
   System.out.println(num[3][3]);   // ArrayIndexOutOfBoundsException
}
```

The IndexOutOfBoundsException Class

The `IndexOutOfBoundsException` is thrown when an index is out of range.

Here's an example:

```
public void forceIndexOutOfBoundsException() {
  List<String> gorillaSpecies = new LinkedList<>();
  gorillaSpecies.add("Eastern");
  gorillaSpecies.add("Western");
  System.out.println(gorillaSpecies.get(1));
  System.out.println(gorillaSpecies.get(2)); // IndexOutOfBoundsException
}
```

The NullPointerException Class

The `NullPointerException` is thrown when an application is required to use an object but finds `null` instead.

Here's an example:

```
public void forceNullPointerException() {
  String iceCreamFlavor = "vanilla";
  iceCreamFlavor = null;
  System.out.println(iceCreamFlavor.length());   // NullPointerException
}
```

The IllegalStateException Class

The `IllegalStateException` is thrown when a method has been invoked at an illegal or inappropriate time due to being in an inappropriate state.

Here's an example:

```
public void forceIllegalStateException() {
  List<String> chord = new ArrayList<>();
  chord.add("D");
  chord.add("G");
  chord.add("B");
  chord.add("G");
  Iterator it = chord.iterator();
  while (it.hasNext()) {
    it.next();
    it.remove();
    it.remove(); // IllegalStateException (remove depends on next)
  }
}
```

The ClassCastException Class

The ClassCastException is thrown when the code attempts to cast an object to a subclass of which it is not an instance.

Here's an example:

```
public void forceClassCastException() {
  Object x = new Float("1.0");
  System.out.println((Double) x);
  System.out.println((String) x); // ClassCastException
}
```

The ArithmeticException Class

The ArithmeticException is thrown when an exceptional arithmetic condition has occurred.

Here's an example:

```
public void forceArithmeticException() {
  int apple;
  apple = (4 / 2);
  apple = (4 / 0); // ArithmeticException
}
```

Common Errors

Common (unchecked) errors include the following: AssertionError, ExceptionInInitializeError, VirtualMachineError, OutOfMemoryError, and NoClassDefFoundError. These errors, as well as

FIGURE 9-4   Common errors

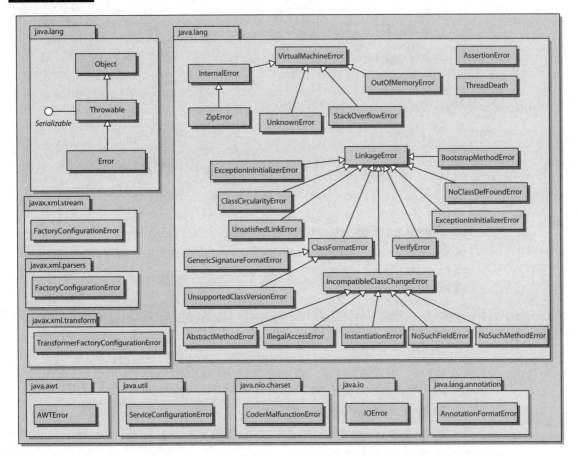

many others, of the error classes in JDK 8 are visualized in Figure 9-4. The five common errors are detailed in the following sections.

The AssertionError Class

The `AssertionError` is thrown upon a failed assertion.

The ExceptionInInitializeError Class

The `ExceptionInInitializeError` is thrown when an unexpected exception occurs in a static initializer.

The VirtualMachineError Class

The `VirtualMachineError` is thrown when a JVM error occurs.

The OutOfMemoryError Class

The `OutOfMemoryError` is thrown when garbage collection is performed but is unable to free up any space.

The NoClassDefFoundError Class

The `NoClassDefFoundError` is thrown when the JVM cannot find a class definition that was found at compile time.

EXERCISE 9-4

Creating an Error Condition

Errors are not typically encountered, but when they are, your application is probably doomed. To demonstrate creating an error, the following code causes an `OutOfMemoryError` ("Exception in thread 'main' java.lang.OutOfMemoryError: Java heap space"):

```
public void forceStackOverFlowError() {
  Integer counter = 0;
  ArrayList<Integer> unstoppable = new ArrayList<>();
  while (true) {
    unstoppable.add(counter);
    counter++;
    if (counter % 10000 == 0) {
      System.out.println(counter);
    }
  }
}
```

It's now your turn.

1. Select an error you'd like to force from Figure 9-4.

2. Study the error in the Javadoc documentation. You can find documentation for the subclasses of the `Error` class here: http://docs.oracle.com/javase/8/docs/api/.

3. Develop and execute a simple application.

4. Do whatever it takes to impress your selected `Error` on the application.

5. Share what you did with the JavaRanch at this thread, "Various examples of having errors thrown relative to the Error class," at www.coderanch .com/t/583633/java-SCJA/certification/Various-examples-having-errors-thrown#2656332.

CERTIFICATION SUMMARY

This chapter discussed the exception handling hierarchy in Java. We went over the different types/categories of exceptions in Java. We discussed the various `try` block statements and how to throw, catch, and handle exceptions. Finally, we discussed the various types of common exceptions and errors that you'll see when working with the Java programming language.

When you sit the OCA exam, you will see several questions on exception handling, most of them dealing with presented code samples. Your knowledge of working with exceptions must be strong or you will feel defeated even before you finish the exam. If after reading this chapter, you still think your knowledge is weak on exceptions, read it through again, making sure you complete all the exercises. Also, for this chapter as well as the others, you should always feel comfortable with going straight into the Java Language Specification for clarity or information: http:// docs.oracle.com/javase/specs/jls/se8/jls8.pdf.

Finally, mastering exception handling won't be important just for the exam; you'll be using it a lot in your own code for your projects at work, at school, and anywhere else.

TWO-MINUTE DRILL

Understand the Rationale and Types of Exceptions

- ☐ All exceptions and errors inherit from the `Throwable` class.
- ☐ Types include checked exceptions, unchecked exceptions, and errors.
- ☐ Checked exceptions are checked by the compiler at compile time.
- ☐ Checked exceptions are all subclasses to the `Exception` class; however, `RuntimeException` and its subclasses are not part of the `Exception` class.
- ☐ Unchecked exceptions are checked at runtime, not compile time.
- ☐ Unchecked exceptions are all subclasses to the `RuntimeException` class, including `RuntimeException` itself.
- ☐ Unchecked exceptions and errors do not need to be caught.
- ☐ Errors represent extreme conditions and will typically cause your application to fail.

Understand the Nature of Exceptions

- ☐ Code cannot be placed between the `try` and `catch` blocks, `try` and `finally` blocks, or `catch` and `finally` blocks—that is, extra code cannot be immediately placed before or after the curly braces that separate the blocks in these statements.
- ☐ The common naming convention for `catch` clause arguments is the representation of a string containing the first letter of each word of the exception being passed.
- ☐ Exceptions are thrown with the `throw` keyword.
- ☐ The `throws` keyword is used in definitions of methods that throw an exception.
- ☐ Methods of the `Throwable` class provide support for gathering information about a thrown exception. The methods `getMessage`, `toString`, and `printStackTrace` are commonly used.
- ☐ Thrown exceptions move up the call stack until they are caught. If they are not caught and reach the main method, the application will end.

Alter the Program Flow

☐ The `try` block must contain code that can throw an exception.

☐ The `try` block must have one `catch` or `finally` block.

☐ The `try-with-resources` statement declares resources that can be automatically closed. The objects must implement `AutoCloseable`.

☐ The `catch` block must be ordered by subtypes first.

☐ The `multi-catch` feature allows for multiple exception types to be caught in one `catch` block.

☐ The `try-catch` statement is a valid statement that does not include a `finally` clause.

☐ The `finally` block of the `try-catch-finally` and `try-finally` statements are always invoked, unless the JVM terminates first.

☐ The `finally` block is typically used for releasing resources.

Recognize Common Exceptions

☐ Common checked exceptions include `CloneNotSupportedException`, `ClassNotFoundException`, `NoSuchMethodException`, `IOException`, `FileNotFoundException`, `SQLException`, `InterruptedIOException`, and `FontFormatException`.

☐ Common unchecked exceptions include `IllegalArgumentException`, `NumberFormatException`, `ArrayIndexOutOfBoundsException`, `IndexOutOfBoundsException`, `NullPointerException`, `IllegalStateException`, `IllegalStateException`, `ClassCastException`, and `ArithmeticException`.

☐ Common (unchecked) errors include `AssertionError`, `ExceptionInInitializeError`, `VirtualMachineError`, `OutOfMemoryError`, and `NoClassDefFoundError`.

SELF TEST

Understand the Rationale and Types of Exceptions

1. Which class has the fewest subclasses: `Exception`, `RuntimeException`, or `Error`? Select the correct statement.
   A. The `Exception` class has fewer subclasses than the `RuntimeException` and `Error` classes.
   B. The `RuntimeException` class has fewer subclasses than the `Exception` and `Error` classes.
   C. The `Error` class has fewer subclasses than the `Exception` and `RuntimeException` classes.

2. Of the following types of exceptions, which will an IDE help you in catching, if it is not handled in your code?
   A. Checked exceptions.
   B. Unchecked exceptions.

3. Which statement about the `Throwable` class is not correct?
   A. The `Throwable` class extends the `Object` class.
   B. The `Throwable` class implements the `Serializable` interface.
   C. Direct subclasses to the `Throwable` class include the `RuntimeException` and `Error` classes.
   D. The `Throwable` class is in the `java.lang` package.

4. Exceptions fall into three categories. Which is not an exceptions category?
   A. `Check Exceptions`
   B. `Unchecked Exceptions`
   C. `Assertions`
   D. `Errors`

5. Which classes are subclasses of the `IOException` class? (Choose three.)
   A. `FileNotFoundException`
   B. `SQLException`
   C. `ClassNotFoundException`
   D. `InterruptedIOException`

6. Which of the following code fragments will throw a `NumberFormatException`?

   A. `Integer.parseInt("INVALID");`

   B. `int e = (2 / 0);`

   C. `Object x = new Float("1.0"); Double d = (Double) x;`

   D. `String s = null; int i = s.length();`

Understand the Nature of Exceptions

7. Which of the following classes can be thrown? (Choose all that apply.)

   A. `throw new Error();`

   B. `throw new RuntimeException();`

   C. `throw new Exception();`

   D. `throw new Assertion();`

   E. `throw new Throwable();`

8. Given:

```
public static void testMethod1() {
  try {
    testMethod2();
  } catch (ArithmeticException ae) {
    System.out.println("Dock");
  }
}

public static void testMethod2() throws ArithmeticException {
  try {
    testMethod3();
  } catch (ArithmeticException ae) {
    System.out.println("Dickory");
  }
}

public static void testMethod3() throws ArithmeticException {
  throw new ArithmeticException();
  System.out.println("Hickory");
}
```

What will be printed when the `testMethod1` is invoked (after allowing the code to run with compilation warnings)?

A. "Hickory Dickory Dock" is printed.

B. "Dickory" is printed.

C. "Dock" is printed.

9. Given:

```
public static void test() throws FileNotFoundException {
   try {
      throw FileNotFoundException();
   } finally {
   }
}
```

Determine why it will not compile. Which statement is correct?

A. The code will not compile without a `catch` clause.

B. The code needs the `new` keyword after the `throw` keyword.

C. The `finally` clause should be the `final` clause.

D. There is no class called `FileNotFoundException`.

10. Can a method throw more than one exception?

A. Yes, a method can throw more than one exception.

B. No, a method cannot throw more than one exception.

11. Following the common convention of naming the parameter in the `catch` clause, what would the parameter be for the exception `EnumConstantNotPresentException`?

A. e

B. ex

C. ee

D. ecnpe

Alter the Program Flow

12. What new features came with Java 7 to enhance exception handling capabilities? (Choose all that apply.)

A. The `multi-catch` feature

B. The `boomerang` feature

C. The `try-with-resources` feature

D. The `try-with-riches` feature

13. Given:

```
try {
  throw new IIOException();
} catch (IIOException iioe) {
} catch (IOException ioe) {
} catch (Exception e) {
} finally {
}
```

This code will not compile. Why?

A. Although it's a best practice that `Exception` classes have a no argument constructor, this isn't always followed, as in the case of the `IIOException` class that does not have a no argument constructor.

B. The exceptions listed in the `catch` blocks should be in the reverse order. The `catch` blocks should be ordered like so: `Exception`, followed by `IOException`, followed by `IIOException`.

C. The `finally` block must include statements.

D. The `throws` keyword should be used in place of the `throw` keyword.

Recognize Common Exceptions

14. What do the `InternalError`, `OutOfMemoryError`, `StackOverflowError`, and `UnknownError` classes have in common? (Choose all that apply.)

A. They are all subclasses to the `VirtualMachineError` class.

B. They all have a no argument constructor.

C. They all have a constructor that accepts a single `String` argument.

D. They are all subclasses to the `RuntimeException` class.

E. All of the above

15. The `bytesTransferred` field of which checked exception provides information on how many bytes were transferred successfully before a disruption occurred?

A. `IOException`

B. `InterruptedIOException`

C. `IntrospectionException`

D. `TimeoutException`

16. Given:

```
String typeOfDog = "Mini Australian Shepherd";
typeOfDog = null;
System.out.println(typeOfDog.length);
```

Which of the following is true?

A. A `NullPointerException` will be thrown.

B. An `IllegalStateException` will be thrown.

C. An `IllegalArgumentException` will be thrown.

D. A compilation error will occur.

17. Which of the following is not a valid Java exception?

A. `IOException`

B. `InterruptedIOException`

C. `CPUProcessException`

D. `CloneNotSupportedException`

E. `ClassNotFoundException`

SELF TEST ANSWERS

Understand the Rationale and Types of Exceptions

1. Which class has the fewest subclasses: `Exception`, `RuntimeException`, or `Error`? Select the correct statement.
   A. The `Exception` class has fewer subclasses than the `RuntimeException` and `Error` classes.
   B. The `RuntimeException` class has fewer subclasses than the `Exception` and `Error` classes.
   C. The `Error` class has fewer subclasses than the `Exception` and `RuntimeException` classes.

   Answer:

   ☑ **C**. The `Error` class has fewer subclasses than the `Exception` and `RuntimeException` classes.

   ☒ **A** and **B** are incorrect. **A** is incorrect because the `Exception` class has the most subclasses compared to the `RuntimeException` class and the `Error` class. Remember that `RuntimeException` is a subclass of the `Exception` class. **B** is incorrect because the `RuntimeException` class has more subclasses than the `Error` classes.

2. Of the following types of exceptions, which will an IDE help you in catching, if it is not handled in your code?
   A. Checked exceptions.
   B. Unchecked exceptions.

   Answer:

   ☑ **A**. An IDE will provide hints to help you catch checked exceptions that are not handled in your code.

   ☒ **B** is incorrect. An IDE will not provide hints to catch unchecked exceptions that are not handled in your code, as unchecked exceptions are not required to be caught.

3. Which statement about the `Throwable` class is not correct?

  A. The `Throwable` class extends the `Object` class.

  B. The `Throwable` class implements the `Serializable` interface.

  C. Direct subclasses to the `Throwable` class include the `RuntimeException` and `Error` classes.

  D. The `Throwable` class is in the `java.lang` package.

> Answer:
>
> ☑ **C.** Direct subclasses to the `Throwable` class include the `Exception` and `Error` classes. The `RuntimeException` class is a subclass, but not a *direct* subclass.
>
> ☒ **A, B,** and **D** are incorrect. **A** is incorrect because the statement is correct; the `Throwable` class does extend the `Object` class. **B** is incorrect because the statement is correct; the `Throwable` class does implement the `Serializable` interface. **D** is incorrect because the statement is correct; the `Throwable` class is in the `java.lang` package.

4. Exceptions fall into three categories. Which is not an exceptions category?

  A. `Check Exceptions`

  B. `Unchecked Exceptions`

  C. `Assertions`

  D. `Errors`

> Answer:
>
> ☑ **C.** `Assertions` is not an exception category.
>
> ☒ **A, B** and **D** are incorrect. `Check Exceptions`, `Unchecked Exceptions`, and `Errors` are all exception categories in Java.

5. Which classes are subclasses of the `IOException` class? (Choose three.)

  A. `FileNotFoundException`

  B. `SQLException`

  C. `ClassNotFoundException`

  D. `InterruptedIOException`

Answer:

☑ **A**, **B**, and **D**. `FileNotFoundException`, `SQLException`, and `InterruptedIOException` are all subclasses of `IOException`.
☒ **C** is incorrect. `ClassNotFoundException` is not a subclass of `IOException`; it is a subclass of `ReflectiveOperationException`.

6. Which of the following code fragments will throw a `NumberFormatException`?
   A. `Integer.parseInt("INVALID");`
   B. `int e = (2 / 0);`
   C. `Object x = new Float("1.0"); Double d = (Double) x;`
   D. `String s = null; int i = s.length();`

Answer:

☑ **A**. Evaluation of the statement causes a `NumberFormatException` to be thrown.
☒ **B**, **C**, and **D** are incorrect. **B** is incorrect because evaluation of the statement causes an `ArithmeticException` to be thrown. **C** is incorrect because evaluation of the statement causes a `ClassCastException` to be thrown. **D** is incorrect because evaluation of the statement causes a null pointer exception.

Understand the Nature of Exceptions

7. Which of the following classes can be thrown? (Choose all that apply.)
   A. `throw new Error();`
   B. `throw new RuntimeException();`
   C. `throw new Exception();`
   D. `throw new Assertion();`
   E. `throw new Throwable();`

Answer:

☑ **A**, **B**, **C**, and **E**. The `Error`, `RuntimeException`, `Exception`, and `Throwable` classes can all be thrown.
☒ **D** is incorrect. There is no `Assertion` class in Java. There is, however, an `AssertionError` class in Java that may be thrown.

8. Given:

```
public static void testMethod1() {
  try {
    testMethod2();
  } catch (ArithmeticException ae) {
    System.out.println("Dock");
  }
}
public static void testMethod2() throws ArithmeticException {
  try {
    testMethod3();
  } catch (ArithmeticException ae) {
    System.out.println("Dickory");
  }
}
public static void testMethod3() throws ArithmeticException {
  throw new ArithmeticException();
  System.out.println("Hickory");
}
```

What will be printed when the testMethod1 is invoked (after allowing the code to run with compilation warnings)?

A. "Hickory Dickory Dock" is printed.

B. "Dickory" is printed.

C. "Dock" is printed.

Answer:

☑ **B.** "Dickory" is printed.

☒ **A** and **C** are incorrect. **A** is incorrect because the "Hickory" statement is never reached and an exception is not thrown to the testMethod2 invocation. **C** is incorrect because an exception is not thrown to the testMethod2 invocation, which would have been necessary to print out "Dock".

9. Given:

```
public static void test() throws FileNotFoundException {
  try {
    throw FileNotFoundException();
  } finally {
  }
}
```

Determine why it will not compile. Which statement is correct?

A. The code will not compile without a `catch` clause.

B. The code needs the `new` keyword after the `throw` keyword.

C. The `finally` clause should be the `final` clause.

D. There is no class called `FileNotFoundException`.

> **Answer:**
>
> ☑ **B.** The code needs the `new` keyword after the `throw` keyword in this example.
>
> ☒ **A, C,** and **D** are incorrect. **A** is incorrect because a `catch` clause is not needed if a `finally` clause is provided. **C** is incorrect because using `finally` instead of `final` is correct. **D** is incorrect because there is an `Exception` class called `FileNotFoundException`.

10. Can a method throw more than one exception?

A. Yes, a method can throw more than one exception.

B. No, a method cannot throw more than one exception.

> **Answer:**
>
> ☑ **A.** There are no restrictions on how many different types of exceptions a method can throw.
>
> ☒ **B** is incorrect because methods can throw one or more exceptions.

11. Following the common convention of naming the parameter in the `catch` clause, what would the parameter be for the exception `EnumConstantNotPresentException`?

A. e

B. ex

C. ee

D. ecnpe

Answer:

☑ **D.** ecnpe would be the parameter name for EnumConstantNotPresentException in the catch clause, with each letter representing one of the words in the exception.

☒ **A, B,** and **C** are incorrect. **A** is incorrect because e does not follow the convention for the parameter name for EnumConstantNotPresentException in the catch clause. **B** is incorrect because ex does not follow the convention for the parameter name for EnumConstantNotPresentException in the catch clause. **C** is incorrect because ee does not follow the convention for the parameter name for EnumConstantNotPresentException in the catch clause.

Alter the Program Flow

12. What new features came with Java 7 to enhance exception handling capabilities? (Choose all that apply.)

A. The multi-catch feature
B. The boomerang feature
C. The try-with-resources feature
D. The try-with-riches feature

Answer:

☑ **A** and **C.** Java 7 introduced the multi-catch and try-with-resources features.

☒ **B** and **D** are incorrect. **B** is incorrect because there is no boomerang feature. **D** is incorrect because there is no try-with-riches feature.

13. Given:

```
try {
   throw new IIOException();
} catch (IIOException iioe) {
} catch (IOException ioe) {
} catch (Exception e) {
} finally {
}
```

This code will not compile. Why?

A. Although it's a best practice that `Exception` classes have a no argument constructor, this isn't always followed, as in the case of the `IIOException` class that does not have a no argument constructor.

B. The exceptions listed in the `catch` blocks should be in the reverse order. The catch blocks should be ordered like so: `Exception`, followed by `IOException`, followed by `IIOException`.

C. The `finally` block must include statements.

D. The `throws` keyword should be used in place of the `throw` keyword.

Answer:

☑ **A.** Although it's a best practice that `Exception` classes have a no argument constructor, this isn't always followed. In this case, the `IIOException` class does not have a no argument constructor and will fail compilation.

☒ **B, C**, and **D** are incorrect. **B** is incorrect because the `catch` blocks are ordered appropriately, with the subclasses listed first in the appropriate hierarchical manner. **C** is incorrect because the `finally` block does not have to include any statements—that is, it can remain empty. **D** is incorrect because the `throw` keyword is used appropriately.

Recognize Common Exceptions

14. What do the `InternalError, OutOfMemoryError, StackOverflowError`, and `UnknownError` classes have in common? (Choose all that apply.)

A. They are all subclasses to the `VirtualMachineError` class.

B. They all have a no argument constructor.

C. They all have a constructor that accepts a single `String` argument.

D. They are all subclasses to the `RuntimeException` class.

E. All of the above

Answer:

☑ **A, B**, and **C. A** is correct because `InternalError`, `OutOfMemoryError`, `StackOverflowError`, and `UnknownError` are all subclasses to the `VirtualMachineError` class. **B** is correct because `InternalError`, `OutOfMemoryError`, `StackOverflowError`, and `UnknownError` all have a no argument constructor. **C** is correct because `InternalError`, `OutOfMemoryError`, `StackOverflowError`, and `UnknownError` all have a constructor that accepts a single `String` argument.

☒ **D** and **E** are incorrect. **D** is incorrect because `InternalError`, `OutOfMemoryError`, `StackOverflowError`, and `UnknownError` are not subclasses to the `RuntimeException` class. **E** is incorrect because all of the answers are not correct.

15. The `bytesTransferred` field of which checked exception provides information on how many bytes were transferred successfully before a disruption occurred?

A. `IOException`

B. `InterruptedIOException`

C. `IntrospectionException`

D. `TimeoutException`

Answer:

☑ **B**. The `InterruptedIOException` class includes a `bytesTransferred` field that provides information on how many bytes were transferred successfully before the interruption occurred.

☒ **A, C**, and **D** are incorrect. **A** is incorrect because `IOException` does not have a `bytesTransferred` field. **C** is incorrect because `IntrospectionException` does not have a `bytesTransferred` field. **D** is incorrect because the `TimeoutException` does not have a `bytesTransferred` field.

16. Given:

```
String typeOfDog = "Mini Australian Shepherd";
typeOfDog = null;
System.out.println(typeOfDog.length);
```

Which of the following is true?

A. A `NullPointerException` will be thrown.

B. An `IllegalStateException` will be thrown.

C. An `IllegalArgumentException` will be thrown.

D. A compilation error will occur.

Answer:

☑ **D.** A compilation error will occur. To make use of the `length` method of the `String` class, parentheses must be used. The statement should have read, `System.out.println (typeOfDog.length());` and not `System.out.println(typeOfDog.length);`.

☒ **A**, **B**, and **C** are incorrect. **A** is incorrect because a `NullPointerException` will not be thrown. Note that the statement wouldn't have been incorrect if the `length` method were used properly. **B** is incorrect because an `IllegalStateException` will not be thrown. **C** is incorrect because an `IllegalArgumentException` will not be thrown.

17. Which of the following is not a valid Java exception?

A. `IOException`

B. `InterruptedIOException`

C. `CPUProcessException`

D. `CloneNotSupportedException`

E. `ClassNotFoundException`

Answer:

☑ **C.** `CPUProcessException` is not a valid Java exception

☒ **A**, **B**, **D**, and **E** are incorrect. They are all valid Java exceptions.

10
Programming with the Date and Time API

O racle's exam topics include working with selected classes from the Java SE API. In this chapter and the next, we cover the objectives related to the new features of Java SE 8. The new Date and Time API is covered in this chapter, and new lambda expressions are covered in Chapter 11.

Because most applications rely heavily on calendar data, most people need to be familiar with this API. Whether calendar data is being presented on a web page, persisted in a database, or present in logging records or filenames, calendar data is everywhere when it comes to software applications. The rich, robust, and fluent Java SE 8 Date and Time API makes it easy for coders to work with calendar data.

Objectives related to APIs originating in Java versions previous to Java 8 are covered in prior chapters. This additional external coverage includes the following:

- Creating and manipulating strings (see Chapter 3)
- Manipulating data using the `StringBuilder` class and its methods (see Chapter 3)
- Declaring and using an `ArrayList` of a given type (see Chapter 6)

CERTIFICATION OBJECTIVE

Understand the Date and Time API

Exam Objective   Create and manipulate calendar data using classes from java .time.LocalDateTime, java.time.LocalDate, java.time.LocalTime, java.time.format .DateTimeFormatter, java.time.Period

Date, time, and calendar calculations are supported by the Date and Time API (Java Special Request [JSR] 310), which is provided by the ThreeTen Project (www .threeten.org) as its reference implementation (RI). JSR 310 is available in Java 8. The Date and Time API includes five calendar-related packages: `java.time`, `java .time.chrono`, `java.time.format`, `java.time.temporal`, and `java .time.zone`. For the OCA 8 exam, you will need to be acquainted with only a few classes in the `java.time` package—`LocalTime`, `LocalDate`, `LocalDateTime`, `DateTimeFormatter`, and `Period`—all of which are covered in this chapter.

The International Organization for Standardization date and time data exchange mode (ISO 8601) is used by the Date and Time API. ISO 8601 is properly named,

"Data elements and interchange formats – Information interchange – Representation of dates and times." The Gregorian calendar sets the basis for ISO 8601 and for the Date and Time API.

This chapter explores the Date and Time API through calendar data creation, calendar data manipulation, period support, and calendar data formatting support. Each area of coverage is provided in its own section.

Calendar Data Creation

Prior to Java 8, calendar data creation was supported with the `Date`, `Calendar`, and `GregorianCalendar` classes. Moving forward, we are leaving these classes in the past and aim to create our calendar data with a new set of classes. For the exam, you will need to master three calendar data creation classes: `LocalDate`, `LocalTime`, and `LocalDateTime`.

Before stepping through each one of these classes, let's take a look at the main classes in the API used in association with calendar data creation. These classes are shown in Table 10-1.

TABLE 10-1   Calendar Creation–Related Classes

Classes	Description
`LocalDate`, `LocalTime`, and `LocalDateTime`	Provides an immutable date-time object represented as year-month-day, hour-minute-second, and year-month-day-hour-minute-second
`OffsetTime`	Provides an immutable date-time object representing a time as hour-minute-second-offset
`OffSetDateTime`	Provides an immutable date-time with an offset for Greenwich/UTC
`ZonedDateTime`	Provides an immutable date-time object represented with a time-zone offset
`ZonedOffset`	Provides the amount of time that a time zone differs from Greenwich/UTC
`Year`, `YearMonth`, and `MonthDay`	Provides immutable date-time objects represented as a year, YearMonth, and MonthDay
`DayOfWeek` and `Month`	Provides enumerations for weekdays and months
`Period` and `Duration`	Provides a date-based amount of time in years, months, and days and a time-based amount in days, hours, minutes, seconds, and nanoseconds
`Instant`	Provides an instantaneous point (timestamp) of the timeline measured from the Java epoch of 1970-0101T00:00:00Z
`Clock`	Provides access to the current instant, date, and time using a time zone
`DateTimeException`	Exception class that is thrown when an error occurs in calendar calculations

Many say Java reads like a book, and so do we. The Date and Time API makes use of the fluent API design to influence the implementation of its API. A fluent API, also known as a fluent interface, makes code more readable and maintainable. The usability goals of fluent APIs are achieved using *method chaining*, which allows objects to be wired together. Here's an example:

```
// Method Chaining
LocalDateTime ldt =
    LocalDateTime.now().plusYears(14).plusMonths(2).plusDays(10);
```

The method prefixes in Table 10-2 are seen throughout the API when creating, manipulating, and formatting calendar data and when working with the `Period` class.

TABLE 10-2	Date and Time API Method Prefixes	
Prefix	**Use**	**Example**
of	Used with static factory methods	`LocalDate.of(2015, Month.JANUARY, 1);`
parse	Used to parse a text representation of a period	`Period.parse("P3M"); // Three months`
get	Used for getting a value	`Duration d = Duration.ofSeconds(2);` `System.out.println(d.getSeconds());`

is	Used to check for true or false	`LocalTime lt1 =`
		`    LocalTime.parse("11:30");`
		`LocalTime lt2 = LocalTime.NOON;`
		`System.out.println(lt1.isAfter(lt2));`

with	Used as the immutable equivalent of a setter	`LocalDateTime.now().withYear(2001);`
plus	Used to add an amount to an object	`Period period = Period.of(5, 2, 1);` `period = period.plusDays(1);`
minus	Used to subtract an amount from an object	`Period period = Period.of(5, 2, 1);` `period = period.minusDays(1);`
to	Used to convert an object to another type	`LocalTime lt1 = LocalTime.MAX;` `System.out.println(lt1.toSecondOfDay());`

at	Used to combine an object with another	`LocalTime lt1 = LocalTime.MIDNIGHT;`
		`LocalDateTime ldt =`
		`    lt1.atDate(LocalDate.now());`

When creating dates, the `of`, `parse`, and `now` methods are commonly used for the `LocalTime`, `LocalDate`, and `LocalDateTime` classes.

LocalTime Class

The `LocalTime` class includes several method declarations in support of creating a time (without a date or time zone).

Here are some of the `LocalTime` class's method declarations:

```
public static LocalTime now() {…}
public static LocalTime of(int hour, int minute) {…}
public static LocalTime of(int hour, int minute, int second) {…}
public static LocalTime parse(CharSequence text) {…}
public static LocalTime parse(CharSequence text, DateTimeFormatter formatter) {…}
```

Here are some examples:

```
LocalTime lt1 = LocalTime.now();
LocalTime lt2 = LocalTime.parse("12:00");  // Hour
LocalTime lt3 = LocalTime.of(12,0); // Hour, minutes
LocalTime lt4 = LocalTime.of(12,0,1); // Hour, minutes, seconds
LocalTime lt5 = LocalTime.NOON;  // MIN, MAX, MIDNIGHT as well
LocalTime lt6 = LocalTime.of(12,0,0,1); // Hour, minutes, seconds, nanos
LocalTime lt7 = LocalTime.now(ZoneId.of("Asia/Tokyo")); // Locale
LocalTime lt8 = LocalTime.parse("12:00", DateTimeFormatter.ISO_TIME);
```

LocalDate Class

The `LocalDate` class includes several method declarations in support of creating a time without a time or time zone.

Here are some of the `LocalDate` class's method declarations:

```
public static LocalDate now() {…}
public static LocalDate of(int year, Month month, int dayOfMonth) {…}
public static LocalDate of(int year, int month, int dayOfMonth) {…}
public static LocalDate parse(CharSequence text) {…}
public static LocalDate parse(CharSequence text, DateTimeFormatter formatter) {…}
```

Here are some examples:

```
LocalDate ld1 = LocalDate.now();
LocalDate ld2 = LocalDate.parse("2015-01-01"); // Date
LocalDate ld3 = LocalDate.of(2015, 1, 1); // Year, Month, Day
LocalDate ld4 = LocalDate.of(2015, Month.JANUARY, 1); // Year, Month, Day
LocalDate ld5 = LocalDate.now(ZoneId.of("Asia/Tokyo"));  // Locale
LocalDate ld6 = LocalDate.parse("2015-01-01", DateTimeFormatter.ISO_DATE);
```

LocalDateTime Class

The `LocalDateTime` class includes several method declarations in support of creating a date-time without a time zone.

Here are some of the `LocalDateTime` class's method declarations:

```
public static LocalDateTime now() {…}
public static LocalDateTime of(int year, Month month, int dayOfMonth,
  int hour, int minute) {…}
public static LocalDateTime of(int year, Month month, int dayOfMonth,
  int hour, int minute, int second) {…}
public static LocalDateTime of(int year, int month, int dayOfMonth,
  int hour, int minute, int second) {…}
public static LocalDateTime of(int year, int month, int dayOfMonth,
  int hour, int minute, int second, int nanoOfSecond) {…}
public static LocalDateTime parse(CharSequence text) {…}
public static LocalDateTime parse(CharSequence text, DateTimeFormatter formatter) {…}
```

Here are some examples:

```
LocalDateTime ldt1 = LocalDateTime.now();
LocalDateTime ldt2 = LocalDateTime.parse("2015-01-01T12:00:00");
LocalDateTime ldt3 = LocalDateTime.of(2015, 1, 1, 12, 0);
LocalDateTime ldt4 = LocalDateTime.of(2015, Month.JANUARY, 1, 12, 0);
LocalDateTime ldt5 = LocalDateTime.of(2015, 1, 1, 12, 0, 1);
LocalDateTime ldt6 = LocalDateTime.now(ZoneId.of("Asia/Tokyo"));
LocalDateTime ldt7 = LocalDateTime.parse("2015-01-01 12:00",
  DateTimeFormatter.ofPattern("yyyy-MM-dd HH:mm"));
```

Legacy Date/Time Support

Legacy calendar classes are supported by new methods to allow integration with JSR 310. These changes include updates to `java.util.Calendar`, `java.util.DateFormat`, `java.util.GregorianCalendar`, `java.util.TimeZone`, and `java.util.Date`. The following code demonstrates the integration of the older classes (such as `Calendar` and `Date`) with the new classes of JSR 310 (such as `Instant` and `LocalDateTime`). This interoperability is not on the exam, but it is helpful to know.

```
Calendar calendar = Calendar.getInstance();
Instant instance = calendar.toInstant();
Date date = Date.from(instance);
LocalDateTime ldt
  = LocalDateTime.ofInstant(date.toInstant(), ZoneId.systemDefault());
```

on the
Job

Four regional calendars are packaged with Java SE 8: Hijrah, Japanese imperial, Minguo, and Thai Buddhist. The API is flexible enough to allow for the creation of additional calendars. For new calendars, the `Era`*,* `Chronology`*, and* `ChronoLocalDate` *interfaces need to be implemented.*

Calendar Data Manipulation

Questions on manipulating calendar data will perhaps be the easiest part of your exam. This section is concerned with adding or subtracting units of time to instances of `LocalTime`, `LocalDate`, and `LocalDateTime`. You should know 16 plus/minus methods that all apply to `LocalDateTime`, eight methods that apply to `LocalDate`, and eight methods that apply to `LocalTime`. Let's look at all of them starting with `LocalDateTime`.

```
LocalDateTime ldt = LocalDateTime.now();
// All plus methods
ldt = ldt.plusYears(1).plusMonths(12).plusWeeks(52).plusDays(365)
  .plusHours(8765).plusMinutes(525949).plusSeconds(0).plusNanos(0);

// All minus methods
ldt = ldt.minusYears(1).minusMonths(12).minusWeeks(52).minusDays(365)
  .minusHours(8765).minusMinutes(525949).minusSeconds(0).minusNanos(0);

// Demonstrating mixing methods
ldt = ldt.plusYears(1).minusMonths(12).plusWeeks(52).minusDays(365)
  .plusHours(8765).minusMinutes(525949).plusSeconds(0).minusNanos(0);
```

Working with the `LocalDate` class, you can add and subtract units of years, months, weeks, and days. In this context, you cannot add or subtract units of hours, minutes, seconds, or nanos.

```
LocalDate ld = LocalDate.now();
// All plus methods
ld = ld.plusYears(1).plusMonths(12).plusWeeks(52).plusDays(365);
// All minus methods
ld = ld.minusYears(1).minusMonths(12).minusWeeks(52).minusDays(365);
```

Working with the `LocalTime` class, you can add and subtract units of hours, minutes, seconds, or nanos. In this context, you cannot add or subtract units of years, months, weeks, or days.

```
LocalTime lt = LocalTime.now();
// All plus methods
lt = lt.plusHours(18765).plusMinutes(525949).plusSeconds(0).plusNanos(0);
// All minus methods
lt = lt.minusHours(1).plusMinutes(1).plusSeconds(1).plusNanos(1);
```

	JSR 310 Type	ANSI SQL Type	XSD Type
TABLE 10-3	LocalDate	DATE	xs:time
	LocalTime	TIME	xs:time
JSR 310, SQL,	LocalDateTime	TIMESTAMP WITHOUT TIMEZONE	xs:dateTime
and XSD Type	OffsetTime	TIME WITH TIMEZONE	xs:time
Mapping in the	OffsetDateTime	TIMESTAMP WITH TIMEZONE	xs:dateTime
Java SE API	Period	INTERVAL	

Look for the exam to try and trip you up in using methods where they do not belong. In the following code segment, plusYears is not a method of the LocalTime class and plusHours is not a method of the LocalDate class. The compiler will let you know accordingly—but you won't have a compiler at the exam.

```
LocalTime lt = LocalTime.now();
lt = lt.plusYears(1); // COMPILER ERROR
LocalDate ld = LocalDate.now();
ld = ld.plusHours(1); // COMPILER ERROR
```

on the job

Interoperability between the calendar types within the java.time and java.sql packages exists in the Java API. Table 10-3 provides the relationships between the JSR 310 types and the SQL types, as well as the XML Schema (XSD) types. Note that there were no changes made to the JDBC API. Instead, you have to use the setObject/getObject to use this new API with JDBC.

Calendar Periods

A calendar Period in Java is a date-based amount made up of years, months, and days. A calendar Duration is a time-based amount made up of days, hours, minutes, seconds, and nanoseconds. The Period class is on the exam, but the Duration class is not. Both classes implement the ChronoPeriod interface. Several methods of the Period class are commonly used, such as the following: of[interval], parse, get[interval], with[interval], plus[interval], minus[interval], is[state], and between methods. These methods and more are detailed in the following section with descriptions, declarations, and examples.

The of[*interval*] Method

The `Period` class of *[interval]* method returns a `Period` from an integer value representing years, months, weeks, or days.

There are five of *[interval]* method declarations:

```
public static Period ofYears(int years) {…}
public static Period ofMonths(int months) {…}
public static Period ofWeeks(int weeks) {…}
public static Period ofDays(int days) {…}
public static Period of(int years, int months, int days) {…}
```

Here are some examples:

```
final Period P1 = Period.ofYears(1);     // 1 year
final Period P2 = Period.ofMonths(12);   // 1 year
final Period P3 = Period.ofWeeks(52);    // 1 year
final Period P4 = Period.ofDays(366);    // 1 year (leap)
final Period P5 = Period.of(1, 12, 366); // 3 years

LocalDate ldt1 = LocalDate.of(2000, Month.JANUARY, 1);
LocalDate ldt2 = null;
ldt2 = ldt1.plus(P1).plus(P2).plus(P3).plus(P4).plus(P5);
System.out.println("Before: " + ldt1 + " After: " + ldt2);
$ Before: 2000-01-01 After: 2007-01-02
```

The parse Method

The `Period` class static `parse` method returns a `Period` from a string PnYnMnD, where P is for period, Y is for years, M is for months, and D is for days. A `Period` is also returned from a string PnW, where P is for period and W is for weeks.

There is one `parse` method declaration:

```
public static Period parse(CharSequence text) {…}
```

Here is an example:

```
/* Creates a period of 41 years, 2 months, and 3 days*/
Period period1 = Period.parse("P41Y2M3D");
System.out.println(period1);
$ P41Y2M3D

// Creates a period of 4 weeks
Period period2 = Period.parse("P4W");
System.out.println(period2.getDays()+ " days");
$ 28 days
```

The get[*interval*] Method

The Period class get [*interval*] method returns a value relative to the type described in the method name.

There are six get [*interval*] method declarations:

```
public long get(TemporalUnit unit) {…}
public List<TemporalUnit> getUnits() {…}
public IsoChronology getChronology() {…}
public int getYears() {…}
public int getMonths() {…}
public int getDays() {…}
```

Here are some examples:

```
Period period = Period.of(5, 1, 14);
int years = period.getYears();
int months = period.getMonths();
long days = period.get(ChronoUnit.DAYS);
System.out.println(years + " years, " + months + " months, " + days + " days");

$ 5 years, 1 months, 14 days
```

The with[*interval*] Methods

The Period class with[*interval*] method returns a copy of the Period object from a specified int that identifies either the years, months, or days value to change.

There are three with[*interval*] method declarations:

```
public Period withYears(int years) {…}
public Period withMonths(int months) {…}
public Period withDays(int days) {…}
```

Here are some examples:

```
Period p1 = Period.of(1, 1, 1); // 1 year, 1 month, 1 day
p1 = p1.withYears(5); // Changes years only
System.out.println(p1); // 5 years, 1 month, 1 day
$ P5Y1M1D

Period p2 = Period.of(1, 1, 1); // 1 year, 1 month, 1 day
p2 = p2.withMonths(5); // Changes months only
System.out.println(p2); // 1 years, 5 months, 1 day
$ P1Y5M1D

Period p3 = Period.of(1, 1, 1); // 1 year, 1 month, 1 day
p3 = p3.withDays(5); // Changes days only
System.out.println(p3); // 1 years, 1 month, 5 day
$ P1Y1M5D
```

The plus[*interval*] Method

The Period class plus [*interval*] method returns a copy of the Period object from a specified long index value or TemporalAmount with the desired amount added.

There are four plus [interval] method declarations:

```
public Period plus(TemporalAmount amountToAdd) {…}
public Period plusYears(long yearsToAdd) {…}
public Period plusMonths(long monthsToAdd) {…}
public Period plusDays(long daysToAdd) {…}
```

Here are some examples:

```
Period period = Period.of(5, 2, 1);
period = period.plusYears(10);
period = period.plusMonths(10);
period = period.plusDays(15);
period = period.plus(Period.ofDays(15));
// Plus a total 10 years, 10 months and 30 days
System.out.println("Period value: " + period);
$ Period value: P15Y12M31D
```

The minus[*interval*] Method

The Period class minus [*interval*] method returns a copy of the Period object from a specified long index value or TemporalAmount with the desired amount added.

There are four minus [interval] method declarations:

```
public Period minus(TemporalAmount amountToSubtract) {…}
public Period minusYears(long yearsToSubtract) {…}
public Period minusMonths(long monthsToSubtract) {…}
public Period minusDays(long daysToSubtract) {…}
```

Here are some examples:

```
Period period = Period.of(15, 12, 31);
period = period.minusYears(10);
period = period.minusMonths(10);
period = period.minusDays(15);
period = period.minus(Period.ofDays(15));
// Minused a total 10 years, 10 months and 30 days
System.out.println("Period value: " + period);
$ Period value: P5Y2M1D
```

The is[*state*] Method

The Period class is[*state*] method returns a boolean from a string PnYnMnD, where P is for period, Y is for years, M is for months, and D is for days.

There are two is[*state*] method declarations:

```
public boolean isZero() {return (this == ZERO);}
public boolean isNegative() { return years < 0 || months < 0 || days < 0; }
```

Here is an example:

```
Period p1 = Period.parse("P10D").minusDays(10);
System.out.println("Is zero: " + p1.isZero());
$ Is zero: true.


// Period equals negative value
Period p2 = Period.parse("P2015M");
p2 = p2.minusMonths(2016); // 2015-2016 is -1 Months
System.out.println("Is negative: " + p2.isNegative());
$ Is negative: true
```

The between Method

The Period class between method returns a Period from two LocalDate arguments.

There is one between method declaration:

```
public static Period between(LocalDate startDateInclusive, LocalDate endDateExclusive) {…}
```

Here is an example:

```
final String WAR_OF_1812_START_DATE =  "1812-06-18";
final String WAR_OF_1812_END_DATE =  "1815-02-18";
LocalDate warBegins = LocalDate.parse(WAR_OF_1812_START_DATE);
LocalDate warEnds = LocalDate.parse(WAR_OF_1812_END_DATE);
Period period = Period.between (warBegins, warEnds);
System.out.println("WAR OF 1812 TIMEFRAME: " + period);
$ WAR OF 1812 TIMEFRAME: P2Y8M
```

EXERCISE 10-1

Using the normalized Method of the Period Class

In this exercise, you will examine the normalized method of the Period class. This method is not on the exam, but this exercise will help get you more familiar with the Period class. The normalized method adjusts the months in tandem with the years so there is never less than zero or more than eleven months, as you see demonstrated here:

```
Period p1 = Period.parse("P0Y13M");
System.out.println("Original: " + p1 + " Normalized: " + p1.normalized());
Original: P13M400D After: P1Y1M

Period p2 = Period.parse("P2Y-1M");
System.out.println("Original: " + p2 + " Normalized: " + p2.normalized());
Original: P2Y-1M Normalized: P1Y11M
```

Both of the Period and Duration classes implement the TemporalAmount interface.

1. Use an IDE (such as NetBeans) to view the contents of the src.zip file that is distributed in JDK 1.8 at C:\Program Files\Java\jdk1.8.0_40\src.zip.

2. Open the package node for java.util and double-click the Period .java class.

3. Examine the Javadoc header and body of the normalized method to get a better idea of exactly how the method operates.

4. Now answer these questions:

   a. As the Period class has a normalized method, does the Duration class have one as well?

   b. If the Duration class does have a normalized method, what does it normalize?

   c. If the Duration class does not have a normalized method, why not?

5. Visit the Javadoc for the Duration class to verify your hypothesis.

Calendar Data Formatting

Calendar data formatting is supported by the DateTimeFormatter class. The API supplies predefined formatters, localized formatting with support of the FormatStyle enumeration type (enum), and specialized formatting (which is your own customization). The following sections examine all three.

Predefined Formatters

Several predefined formatters are included in the DateTimeFormatter class. The constant static variables that associate each formatter can be used directly with the class name, or the static import can be used to remove the class name from inline use, as shown here. This means that `DateTimeFormatter.ISO_WEEK_ DATE` and `ISO_WEEK_DATE` (with `import static java.time.format .DateTimeFormatter.*;`) are essentially the same.

```
import static java.time.format.DateTimeFormatter.*;
…
LocalDate ld = LocalDate.now();

System.out.println("RESULT 1: " + ld.format( DateTimeFormatter.ISO_WEEK_DATE));
System.out.println("RESULT 2: " + ld.format( ISO_WEEK_DATE)););));
$ RESULT 1: 2015-W16-7
$ RESULT 2: 2015-W16-7
```

Several predefined formatters will work for different classes, such as the `OffsetDateTime` and the `ZonedDateTime` classes.

```
OffsetDateTime odt = OffsetDateTime.now();
System.out.println(odt.format(ISO_DATE));
System.out.println(odt.format(ISO_OFFSET_DATE));
System.out.println(odt.format(ISO_OFFSET_DATE_TIME));

$ 2015-04-19-04:00
$ 2015-04-19-04:00
$ 2015-04-19T08:38:48.09-04:00

ZonedDateTime zdt = ZonedDateTime.now();
System.out.println(zdt.format(ISO_DATE_TIME));
System.out.println(zdt.format(ISO_ZONED_DATE_TIME));
System.out.println(zdt.format(DateTimeFormatter.RFC_1123_DATE_TIME));

$ 2015-04-19T08:38:48.09-04:00[America/New_York]
$ 2015-04-19T08:38:48.09-04:00[America/New_York]
$ Sun, 19 Apr 2015 08:38:48 -0400
```

Localized Formatters

Localized `DateTimeFormatter` class formatters with static methods `ofLocalizedTime`, `ofLocalizedDate`, and `ofLocalizedDateTime` use the `FormatStyle` enum values `FormatStyle.SHORT`, `FormatStyle.MEDIUM`, `FormatStyle.LONG`, and `FormatStyle.FULL` to support localized formats. `FormatStyle.LONG` and `FormatStyle.FULL` are not on the exam.

```
    // Localized formatting for LocalDate
    LocalDate ld = LocalDate.now();
    System.out.println("SHORT: " +  ld.format
```

e x a m

ⓦatch

For the scope of the exam, *LocalDateTime class and what the*
you should be familiar with the formatters *formatted results look like.*
that are most commonly used with the

```
ArrayList<DateTimeFormatter> ldtFormattersList = new ArrayList<>();
ldtFormattersList.add(DateTimeFormatter.BASIC_ISO_DATE);
ldtFormattersList.add(DateTimeFormatter.ISO_LOCAL_TIME);
ldtFormattersList.add(DateTimeFormatter.ISO_LOCAL_DATE);
ldtFormattersList.add(DateTimeFormatter.ISO_LOCAL_DATE_TIME);
ldtFormattersList.add(DateTimeFormatter.ISO_TIME);
ldtFormattersList.add(DateTimeFormatter.ISO_DATE);
ldtFormattersList.add(DateTimeFormatter.ISO_DATE_TIME);
ldtFormattersList.add(DateTimeFormatter.ISO_ORDINAL_DATE);

LocalDateTime ldt = LocalDateTime.now();
    ldtFormattersList.forEach(c -> {
      System.out.println(ldt.format(c));
    });

$ 2015-W16-7
$ 20150419
$ 08:40:05.934
$ 2015-04-19
$ 2015-04-19T08:40:05.934
$ 08:40:05.934
$ 2015-04-19
$ 2015-04-19T08:40:05.934
$ 2015-109
```

```
      (DateTimeFormatter.ofLocalizedDate(FormatStyle.SHORT)));
System.out.println("MEDIUM: " +  ld.format
      (DateTimeFormatter.ofLocalizedDate(FormatStyle.MEDIUM)));
System.out.println("LONG: " + ld.format
      (DateTimeFormatter.ofLocalizedDate(FormatStyle.LONG)));
System.out.println ("FULL: " + ld.format
      (DateTimeFormatter.ofLocalizedDate(FormatStyle.FULL)));
SHORT: 4/19/15
MEDIUM: Apr 19, 2015
LONG: April 19, 2015
FULL: Sunday, April 19, 2015
```

In addition to getting the formatted value from passing the localized formatter into the format method of the calendar classes, the formatters have a format method that accepts the calendar instance to achieve the same formatted string results.

```
// Passing Formatter to LocalTime format method
LocalTime lt = LocalTime.now();
System.out.print("SHORT: " + lt.format
  (DateTimeFormatter.ofLocalizedTime(FormatStyle.SHORT)));
System.out.println(", MEDIUM: " + lt.format
  (DateTimeFormatter.ofLocalizedTime(FormatStyle.MEDIUM)));

// Passing LocalTime instance to Formatter's format method
System.out.print("SHORT: " +
DateTimeFormatter.ofLocalizedTime(FormatStyle.SHORT).format(lt));
System.out.println(", MEDIUM: " +
DateTimeFormatter.ofLocalizedTime(FormatStyle.MEDIUM).format(lt));

$ SHORT: 10:44 AM, MEDIUM: 10:44:03 AM
$ SHORT: 10:44 AM, MEDIUM: 10:44:03 AM
```

The three localized methods can be used only with the appropriate calendar classes; otherwise, an UnsupportedTemporalTypeException will be thrown. Also, using FormatStyle.LONG and FormatStyle.FULL where they are not accepted will result in java.time.DateTimeException exceptions being thrown.

```
// Passing Formatters to LocalDateTime format method
LocalDateTime ldt = LocalDateTime.now();
System.out.println(ldt.format
  (DateTimeFormatter.ofLocalizedDateTime(FormatStyle.SHORT)));
System.out.println(ldt.format
  (DateTimeFormatter.ofLocalizedTime(FormatStyle.SHORT)));
System.out.println(ldt.format
  (DateTimeFormatter.ofLocalizedDate(FormatStyle.SHORT)));

$ 4/19/15 10:56 AM
$ 10:56 AM
$ 4/19/15

LocalDate ld = LocalDate.now();
System.out.println(ld.format
  (DateTimeFormatter.ofLocalizedTime(FormatStyle.SHORT)));
$ java.time.temporal.UnsupportedTemporalTypeException:
  Unsupported field: ClockHourOfAmPm
```

Specialized Formatters

Specialized formatters allow the use of letter and symbol sequences to produce custom desired format output.

```
LocalDateTime ldt = LocalDateTime.now();
String dateTime = ldt.format(DateTimeFormatter.
ofPattern("yyyyMMdd"));
Path target = Paths.get("\\opt\\ocaexam\\" + "app_props_"
  + dateTime + ".properties");
// File created with custom date embedded filename
System.out.println(Files.createFile(target).getFileName());
$ app_props_20150419.properties
```

The syntax for the formatting can be found in the `DateTimeFormatter` documentation within the Java 8 Javadoc (https://docs.oracle.com/javase/8/docs/api/java/time/format/DateTimeFormatter.html). However, for the exam, the following code example demonstrates the extent of what you will need to know, being m, mm, h, hh, d, dd, M, MM, MMM, MMMM, MMMMM, y, yy, yyy, and yyyy.

```
String [] minutes = {"m", "mm"};
String [] hours = {"h", "hh"};
String [] days = {"d", "dd"};
String [] months = {"M","MM","MMM","MMMM", "MMMMM"};
String [] years = {"y", "yy", "yyyy"};
String converts = "\u2192"; // Right arrow

LocalDateTime ldt = LocalDateTime.parse("2015-01-01T01:01:01");
System.out.print("Hours:     ");
Arrays.asList(hours).forEach(p -> {

System.out.print(p + converts + ldt.format
  (DateTimeFormatter.ofPattern(p)) + "   ");});
System.out.print("\nMinutes:   ");
Arrays.asList(minutes).forEach(p -> {
System.out.print(p + converts + ldt.format
  (DateTimeFormatter.ofPattern(p)) + "   ");});
System.out.print("\nMonths:    ");
Arrays.asList(months).forEach(p -> {
System.out.print(p + converts + ldt.format
  (DateTimeFormatter.ofPattern(p)) + "  ");     });
System.out.print("\nDays:      ");
Arrays.asList(days).forEach(p -> {
System.out.print(p + converts + ldt.format(DateTimeFormatter.ofPattern(p)) + "   ");
});
```

```
System.out.print("\nYears:     ");
Arrays.asList(years).forEach(p -> {
System.out.print(p + converts + ldt.format
  (DateTimeFormatter.ofPattern(p)) + "   ");
});

// OUTPUT FORMATTED FROM "2015-01-01T01:01:01"
Hours:     h→1    hh→01
Minutes:   m→1    mm→01
Months:    M→1    MM→01    MMM→Jan    MMMM→January    MMMMM→J
Days:      d→1    dd→01
Years:     y→2015   yy→15   yyyy→2015
```

CERTIFICATION SUMMARY

This chapter covered what you need to know about the Date and Time API. We discussed calendar data creation with the `LocalDate`, `LocalTime`, and `LocalDateTime` classes. We also covered calendar data manipulation with the plus/minus methods, and we explored working with the `Period` class and its methods as a way to use a time-based amount composed of days, hours, minutes, seconds, and nanoseconds. Finally, we looked at calendar data formatting with the `DateTimeFormatter` class, utilizing localized formatters and specialized formatters.

Once you are comfortable coding with these classes and their support methods, you will surely do well when presented with questions about the Date and Time API on the exam.

TWO-MINUTE DRILL

Understand the Date and Time API

☐ The Date and Time API belongs to JSR 310 and is packaged in `java.time`, `java.time.chrono`, `java.time.format`, `java.time.temporal`, and `java.time.zone`.

☐ JSR 310 is based on ISO 8601, "Data elements and interchange formats – Information interchange – Representation of dates and times."

☐ Calendar data is created by use of the `LocalTime`, `LocalDate`, and `LocalDateTime` classes.

☐ Calendar data is supported by a fluent API and prefaced methods `of`, `parse`, `get`, `is`, `with`, `plus`, `minus`, `to`, and `at`.

☐ The `Period` class provides various methods to support periods: date-based amounts of time made up of years, months, and days. These include `of[interval]`, `parse`, `get[interval]`, `is[interval]`, `with[interval]`, `plus[interval]`, `minus[interval]`, and `between` methods.

☐ The `Period` class static `parse` method returns a `Period` from a string `PnYnMnD`, where `P` is for period, `Y` is for years, `M` is for months, and `D` is for days.

☐ The `Period` class static `parse` method returns a `Period` from a string `PnW`, where `P` is for period and `W` is for weeks.

☐ The `DateTimeFormatter` class supports formatting with predefined formatters, localized formatters, and specialized formatters.

☐ Predefined formatters are used with the calendar classes (such as `LocalDateTime` and `ZonedDateTime`) to achieve commonly used formatting.

☐ Localized formatters use the static methods `ofLocalizedTime`, `ofLocalizedDate`, and `ofLocalizedDateTime`, along with the `FormatStyle` enumerations to support localized formats.

☐ Specialized formatters use the characters m, mm, h, hh, d, dd, M, MM, MMM, MMMM, MMMMM, y, yy, yyy, and yyyy to achieve custom formatting of dates and times.

SELF TEST

Understand the Date and Time API

1. Given the following code, what will be the result?

```
Period p = Period.parse("P1Y");
System.out.println(p.getMonths());
```

A. 12 is printed to standard output.

B. 1 is printed to standard output.

C. 0 is printed to standard output.

D. This code will not compile.

2. Given the following code, at what line is an `UnsupportedTemporalTypeException` exception thrown at runtime?

```
LocalDateTime.now().format(DateTimeFormatter.BASIC_ISO_DATE); // LINE 1
LocalDateTime.now().format(DateTimeFormatter.ISO_LOCAL_DATE); // LINE 2
LocalDateTime.now().format(DateTimeFormatter.ISO_DATE);       // LINE 3
LocalDateTime.now().format(DateTimeFormatter.ISO_LOCAL_DATE_TIME); // LINE 4
LocalDateTime.now().format(DateTimeFormatter.ISO_ZONED_DATE_TIME); // LINE 5
```

A. Line 1

B. Lines 2 and 3

C. Lines 4 and 5

D. Line 5

3. Given the following code, what will be the result?

```
LocalDate ld = LocalDate.of (1940, Month.JANUARY, 3 );
ld = ld.minusYears(3).plusMonths(10).plusDays(15);
ld.minusYears(10);
System.out.println(ld.getMonth() + " " + ld.getYear());
```

A. NOVEMBER 1937 is printed to standard output.

B. NOVEMBER 1927 is printed to standard output.

C. JANUARY 1940 is printed to standard output.

D. JANUARY 18 1940 is printed to standard output.

4. Given the following code, what change can be made so the code will not throw a runtime exception?

```
String date1 = "2011-12-03";
DateTimeFormatter formatter1 = DateTimeFormatter.ofPattern("yyyy-MM-dd");
LocalDate localDate1 = LocalDate.parse(date1, formatter1);
System.out.print(localDate1.toString() + " ");
String date2 = "2011-12-03 00:00:00";
DateTimeFormatter formatter2 =
  DateTimeFormatter.ISO_LOCAL_DATE_TIME;
LocalDateTime localDate2 =
  LocalDateTime.parse(date2, formatter2);
System.out.println(date2.toString());
```

A. Change `LocalDate.parse(date1, formatter1)` to `LocalDate`
   `.parse(formatter1, date1)` and change `LocalDate.parse(date2,`
   `formatter2)` to `LocalDate.parse(formatter2, date2)`

B. Change `DateTimeFormatter.ofPattern("yyyy-MM-dd");` to
   `DateTimeFormatter.ofPattern("YYYY-MM-DD");`

C. Change `String date2 = "2011-12-03 00:00:00";` to `String date2 =`
   `"2011-12-03T00:00:00";`

D. No changes are needed.

5. Given the following code, which line of code could replace line 1 with the end result of
`2002-02-02T01:01:00` being printed to standard output?

```
LocalDateTime ldt;
ldt = LocalDateTime.of(2001, Month.JANUARY, 1, 1, 1); // Line 2
Period period = Period.parse("P1Y1M1D");
ldt = ldt.plus(period);
DateTimeFormatter formatter =
  DateTimeFormatter.ISO_LOCAL_DATE_TIME;
System.out.println(ldt.format(formatter));
```

A. `ldt = LocalDateTime.parse("2001-01-00T01:01:01");`

B. `ldt = LocalDateTime.parse("2001-01-01T01:01:00");`

C. `ldt = LocalDateTime.parse("01-01-2001 01:01:01");`

D. `ldt = LocalDateTime.parse("01-01-2001T01:01:00");`

6. Given the following code, which statement is correct?

```
LocalDateTime currentTime = LocalDateTime.now();
LocalTime meetingTime = LocalTime.of(16, 0);
if (meetingTime.isBefore(currentTime.toLocalTime())) {
  System.out.println("You're late!");
} else {
  System.out.print("There is a meeting later today ");
  // CODE SEGMENT 1
  {
  Period p = Period.between (currentTime.toLocalTime(), meetingTime);
  System.out.print("in less than: "+ ++p.getHours() +
    ((a == 1) ? " hour." : " hours."));
  }
  // CODE SEGMENT 2
   {
   long a = ChronoUnit.HOURS.between(currentTime.toLocalTime(), meetingTime);
   System.out.print("in less than " + ++a + ((a == 1) ? " hour." : " hours."));
   }
 }
```

A. Code segments 1 and 2 will achieve the same result.

B. Segment 1 will not compile.

C. Segment 2 will not compile.

D. Neither segment 1 nor segment 2 will compile.

SELF TEST ANSWERS

Understand the Date and Time API

1. Given the following code, what will be the result?

```
Period p = Period.parse("P1Y");
System.out.println(p.getMonths());
```

- A. `12` is printed to standard output.
- B. `1` is printed to standard output.
- C. `0` is printed to standard output.
- D. This code will not compile.

> Answer:
>
> ☑ **C.** `0` is printed to standard output.
> ☒ **A, B,** and **D** are incorrect. **A** is incorrect because `12` is not printed to standard output. **B** is incorrect because `1` is not printed to standard output. **D** is incorrect because the code compiles just fine.

2. Given the following code, at what line is an `UnsupportedTemporalTypeException` exception thrown at runtime?

```
LocalDateTime.now().format(DateTimeFormatter.BASIC_ISO_DATE); // LINE 1
LocalDateTime.now().format(DateTimeFormatter.ISO_LOCAL_DATE); // LINE 2
LocalDateTime.now().format(DateTimeFormatter.ISO_DATE);       // LINE 3
LocalDateTime.now().format(DateTimeFormatter.ISO_LOCAL_DATE_TIME); // LINE 4
LocalDateTime.now().format(DateTimeFormatter.ISO_ZONED_DATE_TIME); // LINE 5
```

- A. Line 1
- B. Lines 2 and 3
- C. Lines 4 and 5
- D. Line 5

Answer:

☑ **D.** The exception `java.time.temporal.UnsupportedTemporalTypeException` is thrown at runtime because of an unsupported field: `OffsetSeconds` relative to line 5.

☒ **A, B,** and **C** are incorrect. **A** is incorrect because no exception is thrown at line 1. **B** is incorrect because no exception is thrown at lines 2 and 3. **C** is incorrect because no exception is thrown at lines 4 and 5.

3. Given the following code, what will be the result?

```
LocalDate ld = LocalDate.of (1940, Month.JANUARY, 3 );
ld = ld.minusYears(3).plusMonths(10).plusDays(15);
ld.minusYears(10);
System.out.println(ld.getMonth() + " " + ld.getYear());
```

A. NOVEMBER 1937 is printed to standard output.

B. NOVEMBER 1927 is printed to standard output.

C. JANUARY 1940 is printed to standard output.

D. JANUARY 18 1940 is printed to standard output.

Answer:

☑ **A.** NOVEMBER 1937 is printed to standard output.

☒ **B, C,** and **D** are incorrect. **B** is incorrect because NOVEMBER 1927 is not printed to standard output. **C** is incorrect because JANUARY 1940 is not printed to standard output. **D** is incorrect because JANUARY 18 1940 is not printed to standard output.

4. Given the following code, what change can be made so the code will not throw a runtime exception?

```
String date1 = "2011-12-03";
DateTimeFormatter formatter1 = DateTimeFormatter.ofPattern("yyyy-MM-dd");
LocalDate localDate1 = LocalDate.parse(date1, formatter1);
System.out.print(localDate1.toString() + " ");
String date2 = "2011-12-03 00:00:00";
DateTimeFormatter formatter2 =
  DateTimeFormatter.ISO_LOCAL_DATE_TIME;
LocalDateTime localDate2 =
  LocalDateTime.parse(date2, formatter2);
System.out.println(date2.toString());
```

A. Change `LocalDate.parse(date1, formatter1)` to `LocalDate`
   `.parse(formatter1, date1)` and change `LocalDate.parse(date2,`
   `formatter2)` to `LocalDate.parse(formatter2, date2)`

B. Change `DateTimeFormatter.ofPattern("yyyy-MM-dd");` to
   `DateTimeFormatter.ofPattern("YYYY-MM-DD");`

C. Change `String date2 = "2011-12-03 00:00:00";` to `String date2 =`
   `"2011-12-03T00:00:00";`

D. No changes are needed.

Answer:

☑ **C.** Changing `String date2 = "2011-12-03 00:00:00";` to `String date2 =`
`"2011-12-03T00:00:00";` will avoid a `DateTimeParseException` from being thrown
a runtime at the related `LocalDateTime.parse()` method. That is, the letter `T` is needed in
the string after the date and before the time.

☒ **A, B,** and **D** are incorrect. **A** is incorrect because the code was fine as it was. **B** is
incorrect because the code was fine as it was. **D** is incorrect because a change is needed so
a `DateTimeParseException` is not thrown.

---

5. Given the following code, which line of code could replace line 1 with the end result of
   `2002-02-02T01:01:00` being printed to standard output?

```
LocalDateTime ldt;
ldt = LocalDateTime.of(2001, Month.JANUARY, 1, 1, 1); // Line 2
Period period = Period.parse("P1Y1M1D");
ldt = ldt.plus(period);
DateTimeFormatter formatter =
   DateTimeFormatter.ISO_LOCAL_DATE_TIME;
System.out.println(ldt.format(formatter));
```

A. `ldt = LocalDateTime.parse("2001-01-00T01:01:01");`

B. `ldt = LocalDateTime.parse("2001-01-01T01:01:00");`

C. `ldt = LocalDateTime.parse("01-01-2001 01:01:01");`

D. `ldt = LocalDateTime.parse("01-01-2001T01:01:00");`

Answer:

☑ **B.** `ldt = LocalDateTime.parse("2001-01-01T01:01:00");` will result in the same result to standard output as line 2.

☒ **A, C,** and **D** are incorrect. **A** is incorrect because `ldt = LocalDateTime .parse("2001-01-00T01:01:01");` will not produce the desired result, throwing a `DateTimeParseException`. **C** is incorrect because `ldt = LocalDateTime .parse("01-01-2001 01:01:01");` will not produce the desired result, throwing a `DateTimeParseException`. **D** is incorrect because `ldt = LocalDateTime .parse("01-01-2001 01:01:00");` will throw a `DateTimeParseException`.

6. Given the following code, which statement is correct?

```java
LocalDateTime currentTime = LocalDateTime.now();
LocalTime meetingTime = LocalTime.of(16, 0);
if (meetingTime.isBefore(currentTime.toLocalTime())) {
  System.out.println("You're late!");
} else {
  System.out.print("There is a meeting later today ");
  // CODE SEGMENT 1
  {
  Period p = Period.between (currentTime.toLocalTime(), meetingTime);
  System.out.print("in less than: "+ ++p.getHours() +
    ((a == 1) ? " hour." : " hours."));
  }
  // CODE SEGMENT 2
   {
   long a = ChronoUnit.HOURS.between(currentTime.toLocalTime(), meetingTime);
   System.out.print("in less than " + ++a + ((a == 1) ? " hour." : " hours."));
   }
  }
```

A. Code segments 1 and 2 will achieve the same result.

B. Segment 1 will not compile.

C. Segment 2 will not compile.

D. Neither segment 1 nor segment 2 will compile.

Answer:

☑   **B.** Segment 1 will not compile because the `between` method of the `Period` class requires `LocalDate` arguments only.

☒   **A, C,** and **D** are incorrect. **A** is incorrect because segment 1 will not compile and segment 2 will compile, so the results of segments 1 and 2 are not the same. **C** is incorrect because segment 2 will compile fine. **D** is incorrect because, although segment 1 will not compile, segment 2 will compile.

11
Understanding Lambda Expressions

T he lambda expressions feature is new in Java 8. This chapter shows you how to write a simple lambda expression that uses the `Predicate` functional interface (FI). Leading up to this coverage, FIs and lambda expressions syntax information is provided and explained. The goal of the chapter is to help ensure that you have a working knowledge of the related lambda expressions features that you may see on the exam. Remember that by studying for a certification exam, you prove your knowledge of a specific skill set such as using lambdas. So prior to reading this chapter, you should already have a basic knowledge of lambda expressions. For the scope of the exam, be prepared for questions on lambda expressions syntax, passing lambda expressions through method arguments, and the typical use of the `Predicate` interface.

Lambda expressions are considered a closure-like construct. These types of constructs are presented in other languages as well, but with different names and varying usages: C has callbacks and blocks, C++ has blocks and function objects, Objective-C 2.0 has blocks; C# and D have delegates; Eiffel has inline agents. Consider reviewing these closure-like constructs of the other programming languages to get a better feel for the concept of closures.

Note that the general concept of closures, including lambda expressions, is the ability to work with a function that can be stored as a variable (for example, a first-class method). With this feature comes the ability to pass around the method (a block of code).

CERTIFICATION OBJECTIVE

Write Lambda Expressions

Exam Objective   Write a simple Lambda expression that consumes a Lambda Predicate expression

Java lambda expressions provide a means to represent anonymous methods using expressions. Lambda expressions provide coders with access to functional programming capabilities in the object-oriented Java space. Lambda expressions are supported by Project Lambda (http://openjdk.java.net/projects/lambda) and the lambda expressions specification as presented in JSR 335 (http://jcp.org/en/jsr/detail?id=335). The outline of JSR 335 includes nine parts, and if you are serious about mastering lambda expressions, you should take the time to read through each part. Part I is excluded from the specification.

- Part A: Functional Interfaces
- Part B: Lambda Expressions
- Part C: Method References
- Part D: Poly Expressions
- Part E: Typing and Evaluation
- Part F: Overload Resolution
- Part G: Type Interference
- Part H: Default Methods
- Part J: Java Virtual Machine

In this chapter, the features of the first two parts of the specification—Part A: Functional Interfaces and Part B: Lambda Expressions—are examined, as the content of these parts are included on the exam. After reviewing Parts A and B of the specification, a working example of lambda expressions and the `Predicate` FI are presented.

Functional Programming

Functional programming is integrated with Java in Java SE 8. Lambda expressions support functional programming in Java and add several benefits that software developers can take advantage of, including ease of use, one of the most important features. Lambdas in Java have long been awaited and their absence criticized. They delightfully provide an alternative to the awkward and difficult-to-understand anonymous inner classes that routinely challenge new developers. In addition to ease of use, lambda expressions offer other values brought from the introduction of functional programming:

- A clear and concise way to represent a method interface using an expression
- Code reduction, typically to a single line
- Improvement to the collections library (easier iteration, filtering, sorting, counting, data extraction, and so on)
- Improvement to the concurrency library (improved performance in multicore environments)
- Lazy evaluation support through streams

There is a trade-off when implementing code with lambda expressions, however; the debugging process is more complex because the call stacks can be considerably longer. When you prefer finer levels of debugging, you may choose to forgo the use of lambda expressions.

Here's an example of code that uses a lambda expression and an FI:

```java
public class Guitar {
  public static void main(String[] args) {
    // Includes Lambda Expression
    Strummable instrument = () -> {System.out.println("strummed!");};
    instrument.strum();
  }
  @FunctionalInterface
  interface Strummable {
    void strum();
  }
}
```

To understand what is going on here, we need to visit functional interfaces.

Functional Interfaces

Lambda expressions must have a functional interface, also called a single abstract method (SAM). FIs provide target types for lambda expressions as well as method references. FIs must also have exactly one abstract method. Because the name of the method is known, the method name is excluded from the actual lambda expression. This concept is explored in the upcoming syntax and example sections.

An FI may have one or more default methods and one or more static methods. Default methods allow for the addition of new code to the interface, ensuring backward compatibility. This ensures that legacy code that implements the interface will not break if the new default methods are not used. (Note that default and static methods in the context of FIs are not on the exam.) An example of an FI that also includes default methods is Java's Predicate FI:

```java
// Copyright (c) 2010, 2013, Oracle and/or its affiliates. All rights reserved
// ORACLE PROPRIETARY/CONFIDENTIAL. Use is subject to license terms.

@FunctionalInterface
public interface Predicate<T> {
  // Abstract method
  boolean test(T t);  // Evaluates this predicate on the given argument.

  // Default methods
  default Predicate<T> and(Predicate<? super T> other) {
      Objects.requireNonNull(other);
```

```
        return (t) -> test(t) && other.test(t);
  }
  default Predicate<T> or(Predicate<? super T> other) {
    Objects.requireNonNull(other);
      return (t) -> test(t) || other.test(t);
  }
  default Predicate<T> negate() {
    return (t) -> !test(t);
  }
}
```

The `Predicate` FI is one of many general-purpose FIs, which are included in the `java.util.function` package for the primary use of features of the JDK. General-purpose FIs are listed in Table H-2 in Appendix H. The `Predicate` FI will be visited later in the chapter, because you will see this FI on the exam.

The Java SE 8 API has several specific-purpose functional interfaces as well, and the number will continue to grow as the API is extended and refined. Various specific-purpose FIs are listed in Table H-1 of Appendix H.

Instances of functional interfaces can be created with method references, constructor references, and lambda expressions.

FIs should be annotated with the `@FunctionalInterface` annotation to aid the compiler in checking for specification adherence and the IDE in features support. An example of IDE features support would be refactoring of anonymous inner classes to lambda expressions.

Lambda Expressions

Lambda expressions allow for the creation and use of single method classes. These methods have a basic syntax that provides for the omission of modifiers, the return type, and optional parameters. Full syntax includes a parameter list with explicit or implicit target types, the arrow operator, and the body with statements. A target type is the type of object in which a lambda is bound. Multiple target types must be enclosed in parentheses. A body with multiple statements must be enclosed in braces. Therefore, syntax for lambda expressions is either of these:

```
(parameter list) -> expression
    or (parameter list) -> { statements; }
```

Various examples of lambda expressions syntax are shown in Table 11-1.

Lambda expressions can appear in any of these contexts: assignments, array initializers, cast expressions, constructor arguments, lambda bodies, method arguments, return statements, ternary expressions, and variable declarations.

TABLE 11-1   Lambda Expressions Syntax Examples

Lambda Expression	Notes
`(Float f1, Float f2) -> {return f1*f2;}`	Full syntax is included.
`(Float f1, Float f2) -> f1*f2`	Curly brackets and the return keyword are optional for single statements in the body.
`(f1, f2) -> {return f1*f2;}`	Implicit target types can exclude the class names.
`(String s) -> {return s.length();}`	Parentheses are required with an explicit target type.
`s -> {return s.length();}`	Parentheses are optional with an implicit target type.

`(x, y) -> {`
`    String msg1 = "leaking";`
`    String msg2 = "sealed";`
`  if (x > y) return msg1`
`  else {`
`    return msg2;`
`  }`
`}`
	The body may include multiple statements.

`() -> 12`	`Runnable` and `Callable` FIs all have abstract methods without parameters, so no target type is included.

The body of lambda expressions that return a value are considered to be value-compatible, and those that do not are considered to be void-compatible.

on the **Ⓙob**

Pipelines and streams are not on the exam, although they work hand-in-hand with lambda expressions. A pipeline is a sequence of aggregate operations, connected through method chaining. Streams are seen with classes that support functional-style operations on streams of elements. The following code demonstrates refactoring of the enhanced-for loop toward use of the implicit `Stream` *interface and a lambda expression. A stream is a sequence of elements that supports sequential and parallel aggregate operations.*

```
// Prints retail prices of branded shoes
for (Shoe s : shoeList) {
  if (s.isBranded()) {
    System.out.println(s.getRetailPrice());
```

```
    }
  }

  // Refactored with a stream and λEs
  shoeList.stream().filter(s -> s.isBranded())
    .forEach(s -> System.out.print(s.getRetailPrice()));
```

Lambda Expressions and FI Example

In this section, we'll demonstrate the use of a lambda expression with a functional interface. We'll take a look at refactoring an anonymous inner class into a lambda expression. For this example, we'll make use of the Comparator FI. To build up to use of the Comparator FI, let's look at the Comparator interface in three contexts:

- Comparator interface implemented from a class
- Comparator interface used with an anonymous inner class
- Comparator functional interface used with a lambda expression

Because objects often need to be compared, methods in the Collections class assume that objects in the collection are comparable—which is the case, for example, when you are sorting an ArrayList. However, if there is no natural ordering, the Comparator interface can be used to specify the desired ordering of the objects.

Comparator Interface Implemented from a Class

If we wanted to compare water from various sources, we'd have to implement a helper class to specify which piece of state would be used for sorting—in this case, the state would be the source.

The helper class would be WaterSort, which implements the Comparator interface.

```
import java.util.Comparator;
// Class with sorting algorithm
public class WaterSort implements Comparator <Water> {
  @Override
  public int compare (Water w1, Water w2) {
    return w1.getSource().compareTo(w2.getSource());
  }
}
```

The Water class represents the value/transfer bean.

```java
// Water Class
public class Water {
  private String source;
  public Water (String source) {
    this.source = source;
  }
  public String getSource() {
    return source;
  }
  public void setSource(String source) {
    this.source = source;
  }
  public String toString() {
    return this.source;
  }
}
```

Let's look at a simple program that exercises the sort and use of the Water transfer object. Here, we build an array list of Water objects and then perform an alphabetical sort on them by instantiating the WaterSort class that implements the Comparator interface.

```java
import java.util.ArrayList;
import java.util.Collections;
import java.util.List;
public class WaterApp {
  public static void main(String[] args) {
    Water hardWater = new Water ("Hard");
    Water softWater = new Water ("Soft");
    Water boiledWater = new Water ("Boiled");
    Water rawWater = new Water ("Raw");
    Water rainWater = new Water ("Rain");
    Water snowWater = new Water ("Snow");
    Water filteredWater = new Water ("Filtered");
    Water reverseOsmosisWater = new Water ("Reverse Osmosis");
    Water deionizedWater = new Water ("Deionized");
    Water distilledWater = new Water ("Distilled");
    // List of Water types
    List <Water> waterList = new ArrayList<> ();
    waterList.add(hardWater);
    waterList.add(softWater);
    waterList.add(boiledWater);
    waterList.add(rawWater);
```

```
    waterList.add(rainWater);
    waterList.add(snowWater);
    waterList.add(filteredWater);
    waterList.add(reverseOsmosisWater);
    waterList.add(deionizedWater);
    waterList.add(distilledWater);
    // Without Sort
    System.out.println("Not Sorted: " + waterList);
    // With Sort
    WaterSort waterSort = new WaterSort();
    Collections.sort(waterList, waterSort);
    System.out.println("Sorted: " + waterList);
  }
}
```

```
$ Not Sorted: [Hard, Soft, Boiled, Raw, Rain, Snow, Filtered,
Reverse Osmosis, Deionized, Distilled]
$ Sorted: [Boiled, Deionized, Distilled, Filtered, Hard, Rain,
Raw, Reverse Osmosis, Snow, Soft]
```

Comparator Interface Used with an Anonymous Inner Class

If you are going to use code only once and you will not reuse it, there is no practical need to maintain it (for example, the WaterSort class) as a stand-alone piece of code. As with this example, it would be most ideal to replace the WaterSort class with an inline anonymous inner class. This means you can remove the WaterSort class altogether and replace the code in the main method, from WaterSort waterSort = new WaterSort();, to this:

```
Comparator <Water> waterSort = new Comparator <Water> () {
  @Override
  public int compare (Water w1, Water w2) {
    return w1.getSource().compareTo(w2.getSource());
  }
};
```

Comparator Functional Interface Used with a Lambda Expression

Comparator isn't just an interface; it's an FI. Remember that FIs have one abstract method originating within its interface. However, FIs can also include public abstract method declarations from java.lang.Object. Again, FIs may optionally have one or more default methods and one or more static methods, but typically they have zero of each.

In the next code listing, the following items are present in Java's Comparator FI:

- The interface is annotated with @FunctionalInterface
- One and only one abstract method; int compare(T o1, T o2);
- Inclusion of the java.lang.Object abstract method declaration boolean equals(Object obj);
- Overloaded default methods: thenComparing
- Static methods: naturalOrder(), overloaded comparing(), comparingInt(), comparingLong(), comparingDouble()

None of these specific details of the Comparator FI will be on the exam, but it is good to see how an FI can be constructed and that it follows the rules, as shown in the next code listing. If any of the rules are broken in the coding of the interface, compiler errors will be thrown, thanks to the inclusion of the @ FunctionalInterface annotation.

```java
// Copyright (c) 2010, 2013, Oracle and/or its affiliates. All rights reserved
// ORACLE PROPRIETARY/CONFIDENTIAL. Use is subject to license terms.

@FunctionalInterface
public interface Comparator<T> {
  int compare(T o1, T o2);  // abstract method
  boolean equals(Object obj); // inherited abstract method
  default Comparator<T> reversed() {
    return Collections.reverseOrder(this);
  }
  default Comparator<T> thenComparing(Comparator<? super T> other) {
    Objects.requireNonNull(other);
    return (Comparator<T> & Serializable) (c1, c2) -> {
      int res = compare(c1, c2);
      return (res != 0) ? res : other.compare(c1, c2);
    };
  }
   default <U extends Comparable<? super U>> Comparator<T> thenComparing(
      Function<? super T, ? extends U> keyExtractor,
      Comparator<? super U> keyComparator)
  {
    return thenComparing(comparing(keyExtractor, keyComparator));
  }
  default <U extends Comparable<? super U>> Comparator<T> thenComparing(
      Function<? super T, ? extends U> keyExtractor)  {
    return thenComparing(comparing(keyExtractor));
```

```
    }
     default Comparator<T> thenComparingInt(ToIntFunction<? super T> keyExtractor) {
      return thenComparing(comparingInt(keyExtractor));
    }
     default Comparator<T> thenComparingLong
        (ToLongFunction<? super T> keyExtractor) {
      return thenComparing(comparingLong(keyExtractor));
    }
    default Comparator<T> thenComparingDouble
        (ToDoubleFunction<? super T> keyExtractor) {
      return thenComparing(comparingDouble(keyExtractor));
    }
     public static <T extends Comparable<? super T>> Comparator<T> reverseOrder() {
      return Collections.reverseOrder();
    }
     @SuppressWarnings("unchecked")
    public static <T extends Comparable<? super T>> Comparator<T> naturalOrder() {
      return (Comparator<T>) Comparators.NaturalOrderComparator.INSTANCE;
    }
     public static <T> Comparator<T> nullsFirst(Comparator<? super T> comparator) {
      return new Comparators.NullComparator<>(true, comparator);
    }
    public static <T> Comparator<T> nullsLast(Comparator<? super T> comparator) {
      return new Comparators.NullComparator<>(false, comparator);
    }
    public static <T, U> Comparator<T> comparing(
        Function<? super T, ? extends U> keyExtractor,
        Comparator<? super U> keyComparator) {
      Objects.requireNonNull(keyExtractor);
      Objects.requireNonNull(keyComparator);
      return (Comparator<T> & Serializable)
        (c1, c2) -> keyComparator.compare(keyExtractor.apply(c1),
                       keyExtractor.apply(c2));
    }
     public static <T, U extends Comparable<? super U>> Comparator<T> comparing(
        Function<? super T, ? extends U> keyExtractor) {
      Objects.requireNonNull(keyExtractor);
      return (Comparator<T> & Serializable)
        (c1, c2) -> keyExtractor.apply(c1).compareTo(keyExtractor.apply(c2));
    }
    public static <T> Comparator<T> comparingInt(ToIntFunction<? super T>
  keyExtractor) {
      Objects.requireNonNull(keyExtractor);
      return (Comparator<T> & Serializable)
        (c1, c2) -> Integer.compare(keyExtractor.applyAsInt(c1),
```

```
keyExtractor.applyAsInt(c2));
   }
   public static <T> Comparator<T> comparingLong
       (ToLongFunction<? super T> keyExtractor) {
    Objects.requireNonNull(keyExtractor);
    return (Comparator<T> & Serializable)
       (c1, c2) -> Long.compare(keyExtractor.applyAsLong(c1),
keyExtractor.applyAsLong(c2));
   }
   public static<T> Comparator<T> comparingDouble
       (ToDoubleFunction<? super T> keyExtractor) {
    Objects.requireNonNull(keyExtractor);
    return (Comparator<T> & Serializable)
       (c1, c2) -> Double.compare(keyExtractor.applyAsDouble(c1),
keyExtractor.applyAsDouble(c2));
   }
}
```

Java SE 8 aims to solve the "vertical" issue of several lines of code with a simpler expressive means with lambda expressions. Thus, the six lines of code shown in the anonymous inner class example can be replaced with the following abbreviated code statement using the Comparator FI in the context of a lambda expression:

```
// Commenting out Anonymous inner class for λE use
// Comparator <Water> waterSort = new Comparator <Water> () {
//    @Override
//    public int compare (Water w1, Water w2) {
//       return w1.getSource().compareTo(w2.getSource());
//    }
// };
Comparator <Water> waterSort = (Water w1, Water w2) ->
   w1.getSource().compareTo(w2.getSource());
Collections.sort (waterList, waterSort);
System.out.println("Sorted: " + waterList);

$ Sorted: [Boiled, Deionized, Distilled, Filtered, Hard, Rain,
Raw, Reverse Osmosis, Snow, Soft]
```

To reduce SLOC (source lines of code) further, Collections.sort() can be used to reduce the use of two lines of code (or statements) to one.

```
Collections.sort (waterList, (Water w1, Water w2) ->
   w1.getSource().compareTo(w2.getSource()));
System.out.println("Sorted: " + waterList);

$ Sorted: [Boiled, Deionized, Distilled, Filtered, Hard, Rain,
Raw, Reverse Osmosis, Snow, Soft]
```

Also, since the target types are known, the expression can be further simplified by removing the class names, so (Water w1, Water w2) would be (w1, w2).

```
Collections.sort (waterList, (w1, w2) ->
  w1.getSource().compareTo(w2.getSource()));
System.out.println("Sorted: " + waterList);

$ Sorted: [Boiled, Deionized, Distilled, Filtered, Hard, Rain,
Raw, Reverse Osmosis, Snow, Soft]
```

Simpler even (and you can probably use this on the job right away) is that the Comparator class provides a comparingWith method that accepts a lambda expression. The return value of this method can be used with the sort method of various collection types (such as ArrayList):

```
waterList.sort(Comparator.comparing(w -> w.getSource()));
System.out.println("Sorted: " + waterList);

$ Sorted: [Boiled, Deionized, Distilled, Filtered, Hard, Rain,
Raw, Reverse Osmosis, Snow, Soft]
```

Predicate Functional Interface

As previously discussed, the Predicate FI is included on the exam. Its general definition is quite simple, with a generic as the target type and the abstract method being test. The test method returns a Boolean value.

```
Public interface Predicate <T>
 Boolean test (T t);
}
```

Three classes are provided here that will collectively help demonstrate the use of lambda expressions through five similar scenarios:

■ PlanetApp   Application that creates planet objects and queries filtered planet lists using the Predicate FI

■ Planet   A value/transfer object representing planets as basic Java Beans

■ PlanetPredicates   A helper class making use of predicates

Let's list the `Planet` class first, because it's just a simple bean showing a `Planet` object with state representing their names, primary color, number of moons, and whether or not the planets have rings.

```java
import javafx.scene.paint.Color;
public class Planet {
  private String name = "Unknown";
  private Color primaryColor = Color.WHITE;
  private Integer numberOfMoons = 0;
  private Boolean ringed = false;
  public Planet(String name, Color primaryColor, Integer numberOfMoons, Boolean ringed) {
    this.name = name;
    this.primaryColor = primaryColor;
    this.numberOfMoons = numberOfMoons;
    this.ringed = ringed;
  }
  public String getName() {
    return name;
  }
  public void setName(String name) {
    this.name = name;
  }
  public Color getPrimaryColor() {
    return primaryColor;
  }
  public void setPrimaryColor(Color primaryColor) {
    this.primaryColor = primaryColor;
  }
  public Integer getNumberOfMoons() {
    return numberOfMoons;
  }
  public void setNumberOfMoons(Integer numberOfMoons) {
    this.numberOfMoons = numberOfMoons;
  }
  public Boolean isRinged() {
    return ringed;
  }
  public void setRinged(Boolean ringed) {
    this.ringed = ringed;
  }
  public String toString() {
    return this.name;
  }
}
```

Next, the `PlanetPredicates` class listing is provided. This class demonstrates different features, such as using predicates in the return statement of methods. These features are examined in more detail against the associated scenarios.

```java
import javafx.scene.paint.Color;
import java.util.List;
import java.util.function.Predicate;
import java.util.stream.Collectors;

public class PlanetPredicates {
  public static Predicate<Planet> hasMoonsMoreThan(Integer moons) {
    return p -> p.getNumberOfMoons() > moons;
  }
  public static Predicate<Planet> hasAColor() {
    return p -> p.getPrimaryColor() != Color.BLACK;
  }
  public static List<Planet> filterPlanets(List<Planet> planetList, Predicate<Planet>
predicate) {
    return planetList.stream().filter(predicate).collect(Collectors.<Planet>toList());
  }

  public static StringBuilder listFilteredPlanets(List<Planet> planetList,
Predicate<Planet> predicate) {
    StringBuilder planets = new StringBuilder();
     planetList.stream().filter((planet) -> (predicate.test(planet))).forEach((planet) ->
{

      planets.append(planet).append(" ");
    });

    // Alternate approach
    // for (Planet planet : planetList) {
    //   if (predicate.test(planet)) {
    //     planets.append(planet).append(" ");
    //   }
    // }
    return planets;
  }
}
```

Now, let's look at the source code for the application. We'll step through each scenario that uses lambda expressions, one at a time. Note that the scenarios provide standard output listings where the `Predicate` FI has been used to assist with the task. The five scenarios are listed here from a general user goal perspective, followed by the overall source code, and then a general description of each scenario.

- Scenario 1: Which planets have rings?
- Scenario 2: Which planets are blue and have moons?
- Scenario 3: Which planets have more than twenty moons?
- Scenario 4: Which planet has a color (other than black)?
- Scenario 5: Which planets have moons?

```java
import java.util.ArrayList;
import java.util.List;
import javafx.scene.paint.Color;
import static com.ocajexam.planets.PlanetPredicates.*;

public class PlanetApp {
  public static void main(String[] args) {
    Planet mercury = new Planet("Mercury", Color.GRAY, 0, false);
    Planet venus = new Planet("Venus", Color.YELLOW, 0, false);
    Planet earth = new Planet("Earth", Color.BLUE, 1, false);
    Planet mars = new Planet("Mars", Color.RED, 2, false);
    Planet jupiter = new Planet("Jupiter", Color.YELLOW, 67, true);
    Planet saturn = new Planet("Saturn", Color.ORANGE, 62, true);
    Planet uranus = new Planet("Uranus", Color.TEAL, 27, true);
    Planet neptune = new Planet("Neptune", Color.BLUE, 14, true);

    List<Planet> planetList = new ArrayList<>();
    planetList.add(mercury);
    planetList.add(venus);
    planetList.add(earth);
    planetList.add(mars);
    planetList.add(jupiter);
    planetList.add(saturn);
    planetList.add(uranus);
    planetList.add(neptune);

    // SCENARIO 1 - Which planets have rings?
    System.out.println("Has one or more rings: " + listFilteredPlanets
      (planetList, (Planet p) -> p.isRinged()));

    // SCENARIO 2 - Which planets are blue and have moons?
    System.out.print("Has moons and is blue: ");
    planetList.stream().filter(p -> p.getNumberOfMoons() > 0 &
      (p.getPrimaryColor() == Color.BLUE)).forEach
```

```
    (s -> System.out.print(s + " "));

    // SCENARIO 3 - Which planets have more than twenty moons?
    System.out.println("\nHas over twenty moons: " + filterPlanets
      (planetList, hasMoonsMoreThan(20)));

    // SCENARIO 4 - Which planet has a color (other than black)
    System.out.print("Has a color not black: ");
    planetList.stream().filter(hasAColor()).forEach(s -> System.out.print(s + " "));

    // SCENARIO 5 - Which planets have moons?
    planetList.removeIf((Planet p) -> {
      return (p.getNumberOfMoons() == 0);
    });
    System.out.println("\nHas one or more moons: " + planetList);
  }
}
```

```
$ Has one or more rings: Jupiter Saturn Uranus Neptune
$ Has moons and is blue: Earth Neptune
$ Has over twenty moons: [Jupiter, Saturn, Uranus]
$ Has a color not black: Mercury Venus Earth Mars Jupiter Saturn Uranus Neptune
$ Has one or more moons: [Earth, Mars, Jupiter, Saturn, Uranus, Neptune]
```

Scenario 1: Which Planets Have Rings?

In this scenario, a lambda expression is passed into a method call as an argument. By using an enhanced for loop, you can see the Planet target type and the test method that belong to the Predicate FI.

```
public static StringBuilder listFilteredPlanets(List<Planet>
  planetList, Predicate<Planet> predicate) {
    StringBuilder planets = new StringBuilder();
    for (Planet planet : planetList) {
    if (predicate.test(planet)) {
       planets.append(planet).append(" ");
    }
  }
  return planets;
}
```

Here the method is called, accepting the Predicate type in the second argument:

```
System.out.println("Has one or more rings: " + listFilteredPlanets
  (planetList, (Planet p) -> p.isRinged()));
$ Has one or more rings: Jupiter Saturn Uranus Neptune
```

Notice that replacing the enhanced `for` loop with a pipeline is beneficial, and in most cases, your IDE can do it for you.

```
// Replaces for loop in listFilteredPlanets method
planetList.stream().filter((planet) ->
  (predicate.test(planet))).forEach((planet) ->
  { planets.append(planet).append(" "); });
```

Scenario 2: Which Planets Are Blue and Have Moons?

Determining which planets are blue and have moons, we use streams, filters, and the `foreach` method. None of these elements is on the exam, but you will surely be using them on the job—that is, if you decide to use functional programming in your Java space.

```
System.out.print("Has moons and is blue: ");
planetList.stream().filter(p -> p.getNumberOfMoons() > 0 &
  (p.getPrimaryColor() == Color.BLUE)).forEach
  (s -> System.out.print(s + " "));
$ Has moons and is blue: Earth Neptune
```

Scenario 3: Which Planets Have More Than Twenty Moons?

Passing lambda expressions can still be a little too implicit, so you may find it beneficial to create helper classes that work with the expressions behind the scenes, as in the supplied `PlanetPredicates` class example. In the main method, a very simple method is called, providing two arguments to produce our list.

```
System.out.println("\nHas over twenty moons: " + filterPlanets
  (planetList, hasMoonsMoreThan(20)));
```

Here, the `filterPlanets()` and `hasMoonsMoreThan()` methods do the work for us, while leveraging off of the use of the lambda expression:

```
public class PlanetPredicates {
   ...
    public static Predicate<Planet> hasMoonsMoreThan(Integer moons) {
   return p -> p.getNumberOfMoons() > moons;
  }
  public static List<Planet> filterPlanets
    (List<Planet> planetList, Predicate<Planet> predicate) {
   return planetList.stream().filter(predicate).collect
     (Collectors.<Planet>toList());
  }
   ...
}
```

Scenario 4: Which Planet Has a Color (Other Than Black)?

This scenario is very similar to scenario 3, except the method used to return lambda expressions through a `Predicate` parameter is done so in a pipeline versus a straight method call.

```
System.out.print("Has a color not black: ");
planetList.stream().filter(hasAColor()).forEach(s -> System.out.print(s + " "));
$ Has a color not black: Mercury Venus Earth Mars Jupiter Saturn Uranus Neptune
```

Scenario 5: Which Planets Have Moons?

To determine which planets have moons, we will be modifying the `ArrayList` to remove all elements that don't have moons. We can do this easily because the `ArrayList` class provides a `removeIf` method that accepts a `Predicate`.

```
removeIf(Predicate<? Super E> filter)
```

In our scenario, the list is simply modified to remove elements where `numberOfMoons` is equal to zero:

```
planetList.removeIf((Planet p) -> {
    return (p.getNumberOfMoons() == 0);
});
   System.out.println("\nHas one or more moons: " + planetList);
$ Has one or more moons: [Earth, Mars, Jupiter, Saturn, Uranus, Neptune]
```

As you should be deeply familiar with the syntax by now, you'll know that the lambda could have been abbreviated even further:

```
planetList.removeIf( p -> p.getNumberOfMoons() == 0);
```

EXERCISE 11-1

IDE Refactoring for Lambda Expressions

In this exercise, you'll use an IDE to refactor an anonymous inner class to a lambda expression.

1. Install the latest version of the NetBeans IDE.

2. Create a new JavaFX project (choose File | New Project, select JavaFX, select JavaFXApplication, click Next, and click Finish). A JavaFX application will be created that includes an anonymous inner class.

3. In the Projects pane, expand the JavaFXApplication, Source Packages, and javafxapplication nodes. Click the JavaFXApplication.java filename so the file is opened in the source code editor. Scroll down to line 26, which begins with `btn.setOnAction`.

4. Click the light bulb in the glyph gutter at line 26. Notice that if you hover the mouse over the light bulb, you will see this message: "This anonymous inner class creation can be turned into a lambda expression."

5. Click Use Lambda Expression. The conversion will be automatic. Examine the conversion to understand what you did.

CERTIFICATION SUMMARY

The goal of this chapter was to solidify your knowledge of using lambda expressions. This chapter reviewed syntax and when and why lambda expressions are used. General-purpose and specific-purpose functional interfaces were included to guide you with an overview of the JDK's supporting interfaces. The `Predicate` interface was discussed in detail and is the only FI you will see on the exam. Lambda expressions are best understood through coding exercises. If you haven't already done so, through our guidance, write a sample program that uses the `Predicate` interface and lambda expressions, while exercising the various allowable syntax. Once you can do this comfortably, you'll be sure to score well on lambda expression–related questions on the exam.

TWO-MINUTE DRILL

Write Lambda Expressions

- ☐ Lambda expressions provide a means to represent anonymous methods using an expression.

- ☐ Lambda expressions allow for the creation and use of single method classes—that is, one and only one abstract method is allowed.

- ☐ Lambda expressions must have a functional interface (FI), preferably annotated with `@FunctionalInterface`.

- ☐ An FI has exactly one abstract method.

- ☐ An FI may optionally have one or more default methods.

- ☐ An FI may optionally have one or more static methods.

- ☐ FIs provide target types for lambda expressions and method references.

- ☐ Lambda expressions typically include a parameter list of target types, a return type, and a body. Parameter types are optional. Curly brackets and the `return` keyword are necessary only when there are multiple statements in the body.

- ☐ Lambda expression acceptable contexts are as follows: assignments, array initializers, cast expressions, constructor arguments, lambda bodies, method arguments, return statements, ternary expressions, and variable declarations.

- ☐ Specific-purpose functional interfaces are included in various packages throughout the Java SE 8 API.

- ☐ General-purpose functional interfaces are included in the `java.util` `.function` package of the Java SE 8 API.

- ☐ The `Predicate` general-purpose FI represents a predicate (`boolean`-valued function) of one argument, whose functional method is `test`.

SELF TEST

Write Lambda Expressions

1. Given the following code, which is a correct syntactical means to refactor with a lambda expression?

```
new Thread ( new Runnable () {
   @Override
   public void run () { processDNA(); }
   }).start();
```

A. `new Thread ( () -> processDNA() ).start();`

B. `new Thread ( {} -> processDNA() ).start();`

C. `new Thread ( () => processDNA() ).start();`

D. `new Thread ( processDNA() ).start();`

2. Given the following code, which statements about the code are valid?

```
PathMatcher matcher1 = (Path p) -> { return (p.toString().contains("DNA")); };
PathMatcher matcher2 = p -> { return
   (p.toString().equals("DNA")); };
PathMatcher matcher3 = (Path p) ->
   p.toString().startsWith("DNA");
PathMatcher matcher4 = p ->
   p.toString().endsWith("DNA");
Path path = FileSystems.getDefault().getPath("\\dna_data\\DNA_results.txt");
System.out.print(matcher1.matches (path));
System.out.print(" " + matcher2.matches (path));
System.out.print(" " + matcher3.matches (path));
System.out.print(" " + matcher4.matches (path));
```

A. When executed, `true false false false` will be printed to standard output.

B. The code will not compile due to a syntactical issue with one of the lambda expressions.

C. The code will throw a runtime exception.

D. `Path` is not the target type for the `PathMatcher` functional interface.

3. What do the specific-purpose functional interfaces `Runnable` and `Callable` have in common?

A. `Runnable` and `Callable` do not contain abstract methods.

B. `Runnable` and `Callable` contain multiple default methods.

C. `Runnable` and `Callable` do not have target types.

D. `Runnable` and `Callable` have multiple target types.

4. Given the following code, what will be printed upon execution?

```
List <String> yHaplogroupList = new ArrayList <> ();
yHaplogroupList.add("I2");
yHaplogroupList.add("L126");
yHaplogroupList.add("R1b");
yHaplogroupList.stream().filter(s -> !s.startsWith("R"))
    .forEach(s -> System.out.print(s + " "));
yHaplogroupList.forEach(s -> System.out.print(s + " "));
yHaplogroupList.removeIf(s -> s.startsWith("R"));
yHaplogroupList.forEach(s -> System.out.print(s + " "));
```

A. I2 L126 I2 L126 R1b I2 L126 R1b

B. I2 L126 I2 L126 I2 L126

C. I2 L126 I2 L126 R1b I2 L126

D. I2 L126 I2 L126 I2 L126 R1b

E. A compiler error will result.

5. Given the following code, what will the compiler output?

```
@FunctionalInterface
public interface Sequenceable <T> {
    public void sequence (T t);
    public boolean test (T t);
}
```

A. "one or more default methods required"

B. "multiple non-overriding abstract methods found in interface Sequenceable"

C. "cannot find symbol class T"

D. "abstract keyword missing for multiple methods"

6. Which of the following is not a default method of the `Predicate` functional interface?

A. `and(Predicate<? super T> other)`

B. `or(Predicate<? super T> other)`

C. `xor(Predicate<? super T> other)`

D. `negate()`

7. What code segment can replace the "MISSING-CODE" section to enable the following source code to compile?

```
String [] birdArray = {"bluebird", "scarlet macaw", "bluejay"};
List <String> birdList = Arrays.asList (birdArray);
list.forEach( MISSING-CODE System.out.println(p.toString().
contains("blue")));
```

   A. `(p1, p2) ->`

   B. `() ->`

   C. `String p ->`

   D. `(String p) ->`

8. The body of a lambda expression can be enclosed in braces (for example, a block statement). Which representation of a lambda expression using a block statement is invalid?

   A. `(p -> {})`

   B. `(p -> {{;}})`

   C. `(p -> {;})`

   D. `(p -> {;;})`

   E. All statements are valid.

SELF TEST ANSWERS

Write Lambda Expressions

1. Given the following code, which is a correct syntactical means to refactor with a lambda expression?

```
new Thread ( new Runnable () {
    @Override
    public void run () { processDNA(); }
    }).start();
```

A. `new Thread ( () -> processDNA() ).start();`

B. `new Thread ( {} -> processDNA() ).start();`

C. `new Thread ( () => processDNA() ).start();`

D. `new Thread ( processDNA() ).start();`

> Answer:
>
> ☑ **A.** Parentheses for a zero argument target type, followed by the arrow operator and the method name, is the acceptable format for lambda expressions.
>
> ☒ **B, C,** and **D** are incorrect. **B** is incorrect because parentheses are required in place of curly brackets. **C** is incorrect because `->` is required in place of `=>`. **D** is incorrect because the lambda expression is incomplete.

2. Given the following code, which statements about the code are valid?

```
PathMatcher matcher1 = (Path p) -> { return (p.toString().contains("DNA")); };
PathMatcher matcher2 = p -> { return
    (p.toString().equals("DNA")); };
PathMatcher matcher3 = (Path p) ->
    p.toString().startsWith("DNA");
PathMatcher matcher4 = p ->
    p.toString().endsWith("DNA");
Path path = FileSystems.getDefault().getPath("\\dna_data\\DNA_results.txt");
System.out.print(matcher1.matches (path));
System.out.print(" " + matcher2.matches (path));
System.out.print(" " + matcher3.matches (path));
System.out.print(" " + matcher4.matches (path));
```

A. When executed, `true false false false` will be printed to standard output.

B. The code will not compile due to a syntactical issue with one of the lambda expressions.

C. The code will throw a runtime exception.

D. `Path` is not the target type for the `PathMatcher` functional interface.

> **Answer:**
>
> ☑ **A.** When executed, `true false false false` will be printed to standard output.
> ☒ **B, C,** and **D** are incorrect. **B** is incorrect because there are no syntactical issues with the code. **C** is incorrect because no runtime exception will be thrown. **D** is incorrect because `Path` is the target type for the `PathMatcher` functional interface.

3. What do the specific-purpose functional interfaces `Runnable` and `Callable` have in common?

A. `Runnable` and `Callable` do not contain abstract methods.

B. `Runnable` and `Callable` contain multiple default methods.

C. `Runnable` and `Callable` do not have target types.

D. `Runnable` and `Callable` have multiple target types.

> **Answer:**
>
> ☑ **C.** The `Runnable` and `Callable` functional interfaces do not have target types.
> ☒ **A, B,** and **D** are incorrect. **A** is incorrect because `Runnable` and `Callable` each contain one abstract method. **B** is incorrect because `Runnable` and `Callable` do not contain default methods. **D** is incorrect because `Runnable` and `Callable` do not have multiple target types.

4. Given the following code, what will be printed upon execution?

```
List <String> yHaplogroupList = new ArrayList <> ();
yHaplogroupList.add("I2");
yHaplogroupList.add("L126");
yHaplogroupList.add("R1b");
yHaplogroupList.stream().filter(s -> !s.startsWith("R"))
  .forEach(s -> System.out.print(s + " "));
yHaplogroupList.forEach(s -> System.out.print(s + " "));
yHaplogroupList.removeIf(s -> s.startsWith("R"));
yHaplogroupList.forEach(s -> System.out.print(s + " "));
```

A. I2 L126 I2 L126 R1b I2 L126 R1b
B. I2 L126 I2 L126 I2 L126
C. I2 L126 I2 L126 R1b I2 L126
D. I2 L126 I2 L126 I2 L126 R1b
E. A compiler error will result.

Answer:

☑ **C.** I2 L126 I2 L126 R1b I2 L126 will be printed to standard output.
☒ **A, B, D,** and **E** are incorrect. **A** is incorrect because it does not represent what is printed to standard output. **B** is incorrect because it does not represent what is printed to standard output. **D** is incorrect because it does not represent what is printed to standard output. **E** is incorrect because no compiler error occurs.

5. Given the following code, what compiler warning will be present?

```
@FunctionalInterface
public interface Sequenceable <T> {
    public void sequence (T t);
    public boolean test (T t);
}
```

A. "one or more default methods required"
B. "multiple non-overriding abstract methods found in interface Sequenceable"
C. "cannot find symbol class T"
D. "abstract keyword missing for multiple methods"

Answer:

☑ **B.** The compiler warning "multiple non-overriding abstract methods found in interface Sequenceable" will be presented.
☒ **A, C,** and **D** are incorrect. **A** is incorrect because default methods are optional. **C** is incorrect because the symbol class T can be found. **D** is incorrect because the abstract keyword does not need to be explicitly provided.

6. Which of the following is not a default method of the `Predicate` functional interface?

A. `and(Predicate<? super T> other)`

B. `or(Predicate<? super T> other)`

C. `xor(Predicate<? super T> other)`

D. `negate()`

Answer:

☑ **C.** `xor()` is not a default method of the `Predicate` functional interface.

☒ **A, B,** and **D** are incorrect. **A** is incorrect because and `()` is a default method of the `Predicate` functional interface. **B** is incorrect because or`()` is a default method of the `Predicate` functional interface. **D** is incorrect because `negate()` is a default method of the `Predicate` functional interface.

7. What code segment can replace the "MISSING-CODE" section to enable the following source code to compile?

```
String [] birdArray = {"bluebird", "scarlet macaw", "bluejay"};
List <String> birdlist = Arrays.asList (birdArray);
list.forEach( MISSING-CODE System.out.println(p.toString().
contains("blue")));
```

A. `(p1, p2) ->`

B. `() ->`

C. `String p ->`

D. `(String p) ->`

Answer:

☑ **D.** `(String p)` -> as provided, with the explicit target type and parentheses, will allow the code to compile.

☒ **A, B,** and **C** are incorrect. **A** is incorrect because only one target type is expected in this context. **B** is incorrect because the `String` target type is expected in this context. **C** is incorrect because explicit target types must be surrounded with parentheses.

8. The body of a lambda expression can be enclosed in braces (for example, a block statement). Which representation of a lambda expression using a block statement is invalid?

A. `(p -> {})`

B. `(p -> {{;}})`

C. `(p -> {;})`

D. `(p -> {;;})`

E. All statements are valid.

Answer:

☑ **E.** All statements are valid.

☒ **A, B, C,** and **D** are incorrect. **A** is incorrect because the statement `(p -> {})` represents a valid lambda expression. **B** is incorrect because the statement `(p -> {{;}})` represents a valid lambda expression. **C** is incorrect because the statement `(p -> {;})` represents a valid lambda expression. **D** is incorrect because the statement `(p -> {;;})` represents a valid lambda expression.

A

Class Relationships

Object relationships are often described in terms of *composition* and *association*. The SCJA exam (predecessor to the OCA exam) included questions that required that you understand the relationship between objects and distinguish between a composition relationship and an association relationship. The OCA exam does not include specific objectives for this skill set, but it is implied that you understand class compositions and associations. As such, we provide this coverage as a bonus to aid in your exam preparation.

Understand Class Compositions and Associations

Composition and association are two general descriptions for object relationships. Composition and association encompass four specific types of relationship descriptors: direct association, composition association, aggregation association, and temporary association. These descriptors are covered in this appendix. By studying the four specific relationship types, you will have a greater understanding of the difference between composition and association. Multiplicities are also discussed. Every object relationship has a multiplicity.

The following topics will be covered in this appendix:

- Class compositions and associations
- Class relationships
- Multiplicities
- Association navigation

Class Compositions and Associations

Composition and *association* are the general terms used to describe a class relationship. An association or composition relationship is formed between two objects when one contains a reference to the other. The reference is often stored as an instance variable. The reference may be in one direction or bidirectional.

An association relationship is a relationship of two objects, where neither one directly depends on the other for its logical meaning. For example, suppose object A has an association relationship with object B. If this relationship was lost, both objects would still retain the same meaning they had before the relationship. These are considered weak relationships. Objects in an association relationship have no dependence on each other for the management of their lifecycle. In other words, the existence of one object is not tied to the existence of the other object in the relationship. Another example would be a `CarFactory` object and a `CarFrame` object. The `CarFactory` object and `CarFrame` object have an association relationship. If this relationship no longer existed, each object could continue to make sense logically and would retain its original meaning on its own.

A composition relationship is stronger than an association relationship. Composition means that one object is composed of another. An object may be composed of one or multiple objects. If, for example, object A is composed of object B, object A depends on object B. This statement does not imply that object A is composed of only object B, however; in fact, object A may also be composed of other objects. If the relationship were lost between object A and object B, the logical meaning of both objects would be lost or significantly altered. In this example, object B—the inner object that object A is composed of—would depend on object A to manage its lifecycle. The existence of object B is directly tied to the existence of object A, so when object A no longer exists, object B would also no longer exist. Object B would also become nonexistent if the relationship between the two objects were lost. Examples of objects that have a composition relationship tend to be more abstract than those with association relationships. Consider a `Car` object and `CarStatus` object, for example. The `Car` object is composed of the `CarStatus` object, and both objects depend on this relationship to define their meanings. The `CarStatus` object also depends on the `Car` object to maintain its lifecycle. When the `Car` object no longer exists, the `CarStatus` object would also no longer exist.

SCENARIO & SOLUTION

You have an object that controls the lifecycle of another object. What term can be used to describe it?	Composition
You have an object that has a weak relationship with another object. What term can be used to describe it?	Association
You have an object that has a strong relationship with another object. What term can be used to describe it?	Composition

In many cases, determining the type of relationship between two objects is not as clear as the preceding examples. Some interpretation is needed to determine the relationship. A composition relationship will always be responsible for an object's lifecycle. Composition relationships also represent a stronger relationship compared to an association. Objects belonging to an association relationship make more sense by themselves than objects in a composition relationship.

Class Relationships

This section will break down the four specific class relationships that are possible. Each represents a different way objects can have relationships. Association and composition relationships are not mutually exclusive. In fact, composition association is one of the detailed relationship types, and it is sometimes referred to as simply composition. The other three detailed relationship types, direct association, aggregation association, and temporary association, are often referred to as simply association.

The following topics will be covered in the next few sections:

- Direct association
- Composition association
- Aggregation association
- Temporary association

Direct Association

Direct association describes a "has a" relationship. This is a basic association that represents navigability. Direct association is a weak relationship and therefore can be generalized to an association. There is no lifecycle responsibility, and each object in the relationship can conceptually be independent. This tends to be the default association when nothing else can accurately describe the relationship.

If a truck was modeled as an object to create a `Truck` object, it may have a `Trailer` object that it has a direct association with. The `Truck` object and `Trailer` object are weakly associated, because each could be used without the other and still maintain its intended purpose. A `Truck` object does not need to have a `Trailer` object, and a `Trailer` object is not required for the construction of the `Truck` object. This direct association relationship is depicted in the Unified Modeling Language (UML) diagram in Figure A-1.

FIGURE A-1

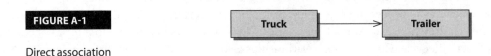

Direct association

Composition Association

Composition associations are used to describe an object's relationship where one object is composed of one or more objects. A composition association is a strong relationship and will be generalized as a composition. The internal object makes conceptual sense only while stored in the containing object. This relationship represents ownership. In a composition association, object A is "composed of" object B. For example, a `Tire` object would be composed of a `RubberStrips` object. The `Tire` object requires a `RubberStrips` object; the `RubberStrips` object is not very useful by itself.

The containing object also has the responsibility of managing the lifecycle of the internal object. It is possible for this object to pass the lifecycle management to another object. Lifecycle management means that the object composed of the second object, or the containing object, must maintain a reference to the inner object; otherwise, the Java virtual machine will destroy it. If the containing object is destroyed, any objects that compose it will also be destroyed. This composition association relationship is depicted in the UML diagram in Figure A-2.

Aggregation Association

An aggregation association is a relationship that represents one object being part of another object. An aggregation association represents a "part of" the whole relationship. In this relationship, even though one object is a part of the other, each object can maintain its own meaning independently if the relationship is lost. Neither object depends on the other for its existence. The aggregation relationship does not require the object to perform lifecycle management for the object that it references. Aggregation association is a weak relationship. It can be generalized as an association.

A `Motorcycle` object would have an aggregation association with a `Windshield` object. The `Motorcycle` object and `Windshield` object are weakly associated, because each could be used without the other and still maintain its intended purpose. The `Windshield` object has a "part of" relationship with the `Motorcycle` object. This aggregation association relationship is depicted in the UML diagram in Figure A-3.

FIGURE A-2

Composition association

FIGURE A-3

Aggregation
association

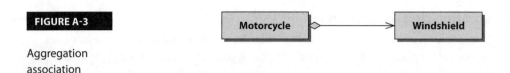

Temporary Association

Temporary association is also known as a dependency. Typically, a temporary association will be an object used as a local variable, return value, or method parameter. It is considered a dependency because object A depends on object B as either an argument, a return value, or at some point, a local variable. A temporary association is the weakest form of association. This relationship will not persist for the entire lifecycle of the object.

For example, a `Car` object may have a method called `startEngine` that has a `Key` object as a parameter. The `Key` object as a parameter would represent a temporary association. This temporary association relationship is depicted in the UML diagram in Figure A-4.

Multiplicities

Every relationship has a multiplicity. *Multiplicity* refers to the number of objects that are part of a relationship. The three general classifications of multiplicity you should know are one-to-one, one-to-many, and many-to-many.

The following topics will be covered in the next few sections:

- One-to-one multiplicity
- One-to-many multiplicity
- Many-to-many multiplicity

Developers often just use the terms "composition" or "association." When they say "composition," they are referring to composition association and a strong relationship. The term "association" is often used to refer to any of the other three weaker relationships: aggregation, direct, and temporary association.

FIGURE A-4

Temporary
association

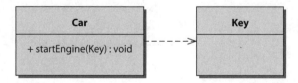

| TABLE A-1 | Object Relationship Characteristics |

	Composition Association	Aggregation Association	Direct Association	Temporary Association
General term is association		✓	✓	✓
General term is composition	✓			
Strong relationship	✓			
Weak relationship		✓	✓	✓
Has lifecycle responsibility	✓			
Persists for most of the object's lifetime	✓	✓	✓	
Is used as a critical part of an object	✓	✓		
Is often a local variable, return variable, or method parameter				✓

Table A-1 shows how each of the four specific relationship types relates to composition and association.

One-to-One Multiplicity

A one-to-one association is a basic relationship where one object contains a reference to another object. All four relationship types may have a one-to-one multiplicity. An example of a one-to-one relationship would be the Motorcycle object that has a relationship with a single Engine object.

One-to-Many Multiplicity

One-to-many relationships are created when one object contains a reference to a group of like objects. The multiple object references are normally stored in an array or a collection. All four relationship types may be one-to-many. The Car object can contain four Tire objects. This would be an aggregation association since the Car and Tire objects have a "part of" association with each other. The Tire objects can be stored in an array or collection. As the name implies, a one-to-many relationship may have many more than four objects. A many-to-one relationship is also possible.

Many-to-Many Multiplicity

Many-to-many relationships are possible only for aggregation associations, direct associations, and temporary associations. Composition association is a strong relationship that implies a lifecycle responsibility for the object that composes it. If many objects have a relationship with an object, it is impossible for any individual object to control the lifecycle of the other object in the relationship. If the car example were broadened to a traffic simulator application, it would include many other Car objects. Each of these Car objects contains references to many other TrafficLight objects. This represents a direct association, since a single Car object does not maintain the lifecycle of the TrafficLight objects. Each car object has a TrafficLight object. The relationship between a Car object and the TrafficLight object is weak. The TrafficLight objects are all shared between all of the Car objects. A many-to-many association does not have to include an equal number of objects on each side of the relationship.

on the **job**

Relationships (for example, aggregation and composition) and multiplicities can be easily depicted with UML. Drawing out class relationships can help you convey design concepts to your fellow employees. UML diagrams are covered in Appendix G.

Association Navigation

Association navigation is a term used to describe the direction in which a relationship can be traveled. An object that is contained within another object is said to be navigable if the containing object has methods for accessing the inner object. Most relationships are navigable in one direction, but if both objects contain references to the other, it is possible to have a bidirectional navigable relationship. Oftentimes, the methods for accessing inner objects are called *getters* and *setters*. A getter is a simple method that just returns an instance variable. A setter is a method that accepts an argument and uses it to set an instance variable.

Class Compositions and Associations in Practice

This section reviews practical examples of association and composition relationships. The following examples and explanations should help provide a solid understanding of these concepts.

These topics are covered in the following sections:

■ Examples of class association relationships
■ Examples of class composition relationships
■ Examples of association navigation

Examples of Class Association Relationships

This section examines associations. The following three examples demonstrate possible multiplicities of an aggregation association. An explanation follows to highlight the important points from the example.

The following topics are covered:

■ One-to-one class association
■ One-to-many class association
■ Many-to-many class association

One-to-One Class Association

The following example shows a `Truck` object and `Trailer` object. This is an example of a one-to-one direct association.

```
public class Truck {
/* This is an example of a one-to-one
direct association */
  Trailer trailer;
  void setTrailer(Trailer t){
       trailer = t;
    }
   /*
    * Remainder of Truck class would be here
    */
}
```

In this example of a one-to-one association, the `Truck` object contains a reference to the `Trailer` object. This is a one-to-one association because the variable `trailer` is a single variable. It is not part of an array or collection. This example is a direct association, because the `Truck` object is not responsible for the lifecycle of the `trailer` variable. Another indication that it is a direct association is that, logically, the `Truck` object "has a" `Trailer` object.

In this example, and in most real-world situations, it is not always easy or even possible to determine if one object controls the lifecycle of another. Oftentimes, you must make the best determination based on the information that is available. In this example, the `trailer` variable is being set by the method `setTrailer`. Since this method is used to set the variable, it can be assumed that other objects contain a reference to the `trailer` object and, therefore, no sole object is responsible for the lifecycle of the other object. Finally, since this was determined to be a direct association, the relationship can be generalized to an association relationship.

One-to-Many Class Association

The next example demonstrates an aggregation association. This example shows a relationship that is one-to-many. Here, `Wheel` objects are "part of" a `Car` object.

```
public class Car {
  Wheel[] wheel = new Wheel[4];
  void setWheels(Wheel w) {
    wheel[0] = w;
    wheel[1] = w;
    wheel[2] = w;
    wheel[3] = w;
  }
  // Remainder of Car class would be here
}
```

This example has an array of four `Wheel` objects. Since there is one `Car` object that contains four `Wheel` objects, this relationship is one-to-many. With a one-to-many relationship, the multiple objects will normally be stored in an array or collection such as a `Vector`. This example is an aggregation association, because the `Wheel` object is "part of" the `Car` object. Because this is a weak relationship and there are no lifecycle responsibilities, this can be generalized as an association.

Many-to-Many Class Association

The many-to-many relationship is more complex than the one-to-one and one-to-many relationships. In this example, the relationship is between a group of `Car` objects and a group of `TrafficLight` objects. The following is the code segment for the two objects:

```
// TrafficLight class
public class TrafficLight {
  int lightID;
    TrafficLight(int ID) {
      lightID = ID;
    }
```

```
  }

// Car class
public class Car {
  TrafficLight[] allTrafficLights;
  Car(TrafficLight[] trafficLights) {
    allTrafficLights=trafficLights;
  }
}
```

This next segment is the code that creates both objects. This segment is important because it shows how the relationships are formed between the objects.

```
public class TrafficSimulator {
  Car[] cars = new Car[3];
  TrafficLight[] trafficLights = new TrafficLight[8];
  public static void main(String[] args) {
    new TrafficSimulator();
  }

  TrafficSimulator() {
    for (int i = 0; i < trafficLights.length; i++) {
      trafficLights[i] = new TrafficLight(i);
    }
    cars[0] = new Car(trafficLights);
    cars[1] = new Car(trafficLights);
    cars[2] = new Car(trafficLights);
  }
}
```

This segment contains a main method. The sole job of main is to create a new TrafficSimulator object. The TrafficSimulator object contains an array of Car objects and an array of TrafficLight objects. First, the TrafficLight objects are created. Each TrafficLight object stores a unique ID. Next, the Car objects are created. Each Car object contains an array of all the TrafficLight objects. This example is many-to-many, because each Car object contains the same group of multiple TrafficLight objects. This relationship can be classified as a direct association because the Car objects have an array of TrafficLight objects.

Examples of Class Composition Relationships

This section is similar to the last section except that composition associations are demonstrated here. Composition associations have only two possible multiplicities. This section shows an example of each followed by an explanation.

One-to-One Class Composition

This example demonstrates a one-to-one composition relationship. This is a composition association because that is the only type of association that can create a composition relationship.

```
public class Tire {
    TireAirPressure tireAirPressure;
        Tire(){
            tireAirPressure = new TireAirPressure();
    }
}
```

In this example, the `Tire` object and the `TireAirPressure` object have a one-to-one relationship. The `Tire` object is "composed of" the `TireAirPressure` object. This represents a composition association. The relationship between the two objects is strong. The `Tire` object has lifecycle management responsibilities to the `TireAirPressure` object. If the `Tire` object was destroyed, the `TireAirPressure` object would also be destroyed.

One-to-Many Class Composition

This final example demonstrates a composition relationship with a one-to-many multiplicity. The following code segment is of a `SensorStatus` class:

```
public class SensorStatus {
  int status;
  public SensorStatus(int newStatus) {
    status = newStatus;
  }
}
```

The next segment demonstrates a `CarComputer` object that is "composed of" an array of five `SensorStatus` objects:

```
public class CarComputer {
  SensorStatus[] sensorStatus = new SensorStatus[5];
  public CarComputer() {
    sensorStatus[0] = new SensorStatus(1);
    sensorStatus[1] = new SensorStatus(1);
    sensorStatus[2] = new SensorStatus(1);
    sensorStatus[3] = new SensorStatus(1);
    sensorStatus[4] = new SensorStatus(1);
  }
}
```

Because there is one `CarComputer` object and five `SensorStatus` objects, this represents a one-to-many relationship. The relationship is composition association. Again, notice how the relationship is strong and that the `SensorStatus` array depends on the `CarComputer` object to manage its lifecycle.

Examples of Association Navigation

Association navigation is the ability to navigate a relationship. The following example demonstrates a `PinStripe` object that is "composed of" a `Color` object:

```
public class PinStripe {
  Color color = new Color(Color.blue);
  Color getColor(){
    return color;
  }
}
```

In this example, any object that had access to the `PinStripe` object could use its `getColor` method, which is considered a getter, to navigate to the `Color` object. In this example, the navigation is only in a single direction.

APPENDIX SUMMARY

This appendix discussed the different relationships that are possible among objects. Association and composition are the general description of relationships and are important for you to be familiar with.

Association is used to describe an object-to-object reference. This type of reference means that object A has a reference to object B and can access object B's public methods and member variables. Object B may or may not have a reference back to object A. A relationship of association means that both objects are independent and neither one relies on the other to maintain its existence. Direct association, aggregation association, and temporary association are all more detailed forms of association.

Composition relationships are a stronger form of association relationships. A composition relationship is a type of association in which an object that is composed of another object is also responsible for the lifecycle management of that object. A composition relationship may have one-to-one or one-to-many multiplicities. Composition association is an example of composition.

Next, this appendix covered each of the four possible relationships in detail. Direct association, aggregation association, and temporary association are three of the four relationship types. Each of these belongs in the general category of association. They imply no responsibility of lifecycle management. Composition association belongs to the category of general composition. Composition association has a lifecycle responsibility.

There may be three different multiplicities of relationships. In a one-to-one relationship, one object contains a reference to another object of a particular type. In a one-to-many relationship, an object contains an array of object references, or a collection such as an `ArrayList` or `Vector`. The final relationship is many-to-many. In this relationship, many objects contain a reference to the same collection or array of objects. The many-to-many relationship is unique for association and cannot exist for a composition relationship.

This appendix concluded with examples of each multiplicity for association and composition relationships. These examples are important for you to understand. In Appendix G of this book, these relationships will be revisited when UML modeling is discussed.

B

Java SE 8 Packages

Because Java is a programming language, the OCA exam focuses on many of the packages and classes within the core Java SE distributions. Light Java EE coverage was included in the precursor SCJA exam but has been removed in the subsequent OCA versions of the exam. The tables provided in this appendix detail the full set of Java SE 8 packages.

You don't need to learn the low-level details of Java packages to perform well on the OCA exam. To a large extent, just knowing what the packages are designed for and what type of functionality they contain will help you achieve a high score.

Java SE 8 provides packages in the following areas:

- **Core packages**   Language, utility, and base packages
- **Integration packages**   Java Database Connectivity (JDBC), Java Naming and Directory Interface (JNDI), Remote Method Invocation (RMI)/RMI-Internet Inter-Orb Protocol (IIOP), and scripting packages
- **User interface packages**   JavaFX, Swing API, Abstract Window Toolkit (AWT) API, sound, image I/O, printing packages, accessibility
- **Security packages**   Security and cryptography packages
- **XML-based packages**   XML-based packages, web services
- **Temporal packages**   Calendar, Date, and Time packages

The documentation for the OMG packages that are part of the Java SE 8 distribution are not listed in this appendix but can be viewed in the Java SE 8 API documentation: http://docs.oracle.com/javase/8/docs/api/.

Core Packages

The following tables detail the core Java packages (that is, language, utility, and base packages). The definitions provided in these tables, as well as the other tables throughout this appendix, are primarily those definitions used in the Java SE 8 API documentation.

TABLE B-1 Language Packages

Language Packages	Description
`java.lang`	Provides classes that are fundamental to the design of the Java programming language.
`java.lang.annotation`	Provides library support for the Java programming language annotation facility.
`java.lang.instrument`	Provides services that allow Java programming language agents to instrument programs running on the JVM.
`java.lang.invoke`	Contains dynamic language support provided directly by the Java core class libraries and virtual machine.
`java.lang.management`	Provides the management interfaces for monitoring and management of the JVM and other components in the Java runtime.
`java.lang.ref`	Provides reference-object classes, which support a limited degree of interaction with the garbage collector.
`java.lang.reflect`	Provides classes and interfaces for obtaining reflective information about classes and objects.
`javax.lang.model`	Provides classes and hierarchies of packages used to model the Java programming language.
`javax.lang.model.element`	Provides interfaces used to model elements of the Java programming language.
`javax.lang.model.type`	Provides interfaces used to model Java programming language types.
`javax.lang.model.util`	Provides utilities to assist in the processing of program elements and types.

TABLE B-2 Utility Packages

Utility Packages	Description
`java.util`	Contains the collections framework, legacy collection classes, event model, date and time facilities, internationalization, and miscellaneous utility classes (a string tokenizer, a random-number generator, and a bit array).
`java.util.concurrent`	Contains utility classes commonly useful in concurrent programming.
`java.util.concurrent.atomic`	Contains a small toolkit of classes that support lock-free thread-safe programming on single variables.

(continued)

TABLE B-2	Utility Packages *(continued)*

Utility Packages	Description
`java.util.concurrent.locks`	Provides interfaces and classes to use as a framework for locking and waiting for conditions that are distinct from built-in synchronization and monitors.
`java.util.function`	Provides functional interfaces that provide target types for lambda expressions and method references.
`java.util.jar`	Provides classes for reading and writing the Java Archive (JAR) file format, which is based on the standard ZIP file format with an optional manifest file.
`java.util.logging`	Provides classes and interfaces of the Java 2 platform's core logging facilities.
`java.util.prefs`	Allows applications to store and retrieve user and system preference and configuration data.
`java.util.regex`	Provides classes for matching character sequences against patterns specified by regular expressions.
`java.util.spi`	Provides service provider classes for the classes in the `java.util` package.
`java.util.stream`	Provides support for functional-style operations on streams of elements.
`java.util.zip`	Provides classes for reading and writing the standard ZIP and GZIP file formats.

TABLE B-3	Base Packages

Base Packages	Description
`java.beans`	Contains classes related to developing *beans*—components based on the JavaBeans architecture.
`java.beans.beancontext`	Provides classes and interfaces relating to bean context.
`java.applet`	Provides the classes necessary to create an applet and the classes an applet uses to communicate with its applet context.
`java.io`	Provides for system input and output through data streams, serialization, and the file system.
`java.nio`	Defines buffers, which are containers for data, and provides an overview of the other NIO (New I/O) packages.
`java.nio.channels`	Defines channels, which represent connections to entities that are capable of performing I/O operations, such as files and sockets; defines selectors for multiplexed, nonblocking I/O operations.

TABLE B-3	Base Packages *(continued)*

Base Packages	Description
`java.nio.charset`	Defines charsets, decoders, and encoders for translating between bytes and Unicode characters.
`java.nio.channels.spi`	Provides service-provider classes for the `java.nio.channels` package.
`java.nio.file`	Defines interfaces and classes for the JVM to access files, file attributes, and file systems.
`java.nio.file.attribute`	Provides interfaces and classes that allow access to file and file system attributes.
`java.nio.file.spi`	Includes service-provider classes for the `java.nio.file` package.
`java.nio.charset.spi`	Includes service-provider classes for the `java.nio.charset` package.
`java.math`	Provides classes for performing arbitrary-precision integer arithmetic (`BigInteger`) and arbitrary-precision decimal arithmetic (`BigDecimal`).
`java.net and javax.net`	Provides the classes for implementing networking applications.
`javax.net`	Provides classes for networking applications.
`javax.net.ssl`	Provides classes for the secure socket package.
`java.text`	Provides classes and interfaces for handling text, dates, numbers, and messages in a manner independent of natural languages.
`java.text.spi`	Provides service provider classes for the classes in the `java.text` package.
`javax.management`	Provides the core classes for the Java Management Extensions.
`javax.management.loading`	Provides the classes that implement advanced dynamic loading.
`javax.management.modelmbean`	Provides the definition of the ModelMBean classes.
`javax.management.monitor`	Provides the definition of the monitor classes.
`javax.management.openmbean`	Provides the open data types and Open MBean descriptor classes.
`javax.management.relation`	Provides the definition of the Relation Service.
`javax.management.remote`	Provides interfaces for remote access to Java Management Extensions (JMX) MBean servers.
`javax.management.remote.rmi`	Provides the RMI connector as a connector for the JMX Remote API that uses Remote Method Invocation (RMI) to transmit client requests to a remote MBean server.
`javax.management.timer`	Provides the definition of the Timer MBean.

(continued)

TABLE B-3   Base Packages *(continued)*

Base Packages	Description
`javax.annotation`	Provides resource support for annotation types.
`javax.annotation.processing`	Provides facilities for declaring annotation processors and for allowing annotation processors to communicate with an annotation processing tool environment.
`javax.tools`	Provides interfaces for tools that can be invoked from a program—for example, compilers.
`javax.activation`	Provides interfaces and classes used by the JavaMail API to manage MIME data.
`javax.activity`	Contains service activity–related exceptions thrown by the Object Request Broker (ORB) machinery during unmarshalling.

Integration Packages

The following tables detail the integration Java packages (JDBC, JNDI, RMI/RMI-IIOP, scripting, and transactions packages).

TABLE B-4   Java Database Connectivity (JDBC) Packages

Java Database Connectivity (JDBC) Packages	Description
`java.sql`	Provides the API for accessing and processing data stored in a data source (usually a relational database) using the Java programming language.
`javax.sql`	Provides the API for server-side data source access and processing from the Java programming language.
`javax.sql.rowset`	Provides standard interfaces and base classes for JDBC RowSet implementations.
`javax.sql.rowset.serial`	Provides utility classes to allow serializable mappings between SQL types and data types in the Java programming language.
`javax.sql.rowset.spi`	Provides standard classes and interfaces that a third-party vendor must use in its implementation of a synchronization provider.

| TABLE B-5 | Java Naming and Directory Interface (JNDI) Packages |

Java Naming and Directory Interface (JNDI) Packages	Description
`javax.naming`	Provides the classes and interfaces for accessing naming services.
`javax.naming.ldap`	Provides support for Lightweight Directory Access Protocol (LDAPv3) extended operations and controls.
`javax.naming.event`	Provides support for event notification when accessing naming and directory services.
`javax.naming.directory`	Extends the `javax.naming` package to provide functionality for accessing directory services.
`javax.naming.spi`	Provides additional interfaces and classes for naming support.

| TABLE B-6 | Remote Method Invocation (RMI) Packages |

Remote Method Invocation (RMI) Packages	Description
`java.rmi`	Provides the RMI package.
`java.rmi.activation`	Provides support for RMI Object Activation.
`java.rmi.dgc`	Provides classes and interface for RMI distributed garbage collection (DGC).
`java.rmi.registry`	Provides a class and two interfaces for the RMI registry.
`java.rmi.server`	Provides classes and interfaces for supporting the server side of RMI.
`javax.rmi`	Contains user APIs for RMI-IIOP.
`javax.rmi.CORBA`	Contains portability APIs for RMI-IIOP.
`javax.rmi.ssl`	Provides implementations of `RMIClientSocketFactory` and `RMIServerSocketFactory` over the Secure Sockets Layer (SSL) or Transport Layer Security (TLS) protocols.

| TABLE B-7 | Scripting Packages |

Scripting Packages	Description
`javax.script`	Provides the scripting API that includes interfaces and classes that define Java Scripting Engines and provides a framework for their use in Java applications.

TABLE B-8   Transactions Packages

Transactions Packages	Description
`javax.transactions.xa`	Provides the API that defines the contract between the transaction manager and the resource manager, which allows the transaction manager to enlist and delist resource objects (supplied by the resource manager driver) in Java Transaction API (JTA) transactions.
`javax.transactions`	Contains three exceptions thrown by the ORB machinery during unmarshalling.

User Interface Packages

The following tables detail the user-interface Java packages (JavaFX API, Swing API, Abstract Window Toolkit [AWT] API, image I/O, sound, printing, and accessibility packages).

TABLE B-9   JavaFX API Packages

Swing API Packages	Description
`javafx.animation`	Provides the set of classes for ease of use transition–based animations.
`javafx.application`	Provides the application lifecycle classes.
`javafx.beans`	Provides the interfaces that define the most generic form of observability.
`javafx.beans.binding`	Provides characteristics of bindings.
`javafx.beans.property`	Provides the definition of read-only properties and writable properties, plus a number of implementations.
`javafx.beans.property.adapter`	Provides the property adapter.
`javafx.beans.value`	Provides the two fundamental interfaces `ObservableValue` and `WritableValue` and all of its subinterfaces.
`javafx.collections`	Provides the JavaFX collections and collection utilities.
`javafx.collections.transformation`	Provides transformation support.
`javafx.concurrent`	Provides the set of classes for `javafx.task`.
`javafx.css`	Provides the API for styling properties via CSS and for supporting pseudo-class state.

TABLE B-9	JavaFX API Packages *(continued)*

Swing API Packages	Description
`javafx.embed.swing`	Provides the set of classes to use JavaFX inside Swing applications.
`javafx.embed.swt`	Provides the set of classes to use JavaFX inside SWT applications.
`javafx.event`	Provides the basic framework for FX events, their delivery, and handling.
`javafx.fxml`	Provides classes for loading an object hierarchy from markup.
`javafx.geometry`	Provides the set of 2D classes for defining and performing operations on objects related to two-dimensional geometry.
`javafx.print`	Provides public classes for the JavaFX Printing API.
`javafx.scene`	Provides a set of base classes for the JavaFX Scene Graph API.
`javafx.scene.canvas`	Provides a set of classes for canvas, an immediate mode style of rendering an API.
`javafx.scene.chart`	Provides a set of chart components, which are a very convenient way for data visualization.
`javafx.scene.control`	Provides specialized nodes in the JavaFX scene graph that are especially suited for reuse in many different application contexts.
`javafx.scene.control.cell`	Provides cell-related classes.
`javafx.scene.effect`	Provides classes for attaching graphical filter effects to JavaFX scene graph nodes.
`javafx.scene.image`	Provides classes for loading and displaying images.
`javafx.scene.input`	Provides classes for mouse and keyboard input event handling.
`javafx.scene.layout`	Provides classes to support user interface layout.
`javafx.scene.media`	Provides classes for integrating audio and video into Java FX applications.
`javafx.scene.paint`	Provides classes for colors and gradients used to fill shapes and backgrounds when rendering the scene graph.
`javafx.scene.shape`	Provides a set of 2D classes for defining and performing operations on objects related to two-dimensional geometry.
`javafx.scene.text`	Provides classes for fonts and renderable text nodes.
`javafx.scene.transform`	Provides a set of convenient classes to perform rotating, scaling, shearing, and translation transformations for affine objects.
`javafx.scene.web`	Provides a means for loading and displaying web content.
`javafx.stage`	Provides the top-level container classes for JavaFX content.
`javafx.util`	Provides utilities and helper classes.
`javafx.util.converter`	Provides standard string converters for JavaFX.

TABLE B-10   Swing API Packages

Swing API Packages	Description
`javax.swing`	Provides a set of "lightweight" (all-Java language) components that, to the maximum degree possible, work the same on all platforms.
`javax.swing.border`	Provides classes and interfaces for drawing specialized borders around a Swing component.
`javax.swing.colorchooser`	Contains classes and interfaces used by the `JColorChooser` component.
`javax.swing.event`	Provides for events fired by Swing components.
`javax.swing.filechooser`	Contains classes and interfaces used by the `JFileChooser` component.
`javax.swing.plaf`	Provides one interface and many abstract classes that Swing uses to provide its pluggable look-and-feel capabilities.
`javax.swing.plaf.basic`	Provides user interface objects built according to the basic look and feel.
`javax.swing.plaf.metal`	Provides user interface objects built according to the default Java look and feel (once code-named *Metal*).
`javax.swing.plaf.multi`	Provides user interface objects that combine two or more look and feels.
`javax.swing.plaf.nimbus`	Provides user interface objects built according to the cross-platform Nimbus look and feel.
`javax.swing.plaf.synth`	Provides a skinnable look and feel, in which all painting is delegated.
`javax.swing.table`	Provides classes and interfaces for dealing with `javax.swing.JTable`.
`javax.swing.text`	Provides classes and interfaces that deal with editable and noneditable text components.
`javax.swing.text.html`	Provides the class `HTMLEditorKit` and supporting classes for creating HTML text editors.
`javax.swing.text.html.parser`	Provides the default HTML parser, along with support classes.
`javax.swing.text.rtf`	Provides a class (`RTFEditorKit`) for creating Rich Text Format (RTF) text editors.
`javax.swing.tree`	Provides classes and interfaces for dealing with `javax.swing.JTree`.
`javax.swing.undo`	Allows developers to provide support for undo/redo in applications such as text editors.

TABLE B-11   AWT API Packages

AWT API Packages	Description
java.awt	Contains all of the classes for creating user interfaces and for painting graphics and images.
java.awt.color	Provides classes for color spaces.
java.awt.datatransfer	Provides interfaces and classes for transferring data between and within applications.
java.awt.dnd	Provides a mechanism to transfer information by dragging and dropping in the user interface.
java.awt.event	Provides interfaces and classes for dealing with different types of events fired by AWT components.
java.awt.font	Provides classes and interfaces relating to fonts.
java.awt.geom	Provides the Java 2D classes for defining and performing operations on objects related to two-dimensional geometry.
java.awt.im	Provides classes and interfaces for the input method framework.
java.awt.im.spi	Provides interfaces that enable the development of input methods that can be used with any Java Runtime Environment.
java.awt.image	Provides classes for creating and modifying images.
java.awt.image.renderable	Provides classes and interfaces for producing rendering-independent images.
java.awt.print	Provides classes and interfaces for a general printing API.

TABLE B-12   Java Image I/O Packages

Java Image I/O Packages	Description
javax.imageio	Provides the main package of the Java Image I/O API.
javax.imageio.event	Deals with synchronous notification of events during the reading and writing of images.
javax.imageio.metadata	Deals with reading and writing metadata.
javax.imageio.plugins.bmp	Contains the public classes used by the built-in Bean-Managed Persistence (BMP) plug-in.
javax.imageio.plugins.jpeg	Provides classes supporting the built-in JPEG plug-in.
javax.imageio.spi	Contains the plug-in interfaces for readers, writers, transcoders, and streams, and a runtime registry.
javax.imageio.stream	Deals with low-level I/O from files and streams.

TABLE B-13   Sound API Packages

Sound API Packages	Description
`javax.sound.midi`	Provides interfaces and classes for I/O, sequencing, and synthesis of MIDI (Musical Instrument Digital Interface) data.
`javax.sound.midi.spi`	Supplies interfaces for service providers to implement when offering new MIDI devices, MIDI file readers and writers, or sound bank readers.
`javax.sound.sampled`	Provides interfaces and classes for capture, processing, and playback of sampled audio data.
`javax.sound.sampled.spi`	Supplies abstract classes for service providers to subclass when offering new audio devices, sound file readers and writers, or audio format converters.

TABLE B-14   Java Print Service API Packages

Java Print Service API Packages	Description
`javax.print`	Provides the principal classes and interfaces for the Java Print Service API.
`javax.print.attribute`	Provides classes and interfaces that describe the types of Java Print Service attributes and how they can be collected into attribute sets.
`javax.print.attribute.standard`	Contains classes for specific printing attributes.
`javax.print.event`	Contains event classes and listener interfaces.

TABLE B-15   Accessibility Package

Accessibility Package	Description
`javax.accessibility`	Defines a contract between UI components and an assistive technology that provides access to those components.

Security Packages

The following tables detail the security-related Java packages (such as cryptography packages).

| **TABLE B-16** | Security Packages |

Security Packages	Description
`java.security`	Provides the classes and interfaces for the security framework.
`java.security.acl`	The classes and interfaces in this package have been superseded by classes in the `java.security` package.
`java.security.cert`	Provides classes and interfaces for parsing and managing certificates, certificate revocation lists (CRLs), and certification paths.
`java.security.interfaces`	Provides interfaces for generating RSA (Rivest, Shamir, and Adleman asymmetric cipher algorithm) keys as defined in the RSA Laboratory Technical Note PKCS#1, and DSA (Digital Signature Algorithm) keys as defined in NIST's FIPS-186.
`java.security.spec`	Provides classes and interfaces for key specifications and algorithm parameter specifications.
`javax.security.auth`	Provides a framework for authentication and authorization.
`javax.security.auth.callback`	Provides the classes necessary for services to interact with applications to retrieve information (authentication data including usernames or passwords, for example) or to display information (error and warning messages, for example).
`javax.security.auth.kerberos`	Contains utility classes related to the Kerberos network authentication protocol.
`javax.security.auth.login`	Provides a pluggable authentication framework.
`javax.security.auth.X500`	Contains the classes that should be used to store X500 Principal and X500 Private Credentials in a *Subject*.
`javax.security.auth.spi`	Provides the interface to be used for implementing pluggable authentication modules.
`javax.security.sasl`	Contains classes and interfaces for supporting Simple Authentication and Security Layer (SASL).
`javax.security.cert`	Provides classes for public key certificates.
`org.ietf.jgss`	Presents a framework to make use of security services such as authentication, data integrity, and data confidentiality from a variety of underlying security mechanisms such as Kerberos, using a unified API.

TABLE B-17	Cryptography Packages

Package	Description
`javax.crypto`	Provides the classes and interfaces for cryptographic operations.
`javax.crypto.interfaces`	Provides interfaces for Diffie-Hellman keys as defined in RSA Laboratories PKCS #3.
`javax.crypto.spec`	Provides classes and interfaces for key specifications and algorithm parameter specifications.

XML-based Packages

The following table details the XML-related Java packages.

TABLE B-18	XML-based Packages

XML-based Packages	Description
`javax.xml`	Provides Extensible Markup Language (XML) support and constants.
`javax.xml.bind`	Provides a runtime binding framework for client applications, including unmarshalling, marshalling, and validation capabilities.
`javax.xml.bind.annotation`	Defines annotations for customizing Java program elements to XML Schema mapping.
`javax.xml.bind.annotation.adapters`	Provides XmlAdapter and its spec-defined subclasses to allow arbitrary Java classes to be used with Java Architecture for XML Binding (JAXB).
`javax.xml.bind.attachment`	Enables the interpretation and creation of optimized binary data within an MIME-based package format, implemented by a MIME-based package processor.
`javax.xml.bind.helpers`	Provides partial default implementations for some of the `javax.xml.bind` interfaces (JAXB provider use only).
`javax.xml.bind.util`	Provides useful client utility classes.
`javax.xml.crypto`	Provides common classes for XML cryptography.
`javax.xml.crypto.dom`	Provides DOM-specific classes for the `javax.xml.crypto` package.
`javax.xml.crypto.dsig`	Provides classes for generating and validating XML digital signatures.

TABLE B-18   XML-based Packages *(continued)*

XML-based Packages	Description
`javax.xml.crypto.dsig.dom`	Provides DOM-specific classes for the `javax.xml.crypto.dsig` package.
`javax.xml.crypto.dsig.keyinfo`	Provides classes for parsing and processing `KeyInfo` elements and structures.
`javax.xml.crtypto.dsig.spec`	Provides parameter classes for XML digital signatures.
`javax.xml.datatype`	Provides XML/Java Type mappings.
`javax.xml.namespace`	Provides XML Namespace processing.
`javax.xml.parsers`	Provides classes allowing the processing of XML documents.
`javax.xml.soap`	Provides the API for creating and building SOAP messages.
`javax.xml.stream`	Provides interfaces and classes in support of XML streams.
`javax.xml.stream.events`	Provides interfaces in support of XML Streams events.
`javax.xml.stream.util`	Provides interfaces and classes in support of stream events.
`javax.xml.transform`	Defines the generic APIs for processing transformation instructions and performing a transformation from source to result.
`javax.xml.transform.dom`	Implements Document Object Model (DOM)–specific transformation APIs.
`javax.xml.transform.sax`	Implements SAX2-specific transformation APIs.
`javax.xml.transform.stax`	Provides for Streaming API for XML (StAX)-specific transformation APIs.
`javax.xml.transform.stream`	Implements stream- and URI-specific transformation APIs.
`javax.xml.validation`	Provides an API for validation of XML documents.
`javax.xml.ws`	Contains the core Java API for XML Web Services (JAX-WS) APIs.
`javax.xml.ws.handler`	Defines APIs for message handlers.
`javax.xml.ws.handler.soap`	Defines APIs for SOAP message handlers.
`javax.xml.ws.http`	Defines APIs specific to the HTTP binding.
`javax.xml.ws.soap`	Defines APIs specific to the SOAP binding.
`javax.xml.ws.spi`	Defines SPIs for JAX-WS.
`javax.xml.spi.http`	Provides HTTP SPI used for portable deployment of JAX-WS web services in containers.
`javax.xml.ws.wsaddressing`	Defines APIs related to WS-Addressing.
`javax.xml.xpath`	Provides an object-model neutral API for the evaluation of XPath expressions and access to the evaluation environment.

(continued)

TABLE B-18	XML-based Packages *(continued)*

XML-based Packages	Description
org.w3c.dom	Provides the interfaces for the DOM, which is a component API of the Java API for XML processing.
org.w3c.dom.bootstrap	Contains a factory class that enables applications to obtain instances of DOM implementation.
org.w3c.dom.events	Provides interfaces and classes in support of DOM events.
org.w3c.dom.ls	Provides interfaces and exceptions support of DOM factory methods for creating load and save objects.
org.w3c.dom.views	Provides abstract and document views.
org.xml.sax	Provides the core SAX APIs.
org.xml.sax.ext	Contains interfaces to SAX2 facilities that conformant SAX drivers won't necessarily support.
org.xml.sax.helpers	Contains helper classes, including support for bootstrapping SAX-based applications.
javax.jws.soap	Provides support for SOAP bindings.
javax.jws	Provides annotation types in support of Java Web Services.

Temporal Packages

The following table details the time-related Java packages relative to Java 8's new Date and Time API.

TABLE B-19	Temporal-based Packages

Security Packages	Description
java.time	Provides the main API for dates, times, instants, and durations.
java.time.chrono	Provides the generic API for calendar systems other than the default ISO.
java.time.format	Provides classes to print and parse dates and times.
java.time.temporal	Provides access to date and time using fields and units, and date time adjusters.
java.time.zone	Provides support for time zones and their rules.

C

Java Keywords

T he following table represents all of the valid Java keywords.

abstract	continue	for	new	switch
assert	default	goto	package	synchronized
boolean	do	if	private	this
break	double	implements	protected	throw
byte	else	import	public	throws
case	enum	instanceof	return	transient
catch	extends	int	short	try
char	final	interface	static	void
class	finally	long	strictfp	volatile
const	float	native	super	while

Please note the following:

- ◼ Java keywords cannot be used as identifiers.
- ◼ The enum keyword was added in J2SE 5.0 (Tiger).
- ◼ The assert keyword was added in J2SE 1.4 (Merlin).
- ◼ Reserved literals named true, false, and null are not keywords.

Keywords const and goto are reserved Java keywords but are not functionally used. Note that since they are commonly used C language keywords, providing them as keywords allows the IDEs and compilers to provide better error messages when these keywords are encountered in a Java program.

D

Bracket Conventions

Java Bracket Conventions

The Java programming language, like many programming languages, makes strong use of brackets. The OCA exam requires that you be familiar with the different types of brackets. The following table contains each type of bracket that appears throughout this book and in the exam. This table details the bracket names as they are used in the Java Language Specification (JLS) as well as common alternative names.

Brackets	JLS Nomenclature	Alternative Nomenclature	Usage
( )	Parentheses	Round brackets, curved brackets, oval brackets	Surrounds set of method arguments, encloses cast types, adjusts precedence in arithmetic expressions
{ }	Braces	Curly brackets/braces, swirly brackets, squirrelly brackets, fancy brackets, squiggly brackets	Surrounds blocks of code, initializes arrays
[ ]	Box brackets	Square brackets, closed brackets	Used with arrays, initializes arrays
< >	Angle brackets	Diamond brackets, chevrons	Encloses generics

Miscellaneous Bracket Conventions

Guillemet characters, as represented in the next table, are used in Universal Modeling Language (UML). UML was covered in the SCJA exam but does not appear in the OCA exam. This information is provided here because you may find yourself using UML at some point in your career.

Bracket	Nomenclature	Alternative Nomenclature	Usage
« »	Guillemet characters	Angle quotes	Specifies UML stereotypes

E

Unicode Standard

The Unicode Standard is a character coding system designed to form a universal character set. This standard is maintained by the Unicode Consortium standards organization. The characters in this set are technically known as Unicode scalar values (in other words, hex numbers). Commonly known as Unicode characters, the characters are primarily organized into symbol and punctuation characters, as well as script characters (for example, spoken language characters).

Literal values in Java can be written using Unicode, as shown in the following examples:

```
int i = '\u0043' + '\u0021'; // 100 (67 + 33)
char[] cArray = {'\u004F','\u0043','\u0041'}; // OCA
```

Code charts for Unicode are maintained by the consortium for easy reference. You can access the "Code Charts for Symbols and Punctuation" from http://unicode.org/charts/#symbols. You'll find "The Unicode Character Code Charts by Script" at http://unicode.org/charts/index.html.

Current Oracle release documentation states that Java SE 8 supports the Unicode Standard 6.2.0. Unicode 6.2.0 added support for more characters, scripts, and blocks. Java SE 7 introduced support for Unicode version 6.0.0. The Java SE 6 and J2SE 5.0 API's character information is based on the Unicode standard, version 4.0. The J2SE 1.4 API's character information is based on the Unicode standard, version 3.0. This Unicode compliancy information is found in the documentation of the Character class.

Many Unicode standard groupings of characters exist, such as language characters, currency symbols, Braille patterns, arrows, and mathematical operators. The most commonly used characters are the ASCII punctuation characters.

ASCII Punctuation Characters

The first 128 characters are the same as those in the American Standard Code for Information Exchange (ASCII) character set. The Unicode Consortium references them as ASCII punctuation characters. Table E-1 represents these characters. The values \u0000 to \u001F and 0007F represent nonprintable ASCII characters. The values \u0020 to \u007E represent printable ASCII characters. The character \u0020 represents a blank space. As an example, the space could also be referenced by its decimal equivalent value (that is, 32), its octal equivalent value (040), its HTML equivalent value ( ), or directly by its printable character, as in char c = ' ';.

TABLE E-1		Printable and Nonprintable ASCII Characters					
	000	001	002	003	004	005	006	007
0	NUL	DLE	SP	0	@	P	`	p
1	SOH	DC1	!	1	A	Q	a	q
2	STX	DC2	"	2	B	R	b	r
3	ETX	DC3	#	3	C	S	c	s
4	EOT	DC4	$	4	D	T	d	t
5	ENQ	NAK	%	5	E	U	e	u
6	ACK	SYN	&	6	F	V	f	v
7	BEL	ETB	'	7	G	W	g	w
8	BS	CAN	(	8	H	X	h	x
9	HT	EM	)	9	I	Y	i	y
A	LF	SUB	*	:	J	Z	j	z
B	VT	ESC	+	;	K	[	k	{
C	FF	FS	,	<	L	\	l	|
D	CR	GS	-	=	M	]	m	}
E	SO	RS	.	>	N	^	n	~
F	SI	US	/	?	O	_	o	DEL

The Java tutorials provide more information about the Unicode industry standard in their online trail: http://docs.oracle.com/javase/tutorial/i18n/text/unicode.html.

F

Pseudo-code Algorithms

Pseudo-code algorithms were covered on previous version of the exam. The coverage has been removed for the updated OCA exam. Therefore, we have included this content as a supplement. The pseudo-code algorithms are important for you to be familiar with in the real world and will help if you are reviewing old test materials.

> **Note** *Because you do not need to know about pseudo-code algorithms for the OCA exam, your review of this appendix is optional.*

Implementing Statement-Related Algorithms from Pseudo-code

Pseudo-code is a structured means to allow algorithm designers to express computer programming algorithms in a human-readable format. Pseudo-code is informally written and is compact and high-level in nature. Even though pseudo-code does not need to be tied to any specific software language, the designer will typically script the pseudo-code algorithms based on the structural conventions of the target software language.

You may be thinking, "Hey, pseudo-code sounds great! Where do I get started writing high-quality algorithms in pseudo-code?" Well, don't get too excited. No standards exist for writing pseudo-code, since its main purpose is to help designers build algorithms in their own language. With so many different languages having varying structural differences and paradigms, creating a pseudo-code standard that applies to them all would be impossible. Essentially, writing pseudo-code allows for the quick and focused production of algorithms based on logic, not language syntax.

The following topics presented in the next sections will discuss working with basic pseudo-code and converting pseudo-code algorithms into Java code with an emphasis on statements:

- Pseudo-code algorithms
- Pseudo-code algorithms and Java

Pseudo-code Algorithms

The previous exam presented pseudo-code algorithms to the test candidate. In turn, the candidate had to decide which Java code segment correctly implemented the algorithms. This was tricky, since the pseudo-code algorithms did not need to represent Java syntax in any way, but the Java code segments had to be structurally and syntactically accurate to be correct.

Let's take a look at a pseudo-code algorithm:

```
value := 20
IF value >= 1
  print the value
ELSEIF value = 0
  print the value
ELSE
  print "less than zero"
ENDIF
```

While surfing the Internet, you'll come to the conclusion that there is no universally accepted convention for pseudo-code. For demonstration purposes, Table F-1 gives you a general idea of how a typical representation of pseudo-code can be translated to Java.

TABLE F-1   Pseudo-code Conventions

Pseudo-code Element	Pseudo-code Convention	Java Example
Assignment	`variable := value`	`wreckYear = 1511;`

if statement	`IF condition THEN`
	`  //statement sequence`
	`ELSEIF`
	`  //statement sequence`
	`ELSE`
	`  //statement sequence`
	`ENDIF`
		`if (wreckYear == 1502)`
		`  wreck = "Santa Ana";`
		`else if (wreckYear == 1503)`
		`  wreck = "Magdalena";`
		`else`
		`   wreck = "Unknown";`

switch statement	`CASE expression OF`
	`    Condition A: statement`
	`sequence`
	`    Condition B:`
	`statement sequence`
	`    Default: sequence of`
	`statements`
	`ENDCASE`
		`switch (wreckYear) {`
		`case 1502:`
		`    wreck = "Santa Ana";`
		`    break;`
		`case 1503:`
		`    wreck = "Magdalena";`
		`    break;`
		`default:`
		`    Wreck = "Unknown"`
		`}`

while statement	`WHILE condition`
	`//statement sequence`
	`ENDWHILE`
		`while (n < 4) {`
		`    System.out.println(i);`
		`    n++;`
		`}`

for statement	`FOR iteration bounds`
	`//statement sequence`
	`ENDFOR`
		`for (int i=0; i<j; i++) {`
		`    System.out.println(i);`
		`}`

Pseudo-code Algorithms and Java

Pseudo-code can be a fragment of a complete source file, and it is okay that some primitive declarations may be missing. However, conditional and iteration statements are always represented completely.

Let's take a look at some examples. Here's a pseudo-code algorithm:

```
fishingRods := 5
fishingReels := 4
IF fishingRods does not equal fishingReels THEN
  print "We are missing fishing equipment"
ELSE
  print "The fishing equipment is all here"
ENDIF
```

Here's a Java implementation:

```
int fishingRods = 5;
int fishingReels = 4;
if (fishingRods != fishingReels)
  System.out.print("We are missing fishing equipment");
else
  System.out.print("The fishing equipment is all here");
```

Note that this appendix leveraged off of the "PSEUDOCODE STANDARD" page of the Cal Poly State University web site; the authors did a pretty good job proposing a standard: http://users.csc.calpoly.edu/~jdalbey/SWE/pdl_std.html.

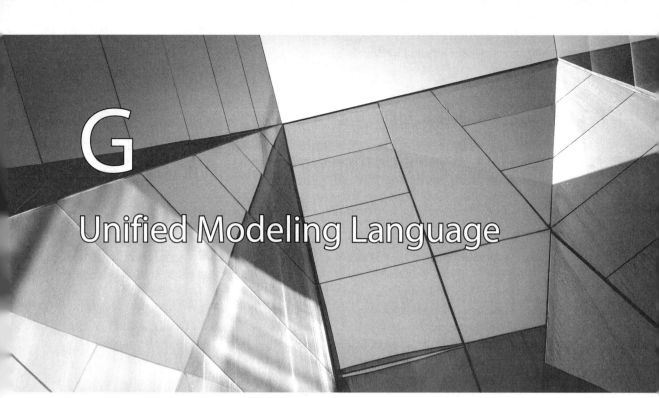

G

Unified Modeling Language

The Unified Modeling Language (UML) specification defines a modeling language for the specification, presentation, construction, and documentation of object-oriented system elements. UML is covered here to offer you a quick understanding to complement the UML diagrams that appear in this book.

The UML standard is the culmination of the works from James Rumbaugh's object-modeling technique, Grady Booch's "Booch method," and Ivar Jacobson's object-oriented software engineering method. The collaborative effort of this trio has earned them the name "The Three Amigos." The origins of their efforts leading to the UML standard are detailed in Table G-1.

The modern UML specification, maintained by the Object Management Group (OMG), has gone through several revisions, as represented in Table G-2. The latest formal specification (UML 2.4.1) comprises four parts. The first two parts are the "OMG UML Infrastructure Specification version 2.4.1" and the "OMG UML Superstructure Specification version 2.4.1." The Infrastructure specification has a tighter focus concerning class-based structures and houses all of the basic information you should know. The Superstructure specification details user-level constructs and cross-references the Infrastructure specification so that the two parts may be integrated into one volume in the future. The remaining parts are the "Object Constraint Language (OCL)" for defining model element rules and the "UML Diagram Interchange" used for defining the exchange of UML 2 diagram layouts. The current versions of the specifications are obtainable from the OMG at www.omg.org/spec/UML/Current. In short, this appendix will teach you how to recognize the main diagram elements and relationships used by UML.

TABLE G-1   Object Methodologies Preceding UML

Methodologists	Method	Emphasis	Circa
James Rumbaugh, Michael Blaha, William Premerlani, Frederick Eddy, William Lorensen	Object Modeling Technique (OMT)	Object-oriented analysis (OOA)	1991
Ivar Jacobson	Objectory, object-oriented software engineering (OOSE) method	Object-oriented software engineering (OOSE)	1992
Grady Booch	Booch method	Object-oriented design (OOD)	1993

TABLE G-2   Evolving UML Specifications

OMG Formal UML Specifications	Release Date	Significant Release Changes
UML 2.5 – Beta 2	September 2013	Beta release, needing two sets of syntactical errors to be corrected in UML 2.6
UML 2.4.1	August 2011	Added URI package attribute, updated actions and events, refined stereotypes, various revisions to 2.3
UML 2.3	May 2010	Added final classifier, updated component diagrams, composite structures, clarified associations, various revisions to 2.2
UML 2.2	February 2009	Adoption of the profile diagram, various revisions
UML 2.1.2	November 2007	Various minor revisions; bug fixes have been resolved
UML 2.1.1	August 2007	Minor updates including implementation of redefinition and bidirectional association
UML 2.0	July 2005	Several changes, enhancements, and additions, including enhanced support for structural and behavioral models
UML 1.3, UML 1.4.X, UML 1.5	Various	Various minor revisions and bug fixes resolved
UML 1.1	November 1997	The OMG formally adopted UML

The complete set of 14 UML diagrams from the UML 2.4 standard is shown in Table G-3.

Two closely related UML focal areas are covered in this appendix. One focal area relates to the recognitions of simple class structure artifacts and basic OO principles. The other relates to depicting UML features related to class relationships.

TABLE G-3   Types of UML Diagrams

Structure Diagrams	Behavior Diagrams	Interaction Diagrams
Class diagram	Activity diagram	Communication diagram
Component diagram	State machine diagram	Interaction overview diagram
Composite structure diagram	Use case diagram	Sequence diagram
Deployment diagram		Timing diagram
Object diagram		
Package diagram		
Profile diagram		

UML package icons

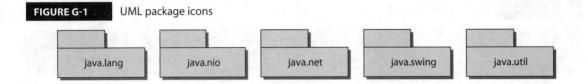

To start with your first UML element—in this case, let's call it an icon—we'll take a look at the basic Java SE package icons represented in Figure G-1. The package icons are typically represented by a folder with the package name located in the top-left compartment (also known as the tab). The package name may also be optionally placed into the larger compartment (as shown in Figure G-1), as is commonly done when no other UML elements are enclosed in the package icon. Note that the package icon is not on the test, but we include it in many of the diagrams to show packages that enclose depicted classes.

This is a good time to look at the core UML information that you should be familiar with. This appendix is filled with details on the representation of these UML elements. After you have read the appendix, you will be able to recognize all of the core UML elements, as well as relationships between elements.

Recognizing Representations of Significant UML Elements

Getting acquainted with the different UML elements can actually be quite fun, and the sense of accomplishment you'll have when mastering the art of reading and writing class relationship diagrams with UML is equally rewarding.

Our initial coverage is geared toward the class diagrams themselves. Attributes and operations compartments and visibility modifiers are also covered. Once you work though this section, you will know how to recognize the basic class elements of UML. These topics will be covered in the following subsections:

- Classes, abstract classes, and interface diagrams
- Attributes and operations
- Visibility modifiers

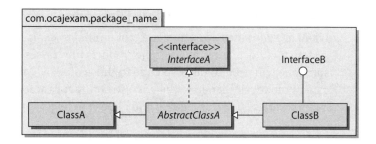

FIGURE G-2

Class diagram

Classes, Abstract Classes, and Interface Diagrams

One of the simplest ways to represent classes and interfaces in UML is to show the class diagrams with only their name compartments. This holds true as well with representing interface implementations and class inheritances. Figure G-2 depicts two interfaces, two classes, one abstract class, and their generalization and realization relationships. Abstract classes, concrete classes, and interfaces are all represented in a rectangle with their names in boldface type. Abstract classes are italicized. Interfaces are prefaced by the word "interface" between guillemot characters (like this: <<interface>>). An interface can be optionally depicted with its name beside the lollipop element (as with InterfaceB in the figure).

The generalization and realization relationships between the classes in Figure G-2 are further explained in the following sections.

Generalization

Generalization is expressed as an *is-a* relationship, where a class allows its more general attributes and operations to be inherited. In Figure G-2, ClassB inherits from *AbstractClassA* and also from ClassA. *AbstractClassA* inherits from ClassA. We can also say ClassB *is-an AbstractClassA*, ClassB *is-a* ClassA, and *AbstractClassA is-a* ClassA. We could also say that ClassA and *AbstractClassA* are superclasses to ClassB, and, appropriately, ClassB would be their subclass. The generalization class relationship is depicted in the figure with a solid line and a closed white arrowhead.

Realization

Realization is the general principle of implementing an interface. *AbstractClassA* implements the InterfaceA interface. ClassB implements the InterfaceB interface. The realization class relationship is depicted with a dotted line and a closed white arrowhead or the lollipop element.

Code Engineering from UML Diagrams

UML provides many benefits; it is not limited to explaining existing code. When a system architect or system designer models the classes for a particular application, someone will need to develop code to those models. Many UML modeling tools can automatically generate the code structure for these models. However, most coders will use UML as a guide and choose to begin their coding from scratch.

Attributes and Operations

Attributes, also known as *member variables*, define the state of a class. *Operations*, sometimes called *member functions*, detail the methods of a class. Let's take a look at adding attributes and operations to a class UML diagram. The following is a code listing for an arbitrary `PrimeNumber` class. We will depict this class with UML.

```java
import java.util.ArrayList;
import java.util.List;
public class PrimeNumber {
  private Boolean isPrime = true;
  private Double primeSquareRoot = null;
  private List<String> divisorList = new ArrayList<>();
  public PrimeNumber(long candidate) {
    validatePrime(candidate);
  }
  public void validatePrime(Long c) {
    primeSquareRoot = Math.sqrt(c);
    isPrime = true;
    for (long j = 2; j <= primeSquareRoot.longValue(); j++) {
      if ((c % j) == 0) {
        divisorList.add(j + "x" + c / j);
        isPrime = false;
      }
    }
  }
  public List getDivisorList() {
    return divisorList;
  }
  public Double getPrimeSquareRoot() {
    return primeSquareRoot;
  }
  public Boolean getIsPrime() {
    return isPrime;
  }
}
```

```
public void setIsPrime(Boolean b) {
   isPrime = b;
}
}
```

Before we actually look at the associated UML diagram(s), let's examine the scope and required format for the information within the attributes and operations compartments.

Attributes Compartment

The attributes compartment houses the classes' attributes, or member variables. The attributes compartment is optionally present under the name compartment of the class diagram. The UML usage for each variable of the attributes compartment is detailed. For the sake of general knowledge, it's good to be familiar with the following condensed attributes format:

```
[<visibility>] <variable_name> [: <type>] [= default_value]
```

Here, visibility defines the optionally displayed visibility modifier. The name would be the variable's name, and the type would be the type of the variable.

Operations Compartment

The operations compartment houses the classes' operations, or member functions or methods. The operations compartment is optionally present under the attributes compartment of the class diagram. If the attributes compartment is excluded, then the operations compartment may reside under the name compartment of the class diagram. The UML usage for each method of the operations compartment is detailed. Again, it's good to be familiar with following condensed operations format:

```
[<visibility>] <method_name> [<parameter-list>] [: <return-type>]
```

Here, visibility defines the optionally displayed visibility modifier. The name would be the method's name, the optionally displayed parameter-list is just as it says, and this is the same for the return-type.

Displaying the Attributes and Operations Compartments

The display of level-of-detail information with regard to most UML elements is optional. This is true for the member variables and methods in the attributes and operations compartments as well. Figure G-3 shows a more complete usage as defined in the compartment sections.

FIGURE G-3

Detailed
attributes and
operations
compartments

PrimeNumber
– divisorList: List<String> = new ArrayList<S...
– isPrime: Boolean = true
– primeSquareRoot: Double = null
+ getDivisorList() : List
+ getIsPrime() : Boolean
+ getPrimeSquareRoot() : Double
+ PrimeNumber(candidate : long)
+ setIsPrime(b : Boolean) : void
+ validatePrime(c : Long) : void

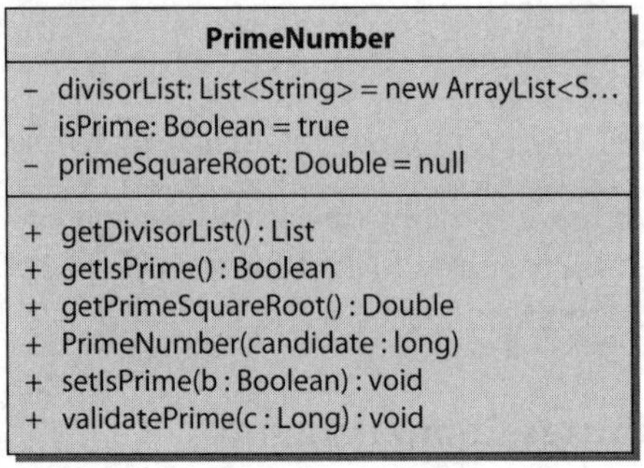

In Figure G-4, a more condensed representation of attributes and operations usages is shown.

Both of the following representations are valid; by taking the time to understand this completely, you can avoid confusion when working with UML.

For attributes: <variable_name> [: <type>]

For operations: <method_name> [<parameter-list>]

Visibility Modifiers

As you are aware, there are four access modifiers: *public*, *private*, *protected*, and *package-private*. These modifiers are depicted with symbols in UML and are used as shorthand in the attributes and operations compartments of a class diagram. These symbols are known as *visibility modifiers* or *visibility indicators*. The visibility indicator for the *public* access modifier is the plus sign (+). The visibility indicator

FIGURE G-4

Abbreviated
attributes and
operations
compartments

PrimeNumber
divisorList: List<String>
isPrime: Boolean
primeSquareRoot: Double
getDivisorList()
getIsPrime()
getPrimeSquareRoot()
PrimeNumber(long)
setIsPrime(Boolean)
validatePrime(Long)

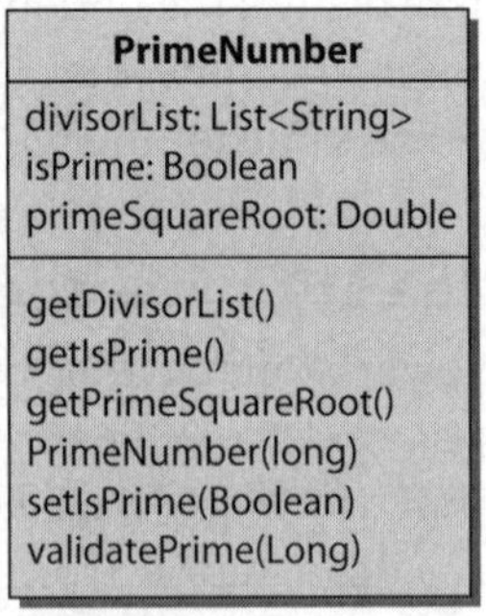

Visibility
modifiers

AccessModifiersClass
+ variable1: int − variable2: int # variable3: int ~ variable4: int
+ method1() : void − method2() : void # method3() : void ~ method4() : void

for the *private* access modifier is the minus sign (–), the visibility indicator for the *protected* access modifier is the pound sign (#), and the visibility indicator for the *package-private* modifier is the tilde (~) modifier. All four visibility modifiers are depicted in Figure G-5 within the attributes and operations compartments. Visibility indicators are also optional and need not be displayed.

Several UML modeling tools are freely and commercially available in the marketplace. Being familiar with these tools will make you more productive in the workplace, will assist in collaboration, and will ultimately give you a more professional edge.

Recognizing Representations of UML Associations

The preceding section solidified your knowledge of basic class diagrams and their main components. This section focuses on the relationships between classes in regard to their associations and compositions. Multiplicity indicators and role names are detailed as well to assist you in specifying the relationships between classes. When you have completed this section, you will know how to recognize connectors used between classes and how to interpret any specified multiplicity indicators and role names. The following topics will be covered:

- Graphic paths
- Relationship specifiers

Graphic Paths

The structure diagram graphic paths, also defined as class relationships, include notations for aggregation, association, composition, and dependency, as depicted in Figure G-6. Generalization and realization graphic paths were covered in the preceding section.

FIGURE G-6   Graphic path notations

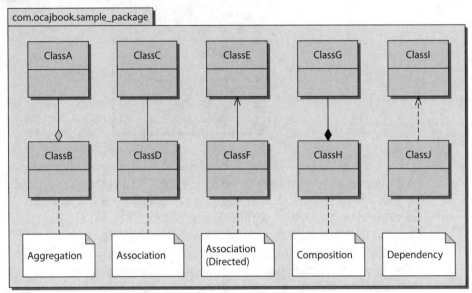

Aggregation Association

Aggregation association depicts one class as the owner of one or more classes. Aggregation is depicted with a solid line and an unfilled diamond. The diamond is on the side of the classifier. In Figure G-6, you could say that a ClassA object is part of a ClassB object.

Association

An association that is not marked by navigability arrows is implied to be navigable in both directions; therefore, each association end is owned by the opposite classifier. Association is depicted with a solid line. In Figure G-6, you could say there is an association between ClassC and ClassD objects.

Directed Association

An association has (directed) navigation when it is marked with a navigability arrow, also described as a stick arrow. This directed association's arrow denotes navigation in the direction of that end, the classifier has ownership of the marked association end, and the unmarked association's end is owned by the association. In addition to the navigability arrow, directed association is depicted with a solid line. In Figure G-6, you could say that a ClassE object has a ClassF object.

Composition

Composition association depicts a class being composed of one or more classes. The component parts/classes live only as long as the composite class. Composition is depicted with a solid line and a filled diamond. The diamond is on the side of the classifier. In Figure G-6, you could say that a ClassH object is composed of one or more ClassG objects.

Dependency

Dependency association depicts one class having a temporary association with another class. Dependency associations occur when a class needs another class to exist or when an object is used as a return value, local variable, or method argument. Dependency is depicted with a dotted line and a stick arrow. In Figure G-6, you could say that a ClassJ object depends on a ClassI object.

Note *As you probably noticed upon reading through the explanations of the relationships, class relationships can be written out using catchphrases between the objects. Common relationship catchphrases include "has-a," "is-a," "is composed of," "is part of," and "uses-a."*

Notes

Notes are represented in UML as a rectangle with a folded upper-right corner. Comments are placed into the notes element, and a dotted line is drawn from the notes element to the artifact being commented on.

Relationship Specifiers

Sometimes depicting class relationships with the basic UML elements such as class diagrams and connectors is not enough to convey the true relationship between classes. A reader may clearly see that a relationship exists but may want to know more with regard to the constraints and high-level interaction. Multiplicity indicators and role names are specifiers used to define and clarify these relationships further.

Multiplicity Indicators

Multiplicity indicators are numerical representations used to depict the number of objects that may or must be used in an association. Table G-4 defines the meanings of the different multiplicity indicators. If an association end does not show a multiplicity indicator, then the value is assumed to be 1. Multiplicity indicators can take the form of a single value or can be represented as a bounded relationship (<lowerbound>..<upperbound>).

Multiplicity indicators in use are represented in Figure G-7. Here you see the following: `ResearchStation` objects must be aware of 20 or more `ResearchBuoy` objects. `ResearchBuoy` objects must be aware of at least

TABLE G-4   Multiplicity Indicators and Their Meanings

Multiplicity Indicator	Example	Meaning of the Multiplicity Indicator
*	*	Object(s) of the source class may be aware of many objects of the destination class.
0	0	Object(s) of the source class are not aware of any objects of the destination class. This notation is not typically used.
1	1	Objects(s) of the source class must be aware of exactly one object of the destination class.
[x]	10	Object(s) of the source class must be aware of the specified number of objects of the destination class.
0..*	0..*	Object(s) of the source class may be aware of zero or more objects of the destination class.
0..1	0..1	Object(s) of the source class may be aware of zero or one object of the destination class.
0..[x]	0..5	Object(s) of the source class may be aware of zero or more objects of the destination class.
1..*	1..*	Objects(s) of the source class must be aware of one or more objects of the destination class.
1..[x]	1..7	Object(s) of the source class must be aware of one or up to the specified number of objects of the destination class.
[x]..[y]	3..9	Object(s) of the source class must be aware of the objects of the destination class within the specified range.
[x].. [y],[z]	4..7,10	Object(s) of the source class must be aware of the objects of the destination class within the specified range or the specified number.

FIGURE G-7

Multiplicity
indicators

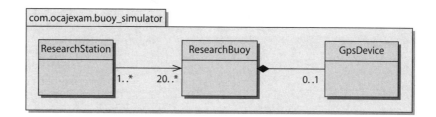

one `ResearchStation`. Each `ResearchBuoy` must be composed of zero or
more `GpsDevice` objects.

Association Role Names

Role names are commonly used to clarify the usage of the associated objects and
their multiplicities. In Figure G-8, we see that the `ResearchStation` object
interrogates the `ResearchBuoy` object. Without this descriptive role name, the
relationship may have been unclear. We can also deduce that the `ResearchStation`
object is aware of 20 `ResearchBuoy` objects, and each `ResearchBuoy` object is
associated with one or more `ResearchStation` objects.

FIGURE G-8

Association role
name

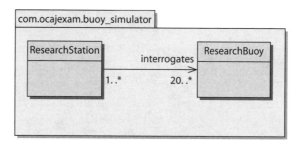

H

Functional Interfaces

J DK 1.8 includes specific-purpose and general-purpose functional interfaces (FIs). An easy way to locate FIs is to search through the source code for the @FunctionalInterface annotation. Java SE 8 source code is included in the src.zip and javafx-src.zip files that are distributed with the JDK.

The following list was produced from "grepping" on the extracted JavaFX source code in the javafx-src directory. The FIs in this listing could be considered JavaFX Specific Purpose FIs (SPFIs). Note that you can run grep on POSIX-based machines or Windows machines with CYGWIN installed.

```
$ grep -r "@FunctionalInterface"
com/sun/javafx/css/parser/Recognizer.java:@FunctionalInterface
com/sun/javafx/iio/bmp/BMPImageLoaderFactory.java:@FunctionalIn-
terface
javafx/animation/Interpolatable.java:@FunctionalInterface
javafx/beans/InvalidationListener.java:@FunctionalInterface
javafx/beans/value/ChangeListener.java:@FunctionalInterface
javafx/collections/ListChangeListener.java:@FunctionalInterface
javafx/collections/MapChangeListener.java:@FunctionalInterface
javafx/collections/SetChangeListener.java:@FunctionalInterface
javafx/event/EventHandler.java:@FunctionalInterface
javafx/util/Builder.java:@FunctionalInterface
javafx/util/BuilderFactory.java:@FunctionalInterface
javafx/util/Callback.java:@FunctionalInterface
```

Specific-Purpose FIs

Specific-purpose FIs are designed to support the packages in which they are included, as you have seen with the JavaFX SPFIs. You can examine the source code for specific-purpose FIs in newer Java distributions (as they are released) to see what additional interfaces become available to use.

Various specific-purpose FIs are listed in Table H-1. Default methods and static methods are optional in FIs. However, of the FIs listed in Table H-1, only the Comparator interface had a need for default and static methods.

TABLE H-1	Specific-Purpose Functional Interfaces

API	Functional Interface – Abstract Method Signature
AWT `java.awt`	`public interface KeyEventDispatcher {` `boolean dispatchKeyEvent(KeyEvent e);}`
AWT `java.awt`	`public interface KeyEventPostProcessor {` `boolean postProcessKeyEvent(KeyEvent e);}`
Basic IO `java.io`	`public interface FileFilter {` `boolean accept(File pathname);}`
Basic IO `java.io`	`public interface FilenameFilter {` `boolean accept(File dir, String name);}`
Concurrency `java.util.concurrent`	`public interface Callable <V> {` `V call() throws Exception;}`
Date and Time `java.time.temporal`	`public interface TemporalAdjuster {` `Temporal adjustInto(Temporal temporal);}`
Date and Time `java.time.temporal`	`public interface TemporalQuery <R> {` `R queryFrom(TemporalAccessor temporal);}`
Language `java.lang`	`public interface Runnable {` `public abstract void run();}`

Logger
`java.util.logging`
	`public interface Filter {`
	`public boolean isLoggable`
	`    (LogRecord record);}`

NIO 2
`java.nio.file`
	`// inside DirectoryStream`
	`public static interface Filter <T> {`
	`boolean accept(T entry) throws IOException;}`

NIO 2 `java.nio.file`	`public interface PathMatcher{` `boolean matches(Path path); }`

Preference
`java.util.prefs`
	`public interface PreferenceChangeListener{`
	`void preferenceChange`
	`    (PreferenceChangeEvent evt);}`

Utilities `java.util`	`public interface Comparator <T> {` `int compare(T o1, T o2);}`

General-Purpose FIs

General-purpose FIs are designed to support the primary features of the JDK. These FIs reside in `java.util.function`. All of the general-purpose FIs available in JDK 1.8-40 are provided in Table H-2, along with their single abstract method signatures.

TABLE H-2	General-Purpose Functional Interfaces

Functional Interface	Abstract Method Signature
Predicate	
`Predicate`	`boolean test(T t);`
`BiPredicate`	`boolean test(T t, U u);`
`DoublePredicate`	`boolean test(double value);`
`IntPredicate`	`boolean test(int value);`
`LongPredicate`	`boolean test(long value);`
Consumer	
`Consumer`	`void accept(T t);`
`BiConsumer`	`void accept(T t, U u);`
`DoubleConsumer`	`void accept(double value);`
`IntConsumer`	`void accept(int value);`
`LongConsumer`	`void accept(long value);`
`ObjDoubleConsumer`	`void accept(T t, double value);`
`ObjIntConsumer`	`void accept(T t, int value);`
`ObjLongConsumer`	`void accept(T t, long value);`
Supplier	
`Supplier`	`T get();`
`BooleanSupplier`	`boolean getAsBoolean();`
`DoubleSupplier`	`double getAsDouble();`
`IntSupplier`	`int getAsInt();`
`LongSupplier`	`long getAsLong();`
Function	
`Function`	`R apply(T t);`
`BiFunction`	`R apply(T t, U u);`
`DoubleFunction`	`R apply(double value);`
`IntFunction`	`R apply(int value);`
`LongFunction`	`R apply(long value);`
`ToDoubleBiFunction`	`applyAsDouble (T t, U u)`
`ToDoubleFunction`	`double applyAsDouble(T t, U u);`
`IntToDoubleFunction`	`double applyAsDouble(int value);`
`LongToDoubleFunction`	`double applyAsDouble(long value);`
`ToIntBiFunction`	`int applyAsInt(T t, U u);`

TABLE H-2	General-Purpose Functional Interfaces *(continued)*

Functional Interface	**Abstract Method Signature**
`ToIntFunction`	`int applyAsInt(T value);`
`LongToIntFunction`	`int applyAsInt(long value);`
`DoubleToIntFunction`	`int applyAsInt(double value);`
`ToLongBiFunction`	`long applyAsLong(T t, U u);`
`ToLongFunction`	`long applyAsLong(T value);`
`DoubleToLongFunction`	`long applyAsLong(double value);`
`IntToLongFunction`	`long applyAsLong(int value);`
Operator	
`BinaryOperator`	`R apply(T t, U u);`
`DoubleBinaryOperator`	`double applyAsDouble` `(double left, double right);`
`IntUnaryOperator`	`int applyAsInt(int operand);`
`IntBinaryOperator`	`int applyAsInt(int left, int right);`
`LongUnaryOperator`	`long applyAsLong(long operand);`
`LongBinaryOperator`	`long applyAsLong(long left, long right);`
`DoubleUnaryOperator`	`double applyAsDouble(double operand);`
`UnaryOperator`	`R apply(T t);`

I

About the CD-ROM

T he CD-ROM included with this book comes complete with Oracle Press Practice Exam software that simulates the 1Z0-808 exam, an Enterprise Architect Project File, code samples from the book, and a free PDF copy of the book. The software is easy to install on any Mac or Windows computer and must be installed to access the Practice Exam feature. You may, however, browse the electronic book or additional content directly from the CD without installation.

System Requirements

The software requires Microsoft Windows XP; Windows Server 2003; Windows Server 2008; Windows Vista Home Premium, Business, Ultimate, or Enterprise (including 64-bit editions) with Service Pack 2; or Windows 7 or Mac OS X 10.6 and 10.7 with 512MB of RAM (1GB recommended). The electronic book requires Adobe Acrobat Reader.

Oracle Press Practice Exam Software

See the following section for information on how to install and run the software using either a Mac or a Windows computer.

Installing the Practice Exam Software

Review the system requirements before proceeding with the installation. Follow the instructions for Windows or Mac OS.

Windows

Step 1   Insert the CD into your CD-ROM drive.

Step 2   After a few moments, the installer will open automatically.

NOTE   *If the installer does not automatically open, from the Start menu, select Run and then enter*

```
X:\Installer.exe
```

(where X is the letter of your CD-ROM drive). Then click OK.

Step 3   Follow the onscreen instructions to install the application.

Mac OS

Step 1   Insert the CD into your CD-ROM drive.

Step 2   After a few moments, the contents of the CD display.

Step 3   Double-click Installer to begin installation.

Step 4   Follow the onscreen instructions to install the application.

NOTE   *If you get an error while installing the software, ensure that your antivirus or Internet security programs are disabled and try installing the software again. You can enable the antivirus or Internet security program again after installation is complete.*

Running the Practice Exam Software

Follow the instructions after you have completed the software installation.

Windows

After installing, you can start the application using either of the two following methods:

- Double-click the Oracle Press Java Exams icon on your desktop.
- From the Start menu, click Programs or All Programs. Click Oracle Press Java Exams to start the application.

Mac OS

Open the Oracle Press Java Exams folder inside your Mac's Application folder and double-click the Oracle Press Java Exams icon to run the application.

Practice Exam Software Features

The Practice Exam Software provides a simulation of the actual exam. The software also features a custom mode that you can use to generate quizzes by exam objective domain. Quiz mode is the default mode. To launch an exam simulation, select one of the OCA exam buttons at the top of the screen, or select the Exam Mode check box at the bottom of the screen and select the OCA exam in the custom window.

The number of questions, types of questions, and the time allowed on the exam simulation are intended to be a representation of the live exam. The custom exam mode includes hints and references, and in-depth answer explanations are provided through the Feedback feature.

When you launch the software, a digital clock display will appear in the upper-right corner of the question window. The clock will continue to count unless you choose to end the exam by selecting Grade The Exam.

Removing Installation

The Practice Exam Software is installed on your hard drive. For best results for removal of programs using a Windows PC, use the Control Panel | Uninstall A Program option and then choose Oracle Press Java Exams to uninstall.

For best results for removal of programs using a Mac, go to the Oracle Press Java Exams folder inside your Applications folder and drag the Oracle Press Java Exams icon to the trash.

Help

A help file is provided through the Help button on the main page in the top-right corner. A readme file is also included in the Bonus Content folder, which provides more information about the additional content available with the book.

Free PDF Copy of the Book

The entire contents of the Study Guide are provided in PDF format. Download Adobe Acrobat Reader from www.adobe.com.

Enterprise Architect Project File

Enterprise Architect (EA) is a CASE tool that supports UML modeling and reverse source code engineering. EA was used to create the draft UML diagrams for this book. Because knowing UML is a requirement for the exam, the authors have included the project file for these diagrams on the CD to assist you in your learning.

To open the project file, you must have a version of EA. You can download a 30-day trial version of the application from the Spark Systems web site at http://www.sparxsystems.com/products/ea/trial.html. Once it is installed, you will be able to view and modify each of the UML diagrams. You will find the diagrams to be organized in the EA project as they are presented in each chapter. See Appendix G for detailed information on UML.

Code Samples

Selected samples of code from the book are included on the CD.

Technical Support

Technical support information is provided in the following sections by feature.

Windows 8 Troubleshooting

The following known errors on Windows 8 have been reported. See the following for information on troubleshooting these known issues.

If you get an error while installing the software, such as "The application could not be installed because the installer file is damaged. Try obtaining the new installer from the application author," you may need to disable your antivirus or Internet security programs and try installing the software again. You can enable the antivirus or Internet security program again after installation is complete.

For more information on how to disable antivirus programs in Windows, visit the web site of the software provider of your antivirus program. For example, if you use Norton or MacAfee products, visit the Norton or MacAfee web site and search for "how to disable antivirus in Windows 8." Antivirus programs are different from firewall technology, so be sure to disable the antivirus program, and be sure to re-enable the program after you have installed the Practice Exam software.

Although Windows doesn't include default antivirus software, it can often detect antivirus software installed by you or the manufacturer of your computer, and it typically displays the status of any such software in the Action Center, located in the Control Panel under System and Security (select Review Your Computer's Status). The Windows help feature can also provide more information on how to detect your antivirus software. If the antivirus software is on, check the Help feature that came with that software for information on how to disable it.

Windows will not detect all antivirus software. If your antivirus software isn't displayed in the Action Center, you can try typing the name of the software or the publisher in the Start menu search field.

McGraw-Hill Education Content Support

For questions regarding the PDF copy of the book or the content of the practice exam software, e-mail techsolutions@mhedu.com or visit http://mhp.softwareassist.com.

For questions regarding book content, e-mail customer.service@mheducation.com. For customers outside the United States, e-mail international_cs@mheducation.com.

Glossary

absolute path   The full path to a directory or file from the root directory. For example, C:\NetBeansProject\SampleProject is an absolute path. The paths ..\ SampleProject or Projects\SampleProject are relative paths.

abstract   A modifier that indicates that either a class or a method has some behavior that must be implemented by its subclasses.

access modifiers   Modifiers that define the access privileges of interfaces, classes, methods, constructors, and data members. Access modifiers include *package-private*, `private`, `protected`, and `public`.

accessor method   A method used to return the value of a private field. See also *getter*.

annotation   Metadata that provides additional data about the program but is not directly part of the resulting application. Annotations are always prepended by @.

application server   A (Java EE) server that hosts various applications and their environments.

arithmetic operator   Java programming language operator that performs addition (+), subtraction (-), multiplication (*), division (/), or remainder production (%) operations.

array   A fixed-length group of the same type variables or references that are accessed with an index.

ArrayList   A resizable array implementation of the List interface; an object-oriented representation of an array.

assertions   Boolean expressions that are used to validate whether code functions as expected while debugging.

assignment statement   A statement that allows for the definition or redefinition of a variable by assigning it a value. It is represented by the equal operator (=) in Java code.

attributes   The state of a class's instance and static variables (fields).

autoboxing   A convenience feature in Java that allows a primitive to be used as its wrapper object class without any special conversion by the developer.

AutoCloseable   A Java interface that represents a resource that must be closed when it is no longer needed. Objects that inherit from AutoCloseable may be used with the try-with-resources statement.

AWT   The *Abstract Window Toolkit* is the original package for developing cross-platform user interfaces.

base class   See *superclass.*

bean   A reusable software component that conforms to design and naming conventions.

bitwise operator   A Java programming language operator that may be used to compare two operands of numeric type or two operands of type `boolean`. Bitwise operators include bitwise AND (&), bitwise exclusive OR (^), and bitwise inclusive OR (|).

block   Code placed between matching braces—for example, { int x; }.

boolean   A Java keyword (`boolean`) that is used to define a primitive variable as having a Boolean type with a value of either `true` or `false`. The corresponding wrapper class is `Boolean`.

byte   A Java keyword (`byte`) used to define a primitive variable as an integer with 1 byte of storage. The corresponding wrapper class is `Byte`.

bytecode   The name of a compiled Java binary.

casting   Converting one type to another, such as converting/casting a primitive `long` to a primitive `int`.

char   A Java keyword (`char`) used to define a variable as a specific Unicode character with 2 bytes of storage. The corresponding wrapper class is `Character`.

Checkstyle   A development tool that assists programmers in writing Java code that adheres to coding standards. See http://checkstyle.sourceforge.net/ for information.

child class   See *subclass.*

class   A Java type that defines the implementation of an object. Classes include instance variables, class variables, and methods. Classes also specify the superclass and interfaces in which they inherit and implement. All classes inherit from the `Object` class.

class method   The name of a method that is not static and belongs to a specific class.

class variable   See *static variable.*

classpath   A variable that includes an argument set telling the Java virtual machine where to look for user-defined classes/packages.

comment   Text within a source file that provides explanations of associated code. In Java, comments are delimited with `//` (single line), `/*...*/` (multiple line), or `/**...*/` (multiple line) Javadoc comments.

composition association   A whole–part relationship between classes whereby the whole is responsible for the lifetime of its parts. Composition is also known as *containment* and is a strong relationship.

compound assignment operator   An operator with an abbreviated syntax that is used in place of the assignment of an arithmetic or bitwise operator. The compound assignment operator evaluates the two operands first, and then assigns the results to the first operand.

concatenation operator   An operator (`+`) that is used to concatenate (join) two strings.

concrete class   A class that has all of its methods implemented. Concrete classes can be instantiated.

conditional statement   A decision-making control flow used to execute statements and blocks of statements conditionally. Examples are `if`, `if else`, `if else if`, and `switch`.

constructor   A method that initializes a new object.

DateTimeFormatter   A class in the Date and Time API. The `DateTimeFormatter` class is a formatter for printing and parsing date-time objects.

declaration   A statement that establishes an identifier with associated attributes. A class declaration lists its instance variables and methods. Declarations within methods define the type of local variables.

default constructor   The empty constructor that is automatically used by the compiler if no other constructors are defined.

dereference   A term used to describe when an object loses a reference. This may result from a variable being reassigned or going out of scope.

double   A Java keyword (`double`) that is used to define a primitive variable as a floating-point number with 8 bytes of storage. The corresponding wrapper class is `Double`.

Duration   A class in the Date and Time API. The `Duration` class provides a simple measure of time along the timeline in nanoseconds.

encapsulation   The principle of defining (designing) a class that exposes a concise public interface while hiding its implementation details from other classes.

enumeration type   A type with a fixed set of constants as fields.

Error   A subclass of the class `Throwable`. The `Error` class indicates issues that an application should not try to catch.

Exception   A subclass of the class `Throwable`. The `Exception` class indicates issues that an application may want to catch.

executable JAR   A JAR file containing a manfest.mf in META-INF directory with the `Main-Class` attribute set to a class with a `public static void main(String args[])` method.

expression statement   A statement that changes part of the application's state. Expression statements include method calls, assignments, object creation, pre/post-increments, and pre/post-decrements. An expression statement can be evaluated to a single value.

FI   Acronym for functional interface—an interface that has one abstract method and zero or more default methods.

FindBugs   A program that uses static analysis to look for bugs in Java code; see findbugs.sourceforge.net for more information.

float   A Java keyword (`float`) that is used to define a primitive variable as a floating-point number with 4 bytes of storage. The corresponding wrapper class is `Float`.

functional interface   Also known as a single abstract method (SAM). An interface that has just one abstract method, and thus represents a single function contract.

garbage collection   The name of the Java process that consumes objects that are no longer in scope and frees their memory.

generic   Generics are the term for a generic class or interface that can be passed as a parameter. This allows methods and objects to work with objects of different types while maintaining compile-time data type checks.

getter   A simple public method used to return a private instance variable.

Git   An open-source distributed version control system.

heap   An area in memory where objects are stored.

IDE   Acronym for *integrated development environment*. A development suite that allows developers to edit, compile, debug, connect to version control systems, collaborate, and do much more depending on the specific tool. Most modern IDEs have add-in capabilities for various software modules to enhance capabilities. Popular IDEs include the NetBeans IDE, JDeveloper, Eclipse, and IntelliJ IDEA.

import statement   A statement used in the beginning of a class that allows for external packages to be made available within the class.

inheritance   The ability of one Java class to extend another and gain its functionality.

instance variable   A variable that is declared in the class instead of in a particular method. This variable's lifecycle lasts for the duration of the object's existence. This variable is in scope for all methods.

Instant   A class in the Date and Time API. The `Instant` represents a numerical timestamp.

int   A Java keyword (`int`) that is used to define a primitive variable as an integer with 4 bytes of storage. The corresponding wrapper class is `Integer`.

interface   A definition of public methods that must be implemented by a class.

iteration statement   A control flow through which a statement or block of statements is iterated, based on a maintained state of a variable or expression. The `for` loop, the enhanced `for` loop, and the `while` and `do-while` statements are used for iterating.

J2EE   Acronym for *Java 2 Platform, Enterprise Edition*. The legacy term for Java EE. See *Java EE*.

J2ME   Acronym for *Java 2 Platform, Micro Edition*. The legacy term for Java ME. See *Java ME*.

J2SE   Acronym for *Java 2 Platform, Standard Edition*. The legacy term for Java SE. See *Java SE*.

JAR   Acronym for *Java Archive*. A JAR file is used to store a collection of Java class files. It is represented by one file with the .jar extension in the file system. It may be executable. The JAR file is based on the ZIP file format. A JAR file is created with the jar utility and can contain a manifest file referencing the main class.

Java EE   Acronym for *Java Platform, Enterprise Edition*. A software development platform that includes a collection of enterprise API specifications for Enterprise JavaBeans, servlets, and JavaServer Pages. Java EE compliance is reached when an application server (full compliance) or web container (partial compliance) implements the necessary Java EE specifications.

Java ME   Acronym for *Java Platform, Micro Edition*. A software development platform that includes a collection of APIs designed for embedded devices.

Java SE   Acronym for *Java Platform, Standard Edition*. A software development platform that includes a collection of APIs designed for client application development.

JavaBean   A reusable Java component based on a platform-independent reusable component model in which a standardized means is used to access and modify the object state of the bean.

Javadoc   A tool that produces HTML documentation from extracted comments of Java source code. The comment symbols and annotations in the comments must comply with the Javadoc specification.

JavaFX   A rich client platform that provides a lightweight, hardware-accelerated Java UI platform.

jConsole   A monitoring and management tool that is a part of the JDK. It enables the local or remote monitoring of an application to track CPU and memory usage. It connects and uses information provided via the Java Management Extension (JMX).

JDK   Acronym for *Java Development Kit*. A bundled set of development utilities for compiling, debugging, and interpreting Java applications. The Java Runtime Environment (JRE) is included in the JDK.

JRE   Acronym for *Java Runtime Environment*, an environment used to run Java applications. It contains basic client and server JVMs, core classes, and supporting files.

JVM   Acronym for *Java virtual machine*, the platform-independent environment where the Java interpreter executes.

keyword   A word in the Java programming language that cannot be used as an identifier (in other words, a variable or method name). Java SE 8 maintains 50 keywords, each designed to be used for a specific purpose.

lambda expression   A lambda expression, also known as a closure, provides a means to implement an instance of a one-use anonymous class that has a single method. In other words, a lambda expression provides a means to represent anonymous methods.

library   A set of compiled classes that add functionality to a Java application.

literal   A value represented as an integer, floating-point, or character value that can be stored in a variable. For example, `1115` is an integer literal, `12.5` is a floating-point literal, and   A is a character literal.

local variable   A variable that is in scope only for a single method, constructor, or block.

LocalDate   A class in the Date and Time API. The `LocalDate` class stores a date and time like so: 2015-03-15.

LocalDateTime   A class in the Date and Time API. The `LocalDateTime` class stores a date and time like so: 2015-03-15T12:00.

LocalTime   A class in the Date and Time API. The `LocalTime` class stores a date and time like so: 12:00.

logical operator   Java programming language operators that perform logical operations, such as the Boolean NOT (`!`), conditional AND (`&&`), and conditional OR (`||`).

long   A Java keyword (`long`) used to define a primitive variable as an integer with a storage of 8 bytes. The corresponding wrapper class is `Long`.

method   A procedure that contains the code for performing operations in a class.

method argument   A variable that is passed to a method. A method may have multiple arguments or none.

method parameter   A variable that is in scope for the entire method. It is declared in the method signature and is initialized from the method arguments.

modulus   The remainder production operator (%).

multi-catch   A clause that allows for multiple exception arguments in one catch clause.

mutator method   A method used to set the value of a private field. See *setter*.

null   A Java keyword (`null`) representing a reserved constant that points to nothing. Specifically, a `null` type has a `null` (void) reference represented by the literal `null`.

object   An instance of a class created at runtime from a class file.

object-oriented   The design principle that uses objects and their interactions to design applications. Each object can represent an abstract concept. Related code and data are stored together in these objects. This is in contrast to procedural programming in a language such as C.

operator   A Java element that performs operations on up to three operands and returns a result.

operator precedence   The order in which operators will be evaluated when more than one operator is included in an expression.

overloading   The process of implementing more than one method with the same return type and name, while using various numbers and/or types of parameters to distinguish between them.

overriding   The process of overriding a superclass's method by using the same method signature.

package   A Java keyword (`package`) that begins a statement at the beginning of a class. This statement indicates the package name with which it is associated. The fully qualified name for a class includes this package name.

package-private modifier   The default modifier that allows package-only access to the associated class, interface, constructor, method, or data member.

parent class   See *superclass*.

pass-by-reference   The action of passing an argument to a method in which the Java virtual machine gives the method a reference to the same object that was passed to it. This is how objects are passed.

pass-by-value   The action of passing an argument to a method in which the Java virtual machine copies the value for the method. This is how primitives are passed.

Period   A class in the Date and Time API. The `Period` class expresses an amount of time in units meaningful to humans, such as in years or hours.

polymorphism   A concept that allows data of one type to be handled and referred to by a type that is more general. Generalities can be created by using inheritance and extending classes, or by implementing interfaces.

POSIX   Acronym for *Portable Operating System Interface*. It is a group of standards defined by IEEE (Institute of Electrical and Electronics Engineers) that cover APIs and command-line utilities.

postfix increment/decrement operator   These operators provide a shorthand way of incrementing and decrementing the value of a variable by 1 after the expression has been evaluated.

predicate   A functional interface that determines whether the input object matches given criteria.

prefix increment/decrement operators   Operators that provide a shorthand way of incrementing and decrementing the value of a variable by 1 before the expression has been evaluated.

primitive   A fundamental data type that is not an object. The Java primitives are `byte`, `short`, `int`, `long`, `float`, `double`, `Boolean`, and `char`.

primitive cast   A technique in Java of changing the primitive data type of a variable to another primitive type.

private access modifier   A Java keyword that allows class-only access to the associated constructor, method, or data member.

profile   A term used in Java ME to describe more specific features that a Java virtual machine target implements.

protected access modifier   A Java keyword that allows package-external subclass access and package-only access to the associated constructor, method, or data member.

pseudo-code   A structured means to allow algorithm designers to express computer programming algorithms in a human-readable format.

public access modifier   A Java keyword that allows unrestricted access to the associated class, interface, constructor, method, or data member.

relational operator   A Java programming language operator that performs relational operations such as less than (<), less than or equal to (<=), greater than (>), greater than or equal to (>=), value equality (==), and value inequality (=!).

relative path   A path that is not anchored to the root of a drive. Its resolution depends upon the current path. For example, ../usr/bin is a relative path. If the current path was /home/user/Documents, this path would resolve to /home/usr/bin.

RuntimeException   A subclass of the class Exception. The RuntimeException class is the superclass of those exceptions that can be thrown during normal runtime of the Java virtual machine.

SAM   Acronym for *Single Abstract Method*. See *functional interface*.

scope   The block of code in which a variable is in existence and may be used.

setter   A simple public method that accepts one argument and is used to set the value of an instance variable.

short   A Java keyword (short) that is used to define a primitive variable as an integer with a storage of 2 bytes. The corresponding wrapper class is Short.

statement   A command that performs an activity when executed by the Java interpreter. Common Java statement types include expression, conditional, iteration, and transfer-of-control statements.

static variable   A variable that is declared in the class, such as an instance variable. This variable, however, is common to all objects of the same type. Only one instance of this variable exists for all objects of a particular type. Each instance of the class shares the same variable.

stream   A mechanism used for conveying elements from a data source through a computational pipeline.

String class   A class representing an immutable character string.

StringBuilder   The `StringBuilder` class represents a mutable sequence of characters.

subclass   A class that is derived from another class through inheritance. Also called a *child class*.

super   A Java keyword (`super`) used to invoke overridden methods.

superclass   A class used to derive other classes through inheritance. Also called a *parent class* or *base class*.

SVN   Apache Subversion, an open source version control system.

Swing API   A rich GUI application programming interface complete with an event model that is used for creating and managing user interfaces.

this   A Java keyword that is used to assist in referring to any member of the current object. The `this` keyword must be used from within an instance method or constructor.

transfer-of-control statement   A statement used to change the controlled flow in an application. Transfer-of-control statements include `break`, `continue`, and `return` statements.

try-catch   A statement that contains code to "catch" thrown exceptions from within the `try` block, either explicitly or propagated up through method calls.

try-catch-finally   A `try-catch` statement that includes a `finally` clause.

try-finally   A statement that contains a `finally` clause that is always executed after successful execution of the `try` block.

try-with-resources   A statement that declares resources that can be automatically closed. The objects/resources that are declared must implement `AutoCloseable`.

unboxing   A convenience feature in Java that allows a primitive wrapper object to be used as its native primitive without any special conversion by the developer.

Unicode character   A 16-bit set of characters that make up the Unicode standard.

Unicode Standard   A character coding system designed to form a universal character set. The Unicode Standard is maintained by the Unicode Consortium standards organization.

variable   A term for a symbolic reference to data in Java code.

void   The keyword used to indicate that no data will be returned from a method.

XML   Acronym for *Extensible Markup Language*. A general-purpose specification used for creating markup languages. This specification allows for the creation of custom tags in structured text files. Web-based solutions make common use of XML files as configuration, deployment descriptor, and tag library files.

INDEX

D

E

J

P

U

Join the Largest Tech Community in the World

 Download the latest software, tools, and developer templates

 Get exclusive access to hands-on trainings and workshops

 Grow your professional network through the Oracle ACE Program

 Publish your technical articles – and get paid to share your expertise

Join the Oracle Technology Network
Membership is free. Visit oracle.com/technetwork

🐦 @OracleOTN   f facebook.com/OracleTechnologyNetwork

Reach More than 700,000 Oracle Customers with Oracle Publishing Group

Connect with the Audience that Matters Most to Your Business

Oracle Magazine
The Largest IT Publication in the World
Circulation: 550,000
Audience: IT Managers, DBAs, Programmers, and Developers

Profit
Business Insight for Enterprise-Class Business Leaders to
Help Them Build a Better Business Using Oracle Technology
Circulation: 100,000
Audience: Top Executives and Line of Business Managers

Java Magazine
The Essential Source on Java Technology, the Java
Programming Language, and Java-Based Applications
Circulation: 125,000 and Growing Steady
Audience: Corporate and Independent Java Developers,
Programmers, and Architects

For more information
or to sign up for a FREE
subscription:
Scan the QR code to visit
Oracle Publishing online.

Beta Test Oracle Software

Get a first look at our newest products—and help perfect them. You must meet the following criteria:

- ✓ Licensed Oracle customer or Oracle PartnerNetwork member
- ✓ Oracle software expert
- ✓ Early adopter of Oracle products

Please apply at: pdpm.oracle.com/BPO/userprofile